Impact of Global Issues on International Trade

Ahu Coşkun Özer
Marmara University, Turkey

IGI Global
PUBLISHER of TIMELY KNOWLEDGE

A volume in the Advances in Finance, Accounting, and Economics (AFAE) Book Series

Published in the United States of America by
IGI Global
Business Science Reference (an imprint of IGI Global)
701 E. Chocolate Avenue
Hershey PA, USA 17033
Tel: 717-533-8845
Fax: 717-533-8661
E-mail: cust@igi-global.com
Web site: http://www.igi-global.com

Library of Congress Cataloging-in-Publication Data

Names: Coskun Ozer, Ahu, 1981- editor.
Title: Impact of global issues on international trade / Ahu Coskun Ozer, editor.
Description: Hershey, PA : Business Science Reference, [2022] | Includes bibliographical references and index. | Summary: "This book analyzes the effects of global issues on international trade such as global crises, war, and security issues, global pandemic and acknowledges the necessity of global cooperation to solve the international trade problems"-- Provided by publisher.
Identifiers: LCCN 2021023092 (print) | LCCN 2021023093 (ebook) | ISBN 9781799883142 (hardcover) | ISBN 9781799883159 (paperback) | ISBN 9781799883166 (ebook)
Subjects: LCSH: International trade. | Global Financial Crisis, 2008-2009--Economic aspects. | Security, International. | International business enterprises. | Globalization--Economic aspects.
Classification: LCC HF1379 .I4593 2021 (print) | LCC HF1379 (ebook) | DDC 382--dc23
LC record available at https://lccn.loc.gov/2021023092
LC ebook record available at https://lccn.loc.gov/2021023093

This book is published in the IGI Global book series Advances in Finance, Accounting, and Economics (AFAE) (ISSN: 2327-5677; eISSN: 2327-5685)

British Cataloguing in Publication Data
A Cataloguing in Publication record for this book is available from the British Library.

Advances in Finance, Accounting, and Economics (AFAE) Book Series

Ahmed Driouchi
Al Akhawayn University, Morocco

ISSN:2327-5677
EISSN:2327-5685

Mission

In our changing economic and business environment, it is important to consider the financial changes occurring internationally as well as within individual organizations and business environments. Understanding these changes as well as the factors that influence them is crucial in preparing for our financial future and ensuring economic sustainability and growth.

The **Advances in Finance, Accounting, and Economics (AFAE)** book series aims to publish comprehensive and informative titles in all areas of economics and economic theory, finance, and accounting to assist in advancing the available knowledge and providing for further research development in these dynamic fields.

Coverage

- Labor Economics
- Development Economics
- Finance and Accounting in SMEs
- Entrepreneurship in Accounting and Finance
- Health Economics
- Behavioral Economics
- Economics of Innovation and Knowledge
- Borrowing and Lending
- Economic Indices and Quantitative Economic Methods
- E-finance

IGI Global is currently accepting manuscripts for publication within this series. To submit a proposal for a volume in this series, please contact our Acquisition Editors at Acquisitions@igi-global.com or visit: http://www.igi-global.com/publish/.

The Advances in Finance, Accounting, and Economics (AFAE) Book Series (ISSN 2327-5677) is published by IGI Global, 701 E. Chocolate Avenue, Hershey, PA 17033-1240, USA, www.igi-global.com. This series is composed of titles available for purchase individually; each title is edited to be contextually exclusive from any other title within the series. For pricing and ordering information please visit http://www.igi-global.com/book-series/advances-finance-accounting-economics/73685. Postmaster: Send all address changes to above address.

Titles in this Series

For a list of additional titles in this series, please visit: www.igi-global.com/book-series

Handbook of Research on Developing Circular, Digital, and Green Economies in Asia
Patricia Ordóñez de Pablos (The University of Oviedo, Spain)
Business Science Reference • © 2022 • 400pp • H/C (ISBN: 9781799886785) • US $225.00

Handbook of Research on Climate Change and the Sustainable Financial Sector
Odunayo Magret Olarewaju (Durban University of Technology, South Africa) and Idris Olayiwola Ganiyu (University of KwaZulu-Natal, South Africa)
Business Science Reference • © 2021 • 573pp • H/C (ISBN: 9781799879671) • US $295.00

CSR and Management Accounting Challenges in a Time of Global Crises
Ionica Oncioiu (Titu Maiorescu University, Romania)
Business Science Reference • © 2021 • 305pp • H/C (ISBN: 9781799880691) • US $215.00

Handbook of Research on the Empirical Aspects of Strategic Trade Negotiations and Management
Nuno Crespo (ISCTE – Instituto Universitário de Lisboa, Portugal) and Nadia Simoes (ISCTE – Instituto Universitário de Lisboa, Portugal)
Business Science Reference • © 2021 • 446pp • H/C (ISBN: 9781799875680) • US $265.00

Handbook of Research on Financial Management During Economic Downturn and Recovery
Nuno Miguel Teixeira (Center for Research in Business and Administration, School of Business Sciences, Polytechnic Institute of Setúbal, Portugal) and Inês Lisboa (CARME, School of Management and Technology, Polytechnic of Leiria, Portugal)
Business Science Reference • © 2021 • 566pp • H/C (ISBN: 9781799866435) • US $295.00

Understanding the Active Economy and Emerging Research on the Value of Sports, Recreation, and Wellness
David J. Finch (Mount Royal University, Canada) and David Legg (Mount Royal University, Canada)
Business Science Reference • © 2021 • 312pp • H/C (ISBN: 9781799879398) • US $225.00

Applied Doughnut Economics and Neuroeconomic Psychology for Business and Politics
Torben Larsen (DEALs Online Collaborative Platform, Denmark)
Business Science Reference • © 2021 • 257pp • H/C (ISBN: 9781799864240) • US $195.00

IGI Global
PUBLISHER of TIMELY KNOWLEDGE

701 East Chocolate Avenue, Hershey, PA 17033, USA
Tel: 717-533-8845 x100 • Fax: 717-533-8661
E-Mail: cust@igi-global.com • www.igi-global.com

Editorial Advisory Board

Table of Contents

Detailed Table of Contents

The Pacific Alliance (PA) is an integration process that projects the commercial exchange of value-added products for its members. However, the external and internal crises have made the PA a volatile region in social and economic terms. This chapter analyzes the economic and trade policy trends in PA countries since 1990 and how they faced the different world and regional economic crises. From the particular analysis of the countries, there are similarities and differences in trade trends and the way to control crises. This chapter provides a general framework to review more specific approaches by sectors, industries, and companies.

The aim of this chapter is to analyse the effects of the economic crisis on the trade among the Southeastern European (SEE) countries. The countries were divided into two groups: the EU countries and non-EU countries. Macroeconomic performances and international trade indicators of the 11 observed countries were analysed for the period 2007-2019, and the effects of the economic crisis were present in all the observed countries, particularly the effects on the export performances. The crisis also affected the entire import of the non-EU countries. The EU countries recovered from the crisis faster than the non-EU countries. However, the non-EU countries achieved a more significant inflow of foreign direct investment in the post-crisis period, which significantly improved the position of the balance of payments in these countries. The observed countries had managed to stabilise their trade flows all until the beginning of the COVID-19 crisis. The impact of the current crisis on these countries remains to be estimated in the future.

This chapter attempts to study the impact of the COVID-19 pandemic on the stock markets of the BRICS nations. Such an exercise will have an important bearing on portfolio allocation in the context of the BRICS. The major contribution of the chapter in the extant literature is to examine based on the multifactor model of the capital asset pricing theory, how uncertainty owing to the pandemic interplay with the geopolitical index to impact the stock market of the BRICS. Further, the major macroeconomic factors are used as control variables. The daily observations were used from 31 December 2019 to 30 December 2020. The results based on the quantile regression model demonstrate the asymmetric response of the stock market to the pandemic. The policy implication that follows from this study is the need for strategic intervention of the central bank to ease the liquidity challenges in the crisis period.

In the literature on exports, the question of why some firms decide to export and why others decide to focus on the domestic market has only received fragmented and different answers. The only overemphasized factor, productivity, seems to be a dead end when empirical evidence is given for high productivity firms which decide to remain in the domestic market. This is mainly due to the ignorance of the role of the firm in international trade by the majority of the literature. In this empirical research, the aim of the author is to test the impact of legal, institutional, and financial conditions on the firm decision to export based on the Enterprise Survey by the World Bank for the Turkish Cypriot people, which remained out of the international community for 57 years, where Turkey emerged as its access point to international markets. Hence, the study contributes to the existing literature on export development by highlighting the obstacles in front of the export decisions of firms and addressing a hitherto not addressed case in international economics.

Products and firms are homogeneous in traditional foreign trade theories; products show no horizontal or vertical differentiation. It is observed that growth in exports is only related to an increase in export quantity and that this is not decomposed into margins. Since Melitz's work, there has been an increase in studies that decompose the firms' heterogeneity and export growth in foreign trade into extensive and intensive margins. The concepts are addressed in the literature known as "new-new" foreign trade theories which include extensive margins, the number of exporting firms, the number of new trade partners, and the volume or variety of exported products. In brief, the growth of global trade is the result of new trade relations (extensive margin) or a rise in existing trade relations (intensive margin). As one of the rapidly developing trade theories in international economics, the main purpose of this study is to conduct a literature survey on the extensive and intensive margins of export growth.

This chapter, first, draws an overview of the theoretical and conceptual framework of corporate decisions in the global financial crisis (GFC) context. Then, it shows the connectedness of corporate finance and international trade. Finally, employing a rich dataset, this chapter assesses the impact of international trade as well as the GFC on corporate financial decisions, particularly cash holdings, debt financing, and dividend payouts over the period 2002-2016. The findings show that international trade significantly affects corporate decisions. Firms with higher trade countries have higher debt level but lower cash and dividends across the globe. During the GFC, the positive impact of trade on debt shifts to negative. Also, trade has a positive effect on both cash and debt in the aftermath of the GFC. Taken together, international trade as an institutional setting influences corporate decisions and its role on cash, debt, and dividend differ during and after the GFC.

International trade cannot be considered separate from the current financial system in the context of imports and exports. In this context, the impact on international trade should be analyzed under the financial fragility hypothesis. This chapter aims to analyze the effects of financial fragility on Fragile Five and Troubled Ten countries' economic growth and trade strategies. In this direction, long-term relationships between variables are analyzed by Westerlund panel cointegration tests. According to the result of the panel cointegration tests, there are long-term relationships between exports, imports, gross domestic product, and financial fragility index. After determining the long-term relationships between variables, causality analyses have been carried out to reveal the direction of these relationships. According to Dumitrescu-Hurlin panel causality test results, there are bidirectional causality relationships between financial fragility index and export, import, and gross domestic product.

Globalization has made the whole world a common market for businesses by removing the commercial borders between countries. Increased competition in the global market has pushed businesses that want to operate in this arena to implement new strategies. As a promotion activity, fairs have been the most important assistant of the companies that want to internationalize over the years. Although the concept of fair organizations has changed with the effect of digitalization in the historical process, fairs still continue their main function of bringing buyers and sellers together. The subject of this chapter is how virtual fairs, which have increased their importance in marketing activities with the pandemic, will affect the future of trade fairs. In this context, the history of the fairs, their place and importance in international marketing, virtual fairs, and the impact of the COVID-19 pandemic on the future of international fairs will be discussed.

The COVID-19 pandemic-related economic lockdowns and restrictions have caused socio-economic uncertainties in the world since 2020. The pandemic-induced economic shocks affected world trade, especially the reactions in fragile markets. As a result of the strict rules taken by the countries, the decrease in the supply of intermediate goods inputs used in industries worldwide, supply shock has caused global supply chains and economic problems to spread through supply chains. Due to the increase in demand exceeding the current supply and production capacity, the fragmented production system, which spread throughout the world, led to the risks related to global value chains (GVC). In this context, discussion of the uplift processes within the chain, which expresses the upgrading perspective, has come to the fore again. The solutions in chains, which are applied by industries in the pandemic process, emphasize the importance of backward and forward linkages in the chain.

Preface

Globalization is the internationalization of economic, political, and social relations all over the world. Relations have gone beyond national borders, and the integration process of countries on economic and social and political have begun with globalization. In addition to its positive effects, this process also brings global problems that countries cannot solve alone in terms of economic, political, security and environmental issues.

For example, the SARS epidemic in 2002-2003 spread to 37 countries according to the data of the World Health Organization, but its economic effects were not as much as COVID 19. The global financial crisis that started in the USA in 2008 had a negative impact on all countries of the world. Security problems and terrorist incidents, environmental issues such as global warming, risk of food and water resources have reached international dimensions as problems that countries cannot solve alone. In this book, global financial crises, pandemics that affected the world such as covid-19, problems in the distribution of resources in the world and the effects of these issues on international trade were evaluated. The authors contributed with their chapters on global supply and value chains and globalization and deglobalization process in the world, the economic situation of the Pacific Alliance countries, impact of the COVID-19 pandemic on the stock markets of the BRICS nation, the effect of the global economic crisis on Southeastern European (SEE) countries, analyse the firms export decision based on the legal, institutional and financial conditions, evaluate the effect of the Covid-19 on world import and export.

Dr. José G. Vargas-Hernández contributes the chapter titled 'Critical Analysis of the Relocation Strategy of Production Between National Protectionist Policies, Global Supply, and Value Chains'. Dr. José G. Vargas- Hernández states that global supply, production and value chains although being economically efficient, are no longer any more secure under national protectionist policies and therefore, the relocation of production processes is mainly due to the increase in the level of income and wages of the developing countries that are the destination and which reduce the advantages to relocate. Also Dr. José G. Vargas-Hernández has a chapter on 'Critical Analysis of The World Economy and Deglobalization Processes in Times of Pandemic', analyze both the world economy and the deglobalization processes under the assumption that they are the result of a dialectical evolution of the economic, financial, political and sanitary crisis. In that chapter, Dr. José G. Vargas-Hernández states that "after a period of intensive economic, trade and financial integration in the creation of a world economic system, suddenly the economic, financial and sanitary dysfunctionalities emerged at the interior and created a reactive deglobalization process. However, what has been at the center are the international cooperation and trade relations determined by the need to expand the possibilities of satisfying human needs, including culture."

Dr. Jahir Lombana, Dr. Lorena A. Palacios-Chacón, Mr. Nestor U. Salcedo and Miss Adriana Cabello Cerna contribute the book with the chapter titled 'Pacific Alliance Facing Crises'. The authors " that "the Pacific Alliance (PA) countries' trade is linked rather to complementary products with already structured domestic value chains. Despite the intra-alliance tariff reduction, neither quantity nor diversification seems to have been motivated, so the response to trade promotion should go beyond costs. The COVID-19 crisis has revealed problems that were not evident but are more extreme; in that sense, the PA initiatives that go beyond tariff reduction, maybe a lifeline for its members."

Dr. Sandra Jednak, Dr. Dragana Kragulj and Mr. Miloš Parežanin, evaluate the effect of the global economic crisis on Southeastern European (SEE) countries, compare the SEE countries in two different groups as EU members and non-EU Countries, with the chapter titled 'Economic Crisis and Its Effects on International Trade: A Case of Selected EU and Non-EU Countries'. Jednak, Kragulj and Parežanin state that "the non-EU SEE countries achieved a more significant inflow of foreign direct investment in the post-crisis period, which significantly improved the position of the balance of payments in these countries. The observed countries had managed to stabilize their trade flows all until the beginning of the COVID-19 crisis."

Dr. Sudeshna Ghosh, evaluate the impact of the COVID-19 pandemic on the stock markets of the BRICS nations, with a chapter titled 'COVID-19, Stock Market, Exchange Rate, Oil Prices, Unemployment, Inflation, Geopolitical Risk Nexus, the Case of the BRICS Nations: Evidence Quantile Regression'. Dr. Ghosh states that "the research results suggest that both geopolitics and the pandemic contribute to fluctuations in the BRIC markets. We also have supportive findings for elucidations that stress how disruptions in demand and supply chain owing to quarantine mandates, government restrictions and social distancing have led to the jumps in the stock market."

Dr. Burak Erkut analyses the firms export decision based on the legal, institutional and financial conditions with the chapter titled 'Exporting Without Direct Access to International Markets: How Legal, Institutional, and Financial Conditions Affect the Decision to Export'. Dr. Erkut states that "the results of this study reveal that Turkish Cypriot firms decide to export largely as a result of the weak legal and institutional conditions that the Turkish Cypriot community is facing. Exporting firms are turning an unfavorable condition into a favorable one by enjoying the benefits of exporting, but the empirical observation that the interaction of the financial and institutional conditions would discourage them from export gives a different picture. Hence, access to finance and financial support for exporting firms should be isolated from political mechanisms."

Dr. Burcu Berke conducts a literature survey on the extensive and intensive margins of export growth, with a chapter titled 'A Literature Survey on Extensive and Intensive Margins in International Trade'. Dr. Berke states that "products and firms are homogeneous in traditional foreign trade theories. Growth in exports is only related to an increase in export quantity and that this is not decomposed into margins. The growth of global trade is the result of new trade relations or a rise in existing trade relations."

Dr. Hasan Tekin contributes the book with his chapter titled 'How the Global Financial Crisis (GFC) and International Trade Affected Corporate Decisions?' Dr. Tekin states that "international trade significantly affects corporate decisions. Firms with higher trade countries have higher debt levels but lower cash and dividends across the globe. International trade influences corporate decisions and its role on cash, debt and dividend differ during and after the GFC."

Dr. Ayberk Şeker evaluates the effect of financial fragility on international trade with the chapter titled 'Financial Fragility and Its Impacts on International Trade and Economic Growth: New Evidence from Fragile Five and Troubled Ten Countries'. Dr. Şeker states that "according to the result of the panel cointegration tests, it has been determined that there are long-term relationships between exports, imports, gross domestic product and financial fragility index. Also, according to Dumitrescu-Hurlin panel causality test results, it is found that there are bidirectional causality relationships between financial fragility index and export, import, and gross domestic product."

Dr. Mehmet Sami Süygün evaluates the effects of the COVID-19 on trade fairs and the digitalization of trade fairs with his chapter titled 'The Future of Trade Fairs After the COVID-19 Pandemic'. According to the Süygün, fairs have been the most important assistant of the companies that want to internationalize over the years, however, it does not seem easy for virtual fairs to meet and replace the advantages of physical fairs such as touching, seeing, feeling and socializing, which arise from the fact that human beings are social beings. Dr. Süygün states that "virtual fairs can be a complementary element to ensure that visitors who cannot come to the physical fair for any reason participate in the fair."

Dr. Osman Seraceddin Sesliokuyucu has a chapter titled 'Upgrading in the Global Value Chains After COVID-19', which evaluates the effects of the COVID-19 on the global supply chain. Dr. Sesliokuyucu states that "as a result of the strict rules taken by the countries has caused economic problems to spread through supply chains. Diversifying supply chains and increasing connections will enable businesses to become more agile by increasing their mobility in possible crisis."

Dr. Bartolomé Marco-Lajara, Dr. Pedro Seva-Larrosa, Dr. Lorena Ruiz-Fernández, Mr. Javier Martínez-Falcó contribute with the chapter titled 'The Effect of COVID-19 on the Spanish Wine Industry'. The authors state that "against this backdrop, the results of this research suggest that the future for the recovery of the Spanish wine industry lies in boosting online sales, food channels and exports. Also, resilience must be the key capacity of Spanish wineries, since in a sector that is mainly made up of small family businesses, they must be able to develop and strengthen their capacity to adapt to turbulent environments and to search for new markets."

Dr. Reenu Kumari, Dr. Ashwani Sharma evaluate the effect of the COVID-19 on world import, export, manufacturing sector, agriculture sector and service sector with the chapter titled 'Impact of COVID-19 on International Trades: New Evidence From Economic Sectors'. Kumari and Sharma state that "international trade collapsed by COVID-19 but consequences depend on the various factors such as normal behavior changes and interruption of supply in shopping centers, narrow policy adoption in world financial market conditions, shifted purchasing pattern by the public."

Ahu Coşkun Özer
Marmara University, Turkey

Acknowledgment

Academics from 10 different countries around the world contributed to this book project. I would like to thank the authors who contributed to Impact of Global Issues on International Trade with their chapters and also I would like to thank my colleagues who helped me in the reviewing process. I would also like to thank my spouse Teoman Özer and my daughters Ece and Çağla Su, who patiently waited for me during my hard work for this book project.

Ahu Coşkun Özer

Chapter 1
Critical Analysis of the World Economy and Deglobalization Processes in Times of Pandemic

José G. Vargas-Hernández
https://orcid.org/0000-0003-0938-4197
University Center for Economic and Managerial Sciences, University of Guadalajara, Mexico

ABSTRACT

This chapter aims to critically analyze both the world economy and the deglobalization processes under the assumption that they are the result of a dialectical evolution of economic, financial, political, and sanitary crises. This dialectical movement of the history of the globalization and deglobalization processes is always a very complex phenomena of interactions between the economic agents and political actors, leading to both progressive and regressive events of economic growth, social development, and environmental sustainability. After a period of intensive economic, trade, and financial integration in the creation of a world economy system, suddenly the economic, financial, and sanitary dysfunctionalities emerged at the interior and created a reactive deglobalization process. However, what has been at the center are the international cooperation and trade relations determined by the need to expand the possibilities of satisfying human needs, including culture.

INTRODUCTION

Under the concept of world economy or economic globalization (Sapir, 2016, 2011) the benefits and damages caused by the advances in the international economy are analyzed, questioning the achievements of reciprocity and equivalence between the advances in the development of national economies with diametrical differences. What results from international economic relations are very distant from the economic interrelationships of a globalized economic process.

The dialectical movement of history is complex with results that are both progressive and regressive. In world history, the processes of globalization that allow trade over great distances, have played

DOI: 10.4018/978-1-7998-8314-2.ch001

a relevant role in the economic and social growth and development of the peoples involved. In each of these stages, globalization processes have presented different characteristics.

Globalization was conceived by Valéry (1945) as described by "Now the era of the finite world begins", an expression that bears a lot of similarity with the descriptions of the global world of the XIX century (Andretta, 2002). The world was considered by McLuhan (1962) as a global village that is generally used to define the phenomenon of "globalization". The term globalization has been used to describe the economic periods when the foreign direct investment (FDI) and trade flows decline for whatever the reason, such as the global economic crisis. Economic globalization is a process in which organizations, business and countries operate at world scale. Globalization is a process of economic, commercial, and financial interdependence between different countries.

Globalization is a phenomenon that Goldin and Reinsert (2007: 28) define as "an increase in the impact on human activities, due to forces that extend beyond national borders."

The concept of mundialization (World economy) is more precise because it has a connotation related to geography while the concept of globalization is more generic that is related to an increasing interdependence between finance, production, the market and trade, free transit and commercial movements and international finance as a multidimensional socio-historical free trade process.

Globalization is defined by the WHO as the increased interconnectedness and interdependence between different peoples and countries. It includes the inter-related elements of the opening of international borders to flows of goods, services, finance, people, and ideas. Globalization also refers to the changes in national and international institutions and policies aimed to facilitate and promote such flows.

Globalization is a very complex phenomenon that has a considerable influence on contemporary societies. The economic dimensions of globalization have evolved concomitantly with dimensions that have independent dynamics of a nature other than economic determinism, such as social, environmental, etc. The components of globalization and international economic integration processes are creating new challenges to national governments due to such responsible causes as the national diversity of jurisdictions for trade liberalization policies, geographical factors, and institutional quality to enforce regulations. International trade is the exchange of goods and services across borders creating global markets.

As a phenomenon, globalization processes indirectly and subjectively affect the sensitivities of human and social activities that, when objectified as a process of improving people's well-being and living conditions, imply concrete and contrasting measurements in terms of access to markets. In relation to economic globalization, the theories of economic growth and development related to the theories of international economic relations and international trade and the theory of social and personal well-being are closely linked to human development (Tugores, 2002: 233).

The economic development of globalization has been promoted by the most developed countries and multinational companies (Cepal, 2002: 17). However, the cooperation and trade relations at the international level are determined by the need to expand the possibilities of satisfying human needs, including culture.

This paper begins analyzing the dialectical evolution of the world economy to show that the current context is complex and uncertain due to the conflicts between the economic and political powers, sieges and commercial reprisals aggravated by the sanitary crisis which are leading the economic globalization processes in the opposite direction away from the international cooperation. From these points, the analyzes moves to consider the arguments in favor and against the economic globalization to understand the challenges faced by the continuing economic and financial global integration that put it at a crucial turning point. Finally, this analysis offers a discussion related to all the issues treated on this paper and tries to identify some of the main points for a continuing debate on the future development of the world economy.

A DIALECTICAL EVOLUTION OF THE WORLD ECONOMY

Some authors contend that globalization begun about 60,000 year ago when the human history started as inherent phenomenon. Since then and through human history, civilizations have experienced migration, exploration expeditions, military conquests, exchanging trade and developed commercial routes.

The penultimate stage of globalization during the period 1820-1913 presented as relevant elements (Williamson, 2013) in commerce and poverty, when and how the backwardness of the Third World began, he relates that the industrial revolution produced an increase in the demand for raw materials for industrial production that provoke the opening of new international markets generate benefits in favor of the most industrialized countries. It was the colonial expression of the time favored by the emerging technologies of communication and transportation, but with less bellicosity than current globalization (Findlay and O´Rourke, 2007).

The collapse of the economic and financial integration processes during the Great Depression, in the 1930s there were tariff wars between countries with competitive devaluations that culminated in World War II (James, 2001). The Great Economic Depression of the 1930s brought down the economic and global integration that culminated in World War II. van Bergeijk (2010) assess overemphasizing the international trade in similar impact that the Great Depression had despite the different causes of the breakdowns, but he still demonstrates the globalization process was the result of the international trade flows, by the uncertainties of economic and social risks caused by the crisis.

Developing countries have the risks of unfavorable internal and external conditions that constraint the macroeconomic policies aimed to achieve equilibrium for economic globalization. However, this development was confined to very few countries while the nonmarket economies remained isolated and less developed economies choose the import substitution path of development.

International finance market has achieved globalization becoming the most relevant element serving the needs of international investment and trade activities and the most rapidly developing aspect of economic globalization since the 1970's. Far-reaching financial globalization changes in geographical organization and activities since the 1970s. In the 1970s, total trade flows exceeded the historical maximum GDP of the first wave in 1913.

Economic globalization, as we know it today, erupted in the eighties with the promotion of movements and mechanisms for the liberalization of international trade and finance, such as the elimination or reduction of barriers and tariffs, etc. Analyzes of data from economic globalization processes confirm that privatization and liberalization are intensifying with the new free trade agreements and the international financial system that is more globalized and immune to national regulations.

TENSIONS OF THE CURRENT GLOBALIZATION /DEGLOBALIZATION

The wave of globalization beginning in the 1980s was questioned by its stance and long-term incidence (Straw and Glennie, 2012). Economic globalization has not been exempted from complex contradictions of reality. Globalization was possible due to the collapse of the soviet system bringing delocalization, deindustrialization, unemployment, precarious and debt leading to a financial crisis. The processes of economic globalization were driven at a time of power and unipolar euphoria with the announcement of "the end of history" made by Francis Fukuyama after the decline of the USSR, in the interest of postponing the dominance of North America.

FINANCIAL CRISIS AND IMPLICATIONS FOR GLOBALIZATION

Since the nineties, economic interdependence has intensified globalization among countries while causing a debate on the potential benefits in terms of economic growth to the involved countries. The last global trade liberalization agreement was the Uruguay Round, which ended in 1993, which created the World Trade Organization (WTO). During the Mexican financial crisis of 1995, the IMF (International Monetary Fund) limited the space of the Mexican government to impose the macroeconomic policies to facilitate the borrowing needed (Morady, Kapucu, and Yalçinkaya, (Ed.) 2017; CEPAL, 2002).

Private equity consolidated after the dot.com bubble burst in 2000/2001 and it continue increased until the outbreak of the financial crisis of 2008-2009. However, with the rapid rise of China and Russia, a multipolar or pluripolar world is given way, marking the decline of unipolar globalization. The long-term planning of China has taken advantage of globalization dealing with the challenges of supplying labor and reducing production costs at global scale. The construction of an alternative new globalization 2.0 relies more in infrastructure investments based on trade and financial ties.

During the economic and financial crisis of 2008 and 2009, many small businesses also went into financial crisis and finally closed. (Dullien, Kotte, Márquez and Priewe, (Ed.), 2010; Verick, and Islam, 2010). The recent economic and financial crisis of 2008-2009 and the pandemic covid-19, are the two major causes, among others, that have led international trade to undergo at the brink to world economy collapse. Many of these leverages are activated especially during periods of economic crisis. In this regard, conclusive evidence follows from the reaction of highly developed countries (Japan, USA, Germany, France, UK etc.) to the negative effects of globalization.

Keynesian anti-cyclical fiscal and monetary policy was effective in overcoming the Great Depression crisis and the international financial crisis of 2008-2009. However, these types of policies create addictions that end in fiscal deficits and greater indebtedness. Global trade growth in the 10 years before the 2008-2009 financial crisis was about 6 percent, and in the years after 2009 it was about 2.5 percent.

The economic globalization process has the tendency to have been slowing down since 2004 (Bello, 2004) and increasing later after 2008 as the consequence of the economic and financial crisis with a slight decrease of the pace after 2004. The economic crisis led on serious consequences due to the slowdown of the globalization processes experienced not only by developed economies but also by developing economies and their reintegration processes has been stagnating. Amid the economic and financial crisis of 2008-2009, many small businesses closed their operations.

The slowdown in economic activities in the most developed countries is motivated by reductions in exports and imports relative to GDP. Countries that increased their exports and in attracting foreign investment to sustain their economy now face great challenges outside of a model of globalization and free market and trade integration.

It was reported in 2010 that some world globalized cities have declined significantly in relative financial services connectivity as the result (Hanssens, Derudder, Taylor et al. 2010: 11; Derudder, Hoyler and Taylor 2011: 4). Contemporary globalization processes show different traits from previous globalizing trends such as the rate of change in the economy, the speed, quantity, scale, and scope of commercial exchanges, giving rise to a more interdependent system (Ritzer, 2011). However, the risks of globalization have increased with events such as the attack and demolition of the twin towers, the outbreak of the dot-com crisis, the tsunami that destroyed the Fukushima nuclear plant in Japan and the financial collapse of Lehman Brothers. The impact of the crisis on globalization carries enormous risks that imply profound changes at the individual, organizational, government and national levels.

Traditional industries have gone to China because the low labor costs and environmental regulations, but as soon China started to rise them business industries are moving to other places where they can benefit from labor costs and environmental regulations. The winners from globalization processes will be the losers from globalization. In 1916, China achieved reduced rates of economic growth due to lower levels of international trade. To sustain and even revive economic and commercial activities, China implements economic policies. Global investment flows are also slowing down due to tighter regulations. In 2017, global foreign direct investment fell by 16% and in 2018 by 27%. Globalization was at the center of the world economy for a period of four decades in which China became the world's factory.

Economic globalization showed signs of exhaustion in 2019 with the contraction of trade flows, for the first time since 2009. Trade wars, the weakening of multilateralism, the paralysis of trade agreements and treaties are expressions that show the exhaustion of the economic globalization model. International trade flows grew by 1.2% in 2019, the lowest growth rate in the last decade due to certain deglobalizing forces beyond trade wars.

THE IMPLICATION OF THE SANITARY CRISIS IN THE GLOBALIZATION-DESGLOBALIZATION PROCESSES

Economic globalization contracted in 2019 and is exacerbated in 2020 by the health emergency that can cause a prolonged disengagement of commercial and financial activities from the world economy driven by businesses, governments, and households in developed countries. However, the health crisis has immediate and profound effects on the processes of economic globalization that affect all economies.

The processes of economic globalization are in difficulties, showing a contraction in international trade flows in 2019, which are aggravated by the responses that companies have given to the health emergency. The outbreak of the coronavirus pandemic has immediate negative effects with a considerable impact on global trade, investment, and financial flows. Coronavirus is changing the way the world does business for bad o for good. Business corporations and companies are being forced to rethink their global value, production, and logistics chains, shaped to maximize efficiency and profits. Resilience, recovery, and adaptation are becoming relevant in the world economy (Javorcik, 2020).

An analysis was conducted by Abdal, & Ferreira (2021) on the dynamic process of globalization and deglobalization in the context of recent development in the capitalist global economy restructuring processes. Based on the effects of the 2007-2008 financial and economic crisis and the current COVID-19 pandemic, the authors argue that this last crisis tends to accelerate and deepen a global ongoing fragmentation processes of economic, productive, and commercial processes.

The health crisis generated by the pandemic has confirmed that dependence on the provision of resources, goods and services from remote locations has direct effects on global trade. With the impact of the pandemic, the effects on governments, companies and households are devastating in terms of debt, unemployment, loss of income due to slow economic activities and consumption.

The coronavirus crisis plays an important role in deepening the transition of globalization processes from one more phase of international cooperation to a more conflictive one, which began after the economic and financial crisis of 2008-2009 and in which it is perceived that the risks outweigh the benefits. However, it is difficult to sustain the arguments that the health crisis has changed the logic of economic globalization processes. What has become clear is that the pandemic crisis has accelerated the trends that were set in motion since the financial economic crisis of 2008-2009.

Unlike the crisis of 2008-2009, the current health crisis has abruptly and profoundly paralyzed a large part of the markets at all levels. An important indicator to measure the impacts of these two crises is to compare unemployment, which has only taken 6 weeks in the current crisis to reach the same level as in 65 weeks in the 2008-2009 crisis. There are sufficient elements to support with evidence that the global economic scenario is one of a greater collapse in the economic growth of the more developed economies than that of the previous economic and financial crisis of 2008-2009. Among this evidence are the fall in production and demand in international markets in all economies without the possibility of meeting the fall in domestic demand in national markets.

The global economic and financial crisis of 2008-2009 and the health crisis of 2020 deepened the negative effects of globalization, the increase in economic inequality, the dislocation of jobs, the systematic destruction of socio-ecosystems and the loss of biodiversity, uncontrollable and unsustainable consumerism, etc. Trade wars and the coronavirus crisis put the continuity of globalization processes and the international trade system in checkmate. Trade tensions reflect the influence of China's economic management approach with a completely different set of values than the more developed economies, one of the factors that has given rise to trade wars. The health crisis of the pandemic has collapsed global trade and that must be faced with supranational institutions that are weak and without leadership. Human movements, tourism and immigration have been disrupted.

Cross-border lending networks driven by large global banks declined during financial crises, with fewer lending banks and fewer interrelationships. The big global banks occupy the center of the network. The big global banks have reduced their operations by allowing the official banks of China to enter. In other words, with the global financial crisis, cross-border financing networks have shrunk but density has increased with greater risk diversification. Economic and financial crises have a strong impact on global banks that spreads through the networks, affecting loans to developing countries (Conesa, Lotti and Powell, 2020).

The current health crisis has had a greater impact on the world economy because it was accompanied by a drop in the prices of commodities and oil, unlike the crisis of 2008-2009. In this situation of the depression of the commodities market, in the pre-crisis there were difficulties in the financial conditions of the less developed economies, such as Latin America, unlike the crisis of 2008-2009, these countries had low levels of external public debt while some were already running surpluses.

The current context of the international economy shows powers in relations of conflict rather than international cooperation, sieges and commercial reprisals that complicate and make the development of globalization processes complex. The international coordination of governments resolved the international financial crisis 2008-2009. International coordination is essential to establish strategic agreements to determine global demand, production, and income. However, at present this coordination has been very scarce due to the polarization of interests involved in trade wars and the spraying of efforts demanded by the solution to the pandemic crisis.

POLITICAL ACTORS AND ECONOMIC AGENTS

The international economic organizations play a limited role in the economic regulation and control of the economic globalization process, factually leading the globalized world economy in a free and drifting situation. The deterioration of international and multilateral organizations constitutes a challenge for conflict management and humanitarian aid, especially when they are relegated by the West to focus on their domestic crises, increasing the risks of greater global instability. The United Nations has proposed as goals the achievement of the 2030 SDGs, which reinforce the idea of continuity in the processes of economic globalization, since, for example, objective 17 raises the need for global, private, and public alliances of the actors of international economic relations and globalization to achieve the objectives.

The world trade organization is harshly questioned by the rulings it issues that ultimately end in a trade war and threaten the economy with a global economy. Global trade relations are in tension between the countries that operate. The emergence of tensions in trade relations between the most advanced countries and before the health crisis, the indicators already indicated that a maximum point had been reached and that there was a stagnation in the integration of the factors of global systems. The globalization of economic relations is an economic model of the great powers and transnational companies on the less developed economies (Bauman: 2015, 7).

For the current global world to advance, it requires strengthening the coordination and collaboration of international institutions with better information exchange. Management of global risks is limited due to greatly diminished global leadership and international organizations. International cooperation systems with global responses are the way out of global economic crises.

A MNE has been defined as a company that belongs to one specific nationality which owns, in whole or in part, subsidiaries within other host national economies where owns property (Gilpin 2001, p. 278). Multinational and transnational corporations (MNCs) have been the main carriers of economic financial globalization, allocating resources and organizing production and distribution through the application of macroeconomic mechanisms to promote global territorial expansions of markets under the principle of profit maximization.

Many of the factors that benefited the United States and its multinational companies that allowed them to borrow, are linked to the star role of the dollar in the international monetary system, a situation that may change. The demand for dollar-denominated assets sustains the commercial and financial system. Financial globalization increases the profits of multinational companies and offers highly profitable investment instruments. The purchase of strategic sectors for the development of nations by foreign investment worries about the loss of their control. Competition among MNEs corporations improve their efficiency and their economic growth (Iamsiraroj and Ulubaşoğlu, 2015).

MNEs locate in countries with more favorable regulations, where they can benefit from low wages, tax evasions, etc. Multinational companies that settled in other countries did so to evade labor and environment regulations, which are usually laxer than in their countries of origin, as well as to receive tax incentives. Multinational corporations have positive effects when they can contribute to national and local economic growth by creating jobs, although the distribution of these benefits may be unequal and asymmetric.

MNEs expand from a home country to other host countries through FDI flows which have been explained by the ownership competitive advantages, the competitiveness of location specific which benefits their exploitation through internalizing the markets for specific advantages (Dunning 1999). Investments from MNEs increase and improve resources and capabilities stimulating local development, contributes to employment generation and development of human resources, among other benefits (Sanna-Randaccio and Veurgelers, 2003; Barrios et al, 2003; Feldstein, 2000; Gilpin 2001; Bhagwati, 2004; Wolf, 2005; Sala-i-Martin, 2006). A MNE invest abroad either creating new infrastructure in greenfield or in existing one to have control of business activities in services, manufacturing, extraction, and exploitation of natural resources abroad (Gilpin, 2001; Dunning and Narula, 1997).

MNEs and corporations have been harshly criticized for the effects of their activities in the host countries and the cost-benefit analysis (Duran, 2001). Critics against MNEs argue that exploit workers by paying lower wages in less developed countries despite the empirical evidence that proves the opposite (Brown et al, 2002; Graham, 2000). Multinational companies distrust operating principles based on the integration and interconnection of global flows of production, investment and consumption and the resolution of trade and investment disputes by multilateral institutions.

Some activities of MNEs corporations have harmful consequences in damaging the environment, facilitating corruption and bribery, and producing harmful goods and services, while exploiting the local natural resources, the biodiversity, and ecosystems, leaving behind environmental pollution and contamination. However, to defend their interests from the action of local communities and governments, multinational corporations can pay the best lawyers and lobbies in international institutions and organizations that protect them against sanctions in this case, or to apply sanctions against local governments that infringe royalty payments for use of intellectual property rights and patents (Bhagwati, 2004: 276).

These problems affect people and local communities in less developed countries and should be solved using multilateral and unilateral approaches sanctioning denounced abuses of multinationals. International and national laws and the actions of civil society and local communities can have a relevant role to regulate and sanction.

The Globalization Index is based on 25 variables covers the issues of economic, social, political, and cultural globalization flows at national level and their macroeconomic instruments and policies (Swiss Economic Institute 2013). The degree of social globalization includes freedom of information and quality of life with indicators such as internet and telephone use and traffic, movements in the tourism sector, etc. In some national cultures, religion in the local particularization in contemporary globalized society is considered antisocial and conflictual because the autonomous power structures evolved in the way out of secular institutions. In these national cultures, religion in a national society is incompatible with the new global society

However, developed economies have added more restrictive measures for imports and exports, and there are still many barriers to free trade such as tariffs, taxes, subsidies, etc. The increase of SWF could control some developed economies rising concerns for more clear regulations on transparency investment decisions and policies, financial risks control and management, fair competition, and international financial instability (Surendranath et al 2010).

The knowledge network flows on demand and supply relationships provides relevant information on the governing relationships management between the world financial cities and the variety of partners. There are very few studies of World cities and globalization and their role in decision-making capacities in urban systems (Friedmann, 2000, 1986: 70, 73 ff.; Sassen 1991: 127 ff.; Beaverstock, Smith and Taylor 2000: 125 ff.; Derudder, Taylor, Witlox et al. 2003: 876 ff.; Taylor 2004: 175 ff.; Robinson 2005: 757 ff.; Hanssens, Derudder and Taylor et al. 2010: 2 ff.; Lüthi, Thierstein and Goebel 2010: 115 ff.).

Theorists and organizers of anti-globalization movements and for global justice call for action. Anti-globalization movements argue that economic globalization has increased the income inequalities and suggesting the need to design and implement another integration strategy into the international economy and trade.

Economic projections also reinforce the dynamism of economic interactions with the leading role of new actors and change in leadership.

ARGUMENT IN FAVOR OF ECONOMIC GLOBALIZATION

Globalization means good opportunities but also responsibilities. Economic globalization processes have benefits, opportunities, challenges, and problems related to the internationalization of economic activities. Economic globalization has brought challenges and opportunities than have changed the global scenario. However, the consolidation process has had disappointing results in prosperity. The benefits of globalization policies must continue extending openness and economic integration while alleviating their negative side effects. The integration of financial and goods and services markets has evolved faster than the movements of services and labor.

However, some analysts argue that the benefits of globalization have reached everyone equally and because it has deepened dependence on certain raw materials and inputs. The increased dependence of the local economy on other foreign economies also increases the risks of losing control of supplies and supplies of inputs.

The increasing acceleration of economic, trade and investment exchanges has fostered a strong global development and economic growth and created economic wealth uniquely distributed. Economic globalization has direct effects on people's lives by allowing direct access as producers and consumers to goods and services in international markets where local economies contribute what they have comparative and competitive advantages. The global consumer increasingly prefers less standardized and more personalized satisfiers that fit their specific needs, wants and fears.

During this period of ascent of globalization processes, there are advances that cannot be haggled as, for example, the increase in global GDP that has multiplied by 62, global life expectancy has increased from 52 to 72 years. Globalization processes are redefined after three decades of economic growth while promoting economic, commercial, and financial exchanges without borders in a more open society.

The trade liberalization policy mix allows taking advantage of globalization (Gurgul and Lach, 2014). Some empirical studies confirm that national economies with higher level of trade liberalization have increased the living standards (World Bank 2016, Frankel and Romer 1999, Sala-i-Martin, 2002 and 2006, and Dollar & Kraay 2001). Other studies analyze the trade effects though regressions on the GDP per capita growth, although Rodriguez and Rodrik (2000) argue that trade liberalization is measured by the proportion between GDP and foreign trade. There has not been found direct correlation between trade liberalization and economic growth as a factor to reduce global inequalities and between each country.

Empirical studies have found association between financial liberalization and macroeconomic instability, but in the other hand, have not identified a direct relationship between economic and financial liberalization and sustained economic growth in developing countries (Stallings and Studart, 2006, Prasad et al, 2003; OECD, 2013; Tamarauntari and Diseye, 2013; Yahya et al 2015). The so called "Tobin tax" is a proposal made by Tobin, (1978) to tax any financial transaction.

Technological innovation has fostered trade liberalization supported by a decrease in tariffs and taxes which in the long run are associated with facilitating innovation, increasing productivity and positive results in economic growth.

Institutional innovations developed the market economies advantages which resulted in efficiency and legitimacy of markets. The capacity for innovation is the essential characteristic that motivates and energizes the world economy and markets. The capacity for innovation is the essential characteristic that motivates and energizes the world economy and markets. Globalization promised to boost prosperity by enlarging and making more efficient the markets.

Economic globalization has contributed to have more influx of information around the world. Speedy mass communication and dissemination of information through digital means is growing very fast. Local and national cultures are intermingling shared, and people are exposed and learning from other cultures.

Governments and corporations concerned with ecological and environmental sustainability are talking more trying to sort out the responsibilities between each other.

THE TURNING POINT: ARGUMENTS AGAINST THE GLOBALIZATION PROCESSES

The liberal economy and the emerging globalization after the Second World War are currently being seriously questioned, even by the countries that promoted it the most. Although globalization processes promote modernization and economic growth in the winning countries, they also generate inequalities and socio-economic inequalities in the losing peoples that give rise to social tensions (Molano, 2007: 12).

The arguments against economic globalization sustain that countries and people who remain outside of this elitist economic process, should consider the elements of the open flows of trade and foreign investments processes, to identify the way to take advantage of any potential benefit for national economies from their insertion from economic globalization. The growing insecurity in investments and international trade is negatively affected by the lack of effective control mechanisms in strategic sectors.

Economic and financial globalization have effects on all economic activities rising concerns on issues of ecology and sustainable development, use of renewable resources and energy, limitation of gas emissions that accelerate climate change and corporate social responsibility, among others. Climate change is a sign that the wealth of nations is changing in the 21st century from a base of unlimited growth marked by the beginning of the end of an economic expansion that is not compatible with the limits set by the finite resources of the planet, to a different mechanism connected with mitigation and reduction. The UN Climate Action Summit 2019 (COP25) does not refer to growth but to the mitigation and reduction of CO2 emissions.

Economic globalization processes of production, distribution and consumption has negative effects on the depletion of natural resources, loss of biodiversity, destruction of ecosystems and sustainable environmental development. Production exceeds effective demand. Transportation and logistics are responsible of environmental problems such as gas emissions, air pollution, plastic pollution and are the main cause of global warming.

The current processes of unbridled globalization are criticized because the effects have not been as expected because it only benefits a part of the world population and provides opportunities for certain business sectors, but it generates the impoverishment of small and medium-sized local businesses, produces a growing wage reduction accompanied by job insecurity, which is intentionally implemented as a strategy to reduce production costs.

The effects of trade liberalization on economic growth are confusing in some countries that undertake internal reforms, besides the difficulties to determine causality (Rodriguez and Rodrik, 2000; Rodrik,

2007; Steinberg, 2005 and 2007; Dollar and Kraay, 2001a). However, the benefits of trade liberalization are considered ambiguous by the new endogenous growth theory, depending on the comparative advantage provided by the economic resources (Rodrik 2007, p. 219).

Trade and labor market reforms favoring trade liberalization are related with an increase in income inequality (Brohman 1996). It is not clear if income inequality is caused by trade liberalization. Trade competition has hit the lowest paid workers. Globalization by itself does not guarantee the well-being of all. The dynamics of economic globalization have strengthened socio-economic inequalities and hierarchies of authority that victimize workers and local cultures subject to their localities. The loss of national identity, due to globalization processes is argued in favor of a homogenization of global cultural identity. For example, minority local languages tend to disappear.

In those nations where there are no fiscal compensation mechanisms, the benefits of globalization go hand in hand with an increase in the levels of inequality. The lack of fiscal mechanisms to compensate for income inequality makes it more pronounced. Therefore, fiscal policy must be oriented to be redistributive of income that benefits those with fewer resources to increase their consumption and demand and therefore tends to reduce poverty and economic inequality, as well as increase economic growth (Piketty, 2014).

Despite that the orthodox theory argues that free trade promotes increases of income, Berry (1998) argues that in Latin America the income inequality increases when the trade liberalized increases. Free trade is questioned for its compatibility with the principle of equal opportunities. These situations lead to high income disparities, declining wages and higher economic and social inequalities and exclusions being the more unskilled workers the most affected for lack of opportunities and mistreatment. The race-down trend in reducing wages and salaries as a strategy to promote economic growth only reduced private consumption which is required by investments and therefore diminishes the global market (Stockhammer 2012).

The market as the best mechanism to allocate resources that generates economic growth has resulted in non-sustainability. The markets have a very complicated evolution due to the health crisis that has serious implications in logistics and supply problems, work management, erratic impact on demand, oversupply and reduction in consumption, changes in the behavior of consumers who prefer non-perishable products to perishable ones, management at points of sale due to decreed closures, fear, or lack of supply of merchandise.

Inequality is increasing and become deeper, damaging an already unfair society. Global inequality has declined in some countries due to the globalization benefits in economic growth (Sala-i-Martin 2006). Economic globalization has favored the strongest economic sectors and the rapid growth of the so-called BRICS and the inequality between countries seems to have decreased. However, other studies have found the increase of inequality within each country and changes in income distribution may not be related to the development of international trade (Bhalla, 2002; Dollar and Kraay, 2001a; Wolf, 2005, Majeed, 2016).

Longstanding incentive systems and structures of economic globalization have some perverse economic, social, and environmental effects. Economic globalization processes have opportunities, challenges and problems related to the internationalization of economic activities. When the globalization processes blew up, they have caused extensive collateral damage leading to the inevitable backlash.

World economy has integrated countries in very unevenly and different degrees due to the power of international structures and reliance in market forces (UNDP 1999) resulting in tensions, inequalities and socially constructed gendered impacts on components of institutions and organizations of economic globalization. Globalization has created more social and economic inequalities, benefiting the richer who gets richer while creating more poverty.

Since 2008, developed countries are experimenting dysfunctionalities of international financial markets. The processes of globalization are causing the increased volatility of the financial and currency markets, the increase in unemployment and the precariousness of employment, the impoverishment of the middle classes, the mediocre economic growth of emerging economies. Emerging and less developed economies are the most vulnerable to the impact of the global economic crisis because they already had problems of low economic growth, and a high level of dependence on commodities. Emerging economies that had increased their levels of trade since 1990 have been affected by a decrease due to the commercial and financial crisis of 2008.

Most of the trade agreements have cost many jobs, dysfunctionalities, and trade deficits for some countries. The free trade agreements promoted by the globalization processes aimed to eliminate free trade barriers, but some countries have imposed more import and export tariffs, valued added taxes, subsidies, zoogenic and phyto sanitary barriers, etc. Multinational and transnational companies exploit the tax heavens to avoid payment of taxes.

Globalism destroys the sovereignty and borders of nation states. National and local governments have diminished their sovereignty and the institutional efficiency to enforce regulations, establish redistributive policies to improve the social wellness and manage the financial crisis. Globalization is criticized and questioned for its inability to prevent or at least mitigate financial economic crises.

Economic globalization process provides more development opportunities but also is posing enormous risks by expanding the gap between developed and the few developing countries benefited, marking the differences in income per capita, the value of foreign trade, etc. Emerging economies are driven by exports to developed countries of natural resources, raw materials and consumer goods showing signs of exhaustion of the model.

Despite that trade liberalization may have positive effects on economic growth, the effects on income distribution are not clear (Ezcurra and Rodríguez-Pose, 2013). Some developed economies have trade imbalances with negative effects on less developed countries. Developed countries lost jobs by the transferences to lower labor costs countries. Workers have little leverage to face pay-cut demands from their employers in developed countries creating a culture of fear.

Despite that economic globalization processes have contributed to increase the standard of living, has also negative effects on emerging local economies and workers. The middle class in developed economies that used to have economic strength, are dissatisfied from the economic globalization processes which has represented a threat to the living standards. Competition has not always driven prices down because countries can manipulate currency exchanges to get a competitive advantage based on price over other nations. Although globalization has increased the living standards of a large part of the world's population, it has also generated large gaps in economic inequality and a rapid deterioration of biodiversity and socio-ecosystems.

Globalization processes have increased levels of job insecurity due to a considerable reduction in wages as one of the strategies to reduce costs and increase competitiveness at the expense of workers. While consumers benefit from great variety of goods and services, better quality and lower prices, communities that are dependent on jobs outsourced elsewhere have difficulties to sustain competing with lower cost labor markets always under the threat of corporations in a race to the bottom. The imported low-price goods and services do not match the decline of wages and family wage jobs.

Economic globalization processes have led to exploitation and degradation of labor, such as the case of child working with the lowest wage, health, and safety standards in inhuman and insane working conditions, increase of human trafficking for slave labor. Labor skills are marketed around the world which most of the times cause conflicts in local existing labor markets with the wages that are pressured downward. Labor restrictions that prevent the hiring of the best global talent limit the competitiveness of companies and the national competitiveness of the countries that impose them (McGrew, 1990)

Transnational and multinational companies invest in installing manufacturing plants in less developed countries providing employment, while most of the times these jobs are precarious. Multinational and transnational corporations take advantage of their situation in weak and less developed countries where they commit social inequalities and injustices creating unfair working conditions and lower living standards, mismanage and exploitation of natural resources, environmental sustainability, and ecological damages.

The existing WTO rules cannot have control over non-market measures to favor specific trading partners. The international negotiation mechanism has been incapable of mediating international trading disputes.

CHANGES OF THE CURRENT ECONOMIC GLOBALIZATION DUE TO THE PANDEMIC CRISIS: DEGLOBALIZATION

The entire global economic structure is reeling from the health crisis of the pandemic. Governments of Nation states and corporations are assessing the global market as a growing source of disruption of global value, production, and logistics chains, as well as the source of risk and competitive disadvantages. Local governments are retracting global policies of economic integration and are increasing the protectionist policies for repatriation of manufactures Abdal, & Ferreira (2021). However, other national economies have already developed capabilities to become resilient, recovering, restructuring, and enhancing the new institutional governance emerging from the pandemic.

Today's globalization faces challenges that put it at a crucial turning point. The world economy entered a negative growth trend in the last four years with an accumulation of problems such as the indebtedness of individuals, companies, and national governments with high levels of public deficit, disputes and trade wars, changes in the stock markets, etc., among others.

An internal orientation with an inward look at the national economies created the perfect environment for a decreasing trend of reduction of international trade and financial ties in such a way that those who had no other options to modify their economic growth strategy were harmed. The increase in tariffs in each country and trade tensions between the exporting economies, the reduction in the activities and profits of the multinationals, among others, are trends that are aimed at proportionally reducing financial globalization. In economic globalization, nations export goods and services.

The governments of countries with a populist tendency support policy that put an end to the processes of economic globalization, with measures to close borders due to the health emergency, greater control of migratory movements of the population, trade wars and polarization of commercial exchanges. The health crisis of the pandemic results in very negative indicators with the loss of millions of jobs and the bankruptcy of millions of companies, salary falls, increased levels of inequality and poverty, greater concentration, and monopoly control, etc.

The health crisis of the pandemic is affecting all sectors of production, distribution, and consumption, causing major changes in consumer behavior, in the nature and routines of telework, problems of logistics and supply of satisfiers, etc. many of the causes that give rise to consider the scope of the processes of economic globalization. Consumption, for example, is retracted and stopped because of the confinement that implies less exercise and physical activity.

The results of the consolidation of economic globalization processes resulting from the implementation of expansive and invasive strategies have been very different from those expected due to the high disparities in the distribution of wealth that have given rise to staggering levels of poverty. The global health crisis brought de-globalizing implications for the economy with a decrease and slowdown in the processes of integration and interdependence. The processes of world economic integration are in decline in all sectors.

Analysts foresee a period of deglobalization following the pandemic and the lockdown where countries and people tend to stay behind their borders despite that the incomes are going down and costs are going up while individual are getting poorer. Countries are tightening their geographical and commercial borders while increasing their restrictions. Bello (2005, 2013) published deglobalization suggesting that it is possible to give other content. The globalization processes were already in decline before the health crisis of the pandemic dealt the great blow to all national economies and therefore to the global economy, in addition to showing the weaknesses and failures of the system on which it is based.

The coronavirus has spread worldwide as a by-product of globalization processes, showing its weaknesses. The health crisis of the pandemic has negative effects on long-term international trade. National governments are now more aware of strengthening the capacity of public health systems considering it to be a national security imperative.

For other analysts, the de-globalization processes are only a short-term effect of the crisis with a decrease in investments prioritizing the local market. The interests of local elites that converge in the hegemony of local governments legitimize economic policies, although they are not necessarily based on a legitimation of economic behavior. The massive inflow of money into a local economy specialized in primary sectors that are deindustrialized, impoverished, and distorted into Dutch disease also known as abundance disease. This situation leads to deep local financial crises in very different ways (Reinhart and Rogoff, 2013) Many of these links are difficult to disappear.

The processes of economic and financial de-globalization propose that local economies should be reoriented in short circuits towards production for local consumption, avoiding the relocation of companies that generate competition because they seek places where labor costs are lower, production standards and ecological are less restrictive, etc. Financial chaos justifies the concentration of power in financial centers. However, there is no chance that the financial economic elites will be destroyed.

The phenomena of the redefinition of territorial boundaries of the countries and of national identities are not phenomena, although many of the times they are contradictory, that reconfigure globalization processes but rather the continuity of a new stage of the processes of more aggressive, exclusive economic globalization and dangerous than the previous ones for the harmonious and inclusive coexistence of nations. Taking the export of work and the production of companies to other countries and depending on inputs and resources from distant territories, what before was considered an efficient system now turns out to be risky.

Among other important factors for the territorial organization of production, distribution and consumption activities, access to raw materials, availability of skilled labor, costs, strategic location close to global markets, etc., are considered. The manufacturing industry has already begun the return or reshoring of some of its productive operations that it carries out offshoring, due to causes such as the trade war and the coronavirus health crisis. Re-shoring is strengthened with the automation of activities, also allowing the diversification of the supplier base and with the support of the national economic policy.

The systemic risks of economic deglobalization processes can have effects on the economic viability of the business. Among the causes of the processes of slowing down and reducing globalization is the volatility of international markets that has increased in recent years, which causes financial risks to increase with a tendency to decrease international investments and to invest more in local markets, the commercial exchanges in exports and imports are reduced.

This period of deglobalization has implications for international business and companies. Economic policies are shifting towards different forms of globalization promoted by various forms of national production. The national governments of the most developed countries focus their economic policies on favoring domestic demand in their markets.

The Munich Security Conference (MSC) (Munich Security Report 2020) focused on the phenomenon of de-westernization that poses the withdrawal of the world economy as an illiberal trend characterized by the lack of a common strategy that results from disunity. Currently the North American government speaks out against the excesses of the advances of commercial globalization and does not commit itself to the exercise of intellectual leadership.

It can be argued that commercial exchanges are changing form as in the cases of international tourism and migratory movements of people. The process of globalization of the flows of people in a context of global talent has caused a notable migration from emerging economies to develop economies and is expressed in part by the human drama of the refugee crisis, although the total percentage in absolute terms of the migratory population has remained stable for the last 100 years. Greater control of the migratory movements of people, but especially of talent, which is a global resource, has consequences in the labor field, among others, the redefinition of labor relations and the extension of telework as a labor modality.

In the face of deglobalizing uncertainty, autocracies develop a greater capacity to survive the challenges of globalization and take advantage of the freedom of action to review the international order at the cost of weakening the regime of civil liberties and universal human rights. However, these proposals from the extreme right are linked to racist claims and immigration status. Reversing or slowing down the processes of economic globalization will mean changes in the practices and activities of multinational and transnational companies.

The free trade mechanism promoted by globalization is heading towards trade wars between the great trading powers through huge deficits that seek to de-globalize previous advances through a new managed trade. The threats of a trade war weaken the world economy and its impact is uncertain if the current system of international cooperation breaks down. Because of the trade wars, business strategies have been changed; global supply networks are replaced and reconfigured by shorter ones so that they are more resistant to disruptions due to shocks.

All global supply channels that had been established in international trade have been impacted by the closures of national economies, which perceive that they must depend on themselves with economic policies that, before continuing to look abroad, now must look to the outside. The impact of this strategic change in companies is affected by increased costs, reduced efficiency, and increased prices to the final consumer.

The redefinition of globalization processes marks a new way of carrying out cooperative relations and integration of international economic relations.

The left has always opposed the optimistic accounts of the imperialist globalization project and it seems like they are proving their arguments that another world is possible for the explosive growth of poverty and inequality. A viable alternative as a sample is the emergence of large self-centered spaces that are constituted as poles of economic, political, social, cultural and civilization power.

DISCUSSION OF THE IMPLICATIONS FOR GLOBALIZATION

The global economic system has been in chronic crisis for more than half a century. If the world economic history is analyzed, the processes of economic globalization have not been linear. In fact, the dialectical developments of increasing economic, financial, trade, people and ideas toward a more integrated world economy is followed by the opposite movements in the direction of deglobalization. The global economic system has been in chronic crisis for more than half a century. The dynamics of globalization processes have been interrupted by decisions that put into question the world economic system that facilitates exchanges through commercial, financial, people and information flows.

The processes of economic, commercial, and financial globalization have contributed to many nations increasing their wealth with the opening of their markets to international trade, while many nations have been ruined, mainly those that remained closed. History provides evidence that those nations that resist signing free trade agreements under equitable conditions, block their development in some way.

Globalization requires sustaining itself on values, cultures, ideas, ways, and trends that promote the uniformity of tastes and traditions so that they are shared by local communities in such a way as to develop the existence of an international community. Culture, values, traditions, etc., have been changed by the economic globalization. The integration of globalization must be spontaneous and not interference by right or obligation that emerge from the evolution and socio-cultural development of peoples. What has been erroneously called uni-globalization refers to the assimilation of cultures, values, customs, traditions, habits, etc. that are replicated in a single direction and with commercial and economic effect

Economic globalization is becoming deindustrialization of some developed countries due to the outsourcing practices in both manufacturing blue- and white-collar jobs. National economic policies and strategies are designed and implemented to make economic globalization processes more equitable. Economic and financial globalization may be more transformational transition oriented towards more ecological and sustainable world if the environmental concerns are treated as a coordinated response of all agents and actors for a global synergy.

The transition from globalization to the post-global phase is identified with a greater awareness and responsibility for socio-ecosystems, biodiversity, and the quality of life of people and their population-spatial burden, taking the economic side into the background. Some of these concerns that require coordinated efforts are the reduction of gas emissions and waste, transition to renewable energies, etc.

The health and economic crisis have given rise to rethinking the entire business ecosystem. Global competition must play the same rules and regulations (Lascurain and Villafuerte, 2016). Greater global scalability of production in global companies can increase competitiveness but reduce competition and innovation capacity.

International institutions and national governments are redefining their roles as instruments to find better integration processes into the global economy. Globalization processes must redesign institutional structures or create new institutions to build integration based on the socioeconomic and ecosystem needs of nations and communities of all peoples. It is necessary to establish agreements on binding international mechanisms to address economic and financial crises. Also, it is necessary to implement expedited procedures in customs for the import and export of goods that are critical to its sustainability, while promoting and enhancing international agreements and treaties.

Environmental sustainability is one of the great challenges. The recovery from the economic crisis caused by the pandemic and followed by a global recession is an opportunity to reset the world economy based on more sustainable development. Economic globalization processes are leading to the worldwide spreads of human diseases. The initiative to change economic relations in the processes of globalization that originate ecological imbalances, due to an orientation towards greater care for the planet's ecosystems, implies recognizing the finite limits of natural resources and ecosystems, a greater respect for cycles vital of nature and the environment, decarbonize productive activities to preserve the biodiversity of natural resources.

Another challenge of globalization is to achieve a better equitable distribution of global benefits in such a way that it closes the gap of economic and social inequalities and allows people from emerging countries to get out of poverty. Emerging countries require a financial architecture with support mechanisms to regain liquidity and access to international financial markets. Countries that require solvency need to restructure their debt with the support of multilateral institutions and facilities that give more support to their debt markets.

The impact of the processes of economic globalization on the economic growth and social development of the countries explains the increase in inequality. An entirely free global market seems to be an unattainable goal. From 1960 to 1998, the period of rapid growth in international trade and investment economic and social inequalities have worsened. Economic organization is socially digested when it does not involve a destructive acceleration of growth. Multilateral trade relations are under review to guarantee greater autonomy for global economies. Economic globalization processes are not working to benefit most people around the world.

Globalization processes create multiple forms of cooperation. The interests of less developing countries need the development of a new international economic order changing the conditions of the current economic globalization model as the base of an old international economic order that cannot contribute to develop a fairer and reasonable new international economic order to benefit developing countries. The national economy needs the complementation of the international economy to achieve self-sufficiency in agricultural and industrial production. The interests of developing countries must have to be respected and enlarged in such a way that their development may result in larger share of growth.

For this reason, developing nations need to participate and negotiate actively on the economic globalization process to achieve a significant share on development provided the big interests that developed economies must take advantage of the benefits. The benefits obtained from the new international order of the world economy should be made available for the improvement of development to all the participating countries, not only a few ones. However, in the long run the economic interests of developed countries would be affected if developing countries do not benefit.

The debate on globalization points to the implementation of a more inclusive model in such a way that the losers of the more advanced process receive compensation through the implementation of active labor and income protection policies for the unemployed. It is required to analyze the situation, identify the risks inherent to globalization to establish regulation and control measures. The de-frontierization initiative as a proposal for the reconfiguration of the current phase of globalization to allow the free cross-border transit of people, promoting diversity, would be a more solidary and fraternal world, but unfortunately it is utopian.

Achieving an economic recovery to achieve previous levels of income and employment requires reactivation instruments.

Globalization has fostered the attachment to the material and consumerism over the exercise of ethical values and social solidarity.

REFERENCES

Abdal, A., & Ferreira, D. M. (2021). Deglobalization, Globalization, and the Pandemic: Current Impasses of the Capitalist World-Economy. *Journal of World-systems Research*, *27*(1), 202–230. doi:10.5195/jwsr.2021.1028

Barrios, S. (2003). Foreign Direct Investment, Competition and Industrial Development in the Host Country. *European Economic Review*, (49), 1761–1784.

Bauman, Z. (2015). *La globalización, consecuencias humanas*. Ciudad de México: FCE.

Beaverstock, J. V., Smith, R. G., & Taylor, P. J. (2000). World-City Network: A New Metageography? *Annals of the Association of American Geographers*, *90*(1), 123–134. doi:10.1111/0004-5608.00188

Bello, W. (2004). Deglobalization: Ideas for a New World Economy. Zed Books.

Berry, A. (1998). The Impact of Globalization and the Information in Latin America. In A. S. Bhalla (Ed.), *Globalization, Growth and Marginalization*. Macmillan Press. doi:10.1007/978-1-349-26675-3_4

Bhagwati, J. (2004). In Defence of Globalization. Oxford University Press.

Bhalla, S. (2002). *Imagine There's no Country: Poverty, Inequality, and Growth in the Ear of Globalization*. Institute for International Economics.

Brohman, J. (1996). *Popular Development, Rethinking the Theory and Practice of Development*. Backwell Publishers.

Brown. (2002). *The Effects of Multinational Production on Wages and Working Conditions in Developing Countries*. Research Seminar in International Economics, Discussion Paper No. 484, Michigan University.

CEPAL. (2002). *Globalización y desarrollo*. Recuperado el 10 de julio de 2018 de https://repositorio.cepal.org/bitstream/handle/11362/2724/2

Conesa, M., Lotti, G., & Powell, A. (2020). *Resilience and Fragility in Global Banking*. IDB.

Derudder, B., Hoyler, M., & Taylor, P. J. (2011). Goodbye Reykjavik: International banking centres and the global financial crisis. *Area*, *43*(2), 173–182. doi:10.1111/j.1475-4762.2010.00968.x

Derudder, B., Taylor, P. J., Witlox, F., & Catalano, G. (2003). Hierarchical Tendencies and Regional Patterns in the World City Network: A Global Urban Analysis of 234 Cities. *Regional Studies*, *37*(9), 875–886. doi:10.1080/0034340032000143887

Dollar, D., & Kraay, A. (2001). *Growth is Good for the Poor.* Policy Research Working Paper No. 2587, World Bank.

Dollar, D. y Kraay, A. (2001). Comercio exterior, crecimiento y pobreza, Finanzas y Desarrollo. *Revista trimestral del FMI*, *38*(3).

Dullien, S., Kotte, D. J., Márquez, A., & Priewe, J. (Eds.). (2010). The financial and economic crisis of 2008-2009 and developing countries. UNCTAD United Nations.

Dunning, J. H. (1999). Globalization and the Theory of MNE Activity. Discussion Papers in International Investment and Multinationals, Series B, 11(264).

Durán, J. (2001). *Estrategia y Economía de la Empresa Multinacional*. Pirámide.

Ezcurra, R., & Rodríguez-Pose, A. (2013). Does Economic Globalization affect Regional Inequality? A Cross-country Analysis. *World Development*, *52*(December), 92–103. doi:10.1016/j.worlddev.2013.07.002

Feldstein, M. (2000). *Aspects of Global Economic Integration: Outlook for the Future*. NBER, Working Paper No. 7899.

Findlay & O'Rourke. (2007). *Power and Plenty. Trade, War and the World Economy in the second millennium*. Princeton University Press.

Frankel, J., & Romer, D. (1999, June). Does Trade Cause Growth? *The American Economic Review*, *89*(3), 379–399. doi:10.1257/aer.89.3.379

Friedman, T. (2000). *The Lexus and the Olive Tree*. Anchor Books.

Friedmann, J. (1986). The World City Hypothesis. *Development and Change*, *17*(1), 69–83. doi:10.1111/j.1467-7660.1986.tb00231.x

Gilpin, R. (2001). *Global Political Economy: Understanding the International Economic Order*. Princeton University Press. doi:10.1515/9781400831272

Goldin, I., & Reinert, K. (2007). *Globalización para el desarrollo*. Banco Mundial.

Graham, E. (2000). *Fighting the wrong enemy antiglobal activists and multinational enterprises*. Institute for International Economics.

Gurgul, H., & Lach, L. (2014). Globalization and economic growth: Evidence from two decades of transition in CEE. *Economic Modelling*, *36*(January), 99–107. doi:10.1016/j.econmod.2013.09.022

Hanssens, H., Derudder, B., Taylor, P. J., Hoyler, M., Ni, P., Huang, J., Yang, X., & Witlox, F. (2010). The changing geography of globalized service provision, 2000-2008. The Service Industries Journal. doi:10.1080/02642069.2010.503887

Iamsiraroj, S., & Ulubasoglu, M. (2015). Foreign direct investment and economic growth: A real relationship or wishful thinking? *Economic Modelling*, *51*(December), 200–213. doi:10.1016/j.econmod.2015.08.009

James, H. (2001). *The End of Globalization: Lessons from the Great Depression*. Harvard University Press.

Javorcik, B. (2020, Apr. 3). Coronavirus will Change the Way the World Does Business for Good Businesses will be Forced to Rethink their Global Value Chains. *Valor Econômico*.

Lascurain, M., & Villafuerte, L. F. (2016). Primera globalización económica y las raíces de la inequidad social en México. *Ensayos de Economía, 26*(48), 67–90.

Lüthi, S., Thierstein, A., & Goebel, D. (2010). Intra-firm and extra-firm linkages in the knowledge economy: The case of the emerging mega-city region of Munich. *Global Networks, 10*(1), 114–137. doi:10.1111/j.1471-0374.2010.00277.x

Majeed, M. (2016). Economic growth, inequality and trade in developing countries. *International Journal of Development Issues, 15*(3), 240–253. doi:10.1108/IJDI-02-2016-0011

McGrew, A. (1990). A Global Society. In *Modernity and Its Futures*. Polity Press.

McLuhan, H. M. (1962). *La Glaxia Gutemberg*. Available on the web: http://www.ub.edu/procol/sites/default/files/La-Galaxia-Gutenberg-Marshall-Mcluhan-.pdf

Molano, G. (2007, September-December). El interregionalismo y sus límites. *Estudios Internacionales. Revista del Instituto de Estudios Internacionales de la Universidad de Chile*, (158), 12.

Morady, F., & Kapucu, H. (Eds.). (2017). *Development & Growth: Economic Impacts of Globalization. Global Studies, No. 3*. IJOPEC Publication. doi:10.5281/zenodo.1291756

Munich Security Report. (2020). *Westlessness*. Disponible en: https://securityconference.org/en/publications/munich-security-report-2020/

OECD. (2013). *Multidimensional Review of Myanmar* (Vol. 1). Initial Assesment.

Piketty, T. (2014). *El capital en el siglo XXI*. Fondo de Cultura Económica.

Prasad, E. S., Rogoff, K., Wei, S-J., & Ayan Kose, M. (2003). Effects of Financial Globalization on Developing Countries: Some Empirical Evidence. Washington, DC: IMF.

Reinhart, C. M., & Rogoff, K. S. (2013). Banking Crises: An Equal Opportunity Menace. *Journal of Banking & Finance*, *37*(November), 4557–4573. doi:10.1016/j.jbankfin.2013.03.005

Ritzer, G. (2011). *Globalization: The Essentials*. Wiley-Blackwell.

Robinson, J. (2005). Urban geography: World cities, or a world of cities. *Progress in Human Geography*, *29*(6), 757–765. doi:10.1191/0309132505ph582pr

Rodriguez, F., & Rodrik, D. (2000). *Trade Policy and Economic Growth: A Skeptics Guide to the Cross-National Evidence*. NBER Working Paper N° 7081.

Rodrik, D. (2007). *One Economics Many Recipes, Globalization, Institutions and Economic Growth*. Princeton University Press. doi:10.1515/9781400829354

Sala-i-Martin, X. (2002). *The Distributing rise of global income inequality*. NBER Working Paper No. 8904.

Sala-i-Martin, X. (2006). *Globalización y reducción de la pobreza*. FAES.

Sandretto, R. (2002) Globalization and National Sovereignty Defense of an iconoclastic view. In *Seventh International Scientific Conference. The problems of Economic Integration of Ukraine into the European Union.* Globalization and New Economy.

Sanna-Randaccio y Veurgeles, R. (2003). Global Innovation strategies of MNE's: implications for host economies. In J. Cantwell & J. Molero (Eds.), *Multinational Enterprises.* Innovative Strategies and Systems of Innovation, New Horizons in International Business.

Sapir, J. (2011). *La Démondialisation.* Éditions du Seuil.

Sapir, J. (2016). Jacques Sapir: Donald Trump, President of the Demondialisation? *Le Figaro.* http://www.lefigaro.fr/vox/monde/2016/11/10/31002-20161110ARTFIG00233-jacques-sapir-donald-trump-president-de-la-demondialisation.php

Sassen, S. (1991). The global city: New York, London, Tokyo. Princeton.

Stallings, B., & Studart, R. (2006), *Financiamiento para el desarrollo: América Latina desde una perspectiva comparada.* Libros de la CEPAL No. 90.

Steinberg, F. (2005). *Cooperación y Conflicto en el Sistema Comercial Multilateral: La Organización Mundial de Comercio como Institución de Gobernanza Económica Global* (Tesis Doctoral). Presentada en el Departamento de Análisis Económico: Teoría Económica e Historia Económica de la Facultada de Ciencias Económicas y Empresariales de la Universidad Autónoma de Madrid, España.

Steinberg, F. (2007). *Cooperación y Conflicto Cooperación Internacional en la era de la Globalización.* Ediciones Akal.

Stockhammer, E. (2012). Financialization, income distribution and the crisis. Investigación Económica, 71(279).

Straw, W., & Glennie, A. (2012). The Third Wave of Globalization. In *IPPR Review on the Future of Globalization.* Institute for Public Policy Research.

Surendranath, R. (2010). The Role of Sovereign Wealth Funds in Global Financial Intermediation. *Thunderbird International Business Review, 52*(6), 589–604. doi:10.1002/tie.20381

Swiss Economic Institute. (2013). *Press Release, KOF Index of Globalization 2013.* Author.

Tamarauntari, M. K., & Diseye, B. T. (2013). Macroeconomic Uncertainty and Foreign Portfolio Investment: Evidence from Nigeria. *IISTE, 3*(12), 229–236.

Taylor, P. (2004). *World City Network: A global urban analysis.* doi:10.4324/9780203634059

Tobin, J. (1978). A Proposal for International Monetary Reform. *Eastern Economic Journal, 4*(3-4), 153–159.

Tugores, J. (2002). *Economía internacional, globalización e integración regional.* McGraw-Hill.

Valéri, P. (1945). Política del espíritu. Losada.

Van Bergeijk, P. A. G., & Brakman, S. (2010). *The gravity model in international trade: advances and applications.* Cambridge Univ Pr. doi:10.1017/CBO9780511762109

Verick, S., & Islam, I. (2010). *The Great Recession of 2008-2009: Causes, Consequences and Policy Responses.* Discussion Paper No. 4934. IZA Forschungsinstitut zur Zukunft der ArbeitInstitute for the Study of Labor.

Williamson, J. G. (2013). *Trade and Poverty: When the Third World Fell Behind.* MIT Press Books.

Wolf, M. (2005). *Why Globalization Works.* Yale Nota Bene.

World Bank. (2016). *World Bank Data.* http://data.worldbank.org/?display=default

Yahya, W. (2015). Macroeconomic factors and foreign portfolio investment volatility: A case of South Asian countries. *Future Business Journal, 1*(1-2), 65–74. doi:10.1016/j.fbj.2015.11.002

KEY TERMS AND DEFINITIONS

Deglobalization: Process of reduction of international exchanges of goods, services, workers, money, etc.

Economic Growth: It indicates that there is an increase in terms of income or of the goods and services that the

Financial Crisis: It is that economic disturbance that is originated by problems associated with the financial or monetary system of a country. The financial crisis, therefore, is not due to problems in the real economy of a country.

Inequality: The quality of being one thing different from another, or of being distinguished from another by having characteristics, values or traits that make it different. It is the opposite of equality.

International Trade: Is that economic activity that refers to the exchange of goods and services between all the countries of the world.

World Economy: It is that branch of the macroeconomic economy whose mission is to address all the economic actions that a country maintains with the rest of the countries and that can be of a different nature such as: commercial, financial, tourist and technological.

Chapter 2
Critical Analysis of the Relocation Strategy of Production Between National Protectionist Policies and Global Supply and Value Chains

José G. Vargas-Hernández
https://orcid.org/0000-0003-0938-4197
University Center for Economic and Managerial Sciences, University of Guadalajara, Mexico

ABSTRACT

This chapter aims to critically analyze the implications that the national protectionist policies have on the global supply and value chains and the relocation of production. The analysis is based on the assumptions that the global economy is facing the possibility of decoupling of many trade connections, and this trend favors deglobalization processes long promoted by populism, nationalism, and economic protectionism. It is concluded that global supply, production, and value chains, although being economically efficient, are no longer any more secure under national protectionist policies, and therefore, the relocation of production processes is mainly due to the increase in the level of income and wages of the developing countries that are the destination and which reduce the advantages to relocate.

INTRODUCTION

This analysis shows expansive periods of free trade alternate with other periods in which protectionist measures and the relocation of production are part of a process that is called deglobalization and is characterized by a reduction in export growth that is compensated with increased consumption of the domestic market to defend national interests. Some developed economies have trade imbalances with negative effects on less developed countries.

DOI: 10.4018/978-1-7998-8314-2.ch002

The current environment of economic, social, political and health instability has intensified the increase in the economic costs of transaction and coordination of the subsidiaries of multinational companies located in other international host territories, making relocation processes unviable, for which they have initiated processes of repression or de-globalization to return its production to the countries of origin. This situation has meant stagnation, and in some cases a reversal in business strategy to deepen the globalization processes of companies.

The level of economic integration in globalization processes is well advanced, as it has been shown that when production in a province of China is paralyzed, the supply of inputs to other companies from other nations has affected, a situation of vulnerability that has motivated deglobalization as a response that makes relocation more profitable with the repatriation of factories.

This paper first makes a critical analysis of the national protectionist policies and its implications on the global supply and value chains and how these two factors determine the strategy of the relocation of production. Finally, it is offered a discussion on these issues.

NATIONAL PROTECTIONISM POLICY

Protectionism has returned, and it will be having to think about it if it is wanted to reap all the benefits and implement this reasoned "deglobalization" that it called for and that now seems inevitable (Sapir, 2016). The term deglobalization was coined by Sapir (2011) to refer to the protectionism of countries that have a similar level of development and economic growth limited by the commercial and financial dimensions of globalization than through outsourcing and relocation processes of large companies. groups of production centers. Deglobalization processes are characterized by the recovery of the sovereignty of nations, reduction of their interdependence, implementation of automatic and protectionist policies to reduce economic and commercial relations.

In a protectionist policy, countries increase restrictions on the free flow of trade, finance and people, reinforcing their national borders and are oriented towards deglobalization processes that threaten the internationalization of higher education, for example, which remains confined, although It is already advised to deepen the advancement of online education through platforms that reach all places, including the most remote places in the world. The concern about these changes is the depth in which they must occur to save and overcome the advances of globalization, so it can be considered that the advances will be different and different as it had been advancing before, although it is necessary that competition be promoted at the same time that cooperative and collaborative relationships are fostered.

Deglobalization is an inverse process to globalization that is manifested by the protectionist and regulatory economic and trade policies of the nation states as well as the trade wars that are carried out between the great economic and commercial powers. To protect national production, domestic markets increase tariff barriers with the intensification of trade wars between western and eastern markets. What the health crisis has done is accelerate the process.

The international competition on economic systems in the world economy is reduced to economic structures and enterprises mechanisms of macroeconomic players supported by the strengthen functions of the state to stabilize macroeconomics, protect intellectual property rights, to ensure legality and enforcement of contracts, infrastructure provision, and other micro economic policies to stablish incentives and mechanisms for corporate governance, stimulating research and development, investments in human development. Protectionist, nationalist and populist policies can be functional or dysfunctional depending on their correct design and implementation.

Some of the phenomena that disappointed the scope of the globalization economy were job insecurity and flexibility due to stagnant wages and rising unemployment. The far right has channeled discontent to promote protectionist measures. These situations have given rise to deglobalization processes through the implementation of protectionist economic policies. A greater presence of the State is necessary in the face of the challenges of economic growth, greater economic and social equality, social inclusion, environmental sustainability, protection of biodiversity and conservation of socio-ecosystems, the energetic and climate crisis, etc.

During the inter war era from 1914 to 1945, from the outbreak of World War I until the end of World War II, globalization processes were in retreat from the first time, after a period of increased economic integration from 1870 until 1914. After the First World War, protectionism and nationalism were on the rise as international institutions and organizations weakened, but the economic depression deepened. After the year 1918, with the rise of nationalism, international organizations were weakened, an economic depression arose that drove national states to protective economic models.

The abandonment of global economic integration is an option for nation states framed by a Keynesian scheme through the implementation of protectionist trade measures and maintaining democracy. These methods favored the economic growth of some developed countries that later embraced economic globalization (Rodrik 2000 and 2007; Steinberg, 2007, p. 45). The countries that remained with borders closed to trade through protectionist and nationalist measures were imposed asymmetric trade conditions, as was the case with the colonies. When these nations achieved their independence, they could already take off in their economic and social development.

After the Second World War, a system of international governance institutions was established with the programs of the Marshall Plan, the Bretton Woods institutions, the United Nations (UN) and the General Agreement on Customs Tariffs (GATT). During this period of globalization retreatment and economic dislocation led to reduced integration, the Great Depression and protectionism as the solution. After World War II, and until the 1980s, new global institutions for economic cooperation were created and developed to promote economic integration and enabling national economies to be opened to foreign markets. In 1989 the slow food movement was created to protect the consumption of local products, cultures, traditions and gastronomic customs perceived as healthier and safer. The movement aims to create awareness of decisions for food consumption and its origin.

During the international financial crisis of 2008 and 2009, the leaders of the most advanced economies managed adequately to avoid the trend of protectionist economic nationalism. The national state recovers functions that were taken from it and together with international institutions assume responsibilities to protect national economies and societies. In 2017, China promoted globalization as a mechanism for economic integration, generating wealth and multilateral cooperation, while the United States promoted trade protectionism. Protectionist trade policies used as an instrument for multilateral and bilateral negotiations do not always result in benefits for the country that promotes them, as has been recently demonstrated in the case of the United States, which has encountered strong resistance from the trend of economic globalization processes.

In 2018, many North American companies announced the relocation and transfer of their production plants back to the national territory. In 2019, the Kearney index detected a strategic trend in company production towards a greater weight of the "made in America" content of manufacturing production. In part this was achieved by the warning that if they wanted to receive the protection of the American legal system they should return the jobs. European countries grant aid through anti-crisis plans to their companies that disengage from tax havens.

Following North American policy, France encourages the repatriation of its companies while Japan favors its companies that return from China with incentives. Nation states have difficulty regulating the financialization that dominates the real economy and offshore strategies, as well as putting limits on the power of monopolies in the digital economy.

The unilateral discourses practiced by some powers attempt to control the world agenda of globalization processes through neo-protectionist mechanisms under the world economy revolving around a multipolarity. Geo-economics and geopolitical analyzes show a transition of leadership from the global economy to China. Now the United States plays the option of a more protectionist economy that drastically affects the economies that are more dependent on global trade. However, the slowdown in economic globalization began long before the pandemic, which has contributed to accelerating it by declining national economies.

The goal of the new United States government to eliminate the trade deficit through the implementation of protectionist and nationalist fiscal policies, and started a trade war against its trading partners, but above all with China, its main competitor, but which had repercussions worldwide, because it drastically reduced world trade. The elimination of the deficit simply to date, has not been achieved, but also worsened and deepened. The coronavirus health crisis imposed a truce on the trade war that paralyzes the negotiations of trade relations. However, the largest production of medical supplies is in China. With the health crisis, countries want to maintain their own economic activities and in proximity through protectionism. Consistent with this, multinational companies plan to repatriate in reshoring part of their international production.

The world economy faced threats in its globalization process long before the 2020 health crisis, such as the growing challenge of trade wars and the protectionism of the economies of different national states with the implementation of a tariff war. The health crisis is the result of negative externalities of an interconnected world in globalization processes that is perceived to be linked to physical security in identity and economic spheres, whose responsibility to protect against risks has fallen more on the nation state rather than on the international community.

The health crisis caused by the pandemic has accelerated the protectionist tendencies and the populist and nationalist policies of the nations and has caused tensions and trade wars in the face of the fall in international trade flows and foreign direct investment. The health crisis has accelerated and deepened this trend of economic deglobalization through protectionist actions, reduction of multilateral treaties, etc., with economic consequences that are legible, but uncertain and unpredictable.

The protectionist tensions that lead to a trade war constitute a reconsideration in the opposite direction to the progress of trade liberalization. This situation that arises unilaterally resists the continued opening of markets and international economies to position itself as a closed economy, erodes economic, commercial and political relations with its partners. In other words, the country that was the greatest promoter of economic globalization processes is now the greatest opponent of deepening economic, commercial and financial relations.

The liberalization of regulations of local financial markets that protected the host countries from foreign investments allows MNES to have access to local natural resources and get actively involved in local markets. As a consequence of this deregulation, the global FDI flows had increased regularly until 2000 and since then it had been falling until it reached a pick in 2007 (World Bank, 2016).

Now local governments try to implement different initiatives with protectionist measures against global markets since 2008, as ways to recover the economic growth of their economies, resulting in limitations to international trade. All these initiatives are strengthened to weaken the processes of economic globalization and cry out for deglobalization. After the subprime crisis, citizens demand to governments for protection of their own interests against the globalization interest through the redesign and implementation of more protective economic and financial liberalization policies.

The processes of economic globalization are being pressured by isolationist positions that seek to deepen the self-sufficiency of national states to protect local interests over global interests. These changes in perspective have implications and effects on the harmonious development of peoples. The national state recovers relevant functions in this process of deglobalization for the financial rescue in the face of the economic debacle of important economic actors and agents, such as multinational companies, financial institutions. The new scheme is configured with less market and more state with a geopolitical reconfiguration of national borders evidenced in a return to nationalist protectionism and more controls on cross-border financial transactions.

Factors such as technology-based automation, protectionist practices in national economies, rapid shipments and deliveries, among many other factors, contribute to the acceleration of the processes of slowing down or reversing globalization. Rather, the concern is diverted towards how profound these changes that are already occurring will be, but above all in the way they are going to be managed. These trends are driven by rising wages in countries that previously offered low labor cost advantages, as well as protectionism in local economies.

The restrictive and protectionist economic policy measures that materialize in the deglobalization processes are, among the most common, the increase in tariff rates, the establishment of phytosanitary measures, cross-border labor restrictions, limitations on foreign investment, control of movements immigration, trade wars, etc. As part of protectionist measures, importers raise their tariff barriers in response to the trade war.

Nation states are receding driven by protectionist trends due to falling global trade and investment flows driven by the health crisis. With the health crisis of the pandemic, the nation states enact protectionist, deglobalizing economic policy measures that reduce and retract the advance of globalization processes, such as, for example, the closure of the border to commercial exchange activities and nationalist control of migratory movements of the population. Nation states adopt nationalist, populist and protective economic policies in an attempt to recover their regulatory functions and fields of action in a gradual process of control of globalizing dynamics.

Trade protectionism is the relevant element of deglobalization for protecting the losers of globalization assuring gains though imposing high rates of industrial and trade protection and imposing manufacturing tariffs (Findlay and O'Rourke 2008, 401). Trade protectionism is a relevant action implemented in this deglobalization process. Deglobalization processes have repercussions that damage the economies that promote protectionist economic policies. The lack of leadership in the globalization processes makes it easier for each nation to reverse or at least slow down progress by adopting more protectionist measures.

National markets and economies are now less dependent on international markets and rely on the regulations of national economies to protect themselves. To exploit the advantages offered by the new environment, an emerging strategy has emerged that supports the resurgence of protection measures for national markets. The deglobalization of economic integration processes moves the center of gravity back from the market to the sustainable local market through a commercial policy and the use of fiscal, tariff and quota mechanisms to protect the national production of transnational companies. The uniformity and standardization of commercial regulations threaten regional and local development where the asymmetric is normal for self-protection.

Therefore, the protectionist attempt of an economy has a negative impact on national companies in such a way that the protectionist measures taken unilaterally by a country, damage the competitiveness of its companies and therefore its own economy. It is the same multinational companies that promote the relocation of production, distribution and consumption processes. Countries now attempt to relocate the production of goods within or near their national borders for the benefit of integrated regions through tariff protection measures.

The deglobalization process is supported by the promotion of protectionist measures and is characterized by export flows, investments, migratory movements and technological innovation that are reduced or diminished, are reflected in political and economic decisions to orient themselves to domestic demand with measures with tariffs, cross-border restrictions and limitations on investment and foreign labor.

Greater attention to domestic demand leads governments to reduce the growth of exports through direct or indirect protectionist measures. Countries alone are unlikely to oppose globalization given the omnipotence of global financial markets, so the alternative is to recur to the risks of trade wars more focused on national protectionisms. National governments grant tax incentives that benefit protectionism and populism for the repatriation of manufacturing plants and investments. Manufacturing employment is likely to decline while most forms of services employments are likely to be heavily protected from internationalization, therefore avoiding antiglobalization backlashes focus more on improving the quality and provision.

The same powers that before spread the gospel of open market and free trade are the same that now predicate protectionism and support deglobalization markets. It has been said that the global economic and financial elites pursue the creation of a world government by centralizing order and power by protecting from enemies through a surveillance system based on traceability.

Cultural globalization and an increase of human interactions has been the result of the economic, financial and trade exchanges, contributing to the different values, traditions, customs, habits, etc., are being shared among local communities and other communities in such a way that it is homogenizing a world's culture. Local culture requires protection to maintain its uniqueness at community level, environmental and development social movements and activists need the support of the nation state to defend society to defend and protect society from the destructive capacities of economic globalization and global market to exploit the human and natural resources.

GLOBAL SUPPLY, PRODUCTION AND VALUE CHAINS

Trade openness, economics, financial and commercial liberalization, information and communication technology innovations facilitated the special and operational expansion of transnational and multinational corporations which in turn, contributed to alter the exchange of resources flows and supply chains between intra and inter firm as well as to a global power redistribution. Economic globalization processes accelerated the flow of goods through global supply chains and global trade.

The development of ICTs and the emergence of the Internet accelerated the processes of globalization with world communication in real time, financial digitization and with the logistical development of supply and value chains, accelerated the scope of a global economy. Technological and scientific advances have intensified with economic globalization with the monopolistic emergence of digital companies that control the financialization of processes around global supply and value chains where BRICS countries have become the managers of changes in the global competitiveness (Rosales 2009: 77).

The value chains as well as the supply chains of the companies in a global economy scenario are distributed throughout the world. Mutinational and transnational corporations have established networks of supply chains, subcontractors and logistics around the world. The networking-based global economy is formed by chains developed by a large group of shadow enterprises that are connected for economic activities across the boundaries of countries and making meaningless the concept of distance and national borders.

In a competitive global market, the costs of the entire chain of supply, production and consumption spread worldwide should be the lowest (Bello, 2013). However, the globalization based on the economies of scale and scope due to location of production where is most efficient is over, while the concern is for the fragility of supply-chain diversification, because their processes rely each other to add their value.

The global production and distribution chains show the fragility of the high dependence on the processes of economic globalization to provide products and inputs to the economies that require them to continue their manufacturing processes. This failure in global production chains has exposed the weaknesses of national security and national industry, arguments that support protectionist positions, such as measures to guarantee supply in national markets. The national security policy acquires greater force by pressing for reversions in global production chains encouraged by supply decisions in local markets.

Starting in the 1990s, global production and value chains grew steadily. Since 2007, with the outbreak of the economic and financial crisis, the indicators of globalization processes show a trend of decrease in global production and supply chains, due to a drop in demand from international markets and not so much to the structural changes. Since the financial crisis of 2008-2009, world trade has failed to maintain the level of world GDP, due to the emergence of protectionist policies. Global economic, financial, health, and contingency crises such as natural disasters have a domino effect that has a greater impact on global production and value chains. The example is the tsunami in Japan in 2011 that affected global automobile production chains.

These stagnations in economic globalization processes have negative effects for the global economy due to the relocation of the production chain, although the reorientation may have some positive effects for certain national territories where some phases of this production chain can be carried out to take advantage of low labor costs. Reversing or slowing down the processes of economic globalization will mean changes in the practices and activities of multinational and transnational companies

In 2019 there is a high fragmentation of global supply chains, which is deepened by the 2020 health crisis. The ruptures of global supply chains produce a dislocation of production that produces in response the withdrawal of companies located abroad for The Coronavirus has paralyzed the growth of global trade, which contributes with more than 60% of the domestic product world gross. This situation has been called deglobalization, aggravated by the health crisis, which has made interconnections more difficult for commercial practices between different countries.

The current scenario of the health crisis has affected the complex global supply and value chains of intermediate goods, without being able to stop their fragmentation. This has shown that global supply chains are very vulnerable and complicated for companies to immediately redesign and redirect, which has accelerated de-globalization processes.

The critical situation of the health crisis has forced the space of global logistics and supply chains to be reduced to be replaced by shorter chains in such a way that the localities for the supply of raw materials and production of inputs or parts of a product must be shorter than the places where the final product is assembled. The health crisis has highlighted the limitations of global logistics and supply chains in sectors such as electronics, automotive, aeronautical, medical equipment, pharmaceutical products, textile industry, etc. The health crisis has broken global production chains.

The inability of the globalization processes to find a way out of the relocation of the production and supply chains, as well as the inability of the national industry in many countries to produce the required sanitary material, has complicated the economic scenario. The health crisis has exposed the dysfunctionality of global and multinational supply chains, placing excessively dependent companies at vulnerability. The health crisis has affected the global production chains of countries that are prone to international trade, although it is contradictory that it depends on corporate companies that originally relocated their production processes.

The dependence on imports of inputs for national production through supply chains, have been affected by the health crisis, so many nation-states have accelerated the processes of deglobalization by strengthening the production of inputs and operations in local spaces. Deglobalization processes imply having greater controls over commercial, financial, migration, travel flows, etc., which gives rise to retreats in the global supply and production chains.

Protecting and stimulating national food supply chains can help reduce the impact caused by the health crisis of the pandemic. Global supply and value chains have proven to be inoperative amid the health crisis. Multinational corporations transferred their productive operations to places where costs were lower, achieving supply through long global supply chains, which were suddenly interrupted during the Covid-19 health crisis, with serious threats to paralyze the production of certain essential products such as agro-food.

Deglobalization processes attempt to unlink local production from global supply chains to reorient production towards the internal market supported by movements in favor of food self-sufficiency and sovereignty based on domestic industrial and agricultural production, undertaken by economic policies and progressive commercials and not by right-wing nationalist governments that only serve the interests of the dominant ethnic and cultural group and displace minorities and immigrants.

With the emergence of the health crisis of the pandemic, countries have had to reconsider their supply chains and value of strategic productive activities, as in the case of food production. For this reason, strategic productive industries are a priority for national development, which is why they are considered to be maintained and strengthened with actions such as the development of local, flexible and fast supply chains of value chains.

Globalization undergoes profound changes with the crisis of the coronavirus pandemic and will not be as we knew it before in the modes of production, distribution and consumption and in the global production, supply and value chains. The dynamics of contemporary globalization processes have registered a strong interruption that calls into question the entire international economic system, disrupts global supply and value chains, as well as a slowdown in all economic sectors.

The continuity of the processes of economic globalization requires leading the mitigation of the negative impacts in the production and supply chains in the global economy based on the location in places where costs are lower. The priorities of the productive, distribution and consumption systems are changing their priorities through the location of supply chains as secure as possible rather than as economically as possible as was achieved during globalization. The economic efficiencies of globalization processes are being highly questioned with the dysfunctionality of global supply chains that lead to more protectionist economic and fiscal policies.

Deglobalization is a period of slowdown and decline in international economic, commercial, financial and people flows intensified by the coronavirus that has made companies rethink the risks of global supply chains that occur in remote locations. The economic phenomenon of deglobalization of the world economy is a period marked by a decline in commercial and financial flows, intensified by the coronavirus pandemic that has caused a rethinking of the risks of the global chain of supplies that come from geographically remote locations. Disruption of the supply chains of local companies' dependent on a global system generates economic losses.

With the interruption of global production and supply chains, and due to perceived risks, production and consumption turn to alternative sources of inputs, goods and services from local suppliers, passing the acquisition cost to second term Economic deglobalization, according to Witt (2019), assumes considering the strategic policies that affect the political sustainability of multinational companies, the dynamic organizations of value chain specializations and the national context in which these decisions about strategies, structures and behaviors. The breakdown of global supply chains has direct consequences on the profitability of many of these multinational companies.

The main causes that have given rise to the deglobalization processes, the slowdown in the growth of the global economy, the regression of global supply and value chains and the increase in protectionism of local economies against multilateral processes, to reduce the concerns about external dependence on essential supplies. The regression of global supply and value logistics chains go into regression processes for different causes, such as protectionism, wage increases and the level of income reduce the advantages of countries that were the destination of relocations. If production is less delocalized, flows in global supply and value chains are reduced, along with the investments that accompany them.

The interruption of global supply chains and therefore of value is a consequence of the trade wars started by countries with deficiencies in commercial and financial exchanges The Sino-US trade war is the landmark event for furthering the tendency of deglobalization with the disruption of the global supply chain and a declining global trade flows in value and volume.

The trade wars coupled with the risks of the coronavirus have caused the blockage of global supply chains and international supplies. They have been shortening their global supply and value chains for several years now, as a consequence of trade wars, through the relocation of their plants, production processes and the manufacture of their own components that came from distant locations and through the diversification of the origin of inputs and products. Companies around the world rethink their internationalization decisions as a reaction to dependence on global supply chains that distribute the production of products with the relocation of their plants and their production processes. This situation has shown the vulnerability of companies due to their excessive dependence on these chains.

Deglobalization manifests itself in changes in production systems based on the locations where production is most efficient, leading to many logistical mismatches in supply chains and value in trade connections. The creation of alternative supply chains modifies the rules of globalization processes. For the United States, the intensity of globalization shows vulnerabilities, such as in situations where national economies depend on a single country for the supply of goods, which leads to the blockage of supply chains.

Global supply chains are more complex in the production, distribution and consumption of products that have had to be interrupted or reduced due to the lack of provision of essential components. Globalization is transformed to be different than it was before the pandemic and it is possible that the modes of production, distribution and consumption are transformed due to changes in the global value, provision and supply chains.

Destructuring the networks in which currently major strategic activities are included in supply chains, production, management and distribution on global scale are organized and interconnected in real time on a sophisticated information and communication system. Companies are moving away from just-in-time production systems to more secure supply chains. The reduction of global supply and value chains negatively affects commercial, financial, investment and people flows. The deglobalization processes are pressing the global production, provision and value chains to change in organizational forms subject to local decisions.

Multinational companies are already reconsidering their logistics processes for the transport of goods that include socio-ecosystem concerns to try to shorten geographic distances and links in their global supply chains through the use and development of new technologies that reduce the costs and risks of production, increase quality and respond more quickly to market demand. Multinational companies reconfigure global value chains to strengthen themselves in the face of shocks.

National economies are bounded together in globalization through the supply chains to achieve manufacturing efficiency and better prices in international trade. The flow of international business activities is retracted as global supply and supply chains are reconfigured, prioritizing production over economic efficiency. Business organizations are assessing the location of global supply chains relocating their production elsewhere, which is a globalization trend of natural churn and premises. International trade replicates its operations while reconfiguring its supply chains sacrificing economic efficiencies in exchange for greater security in the provision of its inputs. International trade is territorially withdrawn to the national through the reconfiguration of its production chains and supply, leading to importers raising tariff barriers.

Populist and nationalist nation states have taken up this message, supported by political parties and social organizations to promote actions to deglobalize the economy that attempt to dismantle globalization through withdrawals of global value chains, repatriation of investments and strategic relocation of Business.

Global supply chains are relocated, which implies the reorganization of production, distribution and commercialization activities, reinforced with government policies, especially in sectors considered of national security. Returning plants to the country of origin can be more expensive, but in the current conditions of interrupted global supply chains, it turns out to be more productive and competitive due to savings in logistics risks, transportation, tariffs, etc. The reduction of dependence on the provision of supplies from other geographically distant locations through global chains of manufactured inputs has led to relocation or reshoring trends. Not only are the production sites relocated close to the markets, but also innovation, design, logistics, distribution and marketing activities, etc.

New technologies advance innovations in automation, robotization, artificial intelligence, internet of things, etc., which tend to replace the more routine and cheap labor, which implies that global supply and value chains reduce their importance with a localized and robotic production.

The deglobalization trend converted into regional trade agreements allows economies to be fully integrated and to take advantage of regional and local value chains. From the crisis that economic globalization is going through, companies that have less global supply chains, more regional and therefore shorter with respect to assembly or marketing lines, will emerge strengthened, not necessarily from lower cost suppliers and with minimal inventory levels, which confirms deglobalization. The interruptions of the global supply chains forced people and companies to look for alternative local or regional sources of supply, even though they were more expensive.

The less advanced economies have seen their global value chains reduced with premature processes of deindustrialization, lower economic growth, a commodity boom that has given rise to the Dutch disease phenomenon, non-redistributive and regressive fiscal reforms with an increase in income levels of poverty and inequality. Countries are backtracking in their globalization advances and trying to avoid the continuity of outsourced production chains to maintain strategic productive activities internally or as regionally as possible, with more flexible and faster local value chains.

The blockade of global supply chains represents the opportunity for Mexico to be the beneficiary due to its proximity to the North American market, as has been the case in the automotive, electronics and aeronautical sectors. Without the supplies produced in Mexico by these industrial sectors, the manufacturing of finished products is interrupted. Deglobalization and the T-MEC favor the rapid integration of the sectors of the electrical, automotive, medical equipment, aeronautical, pharmaceutical, aeronautical industries, etc. to the supply chains of North American companies. Complementation among the member countries of the T-MEC facilitates regional integration processes and solves the problem of supply and logistics chains.

Risk assessment focuses on disturbances in production processes mainly due to supply chains of inputs that come from geographically distant locations, or other phenomena such as natural disasters, wars, etc. One of the risks that are run with deglobalization is derived from geopolitical and geoeconomic uncertainty and its impact on investments with repercussions on production levels for global supply chains, exports and market volatility. Companies have reacted to the perception of risks through a strategy of geographic diversification of sources of supply and production that can affect global trade as production is relocated in the country itself.

The inability of the globalization processes to find a way out of the relocation of the production and supply chains, as well as the inability of the national industry in many countries to produce the required sanitary material, has complicated the economic scenario.

RELOCATION OF PRODUCTION

In a free market system under the invisible hand, companies continue to track the location of their production, distribution and consumption systems through offshoring or relocation decisions that mean benefits and cost efficiency. Tensions and trade wars accelerated the de-globalization processes under the premise of relocating the production and supply of resources from sources as close as possible, which confirms the trend towards open regionalism.

The processes of economic and financial de-globalization propose that local economies should be reoriented in short circuits towards production for local consumption, avoiding the relocation of companies that generate competition because they look for places where labor costs are lower, production standards and ecological are less restrictive, etc. On the other hand, foreign direct investment movements facilitate the relocation of production systems in global factories, taking advantage of the advantages offered by other national economies in cheap labor, more direct transport systems, the privatization of public companies, etc. The relocation of production that is manifested in the flows of direct foreign investment (Grunwald, and Flamm, 1985).

The relocation of production processes is mainly due to the increase in the level of income and wages of the developing countries that are the destination and which reduce the advantages to relocate. Delocalized production of companies motivated by lower production costs, are returning to a closer place through relocation or reshoring processes. Discontent over the growing impoverishment of the working middle classes in the most developed countries, the precariousness of employment and labor benefits, and the loss of employment, due to the relocation and flight of companies to locations where labor costs are lower. The advantages for relocating production, distribution and consumption systems have been reduced due to an increase in the income and living standards of workers in the countries that were the destination of these relocations.

There are several reasons that are making the processes of economic globalization dysfunctional to the growth and development of some countries, such as the loss of their political and economic sovereignty, growth in unemployment due to the relocation of production and the increase in automated systems and robotization, which also reduces relocations.

Companies have reacted to the perception of risks through a strategy of geographic diversification of sources of supply and production that can affect global trade as production is relocated in the country itself. Extraterritoriality characterizes economic globalization (Palomares 2006: 30) because of the capacity that transnational companies have to relocate production with geographic fragmentation. In such a way, this trend of regional proximity of production occurs, pointing to a relocation of production processes in countries that belong to the same economic region. The processes of regionalization of production is a trend in proximity to consumer markets that ensures the supply of resources, goods and services in places to consumer markets to respond quickly and flexibly to demand through customization or product customization.

With globalization, companies become more dependent on the places from which the inputs and products necessary for production are provided, so national states are now offering incentives to their companies to return operations that they had relocated in other countries. The continuity of the processes of economic globalization currently marks a break in the breakdown of international economic relations that, although it attempts to relocate production, the competition for the attraction of talent, technology and more advanced production capacity.

Relocation as a strategy of deglobalization processes has as immediate consequences the increase in labor costs due to differentials between nations, but also to the health crisis, with a tendency to reduce economic inequality. Another trend that accelerates as a result of relocation is robotization, which in times of pandemic is positive because it reduces the risks of contagion by eliminating or reducing face-to-face contacts. Another trend is the increase and consolidation of teleworking, with many implications for people's movements and the market for office space, parking lots, etc.

The increase in e-commerce is a trend that increases more with relocation and the health crisis of the pandemic. Pandemics have shown the risks that the globalized economy has under the logic of relocation of production to take advantage of lower costs that are then marketed in other regions of the world without establishing the pertinent health controls.

DISCUSSION

The post-pandemic world economy tends to be less globalized as it is rejected by national governments and populations to protect their national economies. The processes of economic globalization are deepening instead of a gradual process of deglobalization, under the argument of the principle of sovereignty with economic policies and measures that show a tendency towards a nationalist, protectionist and populist retreat. The actions of national states and international organizations promoting globalization processes such as regional integration treaties for free trade tend to weaken the sovereignty of the states. This is somewhat paradoxical in its contradictory processes due to its origin of globalized localisms that have contributed to strengthening hierarchies and inequalities both between nations and between individuals, the creation of victims who lack the protection of the state subject to their localities or forced to abandon them.

The world order that has prevailed since the Second World War has been considered under the conception of linear processes of irreversible economic globalization and has undergone structural changes in the last ten years that require reconfiguration. This reconfiguration has been called a deglobalization stage and corresponds to a regression of global integration processes in the form of retractions in world trade and international financial investments carried out through nationalist, populist and protectionist policies.

The movement of trade protectionism as a retreat from the processes of economic globalization with the renegotiation of trade agreements and trade wars was initiated by the United States. The trade war declared by the United States against China tries to weaken its strategic position in economic growth, cooperation, trade, finance, etc. The phenomenon of deglobalization is a popular political cause motivated by protectionist and reindustrializing economic forces.

The nation states face great challenges to guarantee the protection of the minimum welfare of the citizens. Another consequence of the reversal of the global integration of production processes is the increase in costs and therefore consumer prices, which results in a drop in welfare. From an ethical perspective, deglobalization processes should give higher priority to values over interests, cooperative relationships over competition, and community welfare over efficiency. From this same perspective, real economic thinking strengthens the values of social solidarity, justice, equity and community to subordinate the action of the market.

Local economies must exercise fiscal and economic policy mechanisms for the protection of their own production, distribution and consumption systems, as well as their socio-ecosystems from the subsidized importation of large transnational corporations that establish subsidized and artificial prices. A viable alternative as a sample is the emergence of large self-centered spaces that are constituted as poles of economic, political, social, cultural and civilization power.

The new nationalist and protectionist sentiments that drive the decisions of the n countries have a high impact on migrant workers who seek better economic conditions and greater well-being for their families. Nation states can prevent the flight of endogenous technological talent to other economies by creating institutional and instrumental frameworks for the establishment and protection of competitive advantages through reindustrialization processes.

REFERENCES

Bello, W. (2013). *Capitalism's Last Stand? Deglobalization in the Age of Austerity*. Zed Books. doi:10.5040/9781350218895

Findlay, R., & O'Rourke, K. (2008). *Power and Plenty: Trade, War, and the World Economy in the Second Millennium*. Princeton University Press.

Grunwald, J., & Flamm, K. (1985). The global factory: Foreign assembly in international trade, Brookings Institution. *Washington D., C*, 1985.

Palomares, G. (2006). *Relaciones internacionales en el siglo XXI*. Tecnos.

Rodrik, D. (2000). How far will international economic integration go? *Journal of Economic Perspective*, *14*(1), 177-186.

Rodrik, D. (2007). *One Economics Many Recipes, Globalization, Institutions and Economic Growth*. Princeton University Press. doi:10.1515/9781400829354

Sapir, J. (2011). *La demondialisation*. Seuil.

Sapir, J. (2016). Jacques Sapir: Donald Trump, président de la démondialisation? *Le Figaro*. Available on web: https://www.lefigaro.fr/vox/monde/2016/11/10/31002-20161110ARTFIG00233-jacques-sapir-donald-trump-president-de-la-demondialisation.php

Steinberg, F. (2005). *Cooperación y Conflicto en el Sistema Comercial Multilateral: La Organización Mundial de Comercio como Institución de Gobernanza Económica Global* (Tesis Doctoral). Presentada en el Departamento de Análisis Económico: Teoría Económica e Historia Económica de la Facultada de Ciencias Económicas y Empresariales de la Universidad Autónoma de Madrid, España.

World Bank. (2016). *World Bank Data*. http://data.worldbank.org/?display=default

KEY TERMS AND DEFINITIONS

Deglobalization: The slow-down or reverse of globalization. A political project opposed to neoliberal globalization. In the first definition, the term describes how global flows of trade, investment, and migration can decline.

Global Supply Chain: It is the set of activities, facilities and means of distribution throughout the world necessary to carry out the entire sales process of a product. This is, from the search for raw materials, their subsequent transformation and even the manufacture, transport, and delivery to the final consumer anywhere in the world.

Production Chain: It is a system made up of people and companies related to each other, by a succession of production operations.

Protectionism: Is a commercial policy established by a government that aims to protect the national industry against foreign competition with the application of tariffs or any other type of import restriction.

Relocation of Production: The international displacement of a productive structure.

Value Chains: It is a theoretical model that graphs and allows to describe the activities of an organization to generate value to the end customer and to it.

Chapter 3
Pacific Alliance Facing Crises:
A Trade Perspective (1990–2020)

Jahir Lombana
Universidad del Norte, Colombia

Lorena A. Palacios-Chacón
Insituto Tecnológico y de Estudios Superiores de Monterrey (ITESM), Mexico

Nestor U. Salcedo
https://orcid.org/0000-0002-7253-3581
ESAN Graduate School of Business, Peru

Adriana Cabello-Cerna
Universidad de Chile, Chile

ABSTRACT

The Pacific Alliance (PA) is an integration process that projects the commercial exchange of value-added products for its members. However, the external and internal crises have made the PA a volatile region in social and economic terms. This chapter analyzes the economic and trade policy trends in PA countries since 1990 and how they faced the different world and regional economic crises. From the particular analysis of the countries, there are similarities and differences in trade trends and the way to control crises. This chapter provides a general framework to review more specific approaches by sectors, industries, and companies.

INTRODUCTION

In the 1980s and the 1990s, western bureaucratized governments changed their centralized or nationalized hierarchical order to governments ruled by laws of market, quasi-market, or networks (Bevir, 2009). A more open order meant a confirmation of neoliberal policies, and while networks were configured, they could be framed in neo-institutional policies. Since then and continuing through the beginning of the 21st

DOI: 10.4018/978-1-7998-8314-2.ch003

century, Latin American countries, in particular, have not had a common pattern of behavior confronting trade and crises. Despite its recent establishment in 2011, the PA (made up of Mexico, Peru, Colombia, and Chile) has been one of the most dynamic economic integration groups in the subregion in terms of economic openness and potential for growth of its members (Rodríguez et al., 2019). Another group with leftist governments (Argentina, Brazil, Paraguay and Uruguay) reconsidered the integration processes in a revisionist approach and finally the anti-integration group (Bolivia, Cuba, Ecuador, Nicaragua and Venezuela) which rejected any attempt of open regionalism (Ortiz, 2017; Beltran and Ferrer, 2016). In general, every single country has its own macroeconomic policies, and enterprises adapt accordingly with commercial strategies. Regarding the 4 PA countries compared with Latin America, they represent 23% of area, 34% of population and 43,5% of the GDP (World Bank and IMF, n.d.) Thus, considering such background economic characteristics, and conditions make this region attractive to do research in the field of crises and trade (Aguinis et al., 2020).

This chapter analyses the economic and trade policy trends of the PA countries since 1990 and how they faced different economic crises worldwide (e.g., the global recession in 1991, the financial crisis of 2007–08, and the COVID-19 pandemic; Kose et al., 2020; Reinhart & Rogoff, 2009) and regionally (e.g., Mexican crisis in 1994, the Asian crisis of 1997, Argentina, Brazil, and Ecuador crises 1998–2000, the crisis in Venezuela since 2002) during the last 30 years. Special emphasis is placed on trade and integration policies among its members and bilateral trade exchanges among the signatory countries of the alliance.

In the study period and to achieve this objective, after this short introduction, the first section presents the integration process of Latin America, beginning with a general approach and later to the PA countries specifically. The second section corresponds to the PA orientation to confront crises following a single country perspective of its own macroeconomic policies and the intra-trade policies and trends mainly with their PA partners. The chapter ends with some final remarks using a comparative viewpoint to establish particular and joint trading policies that may contribute to a different performance of intra- and extra-trade.

The sources of information for macroeconomic aspects are drawn from the respective governments, central banks, and international organizations such as the World Bank, the World Trade Organization (WTO), and United Nations Conference on Trade and Development (UNCTAD). Furthermore, secondary sources such as newspapers and magazines were used to complete some data that is not yet available on formal websites.

The information drawn in this chapter could be considered the starting point for future policy decisions that are driven by crises. In this sense, governments would move from a reactive position to an adaptive one based on historical experience.

BACKGROUND

Economic Integration in Latin America

General Approach

In the 1970s, the boom of the price of commodities and a cheap dollar against Latin American currencies provoked a massive attraction of foreign currency to the region. For the governments, the management of fiscal policies (Fitzgerald, 1978) was based on three factors. The first one was an increase in public spending as a share of Gross Domestic Product (GDP), but with fewer social benefits compared to industrialized countries. Second, there was a shift from income and wealth taxes to indirect taxes or taxes on wages. The third factor was an increase in loans to sustain the productive apparatus. This background resulted, almost without exception for Latin American countries, in an external deficit that was financed with debt and which, given its volatility and upward trend, was already unsustainable by the 1980s. This was coupled with the abrupt drop in commodity prices, which, due to its regional effect, derived the so-called "Lost Decade" characterized by hyperinflation and fiscal costs of up to 50% of GDP in several countries of the region (Bértola & Ocampo, 2012).

As a result of the profound crisis of the 1980s and of the Washington Consensus in the early 1990s, developing economies (particularly Latin American) have made their trade policies more open to guarantee development, economic growth, and reduce the gaps with developed countries (Williamson, 2003). This open model has been questioned by Naim (1999) and Stiglitz (2003), who have seen trade liberalization as a reason for widening trade gaps with developed countries and as a loss of control and sovereignty over supranational entities. This discussion is broadened in times of crisis, as policy definitions are a pendulum between protectionism (development inward) and openness (development outward).

Developing countries have sought to shield themselves from gaps with developed economies through integration agreements. Particularly, Latin America and Caribbean countries encourage this trend (Aguilera et al., 2017). Since the "Lost Decade," most Latin American countries have managed to stabilize their economies, at least in the short term. Furthermore, except for Cuba, Nicaragua, and Venezuela, authoritarian regimes were transformed into participatory democracies, with imperfections more linked to social problems that are particularly visible in indicators such as unemployment, inequality, and corruption, and later aggravated by the different crises.

The Inter-American Development Bank (2017) mentions that the opening in the 90s was part of the structural adjustment of the region, where domestic institutional changes would seek to improve access to trade preferences and foreign investment. Likewise, the regional integration orientation is seen as an alternative to the slow or stagnant multilateral dialogues of the WTO.

In the Latin American region, trade relations with developed countries (the US and the European Union) stand out. Developed countries granted unilateral preferences over a long period of time and were based on development policies of "aid for trade" supported by multilateral entities such as UNCTAD and WTO (WTO, n.d.). Due to various circumstances, unilateral preferences evolved into bilateral trade North-South agreements. As a result of these trade relationships, Latin America has created a high degree of dependence with developed countries, based on the number of raw materials they provide and due to the more affordable production factors (i.e., lower labor cost). The dependency has also increased the gap of the terms of exchange for the Latin American region as a net importer of capital goods and as an exporter of raw materials, which makes it difficult to guarantee a surplus in the trade balances (CEPAL, n.d.). Thus, the trade and business strategy for southern economies to generate added value has been oriented toward countries of similar relative development and particularly toward neighboring countries (Llorente & Cuenca, 2016). Therefore, parallel to the North-South agreements, South-South agreements have been established among Latin American countries, including Andean Community, Mercosur, Pacific Alliance, Caribbean Common Market, and Central American Common Market.

Pragmatic Integration in Open Regionalism: A Pacific Alliance Approach

The trade integration process of Latin American countries dates back to the 1960s with the Andean Community, later enforced in the 1970s by the Latin American Association of Free Trade (ALALC in Spanish) and in the 1980s by the Latin American Integration Association (ALADI in Spanish). All institutions provided the basis of the preferential agreements that fostered integration by the Washington Consensus in the 1990s (see Appendix 1). However, in spite of the agreements, they seem to have been less relevant and impactful than their European or Asian counterparts, who intensified the intra-market and even achieved higher and consolidated levels of integration (Michaely, 1996). As we will see in next sections, particularly PA countries are not oriented to Latin American partners but to US, EU and China.

Table 1. Average tariffs from PA countries

Importer country	Exporter country	Simple average (%)	1995	2000	2005	2010	2015	2018
Mexico	World	MFN	13,1	17,9	14,5	8,9	7	6,8
Mexico	Chile	Applied	7,5	20,6	0,1	0,2	7,5	0,3
Mexico	Colombia	Applied	8,6	21	0,5	0,7	7,4	1
Mexico	Peru	Applied	14,4	19,7	10,6	7	8,2	1,4
Colombia	World	MFN	13,7	12,2	12,4	12,5	5,7	6,4
Colombia	Chile	Applied	6,4	14,3	0,5	0,1	7,1	0
Colombia	Mexico	Applied	10,3	12,7	0,9	0,4	4,9	0,1
Colombia	Peru	Applied	14,4	10,7	14,4	12,5	6,9	0
Chile	World	MFN	11	9	6	6	6	6
Chile	Colombia	Applied	6,6	9	0,1	3,5	0	0
Chile	Mexico	Applied	3,6	9	0	3,6	0	0
Chile	Peru	Applied	11	9	0,8	4,1	0	0
Perú	Mundo	NMF	16,5	13,7	10,2	5,4	2,4	2,5
Perú	Chile	Applied	16,8	13,6	1,9	0,5	2,4	0
Perú	Colombia	Applied	16,8	13,1	10,7	6	3,5	0
Perú	México	Applied	16	12,9	8,3	4,4	2,5	0

Source: Authors´ elaboration based on WITS by World Bank (2020a)

Chile, Colombia, Peru, and Mexico have a dissimilar history of integration in terms of periodicity and intensity (see Appendix 1). Chile, being the most open even worldwide, has signed more than 30 bi- and pluri-lateral trade agreements. Among the four countries, trade relations have always existed; in fact, the Andean Community originated with Chile, Colombia, and Peru as founding members. However, it was not until the 1990s and the first decade of the 20th century when relations intensified with agreements.

Table 1 shows that tariffs decreased in all countries of the PA, including the Most Favoured Nation (MFN) partners. This is because the PA partners established an intra-trade tariff of almost 0% in 2015.

The motivation for integrating into the Pacific is much more recent. The concept of the "Pacific Arc" coined by the former Peruvian President Alan García in 2006; it invited the countries of the Americas to integrate with the Pacific coastline but did not have enough echo in the region, mainly due to the changing political currents and the leftist ideologization of several integration attempts of that time (e.g., Bolivarian Alternative for Latin America and the Caribbean - ALBA, the Union of South American Nations – UNASUR, and the Community of Latin American and the Caribbean States - CELAC). All attempts to react against the Free Trade Area of the Americas (FTAA) failed, even though they were once promoted by the US and seen by critics as a continuation of hegemonic policies (Chaves-García, 2018).

In times of intentions for mega-agreements such as the Trans-Pacific Economic Cooperation Agreement or the Transatlantic Trade and Investment Partnership (TPP and TTIP, respectively), the PA finally emerged in 2011 with less ostentation, conceiving trade as a freer orientation but following the rules of the WTO to which its members were also signatories. This gave greater institutionalism to its integration process and sought to deepen and facilitate the negotiation for greater openness to other markets (Licona et al., 2020). However, the more pragmatic approach to open regionalism (Kuwayama, 2019) draws attention to the new deep integration processes (Chaves-García, 2018), which do not necessarily expect to sign documents but to start with direct implementations (e.g., tariff reductions and capital market unification) and reviewing the possibility of integrating into value chains (including labor mobility) with preference to the Asia-Pacific region (Giacalone, 2016; Lejárraga, 2019).

The framework agreement of the PA was signed in 2012 in Antofagasta, Chile. It advanced the free flow of goods, services, capital, people, and in the development of the political articulation oriented toward the Asian-Pacific (Pastrana, 2016). This type of regionalism targets neighboring countries while grouping countries or regions with a higher degree of development. It seems to be a new formula in the face of the stagnation of regional groups such as the Andean Community and Mercosur (Garzón, 2015; Garzón & Nolte, 2018).

Progress in trade policy began concretely in 2014 with the Cartagena de Indias Protocol with a 92% tariff relief for products and with a program for the tariff relief for the remaining 8% until 2030. The creation of the Latin American Integrated Stock-Market (MILA in Spanish) integrates the stock exchanges complements the macro-integrationist effort, which despite having a more modest institutional apparatus than other processes, has quickly reached higher degrees of liberalization showing the reason for its success. Economic advances after 2016 with declarations in favor of free trade have been few, and its mobilization has been rather political with declarations on climate change and political approaches to Mercosur (Mora, 2016) and Asian countries.

Despite the internal problems that PA countries suffered and the constant threat to go against agreements from the US with President Trump since 2017, it strengthens the position of the PA with China and other Asian markets (Foster, 2020). However, China's interest could seem to be less than expected since the trading benefits represent a lower return from the four PA countries. Thus, it is argued that the bilateral interest is oriented into geopolitical issues (Creutzfeldt, 2018). On the other hand, a mutually beneficial trade in regulatory and logistical convergence is seen with Mercosur (Lámbarry, 2016), which, according to the Economic Commission for Latin-America and the Caribbean (in Spanish CEPAL; 2018), it is necessary to avoid a more fragmented economic space for the region, where manufacturing SMEs are the most dependent and beneficiaries from these two markets. Approaches between these two groups were relatively strong between 2014–2018, but protectionist policies in some countries and the pandemic halted that progress. Although PA members are not complementary in their productive structures (except with Mexico), it could establish itself as an intra-industrial manufacturing market with an emphasis on SMEs (García-Pérez et al., 2016) to seek new markets and become a link for the broader regional value chain (Baldwin & López-Gonzalez, 2013).

One problem that the PA linkages may have in the expansion of regional value chains is its heavy reliance on commodities based on comparative advantages. If there is any degree of aggregation, sectors with a high unskilled labor force and low technology knowledge suffer the most. The regional effort would have to focus on adding more regional value to make integration worthwhile (Rosales & Kuwayama, 2012). In this way, Concha and Gómez (2016) perform one of the few exercises that allow to empirically identify investment crossovers to take advantage of such chains. They conclude that in services, although it remains at low levels of participation in total exports, despite having competitive advantages in these areas (e.g., tourism), progress has been rather slow.

The maintenance and further development of regional agreements in Latin America still seem to be highly dependent on the political ideologies of the government in office. Although, the PA seems to be an exception given the unusual enthusiasm and support it has recently had (Kuwayama, 2019). In addition, the proximity to Asian countries is a counterbalance to the relations with the US, which was largely lost under the Trump administration (Mellizo, 2019). If it were up to the PA, it should not be a decision between China or the US, but the clause in the United States–Mexico–Canada Agreement suggests non-association with third countries that do not have a proven "market economy," for leaving the agreement. This calls into question the possibility of the PA to expand smoothly into Asia, particularly to China.

MAIN FOCUS OF THE CHAPTER

PA Countries Confronting Crises

Since 1990, there are three economic crises worldwide: the global recession in 1991, the financial crisis of 2007–08, and the COVID-19 Pandemic (Kose et al., 2020; Reinhart & Rogoff, 2009). There are also several regional crises for PA countries, such as the Mexican crisis in 1994, the Asian crisis of 1997, Argentina, Brazil, Colombia, and Ecuador crises 1998¬–2000, and the crisis in Venezuela since 2002. The impact per country has been different, mainly due to the degree of integration with other economies, dependence/diversification to markets and products, and the economic policies of each country. Because of its recent creation, the actions of the PA as a unified group can only be traced to the crisis produced by the COVID-19 pandemic, but it is understandable that regional crises can also have an effect on these individual economies, which is also analyzed in this chapter. This section describes the macroeconomic aspects of the PA countries in relation to their main partners. It also shows the trade exchanges between PA countries, highlighting the possible effects of the different crises.

PA countries are placed into different levels based on their size. The late recovery from the "lost decade" was a milestone for the entire region, and the first five years of the 90s showed an average growth of 5% for the PA countries (see Figure 1), with a sustained reduction in inflation in Chile and Mexico, a radical reduction in Peru after periods of hyperinflation, and in Colombia with structural inflation in the range of 20–30% (see Figure 2). Finally, unemployment reached the single digits, aside from Colombia (see Figure 3). However, what seemed to be a five-year recovery began to falter again in 1994 with the Mexican crisis and its "Tequila effect." The recession in Mexico had a -6.29% GDP contraction,

34% inflation, and 7% unemployment contrasted with the 5–7% growth and relatively stable inflation and unemployment data of its PA peers. The turn for the Mexican partners was between 1998 (Peru in recession -0.39%) and 1999 (Colombia -4.2%, Chile -0.41%), which, although with stable inflation and relatively low unemployment rates, warns that the data may be biased by high levels of informality and economic inequality.

The first decade of the 21st century was relatively stable for Chile, Colombia, and Peru, with moderate growth rates, inflation, and unemployment (e.g., Colombia at one digit). But again, Mexico had negative growth rates between 2001 and 2002, which shows the endogenization of the economic cycles in the US. In spite of a slight recovery, Mexico is most affected by the international financial crisis in 2009, decreasing -5.28%, followed by Chile with -1.56% and, although with positive but low rates, Colombia (1.13%) and Peru (1.09%). After this huge crisis, the second decade of the 21st century remains relatively stable until 2019, when Mexico suffers from Trump's economic policy, reducing its GDP by -0.05%. The great fall, without exception for the PA, comes with the pandemic and the consequent measures of partial and total closures of non-essential economic activities, rebounding the relatively positive indicators of Chile, Colombia, and Peru and deepening those of Mexico.

PA COUNTRY´S PERSPECTIVE OF CRISES AND TRADE

Chile

Rapid Recovery From Economic Crises

By the last decade of the 20th century and the beginning of the 21st, Chile stood out among the countries of the region for having a robust monetary policy, a relatively stable economy, and being open to internationalization, which allowed it to be the first South American country to join the OECD in 2010. However, it was not exempt from avoiding the COVID-19 crisis. One of Chile's most severe crises was the "Banking Crisis" (1982–1983). This crisis led to the issuance of the General Banking Law of 1986, which introduced greater demands on the creation and operation of these institutions (Berstein & Marcel, 2019).

Between 1990 and 1997, Chile obtained an average growth of 7.13%, but the speed of progress in the first years of the return to democracy (1990–1998) declined between 1998 and 1999 by half (Ffrench-Davis, 2016). For example, in the third quarter of 1998, when the effects of the Asian crisis began to be felt, the year closed with a moderate increase in GDP of 4.3% and a decrease of 0.41% in 1999. The recovery from this crisis was quite fast, obtaining a growth rate of 5.3% in 2000. This crisis triggered Chile to strengthen the macroeconomic framework more transversely; the exchange bands were eliminated, which completely freed the exchange rate, the inflation-targeting framework was strengthened, and the banks got better conditions to participate more actively in the foreign exchange derivatives market (Berstein & Marcel, 2019).

Chile was one of the South American countries least affected by the Subprime Crisis, which can be explained by its lower economic dependence on the US (Hwan et al., 2014), the presence of a well-regulated and capitalized banking, and a significant current account surplus (Ffrench-Davis & Heresi, 2014). Despite this, the economy suffered from the plummeting price of copper, which represented 50% of exports in 2008, and industrial exports dropped due to the falling external demand. Consequently, the

Figure 1. GDP growth (%) pacific alliance countries
Source: Authors´ elaboration based on Databank - World Development Indicators

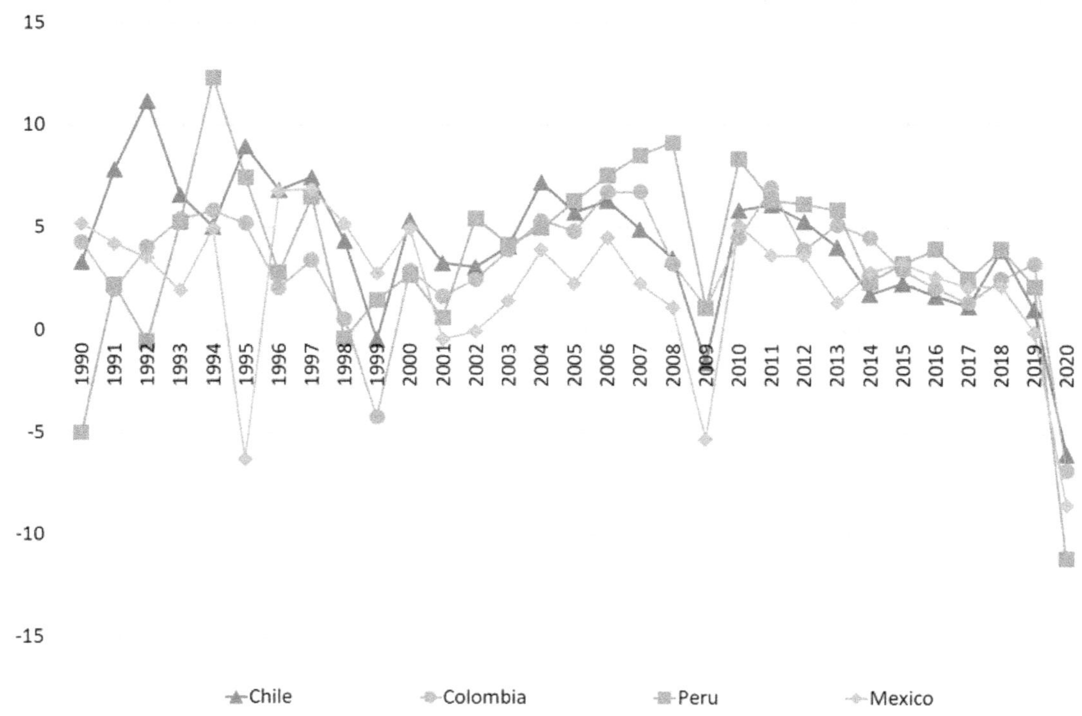

aggregate demand and the employment of labor and productive capital contracted toward the end of 2008 (Ffrench-Davis & Heresi, 2014). The effects of the crisis were felt more strongly in 2009, generating a 1.6% reduction in GDP, mainly due to the decrease in fishing, industrial, and construction activities, and of 5.6% and 14.3% in exports and imports, respectively (Banco Central de Chile, 2010). The drop-in commercial activity generated 11.31% unemployment. However, the effects of this crisis were not long-lasting; in 2010, unemployment and GDP recovered to pre-crisis levels. This rapid recovery was due to corrective economic policies and the increase in the price of copper, mainly driven by Chinese demand (Berstein & Marcel, 2019).

Although poverty has reduced considerably since the financial crisis, a high level of inequality remains (García & Pérez, 2017; OECD, 2021). OECD (2018) highlighted that the quality of life of Chileans improved significantly in recent decades but recognized that the reduction in inequalities had slowed down, and income gaps were one of the most pronounced in member countries. These inequalities plus a generalized discontent toward the current government generated a series of social protests starting in October 2019, called "social outbreak," and were characterized by massive episodes of violence and a collapse of all institutions' approval ratings. The outbreak substantially impacted the country's economy and deteriorated financial market indicators. It was also the starting point for changing the Constitution via a constituent process that is expected to be completed by 2022 (Vial, 2020).

Figure 2. Inflation (annual growth %) pacific alliance countries*
**Data from Peru between 1990 and 1993 excluded for presentation issues. Since the 80s, Peru had a hyperinflation period (50% -3000%) Source: Authors´ elaboration based on Databank - World Development Indicators*

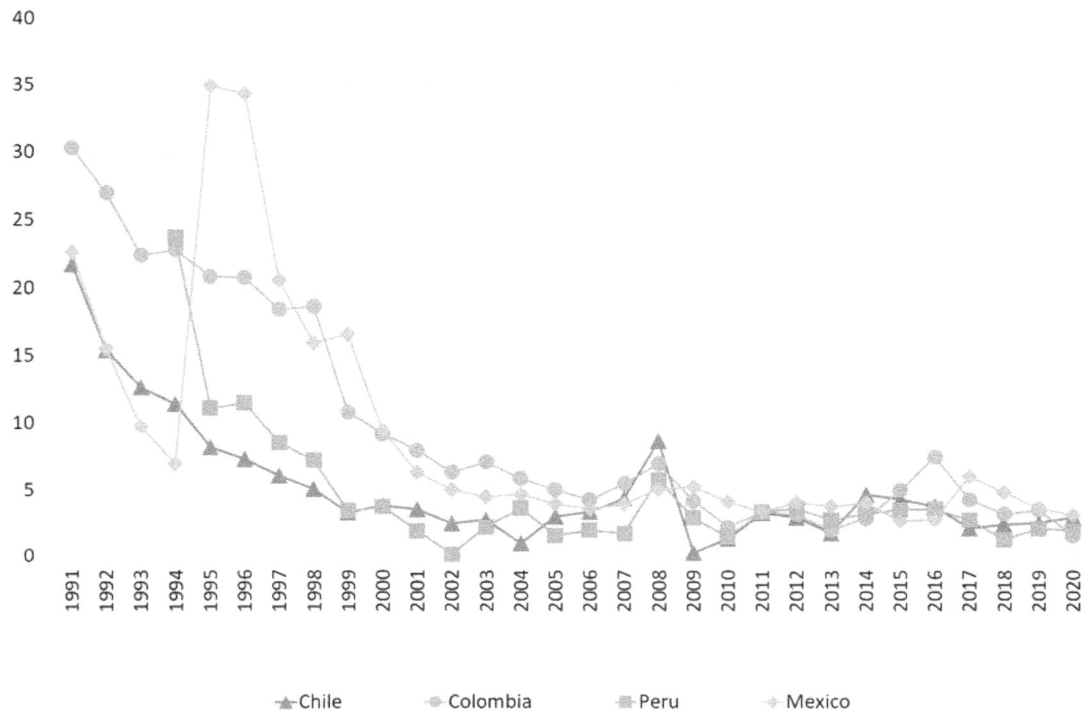

In the first months of 2020, the local economy began to reactivate but suffered a severe setback due to the Coronavirus pandemic; this produced an economic crisis, which is estimated to be the worst recession in the last 40 years (Marcet, 2020). Copper mining, of which Chile is one of the primary world producers, was one of the main supporters of the country's economy in 2020. Still, it did not balance the economy, reaching a decrease in GDP of 5.8% and an unemployment rate of 10.7% (Banco Central de Chile, 2021).

For 2021, the IMF (2021) expects a quick recovery of the Chilean GDP, projecting a growth of 6%, mainly triggered by the successful vaccination plan against COVID-19. The IMF also expects the current account balance to deteriorate in 2021–22 due to the strong import demand associated with the recovery. These expectations can be affected by the internal risks derived mainly from the uncertain outcome of the New Constitution process and a resurgence of unrest. However, the IMF hopes that the country can face them positively due to the remaining fiscal space, the country's robust institutional policy frameworks, the proven solid track record of policy reaction, and the low level of public debt by international standards.

Figure 3. Unemployment (annual average %) pacific alliance countries
Source: Authors´ elaboration based on Databank - World Development Indicators

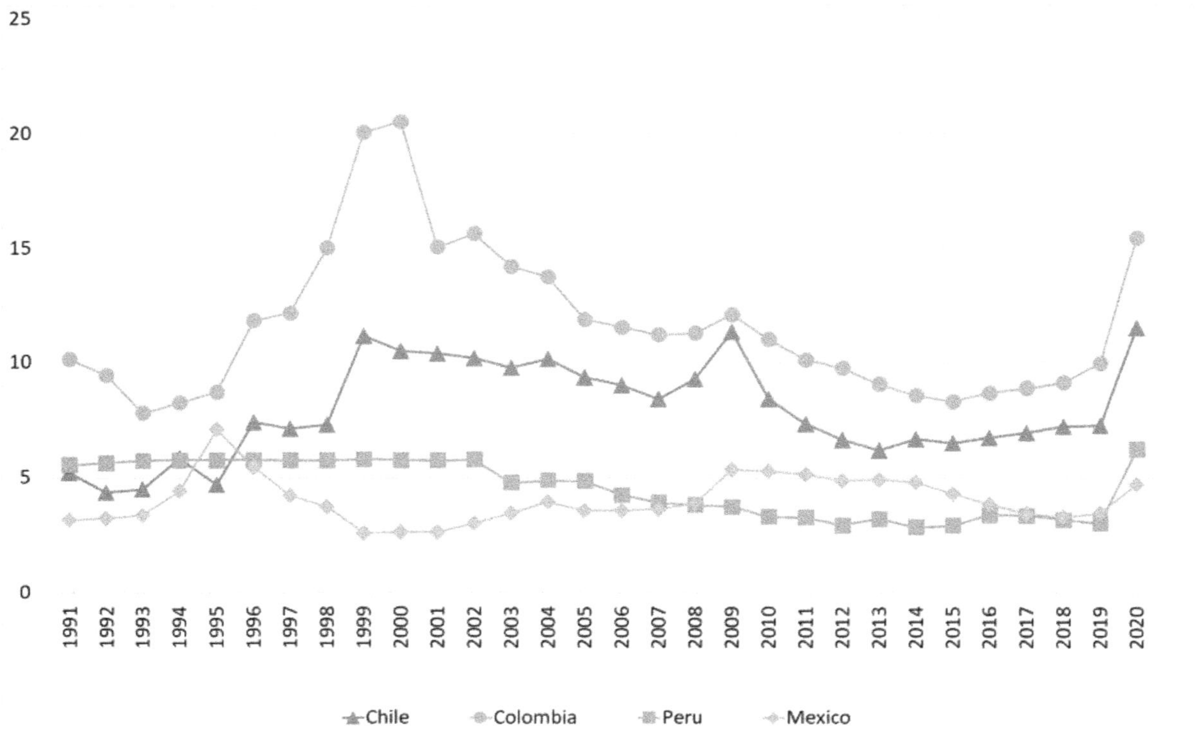

The Most Open Economy Country of the PA

One of the characteristics of Chile is its economic openness to the world. In the 1970s, with the start of the military regime and subsequent substantial changes, Chile went from a highly regulated to a liberalized economy. Some of the main changes accounted for the elimination of almost all subsidies, privatizing most previously nationalized companies, and the liberation of the financial market (Ramos, 2008). One of the objectives was to open the economy up to international trade using initiatives. One of them was a unilateral reduction on tariffs from 90% on average in 1973 to a uniform tariff of 10% by 1979 (Ramos, 2008). Another initiative created ProChile in 1974 to support companies to export, especially in the non-mining sector. Additionally, the issuance in 1974 of Decree-Law No. 600 "Statute of Foreign Investment" gave more protection and confidence to foreign investors to promote inflows of capital and accelerate the development of the economic activity, especially relevant in the mining sector (Hachette, 2000). The measures adopted to boost exports by the military regime diversified the number of destination markets, from 31 in 1970 to 122 in 1990, and increased the number of direct exporters from 150 in 1970 to 4,000 in 1990 (Ramos, 2008). With the arrival of democracy in the country in 1990, international globalization continued to be prioritized, signing trade agreements with neighboring countries. In the mid-1990s, a policy of "open regionalism" was implemented by signing bilateral agreements with more distant countries (Polanco, 2015).

Historically, Chile has been recognized for being one of the main copper exporters since it represents a significant share of the country's income. In 1970, exports of copper and its derivatives represented 75% of total exports (Hachette, 2000), and in 2019, this dependence was close to 48% (OEC, n.d.) due to a more diversified export offer. In 2018, this diversification allowed Chile to be the world's largest exporter in 29 product categories, including fresh grapes, fresh cherries, fresh salmon fillets, fresh blueberries, plums (fresh and dehydrated), frozen trout fillets, sea urchins, and algae for industrial use (Prochile, 2019). Currently, the main export products are copper ore, refined copper, sulfate chemical wood pulp, fish fillets, and pitted fruits (OEC, n.d.).

The destination of exports diversified in recent years. For example, Europe received 60% in 1970, and by 2006, its share fell to 27%, while Asia almost tripled its share, from 12% in 1970 to 34% in 2006 (Ramos, 2008). Currently, Chile's main trading partners are China, the US, Japan, Brazil, and South Korea. During 2020, China consolidated its role as the primary recipient of forestry-agricultural exports and, especially, mining products (SUBREI, 2021a).

Regarding trade with the PA member countries, during 2019, it was the fourth most relevant actor in exports from the agricultural, forestry, fishing, and industrial sectors. The leading trading partner was Mexico, accounting for 41% of trade in that year, followed by Peru (36%) and Colombia (23%) (SUBREI, 2020). The main products exported to PA countries were copper minerals and their derivatives, except for Colombia, where these exports represent only 0.6% and 3.4% during the years 2019 and 2020, respectively (SUBREI, 2021b).

Free trade agreements represent 94.4% of 2020 Chilean exports, although the three principal trading partners were maintained compared to 2019, shipments to the European Union increased by 3.1%, and trade with Peru, Mexico, and Colombia decreased by 15%, displacing the PA from a fourth-place behind the European Union (SUBREI, 2021a).

Trade between Chile and Mexico increased after signing trade agreements; trade between 1999 and 2019 increased 125%. Trade also diversified; the main exports in 1999 to Mexico were copper and articles thereof (38%). By 2019, these products only amounted to 6.8% in 2019 (OEC, n.d.). Mineral or chemical fertilizers, processed foods (e.g., salmon and chicken), cellulose and paper, fruits and vegetables, bottled wine, among other products exported in 2019 and 2020, stand out as new exports to Mexico (SUBREI, 2020; SUBREI, 2021b).

Despite Peru's copper production, it is also the main product imported to Peru from Chile, representing 12.9% of total exports in 2019. Exports to this country increased exponentially in the last decade (400% between 1999 and 2019). Diversification is also important for this destination in products such as iron and steel (7.51%), machine and appliances (7.43%), and plastics and articles thereof (6%; OEC, n.d.).

Finally, Colombia is the PA country with which Chile has the least commercial exchange, despite the fact that exports grew 208% between 1999 and 2019 (OEC, n.d.). During the first years after the trade agreements, the relationship generated a trade surplus for Chile. But as of 2007, the relationship was reversed (Hernández & Muñoz, 2015). The products exported to Colombia are varied. For example, the category representing the highest percentage in 1999 was fruit and nuts (19.2%), followed by wood pulp (12.6%), and by 2019, fruit and nuts represented 18.4%, and fish and crustaceans were 8.07% (OEC, n.d.).

Colombia

Dependence on Commodities and Lack of Regulation

It is not strange that Colombia's economic relations have been subordinated to the political and social problems derived from drug trafficking and armed conflict (Thoumi, 2002). Despite this framework, with economic policies influenced in many ways by institutionalized political crises, it is considered a country with economic stability (Castañeda, 2000). Prior to the period under study, Colombia experienced the lost decade of the 1980s relatively comfortably compared to the rest of Latin America. In 1991, a new political constitution implied profound changes in the institutional framework and, above all, a more open view to the foreign market (i.e., tariff reduction, elimination of barriers to foreign direct investment, and autonomy of the central bank in monetary policy with anti-inflationary and exchange rate objectives). Colombia moved from a crawling-band exchange rate regime in 1994 to a floating one in 1999 (Maya-Muñoz, 2002). However, due to expectations of late tariff reductions and high exchange rates, imports were reduced, while the mini oil and coffee booms gave a temporary trade surplus until 1993 (Villar & Rincón, 2000).

The beginning of the 1990s saw a boom in coffee sales and favorable interest rates, resulting in more liquidity, expansion of consumption, and access to credit (including mortgages) and creating speculative bubbles that later burst (Parra & Salazar, 2000). Between 1998 and 2000, the country's overexposure to external capital, trade deficit due to falling commodity prices on which the country is dependent, unsustainable public and private debt levels, and a structural fiscal deficit, all triggered one of the worst domestic crises with six consecutive quarters of recession (Arango, 2006; Ocampo, 2005; Perez-Reyna, 2017; Urrutia & Llano, 2011; Villar & Rincon, 2000). In addition to the reduction in the price of commodities, the external situation was not the most favorable either, as regional crises in emerging economies caused tensions in the markets and a rush to take resources to supposedly safer and more stable markets (Torres, 2011; Urrutia & Llano, 2011). As a result, in 1999, GDP decreased by 4.5%, and unemployment levels reached 22%, with greater exposure to the financial sector and the collapse of the real estate market. This implied one of the most active interventions by the International Monetary Fund (IMF) in Colombian economic policy in history.

The new century begins for Colombia with sustained growth from 2.2% in 2001 to 7.7% in 2007. Better commodity prices and low interest rates in developed countries encouraged capital inflows to Colombia. That is, until 2008 when the main channel of transmission of the crisis was the reduction of trade exchange, foreign direct investment inflows, and remittances (Mesa, González & Aguirre, 2009). These, combined with the downward pressure on commodity prices, impacted the Colombian economy. As stated by Ocampo (2011), as a result of lessons learned from previous crises, Colombia had less exposure to the financial market (Torres, 2011). In addition, financial control and support entities (Guarantee Fund and Superintendencies) were created and strengthened (Caballero, 2019). Finally, relatively high interest rates made leeway in monetary policy to stabilize the currency in response to speculative attacks. However, Echavarría et al. (2012) argue that external shocks for Colombia may exert greater vulnerability to the extent that it is inserted in international financial markets, as occurred in the 1999 crisis.

Colombia was on a path of growth and recovery in the second decade of the 21st century, with pending issues such as labor and pension reform constantly postponed due to electoral interests. Trade differences between China and the US were at their peak, and Colombia was expecting an abrupt fall in oil prices (Caballero & Machado, 2020). Finally, the COVID-19 crisis and the subsequent total and selective closures of the domestic economy revealed the problems that already existed in terms of economic reaction and the basic needs of the population. Likewise, the loss of employment (21.4% in June), income, and business structure were unprecedented (Rodriguez, 2021). To complicate the situation, the government's actions to increase public spending on the most disadvantaged (including those most affected by health) suffered due to the lack of identification of beneficiaries and transfer mechanisms, especially for the bulk of the population in informal employment. Transfers to this population were estimated for 2020 at almost 2.7% of GDP. As a result, the government's sources of financing shifted to multilateral bank loans since current revenues were not sufficient. The Central Bank lowered intervention interest rates (4.25% pre-pandemic to 1.75% in the pandemic) while guaranteeing its constitutional mandate of sustainable inflation. In addition, for a greater injection of capital, it bought bonds and reduced reserve requirements in commercial banks (Cardenas & Martínez, 2020).

Dependent and Poorly Diversified Trade

Colombia has been more commercially linked to the US and the EU rather than to its own neighbors (García-Parra, 2018). In fact, the most important agreements in relation to the weight of bilateral trade are the ones with these two regions (in force since 2012 and 2013, respectively). The paradigmatic case is that of Venezuela, which was its second-largest trading partner in the 20th century (up to 15% of total exports). Since the diplomatic crisis with that country in 2010, the exchange does not reach 5% of total trade. Trade relations with a relative boom are in the Pacific countries as a result of the impulse of imports and investment from Asia-Pacific, first by imports from Japan (5% average annual participation) in the 90s, and then by China, which has been in absolute terms the country with the highest growth for Colombia in imports (220%) and the second in exports (378%) between 2009 and 2019 (OEC, n.d.). However, efforts to formally join this subregion were put on hold in 1995 with Colombia's application for APEC membership, which is still on hold as of 2021. Thus, the PA appears to be Colombia's only formal trade integration in this geographic area.

Studies on the trade effects of the PA for Colombia are relatively scarce. Of the few, Montoya-Uribe et al. (2016) and Stellian and Danna-Buitrago (2019) review the effects of revealed comparative advantage on Colombia's membership in the PA and that of Caporale, Costamagna, and Rossini (2016), which emphasizes commodities and monetary policies to cover trade deficits. They all emphasize the possibility of trade diversification toward products with higher added value than those traditionally exported. Thus, the following description of exports to PA trade partners details Colombian and recognizes its projection as a destination for diversification and added value products.

The 1990s represented a strong concentration (70%) of exports to Chile in plastics, chemicals, textiles, and food (e.g., sugar). From 1997 to 2006, trade with Chile was mostly in deficit for Colombia, with sporadic appearances of coal exports (1999 and 2004). From 2007 onward, Colombia presented a permanent surplus by adding crude oil to its exportable supply of mining-energy products, which represented 46% of exports that year. In 2013, mining-energy exports reached 70% of the total. Since 2015, the dependence (50% or more) has been on coal, which fluctuates according to international prices. Thus, the ratio of exports has been very marked by the supply of mining-energy products, although in absolute terms, chemicals, plastics, and food have remained a significant portion of exports in the period under study.

Colombia has a permanent trade deficit with Mexico, but exports have been rather diverse. Before 1995, oil (crude and refined), paper products, chemicals, and machinery predominated its exports. After that year, oil exports (only refined) are less representative, and diversification is even greater between

1995 and 1999, with the following additional exports: textiles and clothing, plastics and rubber, and other tools. When the dominance of energy mining in the exportable supply appears again (1999, 2004, 2008, 2010), the relative lower participation of other economic activities becomes noticeable, but not their reduction in absolute terms. However, since 2005, the pronounced deficit for Colombia should be highlighted, with recovery only since 2015. The emergence of automobile exports between 2012 and 2016 ranged from 20% to 30% and remained relatively stable until 2019. Again for 2017–2019, energy mining products reached 40% of exports. In general terms, exports to Mexico have had an important development in terms of added value, but fluctuations occur from Colombia due to the participation of energy mining in sales to this destination.

Finally, in the case of Peru, the conditions resulted in a permanent surplus for Colombia. Until 1997, oil represented more than 50% of exports. Other important products include chemicals, plastics, and foodstuffs (sugar). Between 1998 and 2000, petroleum fell to 35% of exports, with an even more pronounced reduction in participation from 2001 onward, remaining between 10% and 20% until 2019. During this same period, paper products, machinery, and textiles became notorious and were added as exports in the 1990s.

Mexico

Consequences of Globalization and Internalization of the USA's Economic Cycles

From 1994 to 2013, there were some structural reforms in Mexico as a result of the Washington Consensus (Calderon & Hernández, 2017). Since 1994, a flexible exchange rate was predominant. Because of the tequila crisis, the pegged exchange rate policy (1988–1999) changed to inflation targeting policy (1999) as the inflation control tool. By 2003, the inflation targeting lite was implemented, obtaining one-digit inflation, but it slowed the economy down when combined with the restrictive fiscal policy (Carare & Stone, 2003) and more raw materials imports that restructured the productive capacities of the Mexican economy (Calderon & Hernández, 2017).

In the last 30 years, there were five specific periods of crisis. The first one was named the tequila effect (1994). It is called the first globalization crisis, whose causes were of local origin. It resulted from the abundance of external capital inflows derived from structural reforms and the international financial situation (Calderón & Caire, 2012). It was caused by the potential contradictions between a heterodox inflationary policy of stabilization, the export-oriented growth strategy, and the openness to a globalized national monetary and financial system (Calderon & Hernández, 2017). In the first quarter of 1995, Mexico received the most significant amount of financial support in history from the US and other international entities such as the IMF to control the crisis. The crisis represented hyperinflation of around 35%, combined with the highest unemployment rate of the whole period of almost 7% (for more detail, see the Macro Indicators of the PA countries in the previous section). The impact of the 1994 crisis on foreign trade was translated in 1995 into a correction in the trade balance, going from -18,463.6 million dollars in 1994 to 7,008.5 million dollars as a result of the spectacular growth in exports (30.6%) and a notable drop in imports (-8.7%; Banco de México, 1996). This increase was addressed to South America with a 78% increase in exports.

The subsequent three crises of 2001, 2007, and 2012 had an external origin. Some research concludes that they were a consequence of the internalization of the US economic cycles (Calderon & Hernández, 2017). The interrelation between the US and Mexico became stronger after NAFTA. Following the economic boom of the 1990s, especially in countries such as the US, there was a general world deceleration by 2001. The declaration represented a considerable contraction of international trade. In Mexico, there were decreased levels of investment and employment; the recovery started slowly in 2002 (Calderon & Hernández, 2017). The subprime crisis (2007) was better managed by emerging markets in general; nevertheless, providing the closer relationship between Mexico and the US, the Mexican GDP contracted 6% between 2007 and 2009; recovery started in 2010. Finally, the fiscal crisis of 2012 was characterized by a huge fiscal deficit in the US that increased taxes and led to a shortage of public spending. The Mexican economy felt the uncertainty of American elections with a decrease in GDP and employment rate.

The last period of crisis before the COVID-19 pandemic was the tariff crisis of 2019. Following its campaign slogan about "Making America Great Again," Donald Trump implemented strong protectionism policies. In doing so, he renegotiated trade agreements (i.e., from NAFTA to the USMCA), leaving specific trade negotiations such as the Transatlantic Trade and Investment Partnership. Tariff restrictions were also implemented for particular products such as iron and steel from its essential partners: Mexico, Canada, and the European Union. Consequently, there was zero growth in the Mexican GDP in that year, a situation aggravated by the COVID-19 pandemic.

Trade Between Partners: From Raw Materials to Value-Added Products

According to data from the World Bank, raw materials represented 46% of Mexican exports in 1990, followed by oil and consumption products with 37% and 20%, respectively. Following the industrial reconfiguration that started in the late 1980s, it is possible to observe a concentration of manufacturing companies in northern regions close to the US's borders (Vieyra, 2000). Since 1992, consumer products, machinery, electricity, and capital products accounted for more than 90% of Mexican's external trade. From 1999 to 2019, machinery, electricity, and capital products were the leaders in Mexico's international trade, consolidating its leadership in Latin America in value-added products (World Bank, 2020b).

As mentioned above, NAFTA did not just represent Mexico's dependency on the US; it also meant a higher concentration of its international trade. Between 1990 to 1994, Mexico had a trade deficit with the US. However, in 1995, when NAFTA became effective, this trend radically changed to favor Mexican exports; exports increased from 12.3 million dollars to more than 128.3 million in 2018 (World Bank, 2020b). This trade deficit for the US was one of the reasons for renegotiating the agreement. In 2000, the US became the leading Mexican partner, representing 84.7% of its exports, followed by Canada (3.39%) and some Central American countries such as the Antilles, Guatemala, the Dominican Republic, and Costa Rica (OEC, n.d.). From the 2008 crisis to 2019, it is possible to observe a slight diversification in destination countries: US (75.1%), Canada (4.43%), China (1.85%), and Germany (1.82%), while AP partners, Colombia, Chile, and Peru, represented 0.77%, 0.39%, and 0.35% respectively in 2019 (OEC, n.d.).

For international trade between Colombia and Mexico from 1990 to 2004, there was a slight surplus of Mexican exports to Colombia, conformed mainly by intermediate goods such as chemical and plastic products (World Bank, 2020b). Following the tariff reduction plan (2005) from the Group of 3 (G3; which also included Venezuela), Mexican sales to Colombia increased, reaching a peak of about 5,632 million in 2011. This last year, the tariffs for cars reached 0%; therefore, vehicles and their parts became the primary export (32.1%). By 2019, 52.7% of exports from Mexico to Colombia were of manufacturing products (i.e., vehicles and their parts [23.1%], electrical machinery and equipment [20.7%], and machinery and appliances [8.9%]; OEC, n.d.).

In the case of Chile, in 1990, the main export products from Mexico were vehicles and their parts (47.9%; World Bank, 2020b). After the Economic Complementation Agreement (ECA), there was a preference for chemical (23.3%), transport (21.8%), and electrical (16.8%) products in 2000, with a continuous trend until 2019. Some other vital exports included oil, organic and inorganic chemicals, cosmetic or toilet preparations, and spirits such as tequila (OEC, n.d.).

With regard to Peru, the main products imported from Mexico in 1990 were fuels (38%), electrical machinery (28%), and chemicals (19%; World Bank 2020b). In 2000, these products changed to machinery and appliances (14.6%), electrical machinery and equipment (11.5%), pharmaceutical products (9.72%), and plastics and articles thereof (6.58%), among others. In 2011, there was a higher concentration of electrical machinery and equipment (23.4%), vehicles and their parts (19.1%), and machinery and appliances (10.6%; OEC, n.d.). This same composition continued until the end of the period. The ECA between Peru and Mexico was the most recent agreement, which became effective in February 2012. In conclusion, although there was an upward trend of exports from Mexico to the PA trading partners during each of the crises, they have never represented more than 1.7% of Mexico's total international trade. Looking at the general export trends, the positive impact of the PA is evident from when tariff reductions started in 2011.

Peru

Economic Model Changes and Political Crises

By 1990, Peru renewed its presidency with negative economic performance, hyperinflation (7,650%), changing its currency in 1991 (after also changing it in 1985), and facing a former nationalization policy through state-owned companies' privatization to attract foreign capital (Champion, 2001; Reinhart & Savastano, 2003). However, with a majority opposition in parliament, a complex bureaucracy, and excessive market regulations, the presidency had a self-coup in 1992, dissolved parliament, restructured State powers, established a constituent assembly with a parliamentary majority, and promulgated a new Constitution with a free-market model in 1993.

Until 1993, the Peruvian trade balance was mainly in deficit with a falling trend. With the free-market model and an economic shock, exports, mainly extractive, grew until 1997. This growth was mainly due to liberalization measures such as tariff reductions, eliminating taxes, and export restrictions. Therefore, they covered existing trade policy instruments on goods, services, and intellectual property (Lengyel, 2004). By 1999, Peru created the National Fund for the Financing of State Business Activity with 35 unique state-owned companies. Likewise, with the creation of the EU in 1993 and the ALADI in 1980, Peru reinforced international trade markets in the 1990s. This diversification reduced the adverse effects of a potential currency's overvaluation and increased transaction costs. However, Peru continued to suffer slight falls in 1998–1999 due to international crises (Lengyel, 2004). At the end of the decade, the volatile international context (e.g., Asian and Brazilian crises) and the arguments about the vulnerability of the free-market model decreased mineral prices and reduced investment flows.

Moreover, the country went through another crisis in 2000 with a presidential impeachment after its third re-election. Due to severe accusations of institutional corruption, the political parties demanded new elections for parliament and the presidency. With these changes, the presidency, from 2001 to the time of writing this chapter, cannot have a parliamentary majority make significant reforms to trade policies.

Despite internal crises, Peru consolidated foreign trade agreements and diversified its destinations and exportable alternatives. Even under the global financial crisis of 2009, Peru achieved FTA with the US, China, and more than 49 countries. For this reason, Tello (2012) argues that the high level of specialization of the Peruvian economy and the high degree of commercial integration accentuated the effects of the international cycles of the principal partner countries on the local economic cycles. The author suggests that improving economic policies to diversify industries and export markets reduced the potential adverse effects of international crises in the short and long term.

Between 2018 and 2020, Peru underwent two presidential impeachments, a dissolution of parliament, and a referendum on constitutional reforms. Despite its continuous context of crises and changes, Peru maintained one of the best economic performances among the PA members and one of the lowest inflation and unemployment rates until the pandemic in March 2020 (see Graph 1). When COVID-19 appeared, the government's response seemed exemplary with a quick lockdown. Taking advantage of its fiscal surplus, the government launched an ambitious aid program in Latin America, with 12% GDP (Reid, 2020). Unfortunately, the pandemic exposed significant deficiencies and inequalities in health and financial infrastructures. Thus, its economy contracted. These failures have moved to polarized social unrest that has led the country to choose between two extremist populist presidential candidates (Reid, 2021). Indeed, one of them wants to renegotiate or eliminate the trade agreements or alliances created.

Agreements Diversity and Trade Deficit With Its Neighbors

Peru has participated in the globalization process, the free market model, and public investment efficiency since it adopted its last Constitution of 1993. This open orientation allowed its economy to be seen as one of the most stable and with the fastest average annual growth (6.3%) since 2002 in Latin America (Spillan & Virzi, 2017).

From 1990–1995, revenue from privatization as total foreign direct investment averaged 76.7%. The IMF recommended large companies make some transfers to the private sector, with the State maintaining some control (Champion, 2001). In 1992, these steps motivated the strengthening of the Superintendency of the Securities Market and the creation of the National Institute for the Defense of Competition and Intellectual Property Rights, with a Control Commission of Dumping and Subsidies (Lengyel, 2004). In 1996, the government created the Commission for the Promotion of Exports. In parallel, the international context was positive and saw increased prices and demand for primary and non-traditional products.

In 2000, the main exports were refined copper (10.5%), gold (16.1%), pure zinc (5.27%), and fishmeal (12.4%), with the main destinations being the US (27%), UK (8.13%), Switzerland (7.7%), and China (6.24%; OEC, n.d.). By 2001, the EU and the US represented almost 50% of Peru's exports, while ALADI, mainly through the Andean Community of Nations (ACN) and Mercosur, only reached 17% (Lengyel, 2004). In 2008, the year of the global financial crisis, the main exports were gold (17.3%), pure copper (15.2%), refined copper (8.41%), refined petroleum (6.52%), and fishmeal (4.48%), its main destinations being the US (18.5%), China (11.7%), Switzerland (10.6%), Canada (6.23%) and Chile (6.13%; OEC, n.d.).

Moreover, Peru's integration with the global economy grew with its trade agreements. The milestone of this process was the Free Trade Agreement (FTA) with the US (2009), promoting and showing notable growth in exports to the external markets of Latin America since that year (Ariza-Ricaldi, López-Lira, & Giraldo-Mejía, 2019).

Likewise, Peru's trade with Asia has increased since the second decade of the 21st century. One of the reasons is that Peru became a member of the Asia Pacific Economic Cooperation Forum (APEC) in 1998. Since then, exports of primary goods, minerals, and fishmeal have grown. In fact, China, through the FTA, became the largest trading partner and destination of Peruvian exports since 2010 (Aquino Rodríguez, 2015). Subsequently, the country signed FTAs with South Korea (2011) and Japan (2012) and later signed partial agreements with Singapore and Thailand. Then, they expanded the FTA to other countries when they entered the Trans-Pacific Partnership Agreement (TPP). However, its trade with Asia has been asymmetric since it exports raw materials and imports manufactured products.

By 2014, half of Peru's copper exports, almost 100% of iron, and around 70% of fishmeal went to China. Despite this, in 2014, Peru ranked as the seventh fastest-growing emerging economy worldwide and was the second-highest exporter of transformed products in Latin America. Peru diversified its exports to chemicals, textiles, and the agro-industry. Also, industrial production approached 271%, making it the fastest-growing economy in South America (Peña-Vinces et al., 2016).

Considering its relationship with Chile, in 1996, Peru activated the first special tax zones close to Chile: the export processing zone (EPZ) of Ilo and the free zone of Tacna (ZOFRA-Tacna) for international trade. Likewise, under the ALADI framework, they began bilateral negotiations that ended in 1998 by signing the Economic Complementation Agreement (ECA) to strengthen a free trade zone with tariff reductions scheduled for 5, 10, and up to 18 years. In the first two years, 2,600 products, mainly foods, were impacted by tariff reductions and preferences (Lengyel, 2004).

Bilateral trade increased by almost 70% between 1998 and 2001, exports to Chile increased by more than 100%, and Peru's trade deficit with Chile shrunk rapidly since the agreement. In 2006, they replaced the ECA with a FTA. Compared to the PA countries, Peru's exports to Chile were the third most important in the first decade of the 21st century (only surpassed by exports from Mexico to Colombia and from Chile to Mexico) until the global financial crisis. As of 2009, Peru only achieved an export surplus with Chile in 2011 and 2012. Subsequently, the bilateral trade balance has been in deficit for Peru. By 2019, the main exports to Chile were molybdenum (15.6%), sulfuric acid (9.09%), refined petroleum as aviation kerosene and natural gas (8.4%), fruits such as avocados and mangoes (2.4%), unglazed ceramic (2.79%), fish oil (2.08%), plastics such as containers and vinyl floors (1.86%), among others (OEC, n.d.).

On the other hand, Peru's trade relations with Colombia are based on the ACN framework of 1969. This allowed for improvement in 1992 with a Bilateral Trade Agreement and in 1994 with the decision to rejoin the Andean's Free Trade Zone. The bilateral trade balance has been in deficit for Peru for decades, with only higher exports to Colombia in 2014. By 2019, the main exports to Colombia were copper wire (16.5%), raw zinc (5.19%), raw plastic sheeting (5.97%), raw sugar (5.36%), palm oil (4.92%), refined petroleum (4.74%), knitting (3.51%), among others (OEC, n.d.).

Peru's trade relations with Mexico are achieved within the ALADI framework in the 1987 ECA. It was not until the end of 2005 that negotiation, expansion, and deepening of the agreement began, including all goods and creating a basic FTA framework. Finally, in 2011, they signed a Peru - Mexico Trade Integration Agreement, which became effective in 2012. As a result, by 2019, the main exports to Mexico were copper ore (14.6%), refined petroleum (11.2%), zinc ore (6.42%), pepper or paprika (6.42%), grapes (6.35%), rubber tires (5.07%), mollusks (4.14%), raw plastic sheeting (2.93%), knitting (1.16%), among others (OEC, n.d.).

FUTURE RESEARCH DIRECTIONS

In future work, it would be interesting to carry out a more in-depth analysis using econometric techniques to justify the variations in trade within the PA countries and discriminate against the effects of specific agreements and crises. Furthermore, regarding macroeconomic policies would be interesting to review similarities and differences among countries from a more empirical point of view by recognizing for example the establishment of monetary/fiscal policies confronting crises and the effects on trade to test priorities in decision-making policies (e.g. Mundell-Fleming trilemma, inflation-employment dichotomy)

Moreover, the Pacific Alliance has created the first Latin American integrated stock market (MILA in Spanish). This integration of stock markets has allowed listed firms in each country to have the same rules to operate in any of them. Likewise, MILA encourages the standardization of principles, norms, and instruments. A future agenda should contemplate investigations of the behavior of listed firms in MILA engaged in international trade vis-à-vis non-listed firms of the Pacific Alliance. For instance, a neo-institutional economic perspective would be useful to address aspects of institutional complementarity.

CONCLUSION

A Common Approach to Confront Crises in the PA

One of the biggest problems that the PA countries have faced with the constant crises has been structural budget deficits and inflation. Moreover, one thing these countries share is their relative macroeconomic stability by the second decade of the 21st century. Despite the need to maintain social spending, financing the budget deficit represents a serious problem to control inflation. Varon et al. (2017) reviewed how the PA countries financed the deficit. They also discussed how they have resorted to internal and external indebtedness, in some cases to non-structural tax reforms and in no case to monetary issuance, the latter shown as the greatest danger to generate inflation.

The approach to face crises has been similar in all cases. From the macro point of view, there is a structural debt for the PA countries in growth and chiefly on employment. Thus, the best monetary regulation seems to be inflation control via interest rates and capital flow control by an autonomous central bank. However, as stated by the Mundell-Fleming trilemma this has not been out of problems depending on the conditions of the crises, since PA countries have to decide during the crises about the alternatives to use a fix exchange rate, free flow of capital or/and keep an independent monetary policy. Regarding the fiscal sphere, debt dependence has taken a toll on the development of countries, but a different recipe is not seen in the crises they have gone through. Perhaps the most notorious in these countries, excluding Chile in the 90s, is the economic crises due to internal causes, with implications even more significant than worldwide ones.

The effects of crises on trade are perceived in a significant way with its main trading partners, the US, the EU, and China, but have relatively less influence with its counterparts in the PA. This is because their main exports (commodities) have their clients in those large countries/regions. It could be said that the PA countries are a refuge for the products that cannot be sold in the main destinations.

The PA is at a very early stage of integration to show results in the face of long-standing historical relationships. However, due to the evidence of intraregional exchange, the relative weight of this group for individual countries is not much, and their trade is linked rather to complementary products with already structured domestic value chains. Except for the case of Mexico, which has a relationship more closely linked to manufacturing than its peers in the alliance, the dependence on mining (copper and oil) and agricultural products make it difficult to generate greater added value, at least in the short term.

Additionally, exchanges are not sustained, and this shows a premature trading relationship based on the market conditions and not on a structured knowledge of the partners. Despite the intra-alliance tariff reduction, neither quantity nor diversification seems to have been motivated, so the response to trade promotion should go beyond costs. The call to create regional value chains was already on the agenda of governments and companies before the pandemic. However, with the current crisis, the solutions are primarily domestic; there is no short-term glimpse of being able to resume this path, even more so with the internal social crisis than with the pandemic. The COVID-19 crisis has revealed problems that were not evident but are more extreme; in that sense, the PA initiatives that go beyond tariff reduction, may be a lifeline for its members.

REFERENCES

Aguilera, R., Ciravegna, L., Cuervo-Cazurra, A., & González-Pérez, M. (2017). Multilatinas and the internationalization of Latin American firms. *Journal of World Business*, *52*(4), 447–460. doi:10.1016/j.jwb.2017.05.006

Aguinis, H., Villamor, I., Lazzarini, S. G., Vassolo, R. S., Amorós, J. E., & Allen, D. G. (2020). Conducting management research in Latin America: Why and what's in it for you? *Journal of Management*, *46*(5), 615–636. doi:10.1177/0149206320901581

Aquino Rodríguez, C. (2015). El Perú en la Alianza del Pacífico: Cómo poder aprovechar este acuerdo para relacionarnos más con Asia. *Pensamiento Crítico*, *20*(2), 7–23. doi:10.15381/pc.v20i2.11800

Arango, M. (2006). *Evolución y crisis del sistema financiero colombiano. Serie estudios y perspectivas. 11*. CEPAL.

Ariza-Ricaldi, P., López-Lira, A., & Giraldo-Mejía, W. (2019). SME Internationalization in Latin America: Evidence from Mexico and Peru. In Regional Integration in Latin America (pp. 99-111). Emerald Publishing Limited. doi:10.1108/978-1-78973-159-020191008

Baldwin, R., & Lopez-Gonzalez, J. (2013). *Supply-chain trade: A portrait of global patterns and several testable hypotheses.* NBER Working Papers, 18957. National Bureau of Economic Research.

Banco Central de Chile. (2010). *Cuentas Nacionales de Chile 2003-2009.* Author.

Banco Central de Chile. (2021). *Anuario Cuentas Nacionales 2020.* Author.

Banco de México. (1996). *Trade data.* https://www.banxico.org.mx/SieInternet/consultarDirectorioInternetAction.do?sector=1&accion=consultarDirectorioCuadros&locale=es

Beltrán, L. N., & Ferrer, H. E. (2016). Alianza Pacífico: Una perspectiva geopolítica y económica. *Dimensión Empresarial*, *14*(1), 79–94.

Berstein, S., & Marcel, M. (2019). *Sistema Financiero en Chile: Lecciones de la Historia Reciente.* Banco Central de Chile. https://www.bcentral.cl/documents/33528/133323/dpe67.pdf/08b40379-9553-fac0-f077-8ad5083f6a7f?t=1573269248660

Bértola, L., & Ocampo, J. (2012). Latin America's debt crisis and "lost decade". In *The Economic Development of Latin America since Independence.* Oxford University Press. https://sas-space.sas.ac.uk/6500/1/Bertola%20and%20Ocampo%20paper.pdf

Bevir, M. (2009). *Key Concepts in Governance.* SAGE Publications Inc. https://sk.sagepub.com/books/key-concepts-in-governance

Caballero, C., & Machado, G. (2020). De la crisis de 'fin de siglo' a la del 'coronavirus'. La economía colombiana en el siglo XXI. *Coyuntura Económica: Investigación Económica y Social*, *50*, 15–74.

Caballero Argáez, C. (2019). Una visión retrospectiva de dos crisis financieras de los últimos cuarenta años en Colombia. *Revista Desarrollo y Sociedad*, *82*(82), 133–165. doi:10.13043/dys.82.5

Calderón, C., & Caire, G. (2012). Génesis y desarrollo de la crisis macroeconómica de 1995. In C. Calderón & V. M. Cuevas (Eds.), *Macroeconomía abierta en América Latina: teoría y evidencia.* EON.

Calderon, C., & Hernández, L. (2017). Integración económica, crisis económicas y ciclos económicos en México. *Contaduría y Administración*, *62*(1), 64–84. doi:10.1016/j.cya.2016.10.001

Caporale, G. M., Costamagna, R., & Rossini, G. (2016). Competitive devaluations in commodity-based economies: Colombia and the Pacific Alliance group. *CESifo Working Paper Series,* 5907.

Carare, A., & Stone, M. R. (2003). *Inflation targeting regimes.* IMF Working Papers, 03/9. International Monetary Fund.

Cárdenas, M., & Martínez, H. (2020). *COVID-19 in Colombia: Impact and Policy Responses.* Center for Global Development. https://www.cgdev.org/publication/covid-19-colombia-impact-and-policy-responses

Castañeda, J. (2000 January 7). *La Crisis Colombiana. El Tiempo.* https://www.eltiempo.com/archivo/documento/MAM-1295359

Champion, M. Y. (2001). Nationalization and privatization in Peru: Socio-economic images in perpetual conflict? *Journal of Socio-Economics*, *30*(6), 517–532. doi:10.1016/S1053-5357(01)00128-7

Chaves-García, C. A. (2018). Aproximación teórica y conceptual para el análisis de la Alianza del Pacífico. *Desafíos*, *30*(1). doi:10.12804/revistas.urosario.edu.co/desafios/a.5775

Comisión Económica para América Latina y el Caribe. (2018). La convergencia entre la Alianza del Pacífico y el MERCOSUR: enfrentando juntos un escenario mundial desafiante (LC/PUB.2018/10). Author.

Comisión Económica para América Latina y el Caribe. (n.d.). *Statistical Bulletin: International trade in goods in Latin America and the Caribbean.* https://www.cepal.org/en/boletin-estadistico-de-comercio-exterior-de-bienes-en-america-latina-y-el-caribe

Concha, J., & Gómez, O. (2016). Análisis de atracción de inversión extranjera a países de la Alianza del Pacífico. *Estudios Gerenciales*, *32*(141), 369–380. doi:10.1016/j.estger.2016.11.001

Creutzfeldt, B. (2018). *China's Engagement with Regional Actors: The Pacific Alliance*. Wilson Center, Latin *American Programmer*.

Echavarría, J., González, A., López, E., & Rodríguez, N. (2012). Choques internacionales reales y financieros y su impacto sobre la economía colombiana. *Ensayos sobre Política Económica, 30*(69), 14-66.

Ffrench-Davis, R., & Heresi, R. (2014). *La economía chilena frente a la crisis financiera: respuestas contra-cíclicas y desafíos pendientes*. Universidad de Chile, Departmento de Economía.

Fitzgerald, E. V. K. (1978). The Fiscal Crisis of the Latin American State. In J. F. J. Toye (Ed.), *Taxation and Economic Development* (pp. 125–158). Frank Cass.

Foster, K. (2020). The Future of the Pacific Alliance. *Harvard International Review, 24*(March). https://hir.harvard.edu/the-future-of-the-pacific-alliance/

García, P., & Pérez, C. (2017). Desigualdad, inflación, ciclos y crisis en Chile. *Estudos Econômicos, 44*(2), 185–221. doi:10.4067/S0718-52862017000200185

García Parra, P. (2018). La Alianza del Pacífico y Colombia ante la escalada China. *Estudios Politicos, 52*(52), 15–35. doi:10.17533/udea.espo.n52a02

García-Pérez de Lema, D., Gálvez-Albarracín, E., & Maldonado-Guzmán, G. (2016). Efecto de la innovación en el crecimiento y el desempeño de las Mipymes de la Alianza del Pacífico. Un estudio empírico. *Estudios Gerenciales, 32*(141), 326–335. doi:10.1016/j.estger.2016.07.003

Garzón, J. (2015). *Latin American regionalism in a multipolar world.* EUI Working Papers.

Garzón, J., & Nolte, D. (2018). The new minilateralism in regional economic governance. Cross regionalism and the Pacific Alliance. In Handbook of South American Governance. Routledge.

Giacalone, R. (2016). Nuevas propuestas regionales en el tablero latinoamericano. In N. Mellado (Ed.), *Latinoamérica: inserción global e integración regional* (pp. 201–224). Lerner.

Hachette, D. (2000). *La reforma comercial. La transformación económica de Chile*. Centro de Estudios Públicos.

Hernández Bernal, J. A., & Muñoz Angulo, L. G. (2015). Comercio y evolución de la Alianza del Pacífico. *Equidad & Desarrollo*, (24), 97–118. doi:10.19052/ed.3682

Hwang, J. K., Dimkpah, Y., & Ogwu, A. I. (2014). Impacts of the 2008 financial crisis on South American equity markets. *International Business & Economics Research Journal, 13*(3), 573–580. doi:10.19030/iber.v13i3.8594

Inter American Development Bank. (2017). Nuevas tendencias en los tratados comerciales en América Latina. *Módulo, 1*, 1–57.

International Monetary Fund. (2021). *Chile: Staff Concluding Statement of the 2021 Article IV Mission*. Retrieved from: https://www.imf.org/en/News/Articles/2021/03/09/mcs030921-chile-staff-concluding-statement-of-the-2021-article-iv-mission?cid=em-COM-123-42756

International Monetary Fund. (n.d.). *Data.* https://www.imf.org/en/Data

Kose, M., Sugawara, N., & Terrones, M. (2020). *Global Recessions Policy Research Working Paper 9172*. World Bank, Prospects Group. https://openknowledge.worldbank.org/handle/10986/33415

Kuwayama, M. (2019). *Pacific Alliance: A Latin American Version of "Open Regionalism" in Practice.* Discussion Paper Series, DP2019-02, Research Institute for Economics & Business Administration, Kobe University. https://www.rieb.kobe-u.ac.jp/academic/ra/dp/English/DP2019-02.pdf

Lámbarry Vilchis, F. (2016). Análisis estructural de la red económica de exportaciones e importaciones de la Alianza del Pacífico y el Mercado Común del Sur. *Estudios Gerenciales*, *32*(141), 319–325. doi:10.1016/j.estger.2016.10.004

Lejárraga, I. (2019) The Pacific Alliance As an Instrument for Insertion into Global Value Chains: Lessons from a Progressive and Pragmatic Approach. In The Pacific Alliance in a World of Preferential Trade Agreements. Springer. doi:10.1007/978-3-319-78464-9_4

Lengyel, M. (2004). The Latin American Countries and the World Trading System: Addressing Institutional Barriers to Development. In M. Lengyel & V. Ventura-Dias (Eds.), *Trade Policy Reform in Latin America: Multilateral Rules and Domestic Institutions* (pp. 191–217). Palgrave/MacMillan. doi:10.1057/9780230523760_9

Licona Michel, A., Rangel Delgado, J., & González García, J. (2020). Article. *México y la Cuenca del Pacífico*, *9*(25), 21–49. doi:10.32870/mycp.v9i25.597

Llorente & Cuenca. (2016). *La diversificación de las exportaciones en América Latina*. https://ideas.llorenteycuenca.com/wp-content/uploads/sites/5/2016/10/161006_DI_IR_divers_productiva_ESP.pdf

Marcet, M. (2020). La economía chilena frente a la pandemia del COVID-19: fortalezas, desafíos y riesgos. *Seminario Visión Económica 2021*. https://www.bcentral.cl/contenido/-/detalle/la-economia-chilena-frente-a-la-pandemia-del-covid-19-fortalezas-desafios-y-riesgos-mario-marcel

Maya-Muñoz, G. (2002). Colombia 1990-2000: Globalización y crisis. *Ensayos de Economía, 12*(20-21). https://revistas.unal.edu.co/index.php/ede/article/view/23930

Mellizo, A. (2019). *Pacific Alliance: Five Challenges in the medium and long term*. EFE/EPA. https://www.efe.com/efe/english/world/50000262

Mesa, R., González, J., & Aguirre, Y. (2009). Se "esfumó" el crecimiento económico colombiano en 2009: Análisis de la coyuntura y perspectivas 2010. *Perfil de Coyuntura Económica*, *14*, 69–111.

Michaely, M. (1996). *Trade Preferential Agreements in Latin America: An Ex-Ante Assessment.* Policy Research Working Paper 1583. The World Bank. https://core.ac.uk/download/pdf/6645169.pdf

Montoya-Uribe, D. A., Gonzalez-Parias, C. H., & Duarte-Herrera, L. K. (2016). Situación y retos de Colombia en materia de comercio exterior, en el marco de la Alianza del Pacífico. *Revista Entramado*, *12*(1), 50–65. doi:10.18041/entramado.2016v12n1.23128

Mora, J. U. (2016). La Alianza del Pacífico y Mercosur: Evidencias de convergencia económica. *Estudios Gerenciales*, *32*(141), 309–318. doi:10.1016/j.estger.2016.10.005

Naim, M. (1999). *Fads and Fashion in Economic Reforms: Washington Consensus or Washington Confusion.* Working Draft of a Paper Prepared for the IMF Conference on Second Generation Reforms, Washington, DC. https://www.imf.org/external/pubs/ft/seminar/1999/reforms/naim.htm

Observatory of Economic Complexity. (n.d.). *Country's profiles.* https://oec.world/en/profile/country

Ocampo, J. (2005). ¿Por qué fue tan severa la crisis económica de fines de los años noventa? *Coyuntura Económica: Investigación Económica y Social,* (1093). https://www.repository.fedesarrollo.org.co/handle/11445/916

Ocampo, J. (2011). ¿Cómo fue el desempeño de América Latina durante la crisis financiera global? *Revista de Ensayos Económicos. Banco Central de la República de Argentina, 61*(62), 1–28.

Organization for Economic Co-operation and Development. (2018). *OECD Economic Surveys: Chile 2018.* OECD Publishing.

Organization for Economic Co-operation and Development. (2021). *OECD Economic Surveys: Chile 2021.* OECD Publishing.

Ortiz, C. (2017). La Alianza del Pacífico como actor regional: factores de éxito para la cohesión regional hacia la proyección internacional. *Desafíos, 29*(1), 49-77. http:// doi:10.12804/revistas.urosario.edu.co/desafios/a.4885

Parra, C., & Salazar, N. (2000). La crisis financiera y la experiencia internacional. *Boletines de Divulgación Económica,* 1. https://colaboracion.dnp.gov.co/CDT/Estudios%20Econmicos/La%20crisis%20financiera%20y%20la%20experiencia%20internacional.pdf

Pastrana, E. (2016). *La Alianza del Pacífico: de cara a los proyectos regionales y las transformaciones globales.* Barcelona/Ciudad de México, Editorial Gedisa.

Peña-Vinces, J. C., Casanova, L., Guillen, J., & Urbano, D. (2016). International competitiveness of small and medium-sized enterprises: Peru, a Latin-American emerging market. *Emerging Markets Finance & Trade, 53*(1), 150–169. doi:10.1080/1540496X.2016.1156525

Perez-Reyna, D. (2017). Crisis de 1999. In J. D. Uribe (Ed.), Historia del Banco de la República 1923-2015 (pp. 437–463). Academic Press.

Polanco, R. (2015). *Chilean Trade and Investment Agreements with Southern Countries: From Bilateral Treaties to the Pacific Alliance.* SECO/WTI Academic Cooperation Project Working Paper Series, 1.

Prochile. (2019). *Liderazgo de Chile en las exportaciones mundiales.* Departamento de Estudios. https://www.prochile.gob.cl/documento-biblioteca/liderazgo-de-chile-en-las-exportaciones-mundiales-2018/#:~:text=Sin%20ir%20m%C3%A1s%20lejos%2C%20Chile,y%20algas%20de%20uso%20industrial

Ramos, J. (2008). El desarrollo exportador chileno: evolución y perspectivas. *Documento de Trabajo de Economía de la Universidad de Chile,* 289. http://repositorio.uchile.cl/handle/2250/144171

Reid, M. (2020, July). Peru is heading towards a dangerous new populism. *The Economist.* https://www.economist.com/the-americas/2020/07/23/peru-is-heading-towards-a-dangerous-new-populism

Reid, M. (2021, April). Two extremists vie in a run-off for Peru's presidency. *The Economist.* https://www.economist.com/the-americas/2021/04/15/two-extremists-vie-in-a-run-off-for-perus-presidency

Reinhart, C., & Rogoff, K. (2009). *The aftermath of financial crises.* NBER Working Paper Series, 14656. https://www.nber.org/papers/w14656

Reinhart, C. M., & Savastano, M. A. (2003). The realities of modern hyperinflation. *Finance & Development*, *40*(2), 20–23. https://www.elibrary.imf.org/view/journals/022/0040/002/article-A007-en.xml

Rodríguez, J. A. (2021). Situación económica, política fiscal y pandemia en Colombia. *Revista de Economia Institucional*, *23*(44), 249–263.

Rodríguez, M. P., Cortez, K., & Méndez, A. B. (2019). Financial and Economic Convergence in Pacific Alliance Countries. In M. Blanco-Jimenez & J. C. Álvarez (Eds.), *Regional Integration in Latin America* (pp. 45–60). Emerald Publishing Limited. doi:10.1108/978-1-78973-159-020191004

Rosales, O., & Kuwayama, O. (2012). *China y América Latina y el Caribe. Hacia una relación económica y comercial estratégica.* Comisión Económica para América Latina y el Caribe (CEPAL). https://www.redalc-china.org/monitor/images/pdfs/Investigacion/15_Rosales_2012.pdf

SICE. (2020). *Foreign Trade Information System.* Organization of American States (OAS). sice.oas.org

Spillan, J. E., & Virzi, N. (2017). Business Opportunities in the Pacific Alliance: The Economic Rise of Chile, Peru, Colombia, and Mexico. Springer. doi:10.1007/978-3-319-54768-8

Stellian, R., & Danna-Buitrago, J. (2019). Revealed comparative advantages and regional specialization: Evidence from Colombia in the Pacific Alliance. *Journal of Applied Econometrics*, *22*(1), 349–379. doi:10.1080/15140326.2019.1627722

Stiglitz, J. (2003). *Globalization and its Discontents.* W.W. Norton Company.

Subsecretaría de Relaciones Económicas Internacionales - SUBREI. (2020). *Informe Anual de Comercio exterior de Chile, 2019.* Dirección de Estudios. https://www.subrei.gob.cl/docs/default-source/estudios-y-documentos/reporte-trimestral/comercio-exterior-de-chile-anual-2019.pdf?sfvrsn=1eb0bb58_0

Subsecretaría de Relaciones Económicas Internacionales - SUBREI. (2021a). *Informe anual de Comercio exterior de Chile, 2020.* Dirección de Estudios.

Subsecretaría de Relaciones Económicas Internacionales - SUBREI. (2021b). *Ficha país.* https://www.subrei.gob.cl/estudios-y-documentos/ficha-pais

Tello, M. D. (2012). Peru: Integration, sectoral specialization and synchronization with international gross domestic product cycles. *CEPAL Review*, *106*(106), 89–106. doi:10.18356/84420f4d-en

Thoumi, F. E. (2002). Illegal Drugs in Colombia: From Illegal Economic Boom to Social Crisis. *The Annals of the American Academy of Political and Social Science*, *582*(1), 102–116. doi:10.1177/000271620258200108

Torres, G. A. (2011). La crisis colombiana de finales del siglo XX: ¿Un choque real o financiero? *Perfil de Coyuntura Económica*, *18*, 79–96.

Urrutia, M., & Llano, J. (2011). La crisis internacional y cambiaria de fin de siglo en Colombia. *Revista Desarrollo y Sociedad*, (67), 11–48. doi:10.13043/dys.67.1

Varón, O., Ríos, H. F. & Chávez, N. M. (2017). Budgetary deficit and inflation: case the Pacific Alliance. *Dimensión empresarial, 16*(1), 135-146. doi:10.15665/dem.v16i1.1899

Vial, J. (2020). *Situación actual y perspectivas de la economía chilena*. Seminario Banco de España, 17 de febrero 2020, Madrid, España. https://www.bcentral.cl/es/web/banco-central/contenido/-/details/situacion-actual-y-perspectivas-de-la-economia-chilena-joaquin-vial-vicepresidente-madrid

Vieyra Medrano, J. A. (2000). Reconversión industrial, gran empresa y efectos territoriales: El caso del sector automotriz en México. *EURE. Revista Latinoamericana de Estudios Urbano Regionales*, *26*(77), 25–47. doi:10.4067/S0250-71612000007700002

Villar, L., & Rincón, H. (2000). *The Colombian Economy in the Nineties: Capital Flows and Foreign Exchange Regimes*. Paper presented at the Conference on "Critical Issues in Financial Reform: Latin American- Caribbean and Canadian Perspectives", University of Toronto. https://www.banrep.gov.co/sites/default/files/publicaciones/archivos/borra149.pdf

Williamson, J. (2003). The Washington Consensus and Beyond. *Economic and Political Weekly*, *38*(15), 1475–1481.

World Bank. (2020a). *Latin America and Caribbean results*. Retrieved from https://www.worldbank.org/

World Bank. (2020b). *Mexico's international trade*. Retrieved from https://wits.worldbank.org/

World Bank. (n.d.). *World Development Indicators* [Data set]. https://databank.worldbank.org/

World Trade Organization. (n.d.). *Aid for Trade*. https://www.wto.org/english/tratop_e/devel_e/a4t_e/aid4trade_e.htm

ADDITIONAL READING

Aizenman, J., Chinn, M. D., & Ito, H. (2013). The "impossible trinity" hypothesis in an era of global imbalances: Measurement and testing. *Review of International Economics*, *21*(3), 447–458. doi:10.1111/roie.12047

Baker & McKenzie. (2017). *La Alianza del Pacífico: Guía al Más Importante Bloque Comercial Latinoamericano Que Probablemente No Conoces*. Baker & McKenzie.

Blanco-Jimenez, M., & Álvarez, J. C. (2019). *Regional integration in Latin America: Dynamics of the Pacific Alliance*. Emerald Publishing Limited. doi:10.1108/9781789731590

Boughton, J. M. (2003). On the origins of the Fleming-Mundell model. *IMF Staff Papers*, *50*(1), 1–9.

Cavallo, E., & Powell, A. (2021). *Oportunidades para un mayor crecimiento sostenible tras la pandemia: Informe macroeconómico de América Latina y el Caribe*. Banco Interamericano de Desarrollo.

Comisión Económica para América Latina y el Caribe. (2020). *Informe sobre el impacto económico en América Latina y el Caribe de la enfermedad por coronavirus (COVID-19)*. CEPAL.

Novak, F., & Namihas, S. (2018). *La Alianza del Pacífico: situación, perspectivas y propuestas de consolidación* (2nd ed.). Konrad Adenauer Stiftung.

Pereira Pacheco, A. E. (2020). *Essays on Corporate Law, Governance and Development in the Pacific Alliance* [Unpublished doctoral dissertation]. University of California, Berkeley, CA, United States.

KEY TERMS AND DEFINITIONS

Commodities: Are goods whose quality may differ slightly, but it is essentially uniform across producers. Commodities are most often used as inputs in the production of other goods or services. Commonly, their prices are defined in international markets.

Complementary Economic Agreement (CEA): Name used by Latin American countries in the bilateral agreements they enter to reciprocally open their markets for all goods. They are part of the legal framework of the Latin American Integration Association (ALADI). They aim to open markets greater than Preferential Agreements/Partial Scope Agreements, but less than Free Trade Agreements.

Customs Union: Level of integration were countries, apart from eliminating tariffs to products originated from their territories, agree on the duties applied to products that come from third parties.

Economic Integration: Is an arrangement among nations which usually starts with the reduction or elimination of trade barriers. It has a logical order of depth that depends on the degree of commitment of liberalization between partner countries.

Free Trade Agreement: Level of integration where countries agree to eliminate tariffs and other restrictive regulations to products originated from their territories.

Most-Favored Nation (MFN): Is one of the principles of non-discrimination of the WTO. In normal conditions, if a member offers a benefit to another country, it must extend the advantage to the rest of the members of the WTO.

Open Regionalism: It seeks to increase integration among neighboring countries, eliminating and reducing at the same time barriers to integrate with the rest of the world. It is considered as a strategy to facilitate international exchange of goods or services and to coordinate trade economic policies between regions.

Partial/Preferential Scope Agreements (PS): It is a basic trade agreement that includes tariff reductions on a specific group of goods, sometimes unilaterally. It is usually seen as the first stage in a long-term larger opening process.

APPENDIX

Table 2. Trade agreements by PA countries

Chile		Colombia		Mexico		Peru	
Customs Union							
		Agreement/ Partner(s) signatory(ies)				**Agreement/ Partner(s) signatory(ies)**	
		Andean Community (Peru, Ecuador, Bolivia, Venezuela, Colombia)	26/05/1969 (subscribed)			Andean Community (Peru, Ecuador, Bolivia, Venezuela, Colombia)	26/05/1969 (subscribed)
Free Trade Agreements							
Agreement/ Partner(s) signatory(ies)	**In force**	**Agreement/ Partner(s) signatory(ies)**	**In force**	**Agreement/ Partner(s) signatory(ies)**	**In force**	**Agreement/ Partner(s) signatory(ies)**	**In force**
United Kingdom	01 January 2021	Pacific Alliance	01-may-16	USMCA (United States-Mexico-Canada)	01 July 2020	Australia	11 February 2020
Indonesia	10 August 2019	European Free Trade Agreement	01 July 2011	Pacific Alliance	01-may-16	Honduras	01 January 2017
Uruguay	13 December 2018	Canada	15 August 2011	Central America (Costa Rica, El Salvador, Guatemala, Honduras y Nicaragua)		Pacific Alliance	01-may-16
Argentina	02-may-19	Chile	08-may-09	Peru (CEA 67)	01 February 2012	European Union	
Hong Kong, China	29 November 2014	South Korea	15 July 2016	Bolivia (CEA 66)	07 June 2010	Japan	01 March 2012
Pacific Alliance	01-may-16	Costa Rica	01 August 2016	Japan	01 April 2005	Costa Rica	01 June 2013
Thailand	05 November 2015	United States	15-may-12	Panama	01 July 2015	Panama	01-may-12
Vietnam	04 February 2014	Israel	11 August 2020	Uruguay (CEA 60)	15 July 2004	Mexico (CEA 67)	01 February 2012
Malaysia	18 April 2012	MERCOSUR PS.CE N° 72	2017-2019	European Free Trade Agreement	01 July 2001	South Korea	01 August 2011
Turkey	01 March 2011	Mexico	01 January 1995	Israel	01 July 2001	China	01 March 2010
Australia	06 March 2009	Northern Triangle (El Salvador, Guatemala y Honduras)	23 September 2009	Chile (CEA 41)	01 August 1999	European Free Trade Agreement	14 July 2010
Japan	03 September 2007	European Union	01 August 2013	European Union (EU)	01 October 2000	Canada	01 August 2009
Colombia	08-may-09			Colombia	01 January 1995	Singapore	01 August 2009
Peru	01 March 2009			TLCAN (Canada - United States - Mexico)	01 January 1994	Chile	01 March 2009
Panama	07 March 2008					United States	01 February 2009
China	01 October 2006					MERCOSUR (CEA 58)	
New Zealand, Singapore and Brunei Darussalam (P4)						Thailand	31 December 2011
European Free Trade Agreement	01 December 2004						

continued on following page

Table 2. Continued

Chile		Colombia		Mexico		Peru	
United States	01 January 2004						
South Korea	01 April 2004						
European Union (EU)	01 February 2003						
Central America (Costa Rica, El Salvador, Guatemala, Honduras y Nicaragua)							
Mexico (CEA 41)	01 August 1999						
Canada	05 July 1997						
MERCOSUR (CEA 35)	01 October 1996						
Preferential Trade Agreements							
Agreement/ Partner(s) signatory(ies)	**In force**	**Agreement/ Partner(s) signatory(ies)**	**In force**	**Agreement/ Partner(s) signatory(ies)**	**In force**	**Agreement/ Partner(s) signatory(ies)**	**In force**
Ecuador (PS.CE N° 65)	05 January 2010	CARICOM (PS. A25TM N°31)		Argentina (CEA N° 6)	01 January 2007	Venezuela	01 August 2013
India	17 August 2007	Colombia - Ecuador - Venezuela - MERCOSUR (PS. CE N° 59)		MERCOSUR (CEA N° 55) - Agreement on vehicles			
Bolivia (PS.CE N° 22)	06 April 1993	Costa Rica (PS. A25TM N°7)		Brazil (PS.CE N° 53)	02-may-03		
Venezuela (PS.CE N° 23)	02 April 1993	Nicaragua (PS. AT25TM N° 6)		Paraguay (PS.R 38)	01 July 1994		
Argentina (PS.CE N° 16)	02 August 1991	Panama (PS. AT25TM N° 29)	18 January 1995	Ecuador (PS 29)	06 August 1987		
		Venezuela (PS.C N° 28)	19 October 2012	MERCOSUR (CEA N° 54) - Framework agreement	05 January 2006		
Subscribed Trade Agreements (not in force)							
Agreement/ Partner(s) signatory(ies)		**Agreement/ Partner(s) signatory(ies)**		**Agreement/ Partner(s) signatory(ies)**		**Agreement/ Partner(s) signatory(ies)**	
Trans-Pacific Partnership		Panama		Trans-Pacific Partnership		United Kingdom	
		United Kingdom		United Kingdom		Trans-Pacific Partnership	
						Guatemala	

Source: Authors´ elaboration based on SICE (2020)

Chapter 4
Economic Crisis and Its Effects on International Trade:
A Case of Selected EU and Non-EU Countries

Miloš Parežanin
Faculty of Organizational Sciences, University of Belgrade, Serbia

Dragana Kragulj
Faculty of Organizational Sciences, University of Belgrade, Serbia

Sandra Jednak
Faculty of Organizational Sciences, University of Belgrade, Serbia

ABSTRACT

The aim of this chapter is to analyse the effects of the economic crisis on the trade among the Southeastern European (SEE) countries. The countries were divided into two groups: the EU countries and non-EU countries. Macroeconomic performances and international trade indicators of the 11 observed countries were analysed for the period 2007-2019, and the effects of the economic crisis were present in all the observed countries, particularly the effects on the export performances. The crisis also affected the entire import of the non-EU countries. The EU countries recovered from the crisis faster than the non-EU countries. However, the non-EU countries achieved a more significant inflow of foreign direct investment in the post-crisis period, which significantly improved the position of the balance of payments in these countries. The observed countries had managed to stabilise their trade flows all until the beginning of the COVID-19 crisis. The impact of the current crisis on these countries remains to be estimated in the future.

DOI: 10.4018/978-1-7998-8314-2.ch004

INTRODUCTION

The international trade expansion and the development of interdependence have influence on the global economic progress and complexity in the global trade relationship. This trend has been present since the 1950s, but with some contraction of economic activities, trade volumes, and capital movements due to regional or global economic crises (Broll & Jauer, 2014). According to classical and neoclassical economists, international trade plays a role in economic growth and development in both developed and developing countries. However, there is an opinion that international trade cannot have a significant impact on economic growth in the developing countries due to their lack of capacity for import and export of goods and services. Import should bring resources unavailable domestically, new products and technology that will lead to the expansion of export and access to the world markets. These countries have a slow progress towards high technology, increased efficiency, and productivity in industries. They specialise in primary goods' production (agriculture, metal, and mineral) and struggle with industrialisation due to the lack of technological innovation. On the other hand, developed countries benefit from the international trade due to trade openness (trade liberalisation), international prices, cost of production, rising income, and comparative advantage. Today, international trade policy helps all the abovementioned countries to gain sustainable economic growth.

It is a fact that various types of crises occur more and more frequently. Economic crises happen in both national and global economies due to weak economic bases, government inability, and poor management. Prior to the global crisis (2007-2008), most crises were of regional character occurring each three years (Reinhart & Rogoff, 2008). It is also a fact that crises have influence on economies and international trade. However, international trade may also transmit crises from one affected country to other countries (contagious effect). Crises bring about the reduction of economic activity and trade, which was particularly prominent during the global financial crisis of 2007-2008 (Levchenko et al., 2010). In 2009, the world trade flows dropped by 12%, and the decrease in the world GDP was 5.4% (Chor & Manova, 2012). There are various types of crises – sovereign default, financial crises, exchange rate crashes, and inflation explosions. All of them cause major issues in the economy. One of the most common issues is the lack of capital, which affects the exchange rate, price, competitiveness, and consumption. Furthermore, crises affect economies, particularly those with development strategies based on export-led growth. When a crisis occurs, many countries apply trade measures to protect their industries and trade. Also, during the global economic crisis, different credit conditions and a slowdown in global demand affected trade volumes (Chor & Manova, 2012). These are the challenges to overcome.

The last crisis influenced both the supply and demand sides of the global economy. The supply-side effects such as restriction of movement and going to work, and/or disruption in the supply of intermediate products influenced the production. The demand side was also affected by a decline in consumption due to a fall in employment and income on one side, and an increase in uncertainty on the other side. The international service sector (tourism, air sector, etc.) suffered the most during the COVID-19 crisis (Gruszczynski, 2020). According to WTO, merchandise trade would have decreased by 13-32% in 2020.

The European Union (EU) is one of the key players in the global trade along with the USA and China. In 2019, the EU, USA and China counted for 43% of the world trade. The EU is the second-largest exporter and importer of goods globally (Eurostat, 2020). The international trade in the EU and non-EU countries is determined by GDP, geographical distance, membership (Beck, 2020), and commercial cooperation (Maciejewski & Wach, 2019). The EU also tackles the crisis. The estimation of WTO for 2020 was that in EU27 the export would drop by 12-33% and import by 10%-25%.

The purpose of the chapter is to present the economic crisis and its influence on international trade. The aim is to analyse the effects of the global economic crisis on international trade in the selected EU and non-EU countries.

The research questions for this chapter are:

RQ1: What are the effects and challenges of international trade in the period during and after the crisis?
RQ2: How does the crisis affect trade flows and competitiveness of the selected EU and non-EU countries respectfully?
RQ3: What is the volume of export and import during and after the crisis in the selected EU and non-EU countries?

This chapter contributes to expanding the literature on the issues of economic crisis impact on international trade in the selected EU and non-EU countries by the selected indicators.

The structure of the chapter is as follows. The introduction is followed by a theoretical framework for international trade and the link between international trade and crises. The following section discusses macroeconomic performances, with the focus on export and import of the selected EU and non-EU countries during and after the global economic crisis. The chapter ends with the conclusion.

BACKGROUND

International Trade

It is very important to make a distinction between the terms "international trade" and "foreign trade". International trade is defined as the economic activity that comprises the exchange of goods, services, and intellectual property products among various national economies and various cohesion entities. International trade abides by the laws different from the laws in domestic trade. It occurs in international environment that includes international institutions, agreements, and arrangements that affect international trade, investment, and knowledge flows as well as trade conditions in certain countries. Furthermore, international trade has its microeconomic aspects – the trade theory and commercial policy theory, and macroeconomic aspects – the mechanisms of adjustment, capital flow, balance of payments, and international monetary system (Kindleberger, 1974).On the other hand, foreign trade includes all the exchanges of goods and services that a country has with other countries, where import and export of goods present the "visible", and import and export of services the "invisible" exchange. Foreign trade does not only imply a classical exchange of goods and services, but also various types of business-technical cooperation, long-term production cooperation, international exchange of technology, etc. All real transactions are followed by international financial and capital transactions. Foreign exchange and domestic demand have become the key factors of trade flows and sustainable economic development in the circumstances of globalization of the world economy and internationalisation of business.

Foreign trade can be a driver of development of a national economy and influence its international economic and political position. Whether a foreign trade within a national economy is successful or not depends both on domestic trade conditions, and on international environment.

Commercial policy is defined as a set of instruments that a country uses to attain to its goals of foreign trade and economic and commercial cooperation with the rest of the world. The goals of foreign trade include the positive influence on production and employment, price stability, convertibility of national currency, balance of payments, national economy that is open to trade with the rest of the world, etc. Since the modern world economy and global market were created, three main economic theories and policies have emerged – liberalism, protectionism, and inventionism. Liberalism, as a form of economic policy in the time of free competition of the capitalist production system, rests on the notions of Adam Smith and David Ricardo. The founders and theoreticians of the classical economic school advocated free trade and unlimited competition in the global market, which basically means removing national borders as the elements of international exchange. From the aspect of the world economy as a whole, the policy of liberalism has a few advantages. It contributes to a faster total economic development of the world economy by intensifying the division of labour and increasing the productivity through specialized production. The policy of liberalisation encourages competitiveness, which influences faster introduction of new technology and a more modern organisation of production. The market expands enabling mass production and reduced costs of production. All this is reflected in the increased living standard of the countries that use the advantages of the international labour division and free trade system. Thus, for example, in the South East European (SEE) countries within the Central European Free Trade Agreement (CEFTA) 2006 trade liberalization influences GDP growth, unemployment, public debt, and budget deficit, but the influence varies from country to country (Kragulj et al., 2018). Liberalist conceptions, however, are not suitable for the economies that are narrowly specialized in the production of only one or only a few goods. Such monocultural countries are often in the situation where they become too dependent on the world market due to the application of liberalist policy, so the slightest of changes in the world market can put that country in a disadvantageous position (Kragulj, 2020).

Unlike liberalism, protectionism is an economic policy that comprises a set of government measures aimed at protecting domestic production from the international competition in order to maintain or gain economic independence. The advocates of the protectionist policy supported, above all, the introduction of the protective customs duty on the import of industrial equipment and final products. They also supported the application of other instruments in the field of foreign trade such as commodity contingents, exchange quotas, export and import permits, etc. Alexander Hamilton, an economist and the first Secretary of the US Treasury, provided the first theoretical elaboration on protectionism in the economic literature trying to defend the economic interests of the USA, which was an underdeveloped economy in the 18th century. The policy of protectionism was further developed in the works of Friedrich List, a German economist who rejected the ideas of free economy introduced by David Ricardo. According to List, the aim of the protectionist policy was to protect national economies in numerous German mini-states from the competitive, industrially developed Great Britain. List pointed out to the fact that the Great Britain also used protectionist measures during the industrial revolution and strong economic development, but when it reached economic advantage over other countries it proclaimed that the ideas of free trade were universal and only correct conceptions.

The contemporary foreign trade policies, especially in the developed countries, apply numerous protectionist measures such as: duty protectionism, quantitative restrictions when importing foreign goods, financial and currency instruments, government procurement/requisitions, and an array of other technical and administrative barriers that limit the free international trade.The positive aspect of the protectionist policy is the fact that domestic economy can develop more easily without possible damage that could be inflicted by the free competition of the developed foreign partners. By using its own production capacities, a country increases its economic power and strengthens its economic and political independence. However, a long-term application of the protectionist measures may cause serious damage, because they destimulate domestic producers to further develop their production and technological processes and raise the level of productivity. In the conditions of growing competitiveness on the global market, protectionist policy can easily turn into interventionism. Along with the classical protectionist instruments such as duties, contingencies, and quotas, the policy of interventionism applies some stronger and more efficient measures such as import and export bans, foreign currency control, price dumping, subsidised export, local currency devaluation, state monopoly on the foreign trade, etc. Such a policy diminishes the benefits of international labour division and negatively influences productivity and efficiency of the world economy.

Open economy represents not only a necessity for international exchange of goods and services, but also the growth of that exchange. At the current level of social and economic development, the autocratic economy, as an extreme form of protectionism, is not possible. Contemporary economies cannot pursue the policy of complete self-sufficiency and use their own production capacities to fulfil all the needs of the population. The process of international exchange becomes particularly important in the conditions of the ongoing globalisation and growing economic interdependences among countries. Countries do not regulate their trade relationships by bilateral contacts only. On the contrary, various international forums and international organisations discuss the problems of global economy and international exchange.

From the aspect of globalisation, but also from the aspect of international exchange the key roles belong to the World Trade Organisation (WTO), International Monetary Fund (IMF), World Bank (WB), and the United Nations (UN). It is of vital interest for each economy to take part in both world and regional institutions, so the measures of state policies have to be steered in that direction. In trade policy practice, different combinations of applying liberalist and protectionist concepts are possible. Nowadays, almost all countries support liberalism and the free trade ideas in theory pointing out to their benefits, while in practice developed and developing countries alike use various protectionist and interventionist measures that they do not want to give up.

The EU foreign trade policy is a complex and very dynamic area. The EU Common Commercial Policy (CCP) is not only one of its most important policies, but also the area where a high degree of integration has been achieved. It belongs to the areas of the exclusive EU authority, i.e. it is of supranational character. This means that the EU has the exclusive right of decision, and the member countries cannot make decisions on any issues even if the EU has not resolved those issues. One of the goals of integration was to remove the obstacles towards the development of international trade. The EU CCP was established at the very beginning of creating this European integration, and its legal framework was set in the Treaty Establishing the European Community (TEC), which was signed on 25 March 1957 in Rome (it came into force on 1 January 1958). The Title 9 of the Treaty was headed "Common Commercial Policy" and includes articles 131 – 134 of the Treaty. The Article 133 of the Treaty determines the competencies of the EU bodies in managing its foreign trade policy. The goal was to create a single market, a single economic space within the member countries where four free commercial movements would function – the free movement of goods, free movement of people, freedom to establish and provide services, and free movement of capital. In order to ensure the free movement of the production factors, economic global integration demands not only trade liberalisation, but also the harmonisation of taxes, wages, foreign exchange, and monetary and fiscal policies (Kindleberger, 1974). The Treaty of Lisbon from 2009 introduced some substantial changes into the CCP of the EU by expanding its goals. The changes are mostly reflected in the fact that it is clearly stated that commercial agreements are related to the exchange of goods and services, commercial aspects of the intellectual property, and foreign direct investment (FDI). The establishment of a single market turned out to be a long and complex process, since some economic and non-economic factors stimulate, while others hinder the commercial integration.

Commercial integration is carried out in accordance with the national economies. Economic integration is conducted in a few phases, where each phase comprises both its previous characteristics and some new elements (Balassa, 1974). The phases include - Free Trade Area (eliminating the tariffs and other barriers to the trade between the members, while keeping their own tariffs towards the non-members), Customs Union (the area of free trade within the customs union, and the common external set of tariffs towards the non-members), Common Market (removing the barriers related to the flows of production factors), Economic Union (along with the common market it implies a better harmonisation of national economies in order to eliminate discrimination), Monetary Union (introducing a common currency and common monetary policy), Economic and Monetary Union (the combination of the two previous phases), and Total Economic Union (a degree of integration similar to a single country)(Molle, 2006). Commercial integration eliminates the discrimination between the goods produced in one country and the goods produced in any other union member. The areas of free trade and customs union make the conditions for the free trade. However, a new discrimination between the goods produced in member and non-member countries is yet about to start. Therefore, the integration has positive effects by eliminating discrimination, but it also has negative effects by causing discrimination. The magnitude of these effects determines whether such a union will lead towards the free trade and have a positive net effect, or it will lead to increased discrimination and have a negative net effect on a global scale.

The EU plays an important role in the world trade where it participates with about 15%. As a signatory of a great number of bilateral and unilateral agreements, the EU makes a significant contribution to the World Trade Organisation. Prior to the crisis, the EU participated in the total world trade with 19.1%, the USA with 19.3%, and China with 9.2%. After the crisis, the participation of the EU and the USA in the world trade decreased, while the participation of China increased. So, in 2019, the EU participated in the world trade with 15.4%, the USA with 17.2%, and China with 13.8% (Eurostat, 2020).

The EU created an institutional mechanism for conducting a common foreign trade policy (CTP). Furthermore, it has developed and used both well-known and lesser-known foreign trade policy instruments such as tariffs, a wide range of non-customs barriers, anti-dumping measures, predatory pricing, quantitative restrictions, voluntary export restraint (VER), levies, export promotion, temporary restrictions on import, countervailing duties, the rule of origin, safeguard clauses, formulating technical standards, setting administrative barriers, economic sanctions, etc. The trade policy of the EU is strongly protectionist in many areas (agriculture, fishing, and certain industries). It has maintained the protectionist environment towards the non-members mostly in the area of non-tariff barriers. The trade protectionism of the EU constitutes discrimination against the non-members because they have to face the competition which is not the result of comparative advantages in the international division of labour. Unfair competition, together with the collective protectionism have created a regime of trade discrimination. Developing countries are particularly affected, since they cannot make up for their losses with the benefits they get from the EU through commercial agreements (Prokopijević, 2005). Very favourable opportunities have opened up for large monopolies to prosper, not only in the markets of individual member countries, but also within the entire Union with aggressive tendencies towards penetrating the world economy. Anti-monopoly measures applied in some areas by the Union bodies have not prevented this trend that has become prominent in the current circumstances.

Economic Crisis and International Trade

Various crises can international trade both positively and negatively. The most common state before a financial crisis occurs is a current account deficit. It triggers the financial crisis due to the increase of foreign debt, a decline of foreign reserve that undermines the trust in domestic currency and exchange rate (Ma & Cheng, 2005). The crisis brings about a recession and a decline in imports, but exports may rise due to a decrease in domestic demand and devaluation of domestic currency. However, weak financial and banking systems can decrease export.

Banking and currency crises are the types of financial crises. During a financial crisis, asset prices drop, businesses and consumers cannot pay their debts, and banks and other financial institutions have liquidity shortages. A banking crisis can start by withdrawing money from bank accounts or by closing, merging, and bailing out financial institutions. After a banking crisis, capital decreases. The currency crisis is accompanied by a current account deficit anda concern whether there are enough foreign exchange reserves to maintain the exchange rate. Some of the reasons for this kind of crisis are - fixed exchange rates, capital flows, loans, moral hazard, real estate boom, banking crisis (Jednak & Jednak, 2018),fiscal deficits, and external shocks. Due to the uncertainty of exchange rates, the currency crisis negatively impacts both export and import in the short run, but it should regain its balance in the long run. According to Ma & Cheng (2005), there are the channels through which banking and currency crises affect international trade. The banking crisis affects international trade through income channel, foreign capital flow channel, and investment demand channel, while the currency crisis affects trade through income channel, substitution effect channel, and wealth channel. The channels influence export and import in different ways. The banking crisis income channel decreases both imports and exports during and after the crisis. The foreign capital flow channel increases export during the crisis, but decreases it after the crisis, and the investment demand channel decreases import, and increases export after the crisis. The currency crisis reduces both export and import through the income channel and substitution effect channel, but import might decrease and export might increase through the wealth channel.

In the periods when countries are affected by crises, they often resort to protectionism which leads towards a lesser volume of commercial exchange (Wynne & Kersting, 2009). In the period 2000-2008 the export of the EU countries had a real growth of 60%. Due to the protectionist measures imposed by the governments since the beginning of the economic crisis, further growth of import was reduced dramatically. The consequences of such economic policy were the reduced growth of export of the EU members towards the destinations outside the EU by 10-20% in the period 2008-2014. It is estimated that the export growth deficit in the EU could have been reduced by half in comparison to China (where it was 35% in the period 2008-2014) had it not been for the protectionist measures (Evenett & Fritz, 2017). The global crisis caused significant differences in growth rates, price adjustments for different goods, and major changes in demand. Furthermore, it caused geographical changes in the trade flows. The decline in the trade volume between Russia and the countries of CIS and EU was larger than the trade volume with China and some of the developing countries. However, it seems that geographical shares of trade, such as sectoral imports and exports remained stable amid major disruptions in trade flows (Shelburne, 2010). Similar effects occurred in Asian countries, especially affecting the Asian companies that financed their export through loans (Coulibaly et al., 2011). The consequences of the global economic crisis of 2007-2009 on the labour market were not short-term, and their effect on the number of jobs is visible even a decade later (Parisi, 2017; Silva et al., 2021).

There are some estimates that the global shock caused by the COVID-19 will bring about 4% drop in the global GDP. It is estimated that developing countries may expect the drop of 2.5% GDP, while the developed countries may expect the drop of 1.8% GDP. The biggest drop is recorded in providing catering and tourist services (Maliszewska et al., 2020). Protectionism still occurs as a response to the crisis, especially in the developed countries (Albertoni & Wise, 2021). Some authors claim that the trade openness of China and its trade flows contributed to the spreading of the COVID-19 across the world (Price & Adu, 2021). The pandemic has also influenced foreign exchange volatility, which consequently has changed the conditions of commercial exchange (Feng et al., 2021).

MAIN FOCUS OF THE CHAPTER

Globalisation has led to the increased importance of trade in the world and brought about the changes in production and trade. Previously, international trade was focused predominantly on exports and imports of final products. Today, these products account for 30%, while intermediate products account for 70% (OECD, 2020) of the world trade. In this way, the structure of the world trade has changed, but the trade flows between countries have also increased. In addition to these changes, international trade faces other challenges such as economic welfare, raising tariffs, government support, new technology, new ways of business practice, environmental issues, global and national crises, etc. (UNCTAD, 2010).

As explained above, economic crises affect economic activities. International trade had different effects and posed different challenges during and after the global economic crisis. The crisis also affected trade flows and competitiveness of both EU and non-EU countries. Finally, the volume of export and import was different during the crisis and after the EU and non-EU countries were hit by the crisis. All the above statements were analysed on the selected EU and non-EU countries using data from international organisations.

SEE countries that are either the EU members or are the candidate countries (countries in the accession process) were selected to conduct the analysis of the crisis effects on the international trade. Namely, Bulgaria, Croatia, Greece, Romania, and Slovenia are the EU member countries, while Albania, Bosnia and Herzegovina, Moldova, Montenegro, North Macedonia, and Serbia are in the EU accession process. In this chapter, the authors compared the two groups of countries. According to various methodologies, there are some differences in ranking countries due to macroeconomic indicators and its development (Jednak et al., 2018).

The data were collected from the IMF, Eurostat, and the World Bank. The main macroeconomic indicators (GDP, GPD pc, inflation, unemployment, etc.), trade flows (import and export), current account, and FDI for the observed countries will be presented and discussed for the period during and post-global economic crisis. It will be presented how the observed countries tackled the crisis and which mechanisms they used to protect their economy and trade.

RESULTS

The presented theoretical considerations on trade and economic crisis provided the answer to the RQ1 about the effects and challenges of international trade in the period during and post-crisis. Furthermore, in order to complete the answer to RQ1 and provide answer to RQ2 (i.e. gain insight into the international competitiveness of economies) it is important to observe their macroeconomic performances. The period 2007-2019 was analysed in order to see the effects during and after the crisis. The main indicators were GDP growth, GDP per capita, general government net lending/borrowing, inflation, and unemployment rate. SEE countries were divided into two groups. The first group comprised the EU member countries, while the second group comprised the non-members that were in different phases of the EU accession process.

After the initial effects of the economic crisis, the first major negative effect occurred in 2009 (Table 1). In 2009, all the observed SEE countries that are the EU members had negative influence on GDP reflected in the negative rates of GDP growth. The largest drop was recorded in Slovenia (-7.5%) and Croatia (-7.3%). In 2010, the economies started their slow recovery, and Bulgaria and Slovenia achieved positive GDP growth rates. Greece was the exception, because there the economic crisis reached its full effect in 2011 when GDP growth was -9.1%. The effects of the economic crisis had been present all until 2014 when all the observed countries started their recovery. The effects were particularly devastating in Greece which, according to GDP per capita, had been the leader among the SEE countries until 2013 when Slovenia took over the leading position. General government net borrowing increased in almost all observed countries in the period 2009-2011. The exception is Slovenia, which had the largest government borrowing in 2013 due to the recapitalization of state-owned banks. One of the major effects of the crisis was the loss of jobs. Unemployment rate had been increasing in all the observed countries until 2014, when it started to decline. There was no general trend of inflation, but it is evident that the inflation was at its highest in 2008, at the peak of economic crisis. Bulgaria (12.3%) and Romania (7.9%) had the highest inflation.

As for the group of SEE countries that are not the EU members, 2009 was also the year where economic crisis had the strongest effects on economic growth (Table 2). The economies of these countries started to recover after 2013. The exception is Serbia that after the positive economic growth in 2013 recorded a 1.9% drop in economic activity in 2014. All the countries from this group recorded the growth of GDP per capita despite the economic crisis. However, these results are in accordance to all the developing countries. General government net borrowing increased during the crisis in Bosnia and Herzegovina, Moldova and Montenegro. In the remaining countries of this group, the effect of the economic crisis on this indicator is not present. The inflation followed the trend of the first group of countries, reaching its peak in 2008 in all the observed countries. This group also started the recovery of their labour market after 2014. All the countries had the lowest rates of unemployment in the period 2018-2019. In Bosnia and Herzegovina, North Macedonia, and Serbia the unemployment was reduced by half if compared to the period during the crisis. The acquired data show no substantial differences between the two groups of countries concerning the effects of the economic crisis on the macroeconomic indicators. The main difference is that most non- EU started their recovery in 2013, while the EU countries started their recovery a year after. There are significant differences in the amount of GDP per capita between the two observed groups of countries in favour of the EU countries.

The influence of the international trade on a country can be aggregately presented through the current account. Table 3 presents the current account balance in the observed countries for the period 2007-2019. On the basis of the acquired data, it can be concluded that during the economic crisis 2007-2008, the deficit was at its highest level in all the observed countries. In the EU member countries, it was the highest in Bulgaria and Greece. The situation with the current account deficit improved in all the observed EU countries after the economic crisis. Slovenia, Croatia, and Romania achieved surplus current account over the last few observed years.

Table 1. Macroeconomic indicators of SEE countries (EU members)

	2007	2008	2009	2010	2011	2012	2013	2014	2015	2016	2017	2018	2019
Bulgaria													
GDP growth (annual %)	6.6	6.1	-3.4	0.6	2.4	0.4	0.3	1.9	4.0	3.8	3.5	3.1	3.7
GDP per capita (constant 2010 US$)	6478	6920	6730	6812	7018	7084	7147	7323	7664	8013	8354	8675	9059
General government net lending/borrowing (% of GDP)*	3.1	2.7	-0.9	-3.8	-1.8	-0.4	-1.8	-3.7	-2.8	1.5	0.8	0.1	-0.9
Inflation. consumer prices (annual %)	8.4	12.3	2.8	2.4	4.2	3.0	0.9	-1.4	-0.1	-0.8	2.1	2.8	3.1
Unemployment (% of total labour force)	6.9	5.6	6.8	10.3	11.3	12.3	12.9	11.4	9.1	7.6	6.2	5.2	4.2
Croatia													
GDP growth (annual %)	5.1	1.9	-7.3	-1.3	-0.2	-2.4	-0.4	-0.3	2.4	3.5	3.4	2.8	2.9
GDP per capita (constant 2010 US$)	14918	15202	14103	13949	13970	13677	13654	13663	14111	14707	15397	15971	16510
General government net lending/borrowing (% of GDP)*	-2.2	-2.8	-6.1	-6.5	-7.9	-5.3	-5.3	-5.3	-3.3	-0.9	0.8	0.2	0.4
Inflation. consumer prices (annual %)	2.9	6.1	2.4	1.0	2.3	3.4	2.2	-0.2	-0.5	-1.1	1.1	1.5	0.8
Unemployment (% of total labour force)	9.9	8.5	9.2	11.6	13.7	15.9	17.3	17.3	16.2	13.1	11.2	8.4	6.6
Greece													
GDP growth (annual %)	3.3	-0.3	-4.3	-5.5	-9.1	-7.3	-3.2	0.7	-0.4	-0.2	1.5	1.9	1.9
GDP per capita (constant 2010 US$)	30055	29875	28515	26918	24496	22831	22251	22566	22615	22666	23053	23547	24024
General government net lending/borrowing (% of GDP)*	-6.7	-10.3	-15.3	-11.3	-10.5	-6.7	-3.6	-4.1	-2.8	0.6	1.1	0.9	0.6
Inflation. consumer prices (annual %)	2.9	4.2	1.2	4.7	3.3	1.5	-0.9	-1.3	-1.7	-0.8	1.1	0.6	0.3
Unemployment (% of total labour force)	8.4	7.8	9.6	12.7	17.9	24.4	27.5	26.5	24.9	23.5	21.5	19.3	17.3
Romania													
GDP growth (annual %)	7.2	9.3	-5.5	-3.9	1.9	2.0	3.8	3.6	3.0	4.7	7.3	4.5	4.2
GDP per capita (constant 2010 US$)	8024	8918	8497	8214	8412	8622	8980	9339	9660	10173	10982	11541	12092
General government net lending/borrowing (% of GDP)*	-3.0	-4.6	-6.9	-6.4	-4.3	-2.5	-2.5	-1.7	-1.4	-2.4	-2.8	-2.8	-4.6
Inflation. consumer prices (annual %)	4.8	7.9	5.6	6.1	5.8	3.3	4.0	1.1	-0.6	-1.5	1.3	4.6	3.8
Unemployment (% of total labour force)	6.4	5.8	6.9	7.0	7.2	6.8	7.1	6.8	6.8	5.9	4.9	4.2	3.9
Slovenia													
GDP growth (annual %)	7.0	3.5	-7.5	1.3	0.9	-2.6	-1.0	2.8	2.2	3.2	4.8	4.4	3.2
GDP per capita (constant 2010 US$)	24607	25430	23299	23510	23663	22990	22722	23328	23826	24569	25730	26760	27427
General government net lending/borrowing (% of GDP)*	-0.1	-1.4	-5.8	-5.6	-6.6	-4.0	-14.6	-5.5	-2.8	-1.9	-0.1	0.7	0.5
Inflation. consumer prices (annual %)	3.7	5.6	0.8	1.8	1.8	2.6	1.8	0.2	-0.5	-0.1	1.4	1.7	1.6
Unemployment (% of total labour force)	4.8	4.4	5.9	7.2	8.2	8.8	10.1	9.7	9.0	8.0	6.6	5.1	4.4

Source: (World Bank, 2021; IMF*, 2020)

Table 2.Macroeconomic indicators of SEE countries (non-EU countries)

	2007	2008	2009	2010	2011	2012	2013	2014	2015	2016	2017	2018	2019
Albania													
GDP growth (annual %)	6.0	7.5	3.4	3.7	2.5	1.4	1.0	1.8	2.2	3.3	3.8	4.1	2.2
GDP per capita (constant 2010 US$)	3485	3776	3928	4094	4210	4277	4327	4413	4524	4682	4864	5075	5211
General government net lending/ borrowing (% of GDP)*	-5.3	-2.0	-3.4	-0.2	-0.4	-0.3	-2.0	-2.6	-1.6	0.9	0.7	0.9	0.1
Inflation. consumer prices (annual %)	2.9	3.4	2.2	3.6	3.4	2.0	1.9	1.6	1.9	1.3	2.0	2.0	1.4
Unemployment (% of total labour force)	16.0	13.1	13.7	14.1	13.5	13.4	15.9	18.1	17.2	15.4	13.6	12.3	11.5
Bosnia and Herzegovina													
GDP growth (annual %)	5.9	5.4	-3.0	0.9	1.0	-0.8	2.3	1.2	3.1	3.1	3.2	3.7	2.7
GDP per capita (constant 2010 US$)	4425	4677	4558	4636	4737	4771	4969	5114	5353	5592	5829	6097	6304
General government net lending/ borrowing (% of GDP)*	0.8	-3.4	-4.8	-3.5	-2.1	-1.9	-0.6	-2.1	0.6	1.2	2.6	2.4	2.1
Inflation. consumer prices (annual %)	1.5	7.4	-0.4	2.0	3.7	2.1	-0.1	-0.9	-1.0	-1.6	0.8	1.4	0.6
Unemployment (% of total labour force)	29.0	23.4	24.1	27.3	27.6	28.0	27.5	27.5	27.7	25.4	20.5	18.4	15.7
Moldova													
GDP growth (annual %)	3.0	7.8	-6.0	7.1	5.8	-0.6	9.0	5.0	-0.3	4.4	4.7	4.3	3.6
GDP per capita (constant 2010 US$)	2237	2416	2274	2438	2581	2566	2799	2940	2954	3120	3322	3527	3720
General government net lending/ borrowing (% of GDP)*	1.3	0.3	-5.0	-1.5	-1.4	-1.3	-1.1	-1.1	-1.2	-0.4	0.5	-0.1	-0.7
Inflation. consumer prices (annual %)	12.4	12.8	-0.1	7.5	7.7	4.5	4.6	5.1	9.7	6.4	6.6	3.0	4.8
Unemployment (% of total labour force)	5.1	4.0	6.4	7.4	6.7	5.6	5.1	3.9	3.7	4.2	4.1	4.1	5.1
Montenegro													
GDP growth (annual %)	6.8	7.2	-5.8	2.7	3.2	-2.7	3.5	1.8	3.4	2.9	4.7	5.1	4.1
GDP per capita (constant 2010 US$)	6482	6938	6522	6688	6897	6703	6935	7051	7286	7500	7852	8253	8590
General government net lending/ borrowing (% of GDP)*	9.5	-1.5	-5.9	-3.9	-5.3	-4.0	-2.4	-1.6	-3.6	-4.0	-4.4	-4.1	-0.3
Inflation. consumer prices (annual %)	4.3	8.8	3.5	0.7	3.5	4.1	2.2	-0.7	1.5	-0.3	2.4	2.6	0.4
Unemployment (% of total labour force)	19.4	17.1	19.1	19.6	19.7	20.0	19.5	18.0	17.5	17.7	16.1	15.2	15.1
North Macedonia													
GDP growth (annual %)	6.5	5.5	-0.4	3.4	2.3	-0.5	2.9	3.6	3.9	2.8	1.1	2.9	3.2
GDP per capita (constant 2010 US$)	4193	4418	4399	4543	4645	4620	4751	4920	5105	5247	5301	5452	5625
General government net lending/ borrowing (% of GDP)*	1.4	-0.3	-2.0	-1.7	-1.7	-2.9	-2.9	-3.2	-2.3	-1.5	-1.4	-0.6	-0.8
Inflation. consumer prices (annual %)	2.3	8.3	-0.7	1.5	3.9	3.3	2.8	-0.3	-0.3	-0.2	1.4	1.5	0.8
Unemployment (% of total labour force)	34.9	33.8	32.2	32.0	31.4	31.0	29.0	28.0	26.1	23.7	22.4	20.7	17.3
Serbia													
GDP growth (annual %)	6.4	5.7	-2.7	0.7	2.0	-0.7	2.9	-1.6	1.8	3.3	2.1	4.5	4.2
GDP per capita (constant 2010 US$)	5473	5807	5671	5735	5899	5887	6087	6018	6157	6396	6565	6898	7230
General government net lending/ borrowing (% of GDP)*	-0.1	-1.2	-2.7	-2.4	-2.7	-4.6	-2.7	-3.1	-0.4	1.8	3.9	2.9	2.0
Inflation. consumer prices (annual %)	6.4	12.4	8.1	6.1	11.1	7.3	7.7	2.1	1.4	1.1	3.1	2.0	1.8
Unemployment (% of total labour force)	18.1	13.7	16.1	19.2	23.0	24.0	22.1	19.2	17.7	15.3	13.5	12.7	10.4

Source: (World Bank, 2021; IMF*, 2020)

The non-EU countries also followed this trend of decreasing the current account deficit in the first few post-crisis years. However, none of the observed non-EU countries achieved current account surplus. Moreover, during the last few observed years, Serbia and Moldova recorded a deficit increase, while Montenegro constantly had a very high current account deficit.

Table 3. Current account balance (% of GDP) in SEE countries

year	2007	2008	2009	2010	2011	2012	2013	2014	2015	2016	2017	2018	2019
EU countries													
Bulgaria	-23.9	-22.1	-8.3	-1.7	0.3	-0.9	1.3	1.2	0.1	3.2	3.5	1.0	3.0
Croatia	-7.8	-10.5	-6.6	-2.2	-1.7	-1.8	-1.1	0.3	3.3	2.1	3.4	1.8	2.8
Greece	-14.0	-14.6	-11.0	-10.0	-10.1	-2.5	-2.6	-2.4	-1.5	-2.4	-2.6	-3.6	-2.2
Romania	-13.6	-11.5	-4.7	-5.1	-5.0	-4.8	-0.8	-0.2	-0.6	-1.4	-2.8	-4.4	-4.7
Slovenia	-4.1	-5.3	-1.1	-0.8	-0.8	1.3	3.3	5.1	3.8	4.8	6.2	5.8	5.6
non-EU countries													
Albania	-10.6	-15.8	-15.4	-11.3	-12.9	-10.2	-9.3	-10.8	-8.6	-7.6	-7.5	-6.8	-8.0
Bosnia and Herzegovina	-9.5	-14.1	-6.4	-6.0	-9.5	-8.6	-5.3	-7.4	-5.1	-4.8	-4.8	-3.4	-3.1
Moldova	-15.2	-16.1	-8.9	-6.9	-10.1	-7.4	-5.2	-6.0	-6.0	-3.5	-5.7	-10.5	-9.4
Montenegro	-40.1	-49.5	-27.7	-20.3	-14.8	-15.3	-11.4	-12.4	-11.0	-16.2	-16.1	-17.0	-15.0
North Macedonia	-6.9	-12.8	-6.8	-2.0	-2.5	-3.2	-1.6	-0.5	-2.0	-2.9	-1.0	-0.1	-3.3
Serbia	-16.0	-19.9	-5.9	-6.0	-8.1	-10.8	-5.7	-5.6	-3.5	-2.9	-5.2	-4.8	-6.9

Source: (IMF, 2020)

The international trade indicators provide a better insight into the conditions presented through the current account balance, which will answer the RQ3 related to the import and export of the observed countries. Table 3 shows that during the economic crisis in the EU countries the share of import and export in GDP was decreased in comparison to the post-crisis period. This does not apply to the share of import in GDP that varied during the entire observed period. If the share of Trade in GDP is observed, it is evident that the economic crisis had its full effect in 2009 when this indicator was at its lowest point for all the observed countries. According to the degree of this indicator, i.e. the degree of openness towards the international trade, the leading positions belong to Slovenia and Bulgaria. Croatia joined these countries in 2018 and 2019.

Table 5 shows the foreign trade indicators in the non-EU countries. As with the EU members, the share of import in GDP was the lowest in 2009. However, unlike the EU members, most non-EU countries also recorded a drop of import in GDP in 2009. The share of Trade in GDP was the lowest in 2009 in all the observed countries except Moldova. From the beginning of the economic crisis until 2019, Moldova had declining trend of this indicator. At the beginning of the crisis, Moldova was the leader among SEE countries in terms of openness towards international trade, i.e. the share of trade in GDP. According to this indicator, the leading countries were North Macedonia, Montenegro, and Serbia.

Table 4. International trade indicators in SEE countries (EU members)

,		2007	2008	2009	2010	2011	2012	2013	2014	2015	2016	2017	2018	2019
Exports of goods and services (% of GDP)	Bulgaria	52.4	52.5	42.2	50.4	59.1	60.7	64.8	64.8	64	64	67.3	65.8	64.2
	Croatia	37.9	36.4	32.7	36.1	38.8	39.5	40.3	43.3	46.4	47.6	49.9	50.2	52
	Greece	22.5	23.4	19	22.1	25.5	28.7	30.4	32.4	31.6	30.1	33	36.1	37.2
	Romania	24.7	26.2	26	32.4	37.1	37.5	40	41.4	41.4	41.8	42	41.9	40.4
	Slovenia	67.9	66.3	57.3	64.3	70.2	72.9	74.2	76.2	77.1	77.6	83.1	84.8	83.7
Imports of goods and services (% of GDP)	Bulgaria	71.2	72.3	50.5	53.3	58.7	63.8	65.3	65.8	63	59.1	62.9	63.3	61
	Croatia	46.3	46.7	38.3	37.8	40.5	41.1	42.4	43.7	46.2	46.5	49.3	51	52.2
	Greece	35	36	28.8	30.7	32.3	33.1	33.2	34.8	31.5	30.8	34	36.4	37.2
	Romania	38.8	39	32.4	39	42.9	42.8	40.9	41.8	42.2	42.8	44.5	45.3	44.2
	Slovenia	69.2	68.4	55.9	63.2	69	69.5	69.5	69.4	69.1	69.1	74.2	76.3	75.3
Trade (% of GDP)	Bulgaria	123.6	124.8	92.7	103.7	117.8	124.5	130.1	130.6	127	123.1	130.2	129.1	125.2
	Croatia	84.2	83.1	70.9	73.9	79.2	80.6	82.7	87	92.5	94.1	99.1	101.2	104.2
	Greece	57.5	59.3	47.7	52.8	57.8	61.8	63.5	67.1	63.1	60.8	67	72.5	74.4
	Romania	63.5	65.2	58.5	71.4	80	80.4	81	83.3	83.6	84.6	86.5	87.1	84.6
	Slovenia	137.1	134.7	113.1	127.5	139.3	142.4	143.8	145.5	146.3	146.7	157.3	161.1	159

Source: (World Bank, 2020)

FDI can improve the balance of payment and decrease created in the current account balance. Furthermore, FDI can significantly improve foreign trade flows. Figure 1 shows the share of FDI in GDP for the EU members. All the observed EU members, except Greece recorded high values of this indicator during the crisis. However, the effects of the economic crisis manifested in the following years when the values of the indicators declined.

The economic crisis had different effects on the SEE countries that are non-EU members (Figure 2). During the crisis this indicator was very high, similarly to the EU members. After the crisis, the effects varied individually for the observed countries. Albania recorded growth in the share of FDI in GDP during the entire observed period. After recording the growth of 37.3% in 2009, Montenegro had a drop in the following year, while keeping FDI at a significantly high level. In Bosnia and Herzegovina and North Macedonia this indicator varied annually. In 2013, Serbia recorded growth of FDI share in GDP, and the highest values were recorded in the last two observed years. However, in the post-crisis period, there was no correlation between the FDI inflows and the observed macroeconomic indicators in Serbia, which is explained as being the consequence of the economic crisis (Parežanin et al., 2016). Moldova recorded a decline in FDI in the post-crisis period.

The results show that the non-EU countries had higher unemployment rates than the EU countries (except Greece and Croatia). During the crisis, all the observed countries had unfavourable macroeconomic performances. After the crisis, the recovery of economic activities and competitiveness in he observed countries varies as presented by the observed indicators. When observing the import and export in the observed countries, both groups were more import than export oriented. In Bulgaria and Slovenia export was more than 50% of GDP, which can be explained by the fact that they were more developed than the rest of the observed countries. Total trade flows were declining during the crisis, but after the crisis

Table 5. International trade indicators in SEE countries (non-EU countries)

		2007	2008	2009	2010	2011	2012	2013	2014	2015	2016	2017	2018	2019
Exports of goods and services (% of GDP)	Albania	28.2	25.3	25.2	28	29.2	28.9	28.9	28.2	27.3	29	31.6	31.6	31.6
	Bosnia and Herzegovina	27.1	26.8	25	29.7	32	32.4	33.7	34	35.5	36.3	40.8	42.1	40.1
	Moldova	45.6	40.8	36.9	27.8	32.5	31.1	32.1	31.2	31.9	32.3	31.1	30.1	31.4
	Montenegro	43	39.5	34.3	37	42.3	43.7	41.3	40.1	42.1	40.6	41.1	42.9	43.7
	North Macedonia	44.1	43.2	32.8	39.8	47.1	45.4	43.4	47.7	48.7	50.7	55.1	60.4	62.3
	Serbia	27.3	28.4	26.3	32.3	33	35.8	39.9	42.1	45.2	48.5	50.5	50.4	51
Imports of goods and services (% of GDP)	Albania	55	52.1	49.9	48.6	52	47.6	47	47.2	44.5	45.8	46.6	45.3	45.3
	Bosnia and Herzegovina	56.5	59.3	48.7	51.3	55.8	55.8	54.2	56.6	53.8	52.9	57	57.1	55.2
	Moldova	97.1	93.6	73.5	60.1	66.1	65.2	63.6	62	57.4	55.3	54.5	55.7	56
	Montenegro	85.7	92.8	65.1	62.7	64.3	68.1	61.4	60	60.6	63.1	64.5	66.7	64.8
	North Macedonia	62	68.3	54.4	58.1	66.1	66.8	61.5	64.9	65	65.5	69	72.8	76.5
	Serbia	48.3	50.2	39.7	44.5	45.8	49.6	48.1	50.2	52.2	53.3	57.1	59.1	61
Trade (% of GDP)	Albania	83.2	77.5	75.1	76.5	81.2	76.5	75.9	75.4	71.8	74.8	78.2	76.9	76.9
	Bosnia and Herzegovina	83.6	86.2	73.7	81	87.8	88.1	87.9	90.6	89.3	89.3	97.9	99.2	95.3
	Moldova	142.7	134.4	110.4	87.9	98.6	96.3	95.7	93.2	89.3	87.6	85.6	85.9	87.4
	Montenegro	128.7	132.3	99.4	99.8	106.7	111.8	102.8	100.1	102.7	103.7	105.6	109.6	108.5
	North Macedonia	106.1	111.6	87.2	97.9	113.2	112.2	104.9	112.5	113.7	116.2	124.1	133.2	138.8
	Serbia	75.6	78.7	66	76.7	78.8	85.5	87.9	92.2	97.4	101.9	107.5	109.5	112.1

Source: (World Bank, 2020)

they regained the levels they had had prior to the crisis. During the crisis, a slowdown was evident in all economic activities of the observed countries. However, the countries (especially the EU members) managed to raise their economic activities toa higher level by implementing adequate economic and trading policies and measures.

SOLUTIONS AND RECOMMENDATIONS

In order to neutralise the effects of the crisis and encourage and promote import, all the countries need to coordinate their measures. The policy of economic protectionism, which was conducted during the crisis, further deepened the crisis and aggravated the already difficult situation. The cooperation between countries and increased volume of export between them is clearly a more adequate response to the crisis, and a good way to reduce its duration. Open economy in the era of globalisation has had positive and negative effects alike, and they spread quickly on both regional and global levels. Economic interventionism does not have to be established so as to exclude countries from international trade flows, but to encourage trade exchange. The errors made during the global economic crisis of 2007-2009 can provide help in overcoming the crisis induced by the COVID-19 pandemic.

Figure 1. Foreign direct investment, net inflows (% of GDP) of EU members (World Bank, 2020)

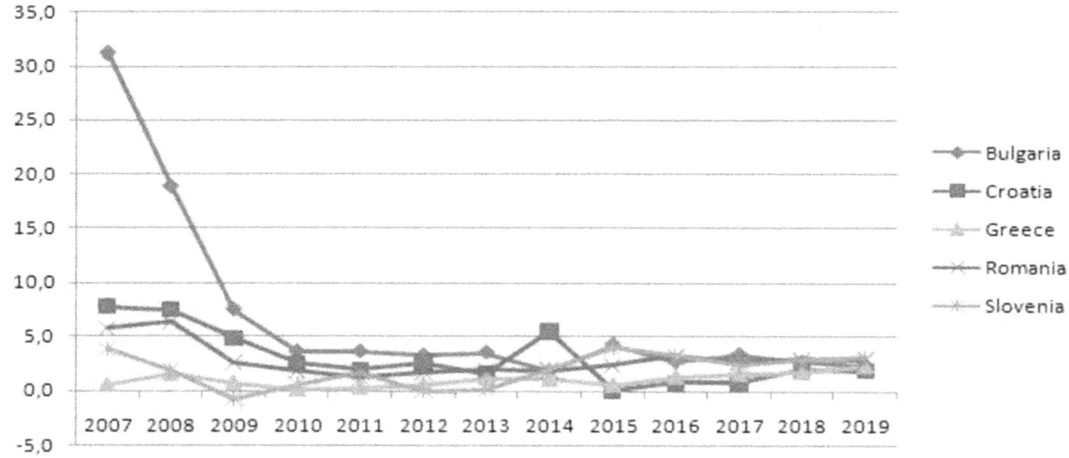

Figure 2. Foreign direct investment, net inflows (% of GDP) of non-EU countries (World Bank, 2020)

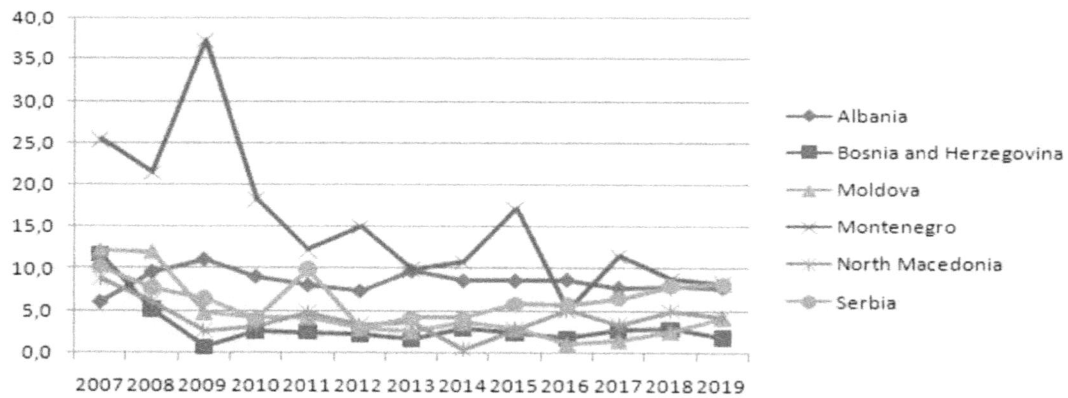

FUTURE RESEARCH DIRECTIONS

The crisis caused by the COVID-19 pandemic is still ongoing, and the data are incomplete. Therefore, the analysis of the current crisis was not thoroughly explained in the chapter. Still, the provided analysis opens possibilities for further research to develop in several directions. First, a research can be conducted on the effects of the COVID-19 crisis on the two SEE groups of countries. Second, a comparison can be made between the effects of the economic crisis presented in this chapter and the COVID-19 crisis to see which of them had more influence on the international trade flows. Finally, other groups of countries can be chosen to conduct a research on the influence of the economic crisis and/or COVID-19 crisis on the international trade.

CONCLUSION

The global economic crisis affected both the EU and non-EU countries. However, the influence of the crisis was not uniform. The economic crisis had impact on the current account balance in all the observed countries. The EU countries recovered their current account balance to a greater degree than the non-EU countries. Total foreign trade flows were on decline during the crisis, but have regained the level prior to the crisis in the past few years. The crisis had the biggest impact on the share of export in GDP. The export into other countries decreased drastically in all the observed countries, while the non-EU countries recorded a decline in import as well. The inflow of FDI was high both during and after the crisis. However, it declined in all the EU member countries after the crisis. This was not the case in the non-EU countries that retained a relatively high level of FDI inflow in the post-crisis period as well.

Although the economic crisis had severe consequences on the international trade, the countries were managing to recover all until the crisis caused by the COVID-19 pandemic. The new crisis is not only a health crisis. Judging by its volume, this crisis threatens to become a more severe economic crisis than the crisis of 2007-2009. The new economic crisis has already affected the volume of international trade and changed the patterns of consumption. Most counties have taken measures to alleviate the effects of the current crisis on supranational, national, and local levels. The degree of success or failure of the undertaken measures, and the effects of the COVID-19 crisis on foreign trade still remain to be estimated in the period after the new crisis has ended.

REFERENCES

Albertoni, N., & Wise, C. (2021). International trade norms in the age of Covid-19 nationalism on the rise? *Fudan Journal of the Humanities and Social Sciences*, *14*(1), 41–66. doi:10.100740647-020-00288-1

Balassa, B. (1974). Types of Economic Integration. *Proceedings of Fouth World Congress of the Integrational Economic Association.*

Beck, K. (2020). What drives international trade? Robust analysis for the European Union. *Journal of International Students*, *13*(3), 68–84. doi:10.14254/2071-8330.2020/13-3/5

Broll, U., & Jauer, J. (2014). *How international trade is affected by the financial crisis: the gravity trade equation* (No. 03/14). Dresden Discussion Paper Series in Economics.

Chor, D., & Manova, K. (2012). Off the cliff and back? Credit conditions and international trade during the global financial crisis. *Journal of International Economics*, *87*(1), 117–133. doi:10.1016/j.jinteco.2011.04.001

Coulibaly, B., Sapriza, H., & Zlate, A. (2011). *Trade credit and international trade during the 2008-09 global financial crisis*. Board of Governors of the Federal Reserve System. doi:10.17016/IFDP.2011.1020

Eurostat. (2020). *International trade data*. Retrieved May 9, 2021, from https://ec.europa.eu/eurostat/web/main/data/database

Evenett, S. J., & Fritz, J. (2017). *Europe fettered: The impact of crisis-era trade distortions on exports from the European Union*. CEPR Press.

Feng, G. F., Yang, H. C., Gong, Q., & Chang, C. P. (2021). What is the exchange rate volatility response to COVID-19 and government interventions? *Economic Analysis and Policy*, *69*, 705–719. doi:10.1016/j.eap.2021.01.018

Gruszczynski, L. (2020). The COVID-19 pandemic and international trade: Temporary turbulence or paradigm shift? *European Journal of Risk Regulation*, *11*(2), 337–342. doi:10.1017/err.2020.29

IMF. (2020). *World Economic Outlook*. Retrieved May 9, 2021, from https://www.imf.org/en/Data

Jednak, S., & Jednak, D. (2018). Financial Integration: Crisis and Economic Development. In Regaining Global Stability After the Financial Crisis (pp. 67-87). IGI Global.

Jednak, S., Kragulj, D., & Bulajic, M. (2018). A comparative analysis of development in Southeast European countries. *Technological and Economic Development of Economy*, *24*(1), 253–270. doi:10.3846/20294913.2016.1212438

Kindleberger, Ch. (1974). *Međunarodnaekonomija*. Beograd, Srbija: VukKaradžić.

Kragulj, D. (2020). *Ekonomija – Osnovimikroekonomskeimakroekonomskeanalize*. Beograd, Srbija: Kragulj.

Kragulj, D., Parežanin, M., & Jednak, S. (2018). Effects of Trade Liberalisation in the SEE Countries: CEFTA 2006 Agreement. In Globalization and Trade Integration in Developing Countries (pp. 1-26). IGI Global.

Levchenko, A. A., Lewis, L. T., & Tesar, L. L. (2010). The collapse of international trade during the 2008–09 crisis: In search of the smoking gun. *IMF Economic Review*, *58*(2), 214–253. doi:10.1057/imfer.2010.11

Ma, Z., & Cheng, L. (2005). The effects of financial crises on international trade. In *International Trade in East Asia* (pp. 253–286). University of Chicago Press. doi:10.7208/chicago/9780226379005.003.0009

Maciejewski, M., & Wach, K. (2019). What determines export structure in the EU countries? The use of gravity model in international trade based on the panel data for the years 1995-2015. *Journal of International Students*, *12*(1).

Maliszewska, M., Mattoo, A., & Van Der Mensbrugghe, D. (2020). The potential impact of COVID-19 on GDP and trade: A preliminary assessment. *World Bank Policy Research Working Paper*, (9211).

Molle, W. (2006). *The Economics of European Integration: theory, practice, policy* (5th ed.). Routledge.

Parežanin, M., Jednak, S., & Kragulj, D. (2016). The Impact of FDI on the Economic Growth of Serbia. *Management: Journal of Sustainable Business and Management Solutions in Emerging Economies*, *21*(78), 25–32.

Parisi, M. L. (2017). Labor market rigidity, social policies and the labor share: Empirical evidence before and after the big crisis. *Economic Systems*, *41*(4), 492–512. doi:10.1016/j.ecosys.2017.08.003

Price, G. N., & Adu, D. P. (2021). Was trade openness with China an initial driver of cross-country human coronavirus infections? *Journal of Economic Studies (Glasgow, Scotland)*, *ahead-of-print*(ahead-of-print). Advance online publication. doi:10.1108/JES-10-2020-0497

Prokopijević, M. (2005). *Evropskaunija: Uvod*. Službeniglasnik.

Reinhart, C. M., & Rogoff, K. S. (2008). This time is different: A panoramic view of eight centuries of financial crises (No. w13882). National Bureau of Economic Research.

Shelburne, R. C. (2010). The global financial crisis and its impact on trade: the world and the european emerging economies. *United Nations Economic Commission for Europe-Discussion Papers Series, 2.*

Silva, T. C., Muniz, F. J., & Tabak, B. M. (2021). Indirect and direct effects of the subprime crisis on the real sector: Labor market migration. *Empirical Economics*, 1–32. PMID:33897095

World Bank Group. (2020). *World Bank Open Data.* Retrieved May 10, 2021, from https://data.worldbank.org/

Wynne, M., & Kersting, E. (2009). Trade, globalisation and the financial crisis. *Economics Letters*, *4*(nov).

ADDITIONAL READING

Ale, B. J., Hartford, D. N., & Slater, D. H. (2020). Dragons, black swans and decisions. *Environmental Research*, *183*, 109127. doi:10.1016/j.envres.2020.109127 PMID:32000008

Baldwin, R., & Di Mauro, B. W. (2020). *Economics in the time of COVID-19: A new eBook.* VOX CEPR Policy Portal.

Behrens, K., Corcos, G., & Mion, G. (2013). Trade crisis? What trade crisis? *The Review of Economics and Statistics*, *95*(2), 702–709. doi:10.1162/REST_a_00287

Cros, M., Epaulard, A., & Martin, P. (2021). *Will Schumpeter Catch Covid-19?* (No. 15834). CEPR Discussion Papers.

Dadush, U., & Wolff, G. B. (2019). *The European Union's response to the trade crisis* (No. 2019/5). Bruegel Policy Contribution.

McGovern, E. (2018). *International trade regulation* (Vol. 1). Globefield Press.

Milanovic, B. (2016). *Global inequality: A new approach for the age of globalisation*. Harvard University Press. doi:10.4159/9780674969797

KEY TERMS AND DEFINITIONS

Balance of Trade: A part of the current account that shows the difference between the monetary value of a country's imports and exports over a given period of time.

Commercial Policy: A set of instruments that a country uses to attain to its goals of foreign trade and economic and commercial cooperation with the rest of the world.:

Customs Union: A higher form of trade integration where a group of countries eliminate customs duties and other forms of trade barriers among themselves, and establish the common external set of tariffs towards the non-members.

Economic Crisis: Economic crisis in a situation when the economy has a slowdown of economic activities due to financial/bank crisis, inflation, currency crushes, or sovereign debt.

Economic Liberalism: The promotion of economic activities that arestrictly regulated by the rules of free trade and competition.

European Union: The European Union was established in Maastricht in 1992 when the Treaty on European Union came into force on 1 November 1993. The European Union was defined through the institutional framework that rests on three pillars. The first pillar comprises European Communities (ECSC, EEZ, and Euroatom). The second pillar is Common Foreign and Security Policy, and the third pillar is the Police and Judicial Co-operation in Criminal Matters.The main EU objectives are: economic and monetary cohesion and common currency, common foreign and security policies and gradual building of a common defence policy, cooperation in judicial and internal affairs, preservation of the community heritage, etc. On 1 December 2009, when the Lisbon Treaty entered into force the difference between the European Community and European Union ceased to exist by removing the term "community".

Four Freedoms: Free movement of people, goods, services, and capital. This is the fundamental pillar upon which the EU common market rests.

International Trade: Economic activity that comprises the exchange of goods, services, and intellectual property products among various national economies.

Interventionism: The situation where the traditional protectionist instruments (such as tariffs, contingents, and quotas) are applied along with some stronger and more efficient measures such as import and export bans, foreign currency control, price dumping, subsidised export, local currency devaluation, state monopoly on the foreign trade, etc.

Protectionism: Economic policy that comprises a set of government measures aimed at protecting domestic production from the international competition in order to maintain or gain economic independence.

Chapter 5
COVID-19, Stock Market, Exchange Rate, Oil Prices, Unemployment, Inflation, Geopolitical Risk Nexus, the Case of the BRICS Nations:
Evidence Quantile Regression

Sudeshna Ghosh
https://orcid.org/0000-0002-2026-1676
Scottish Church College, India

ABSTRACT

This chapter attempts to study the impact of the COVID-19 pandemic on the stock markets of the BRICS nations. Such an exercise will have an important bearing on portfolio allocation in the context of the BRICS. The major contribution of the chapter in the extant literature is to examine based on the multifactor model of the capital asset pricing theory, how uncertainty owing to the pandemic interplay with the geopolitical index to impact the stock market of the BRICS. Further, the major macroeconomic factors are used as control variables. The daily observations were used from 31 December 2019 to 30 December 2020. The results based on the quantile regression model demonstrate the asymmetric response of the stock market to the pandemic. The policy implication that follows from this study is the need for strategic intervention of the central bank to ease the liquidity challenges in the crisis period.

INTRODUCTION

The occurrence of the novel coronavirus, Covid-19 contagion, is declared as a major pandemic, Yang *et al.*, (2020), with approximately 105,935,704 confirmed cases and 2,309,486 deaths as of February 6, 2021. The strict measures imposed by various governments such as closedown of borders, lockdown

DOI: 10.4018/978-1-7998-8314-2.ch005

and movement restrictions have severely impacted the economies and financial markets worldwide. The IMF (International Monetary Fund) in its April 2020 report projected a negative global growth rate worse than that of the global financial crisis of 2007/2009. The economic consequences of the pandemic included disruptions in the supply chain, a plunge in the production process, a decline in consumption activities and a slowdown of investment. Furthermore, the stock markets also experienced downswings particularly due to governmental restrictions on movement. Against this backdrop, the current study attempts to explore the impact of the COVID-19 pandemic upon the stock markets across the major economies of the BRICS nations. According to Salvatore (2020), the COVID-19 has severely impacted the emerging economies of the BRICS nations such as Brazil, Russia, India, China and South Africa which were the major countries contributing to the global share of economic growth. According to Mensi *et al.*, (2014) the BRICS nations is projected to account for more than 40 per cent of global stock market capitalization by 2030. Understanding the current potential dependence of the BRICS nations in the financial world it is worthwhile to investigate the impact upon the BRICS. The study further explores the potential moderating impact of the recent pandemic on the geopolitical risk and how it further impacts the stock market. Geopolitical risks affect business cycles which has adverse implications upon the financial markets, Caldara and Iacoviello (2018). To the best of our knowledge, this chapter is the first of its kind which analyses the moderating role of the Geopolitical index along with the COVID-19 impact upon stock markets. Our chapter contributes to the existing literature as follows. First, our study can be considered as the trailblazer which explores the impact of the COVID-19 pandemic on the performance of the stock market for the BRICS nations. Second the current research examines how the government response measures impacted the stock markets. Third to analyze the responsiveness of the stock market to the pandemic situation the study utilizes the multifactor model, a variant of the Capital Asset Pricing Model postulated by (Sharpe,1964, and Fama and French, 1996). The study further used major macroeconomic variables as control variables to avoid misspecification bias. Fourth this is one of the very few researches to our knowledge that addresses the geopolitical implications and its moderating impact upon the stock market fluctuations. Geopolitical implications impact power structures across nations and this may have interesting implications upon the stock market behaviour in the backdrop of the pandemics. Last, the study used quantile regression (QR) methods to explore how the pandemic impacted the stock market indices across various quantiles. According to Baur (2013), the utilization of the QR methods for studying the implications on stock market behaviour can throw crucial information on the asymmetric and non-linear influences of the conditional variables on the dependent variable.

The hypothesis to be tested is as follows:

1. The COVID-19 pandemics impact the stock market negatively owing to the pessimism associated with the pandemic. Further other macroeconomic factors like unemployment, exchange rate fluctuations and central bank policy rate may have an abnormal impact on stock prices in the backdrop of the pandemic.
2. The announcements of government stringency measures cause stock prices to decline because of associated uncertainties. However, the overall government response index will cause stock prices to rise owing to the public's faith in multi-directional attitude of the government.
3. The declaring of government economic incentive packages and health programmes on testing generate positive sentiments leading to a rise in stock prices.
4. Geopolitical index has a mediating impact on stock prices.
5. The impact of the pandemic will be asymmetric across the stock markets.

The rest of the chapter is organized as follows. Section 2 discusses the relevant literature on stock market performance particularly in the context of uncertainty due to pandemics and other disasters and identifies the major research gaps of the existing literature. Section 3 explains the methodology and data. The major results are found in Section 4. Finally, section 5 concludes.

BACKGROUND

Uncertainty and the Stock Markets

According to (Liu and Zhang, 2015 and Yin *et al.* 2017) fluctuations in the asset price has an important bearing not only in the financial markets but also in the product markets and upon the unemployment rates. These have indirect implications upon the macroeconomic policies of the concerned set of countries. A growing number of papers examine how uncertainty emanating from the Economic Policy Uncertainty (EPU) Index impact the stock markets, for example (Tiwari *et al.*, 2019; Yin *et al.*,2017; and Luo and Zhang, 2020). According to Zhang *et al.* (2019), the theoretical and empirical findings show that the EPU has a considerable impact on the stock market behaviour. The study by Mensi *et al.*, (2014) based on quantile regression (QR) for the period September 1997 to September 2013 in the context of the BRICS countries discussed how the stock markets of these emerging economies are closely associated with the global stock and commodity markets. The study by Guo and You(2018) using QR explored the association between the EPU and returns from stock markets for the set of G7 and BRIC countries. The study finds an asymmetric association between the EPU and returns from stock markets for the countries of Italy and the USA. There is no association in the markets of France and the UK. The impact of the economic policy uncertainty is entirely adversative for China, Japan, India and Germany. The study concluded that such results demonstrated that the markets in the USA and Italy show risk-averse tendency while the markets of China, Japan, India and Germany favour risks. This behaviour has interesting policy suggestions for reducing the contagious effect of the EPU on the stock market behaviour. The research by Hung (2020) using the methodology of DECO-GARCH model examined the accumulative effect of the EPU upon the stock market of the BRICS countries. The results confirm the existence of the bidirectional association between the EPU and returns from the stock markets in the context of the BRICS nations.

Several studies discussed that Geopolitical risks (GPR) impact financial markets and business cycles. According to Caldara and Iacoviello (2018) for financial investors and central bank policy decision making, GPR is a major determinant. The study by Rawat and Arif (2018) discuss using QR methods, how GPR impacted the stock market of the BRICS nations. The study showed that the impact of the GPR is not uniform across the stock markets of the BRICS nations. The paper by Balcilar *et al.,(*2018) using nonparametric causality QR methods explored how the GPR impacted the stock markets in the BRICS nations. The study found a heterogeneous impact in these countries; the impact is negative for the lower quantile than for the higher quantiles. The study by Kannadhasan and Das (2020) throws interesting insights as to how the stock markets respond to the fluctuations in the EPU and GPR for the Asian emerging economies based on QR. The findings show that the EPU has a negative impact across all quantiles but the impact of the GPR is negative on the lower quintiles but positive on the upper quantiles. Such findings confirm the asymmetric behaviour across GPR and the stock market. The discussion by Hoque and Zaidi (2020) explored the nonlinear impact of the country-based GPR upon the stock markets of the major emerging economies like Brazil, India, South Africa, Indonesia and Turkey. The three regime Markov-switching measure showed that the GPR impacted the stock returns of these economies.

The foregoing discussion explained that when the major economies of the world are amalgamated through trade and financial interactions, Ivanov *et al.*, (2016), a shock emanating in one sector will spread rapidly and impact the major financial economies. The impact on the stock market is thus contagious. It is evident from the discussion that negligence of the contagious impact in the stock markets would lead to specious outcomes as far as the expectations of the investors are concerned.

Covid-19 Pandemics, Uncertainty and Stock Markets

The recent pandemic, COVID-19 was associated with mandated closures and precautionary health measures in most countries which generated major economic losses. Furthermore, the stock markets being strongly integrated suffered a negative impact. According to Azimli (2020) the COVID-19 impacted the behaviour of the stock market through two conduits i) high levels of uncertainty was associated with the pandemic that resulted in lower cash flow thereby depressing the markets and ii) the closure of major industries like the tourism, aviation and the hospitality sector caused depreciation in ancillary stock markets. The earlier studies exploring the impact of the outbreak of virus upon the stock market include the works of (Delisle, 2003; Nippani and Washer,2004; and Macciocchi *et al.*,2016). These studies conclude that stock market dynamics are strongly impacted owing to the stress emanating from the health crisis owing to the virus spread.

The current pandemic, COVID-19 has generated uncertainty within the economies of the major nations. In the recent period, the impact of the pandemic COVID-19 upon the performance of the stock market has been explored through diverse methodologies. The study by Salisu and Vo, (2020) discussed the importance of news relating to health made available through Google search and how they impacted the stock market of 20 countries. These countries had a high incidence of deaths owing to COVID-19. The study found an asymmetric impact of health news on stock performance. The study by (Ashraf, 2020; Liu *et a*l., 2020; and Khan *et al.*, 2020)) discussed how the stock market indices responded adversely to the incidence of COVID-19 cases.

According to Wagner (2020) the impact of the pandemic upon the stock market crucially depended on the extent of the economic shutdowns, the governmental response to the adoption of the stringency measures and the sentiments of the investors in the face of uncertainty. The price fluctuations in the stock market are responses to such market uncertainties. The major studies of (Ashraf, 2020; Al-Awadhi *et al.*, 2020; and Baker *et al.*, 2020) discussed the nature of volatile stock markets and the adverse response of the stock index to the pandemic situation. However, World Bank, (2020) observed that the responsiveness of the stock market indices to the uncertain situation emanating from the pandemic is not homogeneous across the countries. The study by Zhang *et al.*, (2020) further discussed that the varied responses of the stock market indices to market uncertainty is due to differences in investors' expectations about future turn in the market movements. The study by Topcu and Gulal (2020) using Driscoll-Kraay estimator obtain the varied impact of the COVID-19 upon the responsiveness of the stock market across regions and across time. The findings showed that the impact of the pandemics is severe in the Asian emerging markets. However, the responsiveness to the uncertain situation is less intense where the governments announced adequate fiscal stimulus measures. The study by Bora and Basistha, (2020) in the context of Indian stock markets over September 3, 2019, to July 10, 2020, obtained that the stock markets were volatile in the post COVID period in comparison to the pre-COVID situation. The study by Choi (2020) used wavelet coherence methodology for the US economy to discuss how the EPU impacted the volatility of the major stock markets during the COVID-19. The study inferred that some sectors are more volatile during the period of the pandemic in comparison to the period of the global financial crisis. The research by Youssef *et al.*, (2021) explored the association between the stock market indices and the EPU for eight countries namely China, Italy, Germany, France, Russia, Spain, the UK and the US. These eight countries according to the study were worst hit by the virus. The results based on the time-varying VAR model showed that the spill-over from the EPU had a severe impact on the stock market during the period of the pandemic. Furthermore, the results from the nonlinear model showed that the impact of the negative news was more severe than the positive one. The study by Sharif *et al.*, (2020) based on the US economy using the wavelet method of Granger causality test discussed how the COVID-19 adversely impacted the stock markets, oil prices, the EPU and GPR of the country. The impact on the GPR of the country according to Sharif *et al.*,(2020) was very intense which called for urgency for proper policy implications so that the asset managers are not pessimistic. The paper by Zaremba *et al.*, (2021) using daily data over January-April 2020 for forty-nine countries explored how governmental intervention measures owing to the pandemic had a significant impact on the volatility of the stock markets. The paper concluded that the closure of business, schools and workplaces negatively impacted the volatility of the stock market however the awareness campaign on the virus had a favourable impact upon the stock markets.

Our study unlike the earlier studies examines the performance of stock markets amidst the pandemic controlling for several macroeconomic and global factors for the major emerging BRICS nations. By employing QR methodology the study examines the asymmetry impact in the multivariate model. This framework allows exploring the differential impact across different quantiles which represents the varying market states. So, the QR model offers new insights as subsequently discussed. Furthermore, we complement the recent findings in the literature for example (Al-Awadhi *et al.* 2020; Wagner 2020; and Zhang *et al.* 2020) by using certain specific features associated with COVID-19 for example the government stringency measures, fiscal packages, health containment measures and economic incentive measures and how they impact the stock prices. We further add to the extant literature by exploring the moderating role of GPR upon the stock market performance.

MAIN FOCUS OF THE CHAPTER

Model Methodology and Datasets

This study attempts to explore the influence of the recent COVID-19 pandemic on the stock prices in the BRICS countries. Further, the connectedness of the macroeconomic variables is also included as control variables to lessen the problems with endogeneity issues. Following the study of Grechi *et al.*,(2017) this study utilizes the multifactor market model which is an alternative version of the Capital Asset Pricing Model. According to the Capital Asset Pricing Model, the returns to any stock index can be stated as in Equation (1)

$$R_{it} = \alpha_i + \beta_t R_{Mt} + e_t \quad (1)$$

Here Ri_t is the excess return of any stock, RM_t is the excess market return of the stock, α denotes the intercept, β is the coefficient and e is the error term.

Since the paper explores how COVID-19 along with other macroeconomic variables impact the stock performance Equation (2) explains the model in the context of the multivariate framework accounting for the moderating role of the geopolitical index.

$$R_t = \alpha_1 + \beta_M R_{Mt} + \beta_1 COVID_t + \beta_2 VIX_t + \beta_3 EX_t + \beta_3 OIL_t + \beta_4 CPI_t \\ + \beta_5 UN_t + \beta_6 CP_t + \beta_7 GP_t + \beta_8 GPI_t + \beta_9 GPI_t * COVID_t + e_t \quad (2)$$

Here t=1,2,.....T; R_t denotes the daily excess return of the stock price index; R_{Mt} is the daily excess market return which could be the drivers of the stock prices of BRICS. This study attempts to use the Dow Jones Industrial Average Stock of the U.S. which is expected to have a positive effect on the stocks of BRICS. $COVID_t$ indicates the impact of the pandemic which specifies respectively the daily confirmed cases, the daily deaths and the government announcement to contain the spread of the virus. It is expected that the daily confirmed cases and the death rates would negatively affect the stock prices. As a proxy to the governmental measures, the study discusses how the stringency index, government stimulus package index, containment and health index and economic support index impact the prices of the stock. VIX_t shows the daily Chicago Board Exchange Volatility index which proxies fear and pessimism of market sentiments, Mishra and Mishra, (2020). A rise in VIX_t is expected to negatively impact the R_t. EX_t denotes the domestic exchange rates against the US dollar, exchange rate fluctuations will bring a downswing in the stock markets, Cardona-Arenas *et al.*, (2020). OIL_t shows the oil price index which may negatively impact stock market returns, Liu *et al.*, (2020). CPI_t denotes inflation rate, in the backdrop of uncertainty inflationary tendency will impact the stock markets. UN_t denotes unemployment owing to work hours lost from restrictions and lockdowns. The rise in the unemployment rates may create pessimism which negatively impacts the stock market. CP_t indicates Central Bank policy rates, a monetary policy variable. It is expected that the monetary response variable will have a positive impact on the stock markets because the measures are initiated to counter adverse circumstances owing to the pandemic. GP_t denotes the gold prices, it is expected that gold prices and stock prices are positively correlated. GPI_t is the geopolitical index. The rise in geopolitical shocks sends bad signals to investors which negatively affects stock prices. Furthermore, the simultaneous impact of the COVID-19 outbreak and geopolitical uncertainty will lead to complicated circumstances of uncertainty adversely affecting the stocks, Sharif *et al.*, (2020). e_t is the usual error term and βi are the coefficients of the explanatory variables.

METHODOLOGY

The study by Assaf and Tsionas (2018) and Badshah *et al.* (2013), discussed that the standard Ordinary Least Square Estimates may create erroneous results since it does not consider the tail ends. To do away with the difficulties the study (Assaf and Tsionas, 2018 and Badshah *et al.,* 2013) explained that the application of Quantile regression Methods would lead to robust estimation. So, the current study adopts the Quantile Estimation Methods to test the hypothesis of the impact of the COVID-19 upon the stock market in the backdrop of the geopolitical situation in the context of BRICS nations.

Considering the expediency of the QR measure the current study applies the QR method postulated by Koenker and Bassett (1978). Equation (3) explains the conditional quantile function for estimating Equation (2):

$$Q_y(\varnothing \mid x) = \inf\{\partial \mid F_y(\partial \mid x) \geq \varnothing\} = \sum_h \beta_h(\varnothing) x_h = x\beta(\varnothing) \quad (3)$$

Here $F_y(\P|x)$ shows the conditional distribution function of y for given x. The QR coefficient $\beta(\varnothing)$ denotes the dependent association between the vector of x and $\varnothing$ th conditional quantile of y.

We explore the effect on the dependent variable across the quantile 0.05, 0.10…….0.90, 0.95. If the values across the quantiles do not change then the dependence configuration is said to be constant, if they fall then the configuration is declining if they rise then the configuration is rising, and lastly, if they are distinct for low and high quantiles then it is asymmetric.

Data Sets

Table (1) presents a precise overview of the possible data repositories. The frequency of observations is daily from 31, December 2019 to 30, December 2020. The data relating to COVID-19 cases and deaths are made available from github website provided by Johns Hopkins University Center for Systems Science and Engineering. Since the earliest data on COVID -19 is found from December 31, 2019, the sample of observations begins from December 31, 2019, and ends on December 30, 2020. The data on governmental measures are made available from the research group of Oxford University. Data on VIX, CPI and EX are available from FRED. Further data on Dow Jones Industrial Average Stock and stock price index for the BRICS is available from Yahoo Finance Data. Data on the oil price index is available from http://oilprice.com. The data on CP is available from of Bank for International Settlements. The GPI data and UN data are made available from Caldara and Iacoviello, (2018) and the International Labour Organization data base respectively.

Table (2) presents the descriptive statistics. All variables are converted into logarithmic forms. The conversion into the natural logarithmic form reduces the difficulties associated with the distributional properties, Alam et al. (2016).

Table 1. Data description

Title	Data Repository	Global persistent identifier	Year
Stock Price	Yahoo Finance Data	https://finance.yahoo.com/	2020/2021
Dow Jones Industrial Average Stock			
The Volatility Index	FRED, Federal Reserve Bank of St. Louis	https://fred.stlouisfed.org/series/	
Exchange Rate			
Inflation*			
Stringency Index	The Oxford COVID-19 Government Response Tracker (OxCGRT)	OxCGRT https://covidtracker.bsg.ox.ac.uk	
Government Response Index			
Confirmed cases and death owing to COVID-19	COVID-19 Data Repository by the Center for Systems Science and Engineering (CSSE) at Johns Hopkins University	https://github.com/CSSEGISandData/COVID-19	
Unemployment Rates*	International Labour Organization	https://www.ilo.org/global/lang--en/index.htm	
Gold Prices	World Gold Council	https://www.gold.org/	
Central Bank Policy Rates*	Bank for International Settlements.	https://www.bis.org/	
Geo-Political Index	Geopolitical Risk Index of Caldara and Iacoviello (2018)	https://www.matteoiacoviello.com/gpr.htm	
Oil Prices	Brent crude oil prices	http://oilprice.com.	
*The observations are converted into daily frequency to keep parity with the other set of observations			

Source: Compilation Author.

Table 2. Descriptive Statistics

	Stock prices	Dow Jones Industrial Average Stock	Cases	Death	Stringency index	Government Response Index	Containment and Health Index	Economic Support Index	VIX	OIL	EX	GPI	CPI	UN	CP	GP
Mean	4.23	4.42	4.47	1.10	1.57	1.60	1.60	1.25	1.42	1.61	1.27	1.94	2.41	0.82	0.59	2.76
Median	4.58	4.44	2.24	0.62	1.85	1.84	1.87	1.69	1.41	1.62	1.16	1.87	2.09	0.89	0.60	2.76
Max	5.07	4.47	4.47	2.91	2	1.98	1.99	1.87	1.91	1.85	1.88	3.06	3.73	1.54	0.81	2.85
Min	3.39	4.26	0.28	0.01	0	0	0	0	1.08	1.29	0.57	1.39	2.04	0.01	0.30	2.70
Standard Deviation	0.64	0.04	1.53	1.01	0.58	0.53	0.56	0.76	0.15	0.01	0.50	0.29	0.65	0.49	0.11	0.04
Skewness	-0.26	-1.34	-0.26	0.32	-1.83	-2.10	-2.01	-0.97	0.33	-0.39	0.07	0.93	1.49	-1.33	-0.87	0.12
Kurtosis	1.26	4.16	1.67	1.54	4.95	6.09	5.63	2.07	4.07	3.40	1.32	3.68	3.24	5.33	4.04	1.61

Source: Compilation Author. Note: Log transformation was log(x+1) because of existence of 0 values in the original set of observations

SOLUTIONS AND RECOMMENDATIONS

Results and Discussion

Tables [3-8] report the estimates of the QR for the BRICS stock markets returns amidst the pandemic situation. Based on the findings of Table (3) we find that the impact of the government stringency index is distinct at the lower and higher quantiles, thereby confirming the asymmetric response. The stock market returns for the lower quantiles is positively impacted by the government stringency index. This shows that market sentiments comprehend government response to be reliable and feel that stringency will contain the pandemic. There will scope for business once it's safe to do so. However, the negative response at the upper quantiles to the government stringency index implies that traders are sceptic when the market is bullish. The behaviour shows that market investors expect higher uncertainty owing to the risk associated with the stringency measures. The stringency measures implied mandated shut down, lockdown and limited mobility making the investors risk-averse. These results support the hypotheses (1), (2) and (5) respectively. The results of Table (4) demonstrate the independence of the stock prices at the lower tails to the government response index however they are sensitive at the upper tails of the quantiles. The response is significant and positive. Such behaviour shows the faith of the investors in the overall response plan of the government to mitigate the pandemic situation. This includes mobilization of resources to build health infrastructure, generating food security and implement new direction for economic urgencies. These results support hypotheses (2) and (5). The results based on Table (5) show that the containment and health index impact the stock prices of the BRICS nations at the upper quantiles significantly and positively. The results in particular support hypotheses (3) and (5). Investment of the government in health care packages generates optimism among investors that the contagion effect of the virus will be arrested. Results of Table (6) show that the stock prices respond positively and significantly for all the quantiles except for the 0.40, 0.50 and 0.60. These results support hypotheses (3) and (5). The stock market is sensitive to the economic support index which includes debt relief, tax holiday and income support for those hard hits. Economic support measures generate positive sentiments in the market signalling investors for better returns. Based on the results of Table (7) and (8) we find that incidence of confirmed cases and deaths owing to the pandemic negatively impact the stock returns. However, the results are insignificant at the lower quantiles but significant at the upper quantiles. These results confirm hypotheses (1) and (5). Since there is in-built heterogeneity under the pandemic situation the association between the incidence of cases and death rates differ across different the distribution of the quantiles. The market appears to be pessimistic under a bullish situation.

As far as the impact of the control variables is concerned oil prices and gold prices impact the stock markets return positively particularly for the higher quantiles. Such results demonstrate asymmetric co-movements of the stock prices with the oil prices and gold prices for the BRICS nations because they are both major consumers (oil and gold India and China) and producers of oil (Brazil) gold (South Africa) respectively. The impact of the exchange rates and volatility index is asymmetric across the quantile range of distribution, it is particularly negative for the higher quantiles. The rise in the volatility index and exchange rates particularly during the onset of the pandemic generates negative market sentiments. The impact of the Dow Jones Industrial Average Stock is asymmetric. The dependence significantly rises at the tail ends. The impact of inflation is significantly positive across the quantile distribution. This signifies co-movement with stock prices, this can occur owing to the disruptions in the demand for durable goods during the pandemic situation. The impact of the Central Bank policy rate is asymmetric across the quantiles. It is negative and significant at the higher quantiles implying that cuts in policy rates lead to liquidity infusion which is expected to boost the economy. The study confirms hypothesis 4 because the geopolitical index has mediating role upon the stock price by negatively impacting the stock prices through interaction with the confirmed cases and death rates particularly at the higher quantiles. The mediating impact is positive through interaction with the economic support index across all quantiles. However, the responsiveness of the stock market to the geopolitical situation is independent at the lower quantiles but significantly negative for the upper quantiles.

Table 3. Impact of COVID-19 on the stock prices of BRICS nations, multivariate model

R_{it} = f(Stringency Index, R_{Mt}, *Control Variables*)											
Explanatory Variable	Q5	Q10	Q20	Q30	Q40	Q50	Q60	Q70	Q80	Q90	Q95
Stringency index	0.02 (0.77) [0.28]	0.01 (0.25) [1.13]	0.03** (0.00) [3.49]	0.06** (0.00) [4.83]	0.02** (0.00) [4.90]	-0.02** (0.99) [-0.01]	-0.01 (0.88) [-0.14]	-0.09** (0.00) [-2.72]	-0.12** (0.00) [-3.79]	-0.19** (0.00) [-7.75]	-0.18** (0.000 [-8.13]
Volatility Index	0.01** (0.00) [4.42]	0.01** (0.01) [3.30]	-0.01** (0.02) [-2.22]	-0.02 (0.15) [-1.41]	-0.01 (0.87) [-0.16]	0.01 (0.64) [0.46]	0.03 (0.22) [1.22]	-0.04** (0.00) [-3.38]	-0.03** (0.01) [-3.37]	-0.01 (0.18) [-1.32]	-0.08 (0.31) [-1.01]
Oil Prices	0.02 (0.18) [1.34]	0.03** (0.02) [2.23]	0.05** (0.04) [2.99]	0.05 (0.08) [1.75]	0.20 (0.10) [1.60]	0.35** (0.00) [3.84]	0.28** (0.01) [2.55]	0.05 (0.25) [1.13]	0.02** (0.03) [3.48]	0.05** (0.01) [3.76]	0.08** (0.00) [5.18]
Exchange Rate	-0.48** (0.00) [-9.90]	-0.04** (0.00) [-9.77]	-0.03** (0.00) [-6.97]	-0.02** (0.00) [-4.85]	0.01 (0.99) [0.41]	0.90 (0.11) [0.93]	0.90** (0.03) [2.12]	-0.14** (0.00) [-16.81]	-0.16** (0.00) [-26.08]	-0.16** (0.00) [-22.24]	-0.16** (0.00) [17.75]
Geo political Index	0.01 (0.80) [0.25]	0.04 (0.19) [1.30]	0.09 (0.12) [1.55]	0.02 (0.46) [0.73]	0.04 (0.69) [0.40]	-0.05 (0.75) [-0.31]	-0.01 (0.76) [-0.30]	-0.02 (0.08) [-1.74]	-0.04** (0.00) [3.01]	-0.08** (0.00) [-7.58]	-0.08** (0.00) [6.81]
Moderating Role of the Geopolitical Index	-0.01** (0.01) [8.97]	-0.02** (0.00) [-9.05]	-0.08** (0.01) [-8.68]	-0.01 (0.35) [-0.92]	-0.02 (0.68) [-0.41]	0.01 (0.96) [0.05]	0.01 (0.92) [0.09]	0.01 (0.11) [1.57]	0.02** (0.00) [2.70]	0.04** (0.00) [6.85]	0.04** (0.00) [6.16]
Inflation	0.81** (0.00) [17.21]	0.82** (0.00) [17.36]	0.83** (0.00) [19.54]	0.84** (0.00) [14.24]	0.82** (0.00) [24.90]	0.97** (0.00) [56.86]	0.96** (0.00) [2.84]	0.55** (0.00) [5.63]	0.31 (0.09) [1.70]	0.12** (0.00) [23.74]	0.12** (0.0)) [23.17]
Unemployment	0.03** (0.00) [4.04]	0.02** (0.00) [3.02]	0.01 (0.40) [0.84]	0.04 (0.81) [0.23]	-0.06 (0.88) [-0.15]	0.02 (0.36) [0.91]	0.03 (0.08) [1.73]	0.02** (0.00) [5.39]	0.03** (0.00) [6.97]	0.03** (0.00) [7.61]	0.02** (0.00) [4.65]
Central Bank Policy Rate	-0.17** (0.00) [-5.13]	-0.19** (0.00) [-6.75]	-0.29** (0.00) [-10.08]	-0.32** (0.00) [-10.38]	-0.39** (0.01) [-2.39]	-0.02 (0.98) [-0.02]	0.03 (0.80) [1.73]	-0.14 (0.10) [-1.64]	-0.08** (0.00) [-4.25]	-0.09** (0.01) [-4.87]	-0.07** (0.00) [-5.06]
Gold Prices	0.03 (0.94) [0.07]	0.03 (0.52) [0.64]	-0.18** (0.01) [-2.43]	-0.24 (0.11) [-1.58]	-0.81** (0.01) [-2.48]	0.63** (0.00) [2.68]	-0.38 (0.21) [-1.23]	0.31** (0.00) [3.53]	0.53** (0.00) [7.87]	0.70** (0.00) [12.93]	0.70** (0.00) [9.70]
Dow Jones Industrial Average Stock of the U.S	0.02 (0.57) [0.56]	0.01 (0.56) [0.57]	0.13** (0.01) [3.26]	0.11 (0.06) [1.84]	0.45** (0.01) [2.41]	0.48** (0.02) [3.13]	0.63** (0.00) [3.34]	0.55** (0.00) [5.63]	0.31 (0.09) [1.70]	-0.09 (0.07) [1.78]	-0.13** (0.00) [2.82]
constant	1.71** (0.00) [8.97]	1.63** (0.00) [9.05]	1.77** (0.00) [8.68]	1.97** (0.00) [4.76]	1.94 (0.12) [1.54]	-0.19 (0.80) [-0.25]	-1.47 (0.35) [-0.92]	1.31** (0.01) [2.44]	1.88** (0.01) [2.56]	3.36** (0.00) [12.60]	3.62** (0.00) [17.68]
Adj R2/ Pseudo R2	0.37	0.37	0.37	0.37	0.37	0.40	0.40	0.45	0.47	0.47	0.37

Note: Figures in the parenthesis are p values. Figures in the squared brackets t statistics. (*), (**) and (***) denotes the level of significance of 1%,5% and 10% respectively. QR denotes quantile regression. Compilation Author.

Table 4. Impact of COVID-19 on the stock prices of BRICS nations, multivariate model

R_{it} = f(Government Response Index, R_{Mt}, *Control Variables*)											
Variable	Q5	Q10	Q20	Q30	Q40	Q50	Q60	Q70	Q80	Q90	Q95
Government Response Index	0.004 (0.58) [0.54]	0.13 (0.77) [1.77]	0.02 (0.10) [1.62]	0.03 (0.83) [0.21]	0.47 (0.13) [1.52]	0.28 (0.13) [1.50]	0.54 (0.06) [1.86]	0.17** (0.00) [5.62]	0.15** (0.00) [4.79]	0.21** (0.00) [6.26]	0.23** (0.00) [6.67]
Volatility Index	0.01** (0.01) [2.38]	0.12 (0.15) [1.41]	-0.08 (0.26) [-1.11]	-0.01 (0.41) [-0.81]	0.06 (0.43) [0.78]	0.92 (0.10) [1.62]	0.05 (0.46) [0.73]	-0.07** (0.00) [-4.98]	-0.05** (0.00) [-3.81]	-0.01** (0.00) [-3.26]	-0.01 (0.31) [-1.00]
Oil Prices	0.01 (0.19) [1.29]	0.03** (0.01) [2.47]	0.01 (0.49) [0.68]	-0.01 (0.77) [-0.29]	-0.37 (0.54) [-0.61]	0.01 (0.95) [0.06]	-0.23 (0.56) [-0.57]	0.08** (0.01) [3.37]	0.04** (0.01) [3.90]	0.09** (0.001) [3.21]	0.07** (0.02) [3.79]
Exchange Rate	-0.05** (0.00) [-9.81]	-0.04** (0.00) [-11.07]	-0.04** (0.00) [-6.88]	-0.02** (0.00) [-4.27]	0.03 (0.83) [0.21]	0.88** (0.00) [11.74]	-0.90** (0.01) [-2.47]	-0.12** (0.00) [-14.13]	-0.14** (0.00) [-15.75]	-0.15** (0.00) [-13.03]	-0.16** (0.00) [-13.89]
Geo political Index	0.01 (0.75) [0.31]	0.05 (0.14) [1.47]	0.02 (0.78) [0.27]	-0.02 (0.80) [-0.24]	-0.14 (0.37) [-0.89]	-0.11 (0.17) [-1.35]	-0.24 (0.07) [-1.79]	-0.04** (0.00) [-3.62]	-0.05** (0.00) [-3.30]	-0.09** (0.00) [-5.90]	-0.11** (0.00) [-6.34]
Moderating Role of the Geopolitical Index	-0.01 (0.65) [-0.44]	-0.03 (0.33) [-0.96]	-0.05 (0.45) [-0.75]	0.08 (0.88) [0.14]	0.07 (0.39) [0.86]	0.05 (0.24) [1.16]	0.12 (0.08) [1.74]	0.02** (0.00) [3.26]	0.02** (0.00) [2.94]	0.05** (0.00) [5.56]	0.06** (0.00) [6.31]
Inflation	0.81** (0.01) [15.61]	0.82** (0.00) [16.10]	0.82** (0.00) [14.00]	0.82** (0.00) [45.48]	0.70** (0.00) [5.33]	0.90** (0.00) [11.08]	0.86** (0.00) [3.07]	0.11** (0.00) [13.06]	0.11** (0.00) [16.63]	0.11** (0.00) [12.16]	0.11** (0.00) [14.01]
Unemployment	0.03** (0.00) [3.62]	0.02** (0.00) [2.89]	0.01 (0.39) [0.85]	0.09 (0.72) [0.35]	0.02 (0.79) [0.26]	0.05 (0.07) [1.77]	0.04 (0.18) [1.32]	0.04** (0.00) [6.13]	0.03** (0.00) [5.67]	0.03** (0.00) [5.16]	0.02** (0.01) [2.46]
Central Bank Policy Rate	-0.15** (0.00) [-4.72]	-0.17** (0.00) [-6.17]	-0.24** (0.00) [-5.00]	-0.43** (0.00) [-4.03]	-1.30 (0.14) [-1.46]	-0.43 (0.37) [-0.89]	-0.69 (0.18) [1.32]	-0.35** (0.00) [-5.21]	-0.20** (0.00) [-5.73]	-0.18** (0.02) [-5.29]	-0.20** (0.01) [-5.69]
Gold Prices	0.10 (0.87) [0.15]	0.01 (0.85) [0.18]	-0.14 (0.06) [-1.84]	-0.19 (0.23) [-1.20]	-0.89 (0.40) [-0.84]	-0.27 (0.60) [-0.52]	0.13 (0.76) [0.30]	0.32** (0.00) [3.45]	0.49** (0.00) [5.42]	0.66** (0.00) [8.30]	0.69** (0.00) [7.00]
Dow Jones Industrial Average Stock of the U.S	0.02 (0.55) [0.59]	0.04 (0.19) [1.29]	0.15 (0.00) [3.90]	0.09 (0.19) [1.30]	0.20 (0.50) [0.66]	0.23 (0.35) [0.92]	0.35 (0.25) [1.15]	0.51** (0.00) [5.41]	0.26** (0.15) [1.41]	0.15** (0.04) [2.05]	0.11** (0.04) [2.03]
constant	1.67** (0.00) [7.57]	1.58** (0.00) [8.68]	1.61** (0.00) [6.71]	2.31** (0.00) [3.55]	5.78 (0.18) [1.31]	1.23 (0.66) [0.44]	0.81 (0.69) [0.40]	1.78* (0.00) [4.19]	2.30** (0.00) [3.08]	3.77** (0.00) [10.55]	3.70** (0.00) [13.29]
Adj R2/ Pseudo R2	0.37	0.37	0.37	0.37	0.38	0.38	0.40	0.43	0.40	0.43	0.44

Note: Figures in the parenthesis are p values. Figures in the squared brackets t statistics. (*), (**) and (***) denotes the level of significance of 1%,5% and 10% respectively. QR denotes quantile regression. Compilation Author.

Table 5. Impact of COVID-19 on the stock prices of BRICS nations, multivariate model

R_{it} = f(Containment and Health Index, R_{Mt}, *Control Variables*)											
Variable	Q5	Q10	Q20	Q30	Q40	Q50	Q60	Q70	Q80	Q90	Q95
Containment and Health Index	0.02 (0.72) [0.36]	0.09 (0.22) [1.22]	0.03** (0.01) [2.54]	0.07 (0.21) [1.25]	0.01** (0.94) [0.07]	0.02 (0.80) [0.25]	0.13 (0.27) [1.08]	0.08** (0.01) [2.54]	0.09** (0.01) [2.39]	0.15** (0.00) [3.70]	0.21** (0.00) [5.79]
Volatility Index	-0.01** (0.00) [-3.54]	-0.01** (0.03) [-2.11]	-0.01** (0.03) [-2.07]	-0.01 (0.35) [-0.92]	-0.04 (0.57) [-0.56]	-0.03 (0.27) [-1.09]	-0.04 (0.13) [-1.50]	-0.05** (0.00) [-3.33]	-0.05** (0.00) [-4.62]	-0.02** (0.01) [-4.30]	-0.01** (0.01) [-5.33]
Oil Prices	0.02 (0.19) [1.29]	0.03** (0.02) [2.23]	0.04 (0.10) [1.63]	0.05 (0.15) [1.44]	0.10 (0.61) [0.50]	0.33** (0.00) [2.69]	0.18** (0.04) [2.46]	0.10** (0.01) [2.55]	0.07** (0.01) [3.51]	0.15** (0.00) [4.11]	0.08** (0.03) [2.14]
Exchange Rate	-0.04** (0.00) [-8.18]	-0.04** (0.00) [-9.61]	-0.03** (0.00) [-6.59]	-0.02** (0.00) [-3.90]	0.06** (0.97) [0.03]	0.89** (0.00) [25.73]	0.90** (0.03) [2.09]	-0.13** (0.00) [-15.04]	-0.16** (0.00) [-19.26]	-0.16** (0.00) [-13.78]	-0.17** (0.00) [-10.93]
Geo political Index	0.01 (0.78) [0.28]	0.04 (0.37) [0.89]	0.08 (0.42) [0.80]	0.03 (0.56) [0.58]	0.05 (0.67) [0.42]	-0.07 (0.85) [-0.18]	-0.05 (0.38) [-0.88]	-0.02 (0.10) [1.62]	-0.03 (0.07) [-1.78]	-0.08** (0.00) [-4.02]	-0.10** (0.00) [5.70]
Moderating Role of the Geopolitical Index	-0.01 (0.69) [-0.39]	-0.02 (0.46) [-0.74]	-0.08 (0.19) [-1.29]	-0.02 (0.44) [-0.77]	-0.33 (0.63) [-0.48]	0.01 (0.98) [0.02]	0.02 (0.42) [0.79]	0.01 (0.10) [1.62]	0.01 (0.09) [1.67]	0.04** (0.00) [3.63]	0.05** (0.00) [5.65]
Inflation	0.81** (0.00) [17.41]	0.82** (0.00) [16.61]	0.83** (0.00) [16.89]	0.84** (0.00) [12.51]	0.80** (0.00) [15.80]	0.96** (0.00) [37.00]	0.93** (0.00) [2.75]	0.13** (0.00) [14.95]	0.13** (0.00) [15.54]	0.12** (0.00) [13.83]	0.11** (0.00) [15.22]
Unemployment	0.03** (0.00) [4.05]	0.02** (0.00) [3.05]	0.01 (0.48) [0.70]	0.06 (0.77) [0.28]	0.01** (0.97) [0.03]	0.03 (0.30) [1.03]	0.03 (0.05) [1.92]	0.03** (0.00) [4.79]	0.03** (0.00) [5.60]	0.03** (0.00) [4.96]	0.01** (0.01) [2.59]
Central Bank Policy Rate	-0.17** (0.00) [-4.16]	-0.19** (0.00) [-5.58]	-0.28 (0.54) [-0.90]	-0.31 (0.61) [-0.41]	-0.59 (0.66) [-0.96]	-0.04 (0.76) [-0.30]	-0.16 (0.34) [-0.94]	-0.14** (0.07) [-5.79]	-0.06** (0.35) [-5.92]	-0.07** (0.25) [-5.13]	-0.10** (0.39) [-5.85]
Gold Prices	0.03 (0.95) [0.06]	0.02 (0.62) [0.49]	-0.17** (0.02) [-2.19]	-0.18 (0.16) [-1.40]	-0.75 (0.08) [-1.74]	-0.56 (0.09) [1.68]	-0.25 (0.49) [-0.69]	0.24** (0.00) [2.65]	0.44** (0.00) [5.37]	0.62** (0.00) [9.36]	0.66** (0.00) [6.95]
Dow Jones Industrial Average Stock of the U.S	0.02 (0.54) [0.61]	0.01 (0.54) [0.60]	0.12 (0.00) [3.03]	0.11 (0.05) [1.95]	0.35 (0.10) [1.61]	0.42** (0.00) [2.90]	0.61** (0.00) [2.86]	0.57** (0.00) [5.56]	0.40** (0.03) [2.11]	-0.10 (0.23) [-1.19]	-0.10 (0.05) [-1.93]
constant	1.71** (0.00) [7.59]	1.64** (0.00) [8.85]	1.75** (0.00) [8.42]	1.77** (0.00) [4.59]	2.51 (0.12) [1.52]	-0.04 (0.96) [-0.04]	-1.14 (0.49) [-0.68]	1.28** (0.00) [2.94]	1.55** (0.03) [2.11]	3.42** (0.00) [8.14]	3.61** (0.00) [10.75]
Adj R2/ Pseudo R2	0.37	0.37	0.37	0.37	0.37	0.38	0.30	0.33	0.30	0.33	0.34

Note: Figures in the parenthesis are p values. Figures in the squared brackets t statistics. (*), (**) and (***) denotes the level of significance of 1%,5% and 10% respectively. QR denotes quantile regression. Compilation Author.

Table 6. Impact of COVID-19 on the stock prices of BRICS nations, multivariate model

R_{it} = f(Economic Support Index, R_{Mt}, *Control Variables*)											
Variable	Q5	Q10	Q20	Q30	Q40	Q50	Q60	Q70	Q80	Q90	Q95
Economic Support Index	0.04** (0.00) [4.87]	0.04** (0.00) [5.47]	0.02** (0.00) [3.11]	0.03** (0.02) [2.31]	0.04 (0.66) [0.43]	0.01 (0.59) [0.53]	0.04 (0.30) [1.03]	0.01** (0.00) [4.77]	0.02** (0.03) [5.13]	0.24** (0.01) [5.37]	0.02** (0.00) [5.86]
Volatility Index	-0.01** (0.00) [-3.66]	-0.01** (0.00) [-3.41]	-0.01 (0.23) [-1.20]	0.02 (0.86) [0.17]	0.05** (0.58) [0.54]	-0.01 (0.70) [-0.38]	0.02 (0.26) [1.12]	-0.02** (0.00) [-3.15]	-0.02** (0.00) [-3.97]	-0.01** (0.01) [-2.58]	0.01** (0.04) [-2.03]
Oil Prices	0.04** (0.00) [3.59]	0.03 (0.05) [1.95]	0.06** (0.00) [2.69]	0.10** (0.001) [3.41]	0.07 (0.54) [0.61]	0.37** (0.00) [6.57]	0.42** (0.00) [3.54]	0.17** (0.00) [5.39]	0.17** (0.00) [3.81]	0.24** (0.00) [9.35]	0.19** (0.00) [7.04]
Exchange Rate	-0.05** (0.00) [-12.67]	-0.05** (0.00) [-11.92]	-0.05** (0.00) [-7.68]	-0.04** (0.00) [-4.94]	0.02 (0.90) [0.11]	0.89** (0.00) [4.42]	0.83 (0.04) [1.98]	-0.14** (0.00) [-25.24]	-0.17** (0.00) [-33.97]	-0.18** (0.00) [-33.82]	-0.19** (0.00) [25.03]
Geo political Index	0.07 (0.12) [1.54]	0.01** (0.00) [2.99]	-0.01 (0.83) [-0.21]	-0.03 (0.73) [-0.34]	-0.05 (0.94) [-0.07]	-0.07 (0.75) [-0.31]	-0.09 (0.61) [-0.50]	-0.01** (0.00) [-3.11]	-0.03** (0.00) [-2.86]	-0.01** (0.00) [-2.65]	-0.01** (0.00) [2.28]
Moderating Role of the Geopolitical Index	-0.09** (0.02) [-2.31]	-0.08** (0.03) [-2.06]	0.03 (0.42) [0.79]	0.01 (0.90) [0.12]	0.07 (0.86) [0.17]	0.09 (0.49) [0.68]	0.09** (0.01) [3.74]	0.02** (0.00) [3.51]	0.03** (0.00) [4.69]	0.02** (0.01) [4.51]	0.01** (0.00) [5.27]
Inflation	0.80** (0.00) [18.80]	0.81** (0..00) [17.99]	0.81** (0.00) [16.51]	0.81** (0.00) [11.81]	0.81** (0.00) [20.55]	0.96** (0.00) [29.36]	0.93** (0.00) [2.84]	0.15** (0.00) [24.65]	0.13** (0.00) [27.69]	0.12** (0.00) [23.72]	0.11** (0.00) [16.43]
Unemployment	0.06 (0.54) [0.60]	-0.01 (0.91) [-0.11]	0.01 (0.97) [0.03]	-0.06 (0.76) [-0.30]	-0.01 (0.79) [-0.25]	0.06 (0.79) [0.26]	-0.05 (0.85) [-0.18]	0.01** (0.00) [5.27]	0.02** (0.00) [10.36]	0.02** (0.00) [8.00]	0.01** (0.12) [1.52]
Central Bank Policy Rate	-0.18** (0.00) [-6.65]	-0.23** (0.00) [-8.98]	-0.29** (0.00) [-6.74]	-0.39 (0.11 [-0.28]	-0.50 (0.54) [-0.57]	-0.02 (0.65) [0.45]	-0.22** (0.01) [-4.91]	0.09** (0.00) [-5.30]	0.01** (0.01) [-5.76]	0.09** (0.00) [-5.37]	-0.10** (0.00) [-5.93]
Gold Prices	-0.45** (0.00) [-3.58]	-0.45** (0.00) [-3.87]	-0.60** (0.00) [-5.58]	-0.71 (0.08) [-0.41]	-1.22 (0.19) [-1.28]	1.06** (0.00) [4.13]	0.82** (0.03) [2.85]	0.21** (0.01) [2.38]	0.40** (0.00) [6.23]	0.61** (0.00) [10.51]	0.72** (0.00) [7.65]
Dow Jones Industrial Average Stock of the U.S	0.09** (0.002) [3.11]	0.13** (0.00) [3.72]	0.22** (0.00) [3.77]	0.08 (0.34) [0.94]	0.43 (0.11) [1.59]	0.70** (0.00) [5.77]	0.88** (0.00) [4.58]	0.58** (0.00) [8.85]	0.38** (0.01) [2.46]	-0.15 (0.06) [-1.88]	0.10 (0.12) [-1.54]
constant	2.64** (0.00) [8.32]	2.49** (0.00) [8.61]	2.55** (0.00) [8.85]	3.46** (0.00) [6.81]	3.30 (0.11) [1.59]	0.02 (0.96) [0.05]	-1.53 (0.27) [-1.10]	1.04** (0.00) [3.41]	1.45** (0.00) [2.74]	3.24** (0.00) [9.81]	2.95** (0.00) [11.66]
Adj R2/ Pseudo R2	0.47	0.47	0.55	0.49	0.49	0.61	0.61	0.37	0.37	0.45	0.45

Note: Figures in the parenthesis are p values. Figures in the squared brackets t statistics. (*), (**) and (***) denotes the level of significance of 1%,5% and 10% respectively. QR denotes quantile regression. Compilation Author.

Table 7. Impact of COVID-19 on the stock prices of BRICS nations, multivariate model

R_{it} = f(Confirmed Cases, R_{Mt}, *Control Variables*)											
Variable	Q5	Q10	Q20	Q30	Q40	Q50	Q60	Q70	Q80	Q90	Q95
Confirmed Cases	-0.05 (0.27) [-1.09]	-0.04 (0.43) [-0.79]	-0.02** (0.02) [-2.19]	-0.10 (0.12) [-1.52]	-0.25** (0.00) [8.13]	-0.04 (0.19) [-1.30]	-0.03 (0.17) [1.37]	-0.02** (0.00) [-4.17]	-0.07** (0.00) [-4.37]	-0.07** (0.00) [-5.03]	-0.01** (0.00) [-5.76]
Volatility Index	0.01** (0.00) [6.06]	0.01** (0.00) [3.11]	-0.01 (0.99) [-0.01]	0.02 (0.56) [0.57]	-0.02 (0.67) [-0.41]	-0.03 (0.91) [-0.11]	0.04 (0.06) [1.87]	-0.02** (0.001) [-3.24]	-0.02** (0.00) [-4.84]	-0.01** (0.00) [--2.72]	0.02** (0.00) [-2.66]
Oil Prices	0.04** (0.01) [3.34]	0.02 (0.17) [1.37]	-0.02 (0.42) [-0.79]	-0.05 (0.48) [-0.70]	0.03 (0.65) [0.44]	0.30** (0.00) [5.06]	0.28** (0.00) [3.23]	0.19** (0.00) [6.46]	0.19** (0.00) [4.07]	0.25** (0.00) [7.69]	0.24** (0.00) [14.26]
Exchange Rate	-0.03** (0.00) [-4.51]	-0.03** (0.00) [-4.07]	0.02 (0.90) [0.12]	0.11 (0.38) [0.87]	0.66** (0.00) [16.30]	0.91** (0.00) [14.45]	-0.85** (0.03) [-2.17]	-0.14** (0.00) [-13.85]	-0.17** (0.00) [-29.42]	-0.18** (0.00) [-19.55]	-0.21** (0.00) [-22.00]
Geo political Index	-0.01 (0.97) [-0.04]	-0.02 (0.74) [-0.32]	-0.01 (0.10) [-1.61]	-0.07 (0.08) [-1.73]	-0.01 (0.80) [-0.24]	-0.01 (0.13) [-1.49]	-0.05** (0.02) [-3.31]	-0.02** (0.03) [2.20]	-0.01** (0.00) [-2.58]	-0.07** (0.01) [-3.37]	-0.09** (0.00) [-3.28]
Moderating Role of the Geopolitical Index	-0.01 (0.62) [-0.49]	-0.01 (0.57) [-0.57]	0.05 (0.25) [1.13]	0.02 (0.12) [1.54]	0.05 (0.73) [0.34]	0.09 (0.37) [0.89]	-0.02 (0.73) [-0.34]	-0.01 (0.58) [-0.54]	-0.01** (0.01) [-4.35]	-0.01** (0.001) [-6.21]	-0.06** (0.00) [-4.26]
Inflation	0.81** (0.00) [12.71]	0.81** (0.00) [13.97]	0.82** (0.00) [10.75]	0.83** (0.00) [35.76]	0.82** (0.00) [78.29]	0.97** (0.00) [44.22]	0.94** (0.00) [3.01]	0.15** (0.00) [13.78]	0.13** (0.00) [20.39]	0.13** (0.00) [14.95]	0.10** (0.00) [9.92]
Unemployment	0.04** (0.00) [6.08]	0.03** (0.00) [3.91]	0.02 (0.15) [1.42]	0.02 (0.45) [0.74]	0.03 (0.26) [1.12]	0.02 (0.15) [1.44]	0.07 (0.66) [0.44]	0.01** (0.00) [3.51]	0.02** (0.00) [7.62]	0.01** (0.00) [5.21]	0.02** (0.00) [2.97]
Central Bank Policy Rate	-0.27** (0.00) [4.36]	-0.30** (0.00) [-5.38]	-0.53** (0.00) [-4.83]	-0.99 (0.09) [-1.68]	-2.87** (0.00) [-20.21]	-0.18 (0.64) [-0.46]	0.28 (0.08) [1.75]	0.05 (0.35) [0.93]	0.01 (0.69) [0.40]	0.03 (0.34) [0.95]	-0.02 (0.00) [2.97]
Gold Prices	0.15** (0.00) [2.87]	0.12** (0.02) [2.27]	-0.01 (0.89) [-0.13]	0.06 (0.73) [0.34]	-0.13 (0.62) [-0.50]	0.38** (0.01) [2.36]	1.30** (0.01) [2.52]	0.11 (0.49) [0.68]	0.49** (0.00) [4.13]	0.64** (0.00) [4.94]	0.87** (0.00) [7.20]
Dow Jones Industrial Average Stock of the U.S	-0.03 (0.18) [-1.33]	0.06 (0.81) [0.24]	0.15** (0.01) [2.51]	0.18** (0.02) [2.32]	0.28** (0.01) [2.39]	0.57** (0.00) [6.29]	0.74** (0.00) [6.25]	0.61** (0.00) [7.89]	0.40** (0.00) [2.79]	-0.15 (0.21) [-1.25]	-0.11 (0.13) [-1.50]
constant	1.57** (0.00) [9.76]	1.53** (0.00) [9.38]	1.53** (0.00) [4.80]	1.57** (0.00) [2.61]	2.44** (0.00) [4.47]	-1.02 (0.13) [-1.49]	0.53 (0.63) [0.48]	1.10** (0.01) [2.55]	1.10** (0.05) [1.89]	3.10** (0.00) [6.18]	2.51** (0.00) [7.84]
Adj R2/ Pseudo R2	0.47	0.47	0.47	0.47	0.50	0.48	0.47	0.40	0.38	0.38	0.34

Note: Figures in the parenthesis are p values. Figures in the squared brackets t statistics. (*), (**) and (***) denotes the level of significance of 1%,5% and 10% respectively. QR denotes quantile regression. Compilation Author.

Table 8. Impact of COVID-19 on the stock prices of BRICS nations, multivariate model

R_{it} = f(Deaths due to COVID-19, R_{Mt}, *Control Variables*)											
Variable	Q5	Q10	Q20	Q30	Q40	Q50	Q60	Q70	Q80	Q90	Q95
Deaths due to COVID-19	-0.01 (0.29) [-1.06]	-0.02 (0.07) [-1.78]	-0.05 (0.01) [-0.49]	-0.09 (0.01) [-0.11]	-0.46** (0.00) [-5.13]	-0.03** (0.49) [-5.68]	-0.11** (0.40) [-5.84]	-0.03 (0.67) [-0.41]	-0.03** (0.21) [-3.24]	-0.06** (0.00) [-3.29]	-0.06** (0.00) [-6.06]
Volatility Index	0.01** (0.00) [3.91]	0.01** (0.00) [3.44]	-0.09 (0.40) [-0.83]	-0.01 0.62) [-0.50]	-0.23** (0.04) [-2.01]	0.08 (0.80) [0.25]	0.03 (0.25) [1.15]	0.01 (0.21) [1.23]	0.01 (0.12) [1.54]	-0.07** (0.01) [-3.88]	-0.09** (0.01) [-3.38]
Oil Prices	0.03** (0.01) [2.42]	0.01 (0.52) [0.63]	-0.03 (0.23) [-1.19]	0.04 (0.91) [0.11]	0.14 (0.18) [1.34]	0.32** (0.00) [5.27]	0.11 (0.58) [0.55]	0.14 (0.25) [1.15]	0.16** (0.00) [3.74]	0.09** (0.06) [3.82]	0.06** (0.15) [3.42]
Exchange Rate	-0.01 (0.54) [-0.61]	-0.02 (0.99) [-0.23]	-0.04 (0.16) [-1.38]	0.01 (0.58) [0.55]	0.88** (0.00) [5.42]	0.91** (0.00) [5.52]	-0.78** (0.01) [-2.45]	-0.13** (0.02) [-2.19]	-0.15** (0.00) [-9.18]	-0.15** (0.00) [-10.09]	-0.15** (0.00) [-12.93]
Geo political Index	-0.03 (0.46) [-0.10]	-0.02 (0.51) [-0.65]	-0.05 (0.46) [-0.73]	-0.01 (0.10) [-1.64]	-0.01** (0.02) [-2.49]	-0.01 (0.30) [-1.02]	-0.05** (0.00) [-4.01]	-0.02** (0.01) [-2.03]	-0.02** (0.01) [-3.53]	-0.02** (0.02) [-3.54]	-0.02** (0.00) [-3.60]
Moderating Role of the Geopolitical Index	-0.03 (0.46) [-0.73]	-0.02 (0.60) [-0.52]	0.03 (0.72) [0.35]	0.09 (0.27) [1.08]	-0.08** (0.00) [-6.32]	-0.01** (0.00) [-8.49]	-0.06** (0.00) [-3.58]	-0.11** (0.00) [-4.49]	-0.13** (0.00) [-3.91]	-0.04** (0.00) [-4.08]	-0.02** (0.00) [-5.11]
Inflation	0.81** (0.00) [12.20]	0.82** (0.00) [12.75]	0.83** (0.00) [14.78]	0.84** (0.00) [36.97]	0.92** (0.00) [33.39]	0.98** (0.00) [38.59]	0.89** (0.00) [3.58]	0.18** (0.00) [2.94]	0.16** (0.00) [8.58]	0.17** (0.00) [11.14]	0.17** (0.00) [14.43]
Unemployment	0.04** (0.00) [4.63]	0.03** (0.00) [2.88]	0.08 (0.57) [0.56]	0.01 (0.69) [0.39]	-0.04 (0.32) [-0.99]	0.01 (0.43) [0.77]	0.02 (0.39) [0.85]	0.02** (0.00) [2.74]	0.02** (0.00) [6.24]	0.03** (0.00) [7.30]	0.03** (0.00) [5.92]
Central Bank Policy Rate	-0.36** (0.01) [-2.35]	-0.46** (0.00) [-3.14]	-0.74 (0.34) [-0.13]	-1.01 (0.24) [-1.16]	-3.87 (0.09) [-0.32]	-0.08 (0.11) [-0.47]	-0.70** (0.04) [-2.40]	-0.30** (0.04) [-2.76]	-- 0.25** (0.01) [-3.61]	-0.37** (0.00) [-3.80]	-0.41** (0.00) [-5.92]
Gold Prices	0.14** (0.02) [2.20]	0.15** (0.02) [2.22]	-0.03 (0.97) [-0.03]	0.02** (0.00) [6.97]	-0.70 (0.12) [2.20]	0.55** (0.01) [2.47]	-1.59 (0.38) [-0.87]	0.33** (0.00) [4.94]	0.23** (0.04) [5.61]	0.49** (0.02 [5.86]	0.39** (0.00) [5.82]
Dow Jones Industrial Average Stock of the U.S	-0.03 (0.24) [-1.17]	0.01 (0.77) [0.29]	0.19** (0.00) [3.37]	0.21** (0.01) [2.45]	0.49** (0.02) [2.20]	0.52** (0.00) [3.76]	0.80** (0.00) [3.00]	0.61** (0.00) [5.09]	0.26 (0.05) [1.93]	0.14** (0.05) [2.98]	0.10** (0.00) [2.69]
constant	1.61** (0.00) [8.71]	1.52** (0.00) [9.37]	1.40** (0.00) [5.70]	1.48** (0.00) [3.74]	3.27** (0.00) [3.81]	0.51 (0.47) [0.72]	1.20 (0.78) [0.27]	2.17 (0.35) [0.92]	3.48** (0.00) [2.61]	4.79** (0.00) [7.71]	4.72** (0.00) [15.43]
Adj R2/ Pseudo R2	0.37	0.37	0.37	0.37	0.40	0.48	0.43	0.45	0.38	0.38	0.42

Note: Figures in the parenthesis are p values. Figures in the squared brackets t statistics. (*), (**) and (***) denotes the level of significance of 1%,5% and 10% respectively. QR denotes quantile regression. Compilation Author.

CONCLUSION

COVID-19 is the worst pandemic of the century that has hit the developed and developing countries. To explore the reaction of the stock market to the COVID-19 pandemic situation the current study utilized the multifactor model. The quantile econometric model building exercise demonstrated that i) costs of human lives reflected through the incidence and death rates owing to the virus; ii) the stringency measures of the government through closures and lockdowns and further (iii) the economic boosters had impacted the stock market severely, however, the impact was not uniform across all quantiles. In addition to the stress, the geopolitical index had a spillover effect on the stock prices thereby aggravating the uncertainty. Our results overall confirm the earlier findings in the literature which has discussed the association with the fear emanating from infectious diseases, health disaster and government policies with stock markets, (Nippani and Washer,2004; and Macciocchi et al.,2016; Zhang et al., 2020, Topcu and Gulal, 2020 and Azimli, 2020)

This study offers an early empirical investigation as to how the stock market of the BRICS nations may be affected by the pandemic situation in the backdrop of the geopolitical situation of the concerned countries. The present study showed that the incidence of confirmed cases and death rates adversely impact the stock prices, particularly at the higher quantiles. Such findings may be explicated owing to the rapid spread of the pandemic across the globe which led to a decline in the economic trend growth. Such instances generated a negative sentiment in the investors' mind thereby strongly impacting stock market investments. Similar to the findings of (Baker et al., 2020 and Wagner 2020) this study obtained that the investors' sentiments are pessimistic and so they are unwilling to take risks. The study by Wagner 2(020 extensively discussed how the pandemic impacts the stock market. The impact is decisive upon the magnitude of mandated shutdowns, governmental decision-making behaviour and responses to handling the health care situation. The steps that were taken by the governments of the BRICS countries to combat the spread of the virus particularly the stringency measures sent negative market signals. According to Mishra and Mishra, (2020), the governments of various countries have adopted expansionary monetary and fiscal policies which were boosters to the economy. The monetary policies included the building of liquidity and easing quantitative restrictions. Such efforts have a positive effect on stock markets. Our study confirms the findings of (Mishra and Mishra (2020). Furthermore, the study in the line with the study by Balcilar *et al.,* (2018) obtain that the geopolitical risk index does not affect the stock markets homogeneously for the BRICS.

Modelling the interactions across the stock markets and the pandemic situation at the backdrop of other associated macroeconomic variables for those of the BRICS countries is a crucial task. Such exercises have far-reaching implications for portfolio allocation for the BRICS. The stock markets more importantly depend significantly upon market fluctuations in the macroeconomy, uncertainty and pessimism owing to disease hazards. The BRICS are important emerging countries as far as stock market investments are concerned. Moreover, they are major consumers/ producers of commodities like gold and oil so changes in the related markets, shocks in the economy and the crisis from the pandemic are transmitted into the stock markets of the BRICS. Furthermore, international investors may be interested in the spillover movements of the geopolitics of the concerned countries. Various empirical econometric methods have been widely used in the existing literature for example the GARCH method, VAR model building method and the quantile regression estimation method to study the impact on the stock markets. The quantile regression estimation method appears to be more suitable because of the flexibility in application. Furthermore, the method allows exploring the response of the dependent variable to various explanatory variables across various quantiles.

This study contributes to the extant seam of literature by evaluating the implications of the shocks from the pandemic COVID-19 owing to the incidence of cases and death rates on the BRICS stock markets across different quantile of the returns of the distribution using daily observations. The period runs from 31, December 2019 to 30, December 2020. Since the earliest detection of the pandemic was found during December, 2019, the sample of observations begins from December 2019. Furthermore, the study also assesses the implications of the stringency measures announced by the government upon the stock returns across the various quantiles of the distribution. Moreover, the impact of the economic policies to boost the economy in the face of a downswing owing to the pandemic is also explored. The set of macro-economic factors used as control include the oil prices, gold prices, volatility index, exchange rate, unemployment rate, monetary policy rate and the Dow Jones Average stock (represents the impact of the global stock market). Moreover, unlike the earlier discussion in the literature, this study also explores the geopolitical implications upon the stock market of the BRICS nations and the moderating impact thereof.

Our results show that there is an asymmetric response of the stock to the government stringency index. The response is significant and negative when the market is bullish thereby confirming the pessimistic sentiments of the investors. However, the responsiveness of the stock market to the containment health index is significant and positive when the market is bullish. Government measures relating to health care signals optimism that the contagion effects of the virus will be arrested. The stock prices respond positively to the economic support index except for the median quantiles. The stock markets react asymmetrically to the incidence of cases and death rates. The response is significant and negative at the upper tail ends. The response of the stock prices of the BRICS to the control variables demonstrates inbuilt heterogeneity of relationship across the stock prices and the concerned variables. There are asymmetric co-movements between the gold and oil prices. The impact of the volatility index and the exchange rate is adverse upon the stock prices, particularly for the higher quantiles. The geopolitical index has a mediating role upon the stock price by adversely affecting the stock prices through interaction with the confirmed cases and death rates at the upper quantiles. Furthermore, the mediating impact is positive through interaction with the economic support index across all quantiles.

Several important policy implications can be drawn from the empirical results of the study. The strong indication of the adverse impact of the pandemic upon the BRICS stock markets and also the evidence of robust interactions across major macro factors call for strategic management of the financial markets. The study shows that the oil and gold markets can protect against further obstacles and risks in investments. Furthermore, the Central Banks of the concerned countries should continue to adhere to the quantitative easing programmes to wane the crisis period. The Central Banks should ensure that stocks facing liquidity challenges should be given the requisite liquidity. The fiscal stimulus should continue as the business recovers. Since the geopolitical impact accelerates the trends of the pandemic, countries need to form small coalitions to pave the way for scientific efforts to combat the pandemic.

LIMITATIONS OF THE STUDY AND SCOPE FOR FURTHER RESEARCH

The study has discussed that the monetary and fiscal policies work to slow down the spread of uncertainty associated with the pandemic thereby mitigating to a certain extent the panic of the investors. However, the current research did not explore how the policy issues would impact long-term expectations. Therefore, future research should be directed towards such directions. Furthermore, the pandemic has exacerbated the geopolitical tensions newer research in future is necessary to explore how the public health sector in conjunction with the climate concerns intersect with the geopolitical situation. Such discussion was beyond the scope of the present study.

REFERENCES

Al-Awadhi, A. M., Alsaifi, K., Al-Awadhi, A., & Alhammadi, S. (2020). Death and contagious infectious diseases: Impact of the COVID-19 virus on stock market returns. *Journal of Behavioral and Experimental Finance*, *27*, 100326. Advance online publication. doi:10.1016/j.jbef.2020.100326 PMID:32292707

Alam, M. S., & Paramati, S. R. (2016). The impact of tourism on income inequality in developing economies: Does Kuznets curve hypothesis exist? *Annals of Tourism Research*, *61*, 111–126. doi:10.1016/j.annals.2016.09.008

Ashraf, B. N. (2020a). Stock markets' reaction to COVID-19: Cases or fatalities? *Research in International Business and Finance*, *54*, 101249. Advance online publication. doi:10.1016/j.ribaf.2020.101249 PMID:34170989

Assaf, A. G., & Tsionas, M. (2018). The estimation and decomposition of tourism productivity. *Tourism Management*, *65*, 131–142. doi:10.1016/j.tourman.2017.09.004

Azimli, A. (2020). The impact of COVID-19 on the degree of dependence and structure of risk-return relationship: A quantile regression approach. *Finance Research Letters*, *36*, 101648. Advance online publication. doi:10.1016/j.frl.2020.101648 PMID:32837368

Badshah, I. U. (2013). Quantile regression analysis of the asymmetric return-volatility relation. *Journal of Futures Markets*, *33*(3), 235–265. doi:10.1002/fut.21551

Baker, S. R., Bloom, N., Davis, S. J., Kost, K., Sammon, M., & Viratyosin, T. (2020). The unprecedented stock market reaction to COVID-19. *Review of Asset Pricing Studies*, *10*(4), 742–758. doi:10.1093/rapstu/raaa008

Balcilar, M., Bonato, M., Demirer, R., & Gupta, R. (2018). Geopolitical risks and stock market dynamics of the BRICS. *Economic Systems*, *42*(2), 295–306. doi:10.1016/j.ecosys.2017.05.008

Baur, D. G. (2013). The structure and degree of dependence: A quantile regression approach. *Journal of Banking & Finance*, *37*(3), 786–798. doi:10.1016/j.jbankfin.2012.10.015

Bora, D., & Basistha, D. (2020). The outbreak of COVID-19 pandemic and its impact on stock market volatility: Evidence from a worst-affected economy. *Journal of Public Affairs*. Advance online publication. doi:10.1002/pa.2623 PMID:33786019

Caldara, D., & Iacoviello, M. (2018). *Measuring geopolitical risk*. FRB International Finance Discussion Paper, (1222).

Cardona-ArenasC. D.Serna-GómezH. M. (2020). COVID-19 and oil prices: Effects on the Colombian peso exchange rate. doi:10.2139srn.3567942

Choi, S. Y. (2020). Industry volatility and economic uncertainty due to the COVID-19 pandemic: Evidence from wavelet coherence analysis. *Finance Research Letters*, *37*, 101783. Advance online publication. doi:10.1016/j.frl.2020.101783 PMID:33013239

Delisle, J. (2003). SARS, greater China, and the pathologies of globalization and transition. *Orbis*, *47*(4), 587–604. doi:10.1016/S0030-4387(03)00076-0 PMID:32287394

Fama, E. F., & French, K. R. (1996). Multifactor explanations of asset pricing anomalies. *The Journal of Finance*, *51*(1), 55–84. doi:10.1111/j.1540-6261.1996.tb05202.x

Grechi, D., Ossola, P., & Tanda, A. (2017). The European tourism industry in crisis: A stock market perspective. *Tourism Analysis*, *22*(2), 139–148. doi:10.3727/108354217X14888192562203

Guo, P., Zhu, H., & You, W. (2018). Asymmetric dependence between economic policy uncertainty and stock market returns in G7 and BRIC: A quantile regression approach. *Finance Research Letters*, *25*, 251–258. doi:10.1016/j.frl.2017.11.001

Hoque, M. E., & Zaidi, M. A. S. (2020). Global and country-specific geopolitical risk uncertainty and stock return of fragile emerging economies. *Borsa Istanbul Review*, *20*(3), 197–213. doi:10.1016/j.bir.2020.05.001

Hung, N. T. (2020). Directional Spillover Effects Between BRICS Stock Markets and Economic Policy Uncertainty. *Asia-Pacific Financial Markets*, 1–20. doi:10.100710690-020-09328-y

Ivanov, I., Kabaivanov, S., & Bogdanova, B. (2016). Stock market recovery from the 2008 financial crisis: The differences across Europe. *Research in International Business and Finance*, *37*, 360–374. doi:10.1016/j.ribaf.2016.01.006

Kannadhasan, M., & Das, D. (2020). Do Asian emerging stock markets react to international economic policy uncertainty and geopolitical risk alike? A quantile regression approach. *Finance Research Letters*, *34*, 101276. Advance online publication. doi:10.1016/j.frl.2019.08.024

Khan, K., Zhao, H., Zhang, H., Yang, H., Shah, M. H., & Jahanger, A. (2020). The impact of COVID-19 pandemic on stock markets: An empirical analysis of world major stock indices. *The Journal of Asian Finance, Economics, and Business*, *7*(7), 463–474. doi:10.13106/jafeb.2020.vol7.no7.463

Liu, H., Manzoor, A., Wang, C., Zhang, L., & Manzoor, Z. (2020). The COVID-19 outbreak and affected countries stock markets response. *International Journal of Environmental Research and Public Health*, *17*(8), 2800. Advance online publication. doi:10.3390/ijerph17082800 PMID:32325710

Liu, L., Wang, E. Z., & Lee, C. C. (2020). Impact of the COVID-19 pandemic on the crude oil and stock markets in the US: A time-varying analysis. *Energy Research Letters*, *1*(1). Advance online publication. doi:10.46557/001c.13154

Liu, L., & Zhang, T. (2015). Economic policy uncertainty and stock market volatility. *Finance Research Letters*, *15*, 99–105. doi:10.1016/j.frl.2015.08.009

Luo, Y., & Zhang, C. (2020). Economic policy uncertainty and stock price crash risk. *Research in International Business and Finance*, *51*, 101112. Advance online publication. doi:10.1016/j.ribaf.2019.101112

Macciocchi, D., Lanini, S., Vairo, F., Zumla, A., Moraes Figueiredo, L. T., Lauria, F. N., ... Ippolito, G. (2016). Short-term economic impact of the Zika virus outbreak. *The New Microbiologica*, *39*(4), 287–289. PMID:28004846

Mensi, W., Hammoudeh, S., Reboredo, J. C., & Nguyen, D. K. (2014). Do global factors impact BRICS stock markets? A quantile regression approach. *Emerging Markets Review*, *19*, 1–17. doi:10.1016/j.ememar.2014.04.002

Mishra, P. K., & Mishra, S. K. (2020). Corona Pandemic and Stock Market Behaviour: Empirical Insights from Selected Asian Countries. Millennial Asia. 10.1177%2F0976399620952354.

Nippani, S., & Washer, K. M. (2004). SARS: A non-event for affected countries' stock markets? *Applied Financial Economics*, *14*(15), 1105–1110. doi:10.1080/0960310042000310579

Rawat, A. S., & Arif, I. (2018). Does geopolitical risk drive equity price returns of BRIC economies? Evidence from quantile on quantile estimations. *Journal of Finance and Economics Research*, *3*(2), 24–36. doi:10.20547/jfer1803202

Salisu, A. A., & Vo, X. V. (2020). Predicting stock returns in the presence of COVID-19 pandemic: The role of health news. *International Review of Financial Analysis*, *71*, 101546. Advance online publication. doi:10.1016/j.irfa.2020.101546

Salvatore, D. (2020). Growth and trade in the United States and the world economy: Overview. *Journal of Policy Modeling*, *42*(4), 750–759. doi:10.1016/j.jpolmod.2020.03.001 PMID:32362694

Sharif, A., Aloui, C., & Yarovaya, L. (2020). COVID-19 pandemic, oil prices, stock market, geopolitical risk and policy uncertainty nexus in the US economy: Fresh evidence from the wavelet-based approach. *International Review of Financial Analysis*, *70*, 101496. Advance online publication. doi:10.1016/j.irfa.2020.101496

Sharpe, W. F. (1964). Capital asset prices: A theory of market equilibrium under conditions of risk. *The Journal of Finance*, *19*(3), 425–442.

Tiwari, A. K., Jana, R. K., & Roubaud, D. (2019). The policy uncertainty and market volatility puzzle: Evidence from wavelet analysis. *Finance Research Letters*, *31*. doi:10.1016/j.frl.2018.11.016

Topcu, M., & Gulal, O. S. (2020). The impact of COVID-19 on emerging stock markets. *Finance Research Letters*, *36*, 101691. Advance online publication. doi:10.1016/j.frl.2020.101691 PMID:32837378

Wagner, A. F. (2020). What the stock market tells us about the post-COVID-19 world. *Nature Human Behaviour*, *4*(5), 440–440. doi:10.103841562-020-0869-y PMID:32242087

World Bank. (2020). *COVID-19 Outbreak: Capital Markets Implications and Response. Equitable Growth, Finance and Institutions: COVID-19 Notes, Finance Series*. https://pubdocs.worldbank.org/en/776691586478873523/COVID-19-Outbreak-Capital-Markets.pdf

Yang, Y., Peng, F., Wang, R., Guan, K., Jiang, T., Xu, G., Sun, J., & Chang, C. (2020). The deadly coronaviruses: The 2003 SARS pandemic and the 2020 novel coronavirus epidemic in China. *Journal of Autoimmunity*, *109*, 102434. Advance online publication. doi:10.1016/j.jaut.2020.102434 PMID:32143990

Yin, L., Yang, Q., & Su, Z. (2017). Predictability of structural co-movement in commodity prices: The role of technical indicators. *Quantitative Finance*, *17*(5), 795–812. doi:10.1080/14697688.2016.1225977

Youssef, M., Mokni, K., & Ajmi, A. N. (2021). Dynamic connectedness between stock markets in the presence of the COVID-19 pandemic: Does economic policy uncertainty matter? *Financial Innovation*, *7*(1), 1–27. doi:10.118640854-021-00227-3

Zaremba, A., Aharon, D. Y., Demir, E., Kizys, R., & Zawadka, D. (2021). COVID-19, government policy responses, and stock market liquidity around the world: A note. *Research in International Business and Finance*, *56*, 101359. Advance online publication. doi:10.1016/j.ribaf.2020.101359 PMID:33343055

Zhang, D., Hu, M., & Ji, Q. (2020). Financial markets under the global pandemic of COVID-19. *Finance Research Letters*, *36*, 101528. Advance online publication. doi:10.1016/j.frl.2020.101528 PMID:32837360

Zhang, D., Lei, L., Ji, Q., & Kutan, A. M. (2019). Economic policy uncertainty in the US and China and their impact on the global markets. *Economic Modelling*, *79*, 47–56. doi:10.1016/j.econmod.2018.09.028

Chapter 6
Exporting Without Direct Access to International Markets:
How Legal, Institutional, and Financial Conditions Affect the Decision to Export

Burak Erkut
https://orcid.org/0000-0001-7746-782X
Bahçeşehir Cyprus University, Cyprus & IREF, France

ABSTRACT

In the literature on exports, the question of why some firms decide to export and why others decide to focus on the domestic market has only received fragmented and different answers. The only overemphasized factor, productivity, seems to be a dead end when empirical evidence is given for high productivity firms which decide to remain in the domestic market. This is mainly due to the ignorance of the role of the firm in international trade by the majority of the literature. In this empirical research, the aim of the author is to test the impact of legal, institutional, and financial conditions on the firm decision to export based on the Enterprise Survey by the World Bank for the Turkish Cypriot people, which remained out of the international community for 57 years, where Turkey emerged as its access point to international markets. Hence, the study contributes to the existing literature on export development by highlighting the obstacles in front of the export decisions of firms and addressing a hitherto not addressed case in international economics.

INTRODUCTION

"Export development is perhaps the most widely studied and least understood aspect of international business" (Bilkey & Tesar, 1977) (p. 93) was the first sentence of the famous Bilkey and Tesar paper published in 1977. 43 years after this publication, export development still remains on the agenda of economics and business scholars alike, with no consensus on its antecedents and impacts in sight (Chen et al., 2016). In particular, (Chen et al., 2016) describe the efforts of focusing on export development as

DOI: 10.4018/978-1-7998-8314-2.ch006

inconsistent and defragmented. With the era of trade liberalization, export-led growth became a catchword for policymaking in different countries across the globe. However, different countries followed their unique strategies to promote export-led growth (Yang, 2018). This heterogeneity in ways of approaching export development lies, among others, in the nature of the heterogeneity of countries in which firms are enterprising, but also in the factors that influence the decision to export.

As (Bernard et al., 2007) states, heterogeneity is not a particular problem for theory per se; however, firm characteristics and export orientation seem to open a new way for international trade to show its influence on productivity. Hence, new empirical evidence to understand this heterogeneity is not only necessary, but also relevant to go beyond the textbook theories of international trade which neglect the role of the firm in trade flows (Bernard et al., 2007). One such case among the heterogeneous cases of export orientation is given by the Turkish Cypriot people of Cyprus, since the economic activities of Turkish Cypriot people are facing embargoes making them remain out of international system for the past 57 years (The World Bank, 2016). The declaration of independence of Turkish Cypriot people occurred in 1983 and the Turkish Republic of Northern Cyprus (TRNC) was established, which is only recognized by the Republic of Turkey (Turan Katircioglu, 2006). Turkey not only serves as the main destination of exports from the TRNC, but also as the access point to the international markets (The World Bank, 2016). After the EU accession of Cyprus and the following attempt to integrate the Turkish Cypriot economy into the common market, a further – yet tough – way is opened for exports (Gokcekus et al., 2012). Recent empirical evidence shows that this small community exhibits a big tendency towards entrepreneurship and new business venturing (Kaya et al., 2019) even with the lack of an entrepreneurial ecosystem that supports these kinds of activities.

While much of the existing literature focused on the fundamental differences between exporter and non-exporter firms regarding productivity, innovativeness, ability to address competition, size, and other factors, there is no consensus on why some firms decide to export, and why others decide rather to focus on the domestic market only. Based on the aforementioned economic and political background, and the identified research gap, the question that remains to be answered is what motivates Turkish Cypriot firms to export. To be more specific, how the legal, institutional and financial environment influences their decision to export remains as a black box. Until now, a reliable data source was not available for exploration and explanation of export behavior of Turkish Cypriot firms. Recently, the World Bank Enterprise Survey was conducted for the Turkish Cypriot people (The World Bank, 2019), which gives a chance to understand the decision to export without a direct access to international markets.

The rest of the chapter is organized as follows: Background information is provided to understand the export decision of firms and the macroeconomic context of the economy of North Cyprus. After the presentation of the background information, the main focus of the chapter is presented, which included data, methodology, results and a discussion. Next comes a section on solutions and recommendations, followed by future research directions and conclusion.

BACKGROUND

Export Decision

The decision to engage in international trade has been on the agenda of economics at least since the contribution of David Ricardo, the theory of comparative advantage, which became a mainstream concept over time. Even though a lot has been written on international trade, economists fell into the trap of neglecting the role of firms that engage in international trade (Bernard et al., 2007). Since the contribution by (Melitz, 2003), the role of the firm started to attract the attention of economics and business scholars alike.

For a firm to engage in international markets, there are different ways; among others, foreign direct investments and exporting are two points of departure for the firm to become internationalized. According to (Deb et al., 2020), firms consider exporting as a better point of departure for internationalization than foreign direct investments, since the latter involves more obligations and threats than the former. In addition, the authors mention that factors such as innovativeness, resources as well as escaping from competitive pressure in the domestic markets can be possible factors of influence for a firm to engage in exporting. In his contribution, (Melitz, 2003) focuses on the firm decision to export, and states that high productivity firms tend to export, whereas low productivity firms tend to produce for the domestic market only. Over time, a number of criticisms addressed the approach by (Melitz, 2003). Empirical evidence provided by (Lileeva & Trefler, 2010) shows that high productivity firms may not choose to export due to a high domestic demand. Therefore, the stream of research around the productivity-export nexus may not be giving us the full picture.

As a critique to the recent empirical micro-level research on internationalization of firms, (Movahedi & Shahbazi, 2020) arise two points that are worth mentioning: First, export process can be gradual and dynamic, indicating that firms do not necessarily engage in exports with optimal quantities, but rather start with small quantities and adjust their quantities over the course of events. This observation implies that the perception of firms regarding the business environment is crucial not only with the starting point of exporting, but throughout the whole process. It also indicates that besides "hard facts" of favorable conditions to export or unfavorable conditions in the domestic market, it is how a firm perceives and evaluates these conditions that is decisive on export behavior. Second, current literature overemphasizes the issue of productivity by implying that high productivity firms are those which export, and low productivity firms are those which remain in the domestic market. The authors give empirical evidence that this may not be always the case. The implication of this second observation is that productivity may not necessarily be enough to explain export decisions of firms. Combining both points raised by the authors (Movahedi & Shahbazi, 2020), in order to understand why some firms exports and others do not, one should take a look at the perceptions of firms regarding the business environment.

Firms, of course, derive these perceptions based on "hard facts". (Erkut, 2016a) identifies two factors that determine the degree of economic freedom, which enables enterprising activities. These are the dimension of market shaping and the dimension of infrastructure. Market shaping is associated with the perceptual components of enterprising, whereas infrastructure is associated with the institutional framework that favors the conditions of enterprising. These two dimensions provide a space to understand the market conditions of an economy. Conditions that support both the perceptions of individuals for enterprising as well as the infrastructural conditions of the economy gives the ideal case of a free and innovative economy (Erkut, 2016a). Regarding export behavior, these results have the following implications (Erkut, 2016a): First of all, the dimension of infrastructure that encompasses intellectual property rights, quick access to utilities, support of science parks, presence of business incubators and reduced bureaucracy indicates that in absence of these conditions, firms may try to target foreign markets to survive. If the infrastructural-institutional support is absent, there may be informal competition hardening competition in the domestic market, bureaucratic procedures to access the domestic market and no support to develop new ideas which may turn into new products. A way out of this can be to focus on foreign markets and adjust the position of the firm accordingly. Second, the dimension of market shaping is associated with the presence of training programs, access to finance and equal opportunities for all. The absence of these implies that not only does the firm lack an orientation, but it also lacks finance and may not be treated equally in comparison to other firms. These may all result in the firm's decision not to export because of a lack of perspectives. Hence, one can read the interplay between market shaping and infrastructural support for enterprising twofold: Favorable conditions in the home country may favor high productivity, which, in turn, may or may not result in exports. Unfavorable conditions in the home country, on the other hand, may hinder firm's access to foreign markets or it may lead the firm to see export as a way out of the unfavorable domestic market conditions. Based on this contribution, the conceptual framework of this chapter is that the market conditions – legal, institutional and financial conditions – are decisive on firm exports.

Hence, although export development has been on the agenda of business and economics scholars since a long time, the role of the firm in this process is largely neglected, and those which focus on the role of the firm overemphasized the role of productivity (Melitz, 2003) in this process. The heterogeneous character of exporting firms, the economies they are based in, and the interaction of these two elements require a microeconomic focus on export decisions and export behavior. As (Kapri, 2019) puts forward, little evidence is present from a microeconomic, empirical perspective that aims to explain the firm's decision to export that goes beyond the mere explanatory factor of productivity. This gap in the literature needs to be addressed under consideration of the perceptions of firms as a point of departure for the decision to export.

Macroeconomic Context

As stated in the introductory part, Turkish Cypriot people remained out of the international system since 57 years, where Turkey serves as a point of access to the international market as well as its most important trade partner (The World Bank, 2019). This section should briefly report about the macroeconomic context of analysis. "North Cyprus is a typical small island state in the Mediterranean Sea" writes (Turan Katircioglu, 2006) (p. 335), emphasizing that both the natural resources and the workforce efficiency remains limited and the nation resembles the characters of a small island economy. The economic activity is largely based on importing goods from other countries. According to trade statistics of the year 2019, a total export of goods worth 43.160.122 $ was made to Turkey, and a total export of goods worth 39.305.257 $ was made to other countries (Ticaret Dairesi, 2019a). In comparison, imports from Turkey are worth 927.163.386 $ and those from other countries are worth 660.757.069 $ (Ticaret Dairesi, 2019b). Regarding the most important export products, the top 10 list of 2019 consists of citrus products, milk products, tobacco, juices, garments, and spirits (Ticaret Dairesi, 2019a).

Regarding export support, a recent competitiveness report by the Turkish Cypriot Chamber of Commerce finds out that support is given for the following (Süreç & Eminer, 2019): Participation in fairs, conducting foreign market research, advertisements in foreign markets, quality and standardization, hiring a store in a foreign market. Furthermore, export premium and freight premium are given as well as a special type of premium for industrial products. The same report gives an idea about the competitiveness of Turkish Cypriot people's economic activities (Süreç & Eminer, 2019): Based on the methodology provided by Global Competitiveness Report, the calculated scores give an overview of the economic profile. Accordingly, there are estimated non-tariff effects on international trade activities, as well as problems associated with access to finance and political instability. The report also finds out that impediments to competition are very big, as well as problems associated with taxation. Overall, obstacles in front of export activities seem to be very obvious based on the most recent findings of the report. The report concludes by stating that incentives, among others, for exports should be improved as the economic activities did not reach to a level of fully realizing the export potential.

Hence, macroeconomic context allows room for discovering the perceived obstacles to firm export behavior. In particular, understanding what encourages or discourages firm exports is not only vital for improving export decisions, but also relevant for exploring the role of the firm in international trade. For the latter point, theoretical and empirical approaches are emerging in the literature; nevertheless, the question of generalizability of these approaches remain valid. On the one hand, the heterogeneity of countries engaging in international trade is present; on the other hand, some structural similarities between countries can be associated (Erkut, 2016b). Hence, the strategy that would be followed should reflect two targets: On the one hand, understanding the decision to export when a community does not have direct access to international markets gives a unique case of export development. On the other hand, firm perceptions on the obstacles in front of export emphasizes the largely neglected role of the firm in trade flows.

MAIN FOCUS OF THE CHAPTER

Data

To examine the perceived obstacles to firm export behavior empirically, this study makes use of the enterprise-level data of the World Bank's "Enterprise Survey". This survey focuses on a representative sample of the private sector of an economy, and covers a broad range of topics that describe the business environment of the firm. Even though surveys are conducted since 2002, the focus on the Turkish Cypriot people is a new one, as the first survey was done in 2019, which is providing the data used in this chapter. The survey covers 105 non-exporting and 15 exporting firms, a total of 120 firms. This is the data that would be used to analyze the obstacles in front of firm export behavior. The survey results are useful because firm managers from small, medium and large enterprises describe what they see as obstacles towards their entrepreneurial activity.

Methodology

To examine export behavior, this study follows the approach by (Singh & Maiti, 2019) describing firm export decision as a nonlinear, unobservable variable. Accordingly, P_j^* is the firm export-to-sales ratio and P_j the unobserved firm export decision, and we can formulate a relation, with which we can derive the firm export decision from the export-to-sales ratio:

$$P_j = \begin{cases} 1, P_j^* > 0 \\ 0, P_j^* = 0 \end{cases} \tag{1}$$

Following the strategy by (Singh & Maiti, 2019), the firm export decision is considered as a binary variable: A firm either decides to export, or not. Following the authors' empirical strategy, a probit model can be utilized to test the obstacles in front of the firm export decision:

$$P_j = \alpha X_j + \varepsilon_j \tag{2}$$

In the above described equation, P_j is a binary variable which takes the value of 1 if the firm is active in exports, whereas it takes the value of 0 if the firm is not an exporting firm. X_j describes variables that can affect the decision to export, and ε_j is the random error term.

In an empirical study on export decision and behavior, (Koenig, 2009) notices that an adequate, qualified workforce as well as a good transportation infrastructure are factors that have a positive impact on the decision to export. (Wignaraja, 2013)also states that both adequate workforce and transportation are factors of influence on the decision to export, in addition to electricity costs and access to finance. By focusing on the Customs Union between Turkey and the European Union, (Adam & Moutos, 2005) identify positive effects for Turkey's access to the single market; hence, removing custom barriers may ease the export decision. On the contrary, the presence of custom barriers may make it difficult for firms to export. (Siba & Gebreeyesus, 2017) explore Ethiopian export performance and share the perspective of (Adam & Moutos, 2005) by stating that easing customs processes such as duty and tax exemptions was a factor of positive influence on Ethiopian firms' decision to export. In addition, the authors state that access to finance and access to land were further factors that influenced the success of Ethiopian export-oriented firms. By reminding that a significant part of economic activities around the globe are occurring in the informal sector, (Deb et al., 2020) analyze whether activities of competing firms in the informal sector may influence the decision of a firm to export. They suggest that informal competition may arise because of weak legal, regulatory and economic systems. Their findings reveal that experiencing informal competition leads the firm to export. Since their implication of informal competition goes back to a weak legal, economic and regulatory system, the presence of strong courts, the absence of corruption and a low level of crime are considered as additional factors of influence. (Flach et al., 2019) find out that taxation is a relevant factor of influence on the decision to export, whereas (Kapri, 2019) shows that political instability leads a firm to decide on exporting. On the contrary, (Fosu, 2003) finds an adverse effect of political instability on export decisions of firms. Following the tradition of (Kumarasamy & Singh, 2018; Manova, 2013; Muûls, 2015; Singh & Maiti, 2019), access to finance is considered as a factor of influence regarding the firm export decision.

Based on these possible factors of influence, the empirical model is formulated as follows:

$$\begin{aligned} Export_i = {} & \alpha_0 + \alpha_1 Electricity_i + \alpha_2 Transport_i + \alpha_3 Customs_i \\ & + \alpha_4 Competitors_i + \alpha_5 Land_i + \alpha_6 Courts_i + \alpha_7 Crime_i + \alpha_8 Tax\ Rates_i \\ & + \alpha_9 Tax\ Administration_i + \alpha_{10} Permissions_i + \alpha_{11} Political\ Instability_i \\ & + \alpha_{12} Corruption_i + \alpha_{13} Access\ to\ Finance_i + \alpha_{14} Inadequate\ Workforce_i + \varepsilon_i \end{aligned} \tag{3}$$

In the above formulated empirical model, $Export_i$ is a binary variable which takes the value of 1 if the firm i's export share in sales is positive, and 0 otherwise. This way of observing export decision of firms is in line with (Kumarasamy & Singh, 2018).

For the right-hand side variables, firms participating in the survey can choose the degree of how big the obstacle is. They can choose among five choices, (0) no obstacle, (1) minor obstacle, (2) moderate obstacle, (3) major obstacle and (4) very severe obstacle. $Electricity_i$ is the variable that describes how big electricity costs are seen as an obstacle, whereas $Transport_i$ is the variable that describes how big transportation is seen as an obstacle in front of exporting. $Customs_i$ describes customs and trade regulations that may prevent the firm to export, whereas $Competitors_i$ describes practices of competitors in the informal sector. $Land_i$ is the variable that explains how easy or difficult it is to have access to land, whereas $Courts_i$ is the variable that describes whether courts are acting in a preventive way to firm operations. $Crime_i$ is about crime, theft and disorder that may prevent the firm to export. $Tax\ Rates_i$ and $Tax\ Administration_i$ are describing whether these two components of the taxation regime are influencing firm operations. $Permissions_i$ is about business licensing and permits, whereas $Political\ Instability_i$ describes whether political instability acts against the decision to export. $Corruption_i$ is about corruption as a possible obstacle in front of exporting. $Access\ to\ Finance_i$ describes whether the lack of access to finance prevents the firm to export, whereas $Inadequate\ Workforce_i$ is about inadequately educated workforce that may prevent the firm to export.

Results

Preliminary Results

Before the presentation of the results of the empirical analysis, a look at the descriptive statistics is useful. All variables that are considered have 0 as minimum value and 4 as maximum value.Descriptive statistics for independent variables are given in Table 1. Apart from basic measures (mean, standard deviation) also the results of T-test statistics are presented for each variable, where the sub-groups were defined as exporter firms and non-exporter firms. These results reveal that for independent variables the differences between exporter and non-exporter firms are statistically significant. This result is in line with the observation of (Bernard et al., 2007) that "firms that trade differ substantially from those that do not" (p. 129).

Empirical Model

The results of the empirical model, estimated as a probit regression (Greene, 2012), are given in Table 2. For the empirical model, McFadden's Pseudo-R2 is calculated as 0.14.

The probit regression analysis indicates that only the variables "courts", "tax rates", "political instability" and "corruption" are relative factors that influence the decision to export in the empirical model formulated based on current literature. Hence, based on the results of the probit regression analysis, the following findings can be highlighted:

The variable "courts" appears to be positively associated with the firm export decision in a statistically significant way. If the courts are seen as obstacles in front of domestic trade, the firm is self-selected to export. This is in line with the literature, since the effectiveness and efficiency of the legal system is important to enforce contracts. With a weak legal system, contracts cannot be enforced, and this has a negative impact on domestic trade (Anderson & Young, 2006).

Table 1. Descriptive statistics

	Non-Exporter		Exporter		T-Test
Variable	**Mean**	**SD**	**Mean**	**SD**	
Electricity	1.54	1.57	1.4	1.59	-2.0907**
Transport	1.2	2.42	0.8	2.57	-2.2745**
Customs	0.61	2.92	0.8	2.51	-2.5323**
Competitors	0.457	3.890	0.4	4.390	-2.6556***
Land	0.29	2.62	0.93	3.37	-3.0491***
Courts	0.92	2.38	1.33	1.59	-2.3656**
Crime	0.13	2.69	0.07	2.22	-2.7954***
Tax Rates	2.29	1.84	2.10	1.10	-1.7132*
Tax Administration	1.25	1.96	1.53	1.36	-2.2119**
Permissions	0.98	2.04	0.87	1.13	-2.3737**
Political Instability	2.34	1.96	2.87	1.36	-1.6355*
Corruption	1.30	2.26	1.13	1.19	-2.2137**
Access to Finance	1.49	1.73	1.07	1.67	-2.1366**
Inadequate Workforce	2.37	1.91	2.10	1.53	-1.6741*

Note: *, ** and *** indicate p=0.1, p=0.05 and p=0.01 respectively.

Table 2. Results of the empirical model

Export>0	Probit (coefficient)	Marginal Effects
Constant	-0.90238**	-
Electricity	-0.06238	-0.0109
Transport	-0.11520	-0.0201
Customs	0.15242	0.0266
Competitors	0.15242	0.0038
Access to Land	-0.03806	-0.0067
Courts	0.20087 *	0.0351
Crime	-0.02119	-0.0037
Tax Rates	-0.34962**	-0.0611
Tax Administration	0.33343	0.0583
Permissions	-0.07969	-0.0139
Political Instability	0.24612 *	0.0430
Corruption	-0.25337**	-0.0443
Access to Finance	-0.17088	-0.0299
Inadequate Workforce	-0.07438	-0.0130

Source: Author's calculation based on World Bank Enterprise Survey Data
Note: *, ** and *** indicate p=0.1, p=0.05 and p=0.01 respectively.

The variable "political instability" seems to be positively associated with the firm export decision in a statistically significant way. If the perceived political instability increases, the firm is self-selected to export. This is in line with the recent findings of (Kapri, 2019) who establishes a positive relationship, and contradicts with the findings of (Fosu, 2003) who establishes a negative relationship.

On the other hand, the variable "tax rates" appears to be negatively associated with the firm export decision in a statistically significant way. If the tax rates are seen as an obstacle, the firm chooses not to export. In this sense, the results contradict with the findings of (Federici & Parisi, 2012) who find that an increase in corporate taxation would lead to the export decision but they support the findings of (Ermolina, 2016) who attributes high tax rates as a factor challenging the business environment and (Flach et al., 2019) who highlight the role of corporate taxation as a competitive factor in case of export behavior.

Finally, the variable "corruption" seems to be negatively associated with the firm export decision in a statistically significant way. If the perceived corruption increases, the firm chooses rather not to export. This is in line with the findings of (Olney, 2016), who states that "corruption reduces the probability that a firm will only sell domestically, since only the more productive domestic firms are able to overcome the additional costs associated with a corrupt business environment" (p. 18).

Empirical Model with Interactions

One point that is worth mentioning from the empirical model is that access to finance is not statistically significant in explaining export decisions. This is contradicting with recent findings (Kumarasamy & Singh, 2018; Manova, 2013; Muûls, 2015; Singh & Maiti, 2019) which highlight the role of access to finance in firm decision to export. Therefore, the question remains whether access to finance really matters. In the following, an interaction model will be tested on whether access to finance affects firm export decision in an indirect way. The target is to identify how access to finance in interaction with transport, customs and regulations, competitor behavior, political instability and inadequate working force affects the firm export decision. Hence, the empirical strategy is formulated as follows:

$$\begin{aligned} Export_i = {} & \alpha_0 + \alpha_1 Electricity_i + \alpha_2 Transport_i + \alpha_3 Customs_i + \alpha_4 Competitors_i + \alpha_5 Land_i \\ & + \alpha_6 Courts_i + \alpha_7 Crime_i + \alpha_8 Tax\ Rates_i + \alpha_9 Tax\ Administration_i + \alpha_{10} Permissions_i \\ & + \alpha_{11} Political\ Instability_i + \alpha_{12} Corruption_i + \alpha_{13} Access\ to\ Finance_i \\ & + \alpha_{14} Inadequate\ Workforce_i + \alpha_{15} Transport \times Access\ to\ Finance_i + \alpha_{16} Customs \\ & \times Access\ to\ Finance_i + \alpha_{17} Competitors \times Access\ to\ Finance_i + \alpha_{18} Political\ Instability \\ & \times Access\ to\ Finance_i + \alpha_{19} Inadequate\ Workforce \times Access\ to\ Finance_i + \varepsilon_i \end{aligned} \tag{4}$$

Based on this empirical strategy, a probit model with interactions (Greene, 2012) is estimated and the results are given in Table 3. For the empirical model with interactions, McFadden's Pseudo-R2 is calculated as 0.23.

In the interaction model, the coefficients of those variables which are not-interacting do not change their behavior in case of their sign or statistical significance. The only exception to this is tax administration which keeps is sign, but has a statistically significant positive impact on export decision. This is in line with the findings of (Ermolina, 2016) who finds that a combination of weak tax administration and high tax rates is a challenge for the business environment, which, in turn, may impede the decision to focus on the domestic market, and instead, switch to foreign markets. Regarding interactions, the interaction between political instability and access to finance has a negative impact on firm decision to export, and it is statistically significant. Hence, it can be said that access to finance has an indirect impact on the decision to export, and this occurs through the political instability channel. The impact is found to be negative, as it is a discouraging factor on the decision to export.

The interaction channel of the indirect impact of access to finance via political instability seems to be a new channel that is, to the best knowledge of the author, hitherto undiscovered. The interpretation of this channel requires macroeconomic contextual knowledge. Based on the Competitiveness Report of the Turkish Cypriot Chamber of Commerce (Süreç & Eminer, 2019), it can be seen that support for exporting firms is provided through different agencies that are influenced by the political context and political decision-makers.

Table 3. Results of the empirical model with interactions.

Export>0	**Probit (coefficient)**
Constant	-0.68574
Electricity	-0.15276
Transport	-0.31947
Customs	0.38977
Competitors	-0.01779
Access to Land	0.02909
Courts	0.24139**
Crime	-0.02807
Tax Rates	-0.57731***
Tax Administration	0.38304**
Permissions	-0.05233
Political Instability	0.57829***
Corruption	-0.36275**
Access to Finance	-0.16945
Inadequate Workforce	-0.25445
Transport x Access to Finance	0.12155
Customs x Access to Finance	-0.07170
Competitors x Access to Finance	0.05146
Political Instability x Access to Finance	-0.20254**
Inadequate Workforce x Access to Finance	0.11129

Source: Author's calculation based on World Bank Enterprise Survey Data
Note: *, ** and *** indicate p=0.1, p=0.05 and p=0.01 respectively.

Discussion of the Results

The results found in this analysis regarding taxation are in line with recent empirical findings, among others, by (Ermolina, 2016; Flach et al., 2019). Regarding taxation, it was found out that the obstacle of tax rates has a negative effect on the decision to export. Hence, once tax rates seem to disappear as an obstacle by introducing a lower corporate taxation policy, it seems that the firms would rethink their decisions to export.

A recent report by the Ministry of Trade of the Republic of Turkey focusing on trade with North Cyprus states that exporting Turkish Cypriot firms need to pay an indirect tax in the form of a contribution to the Price Stability Fond when exporting (TC Ticaret Bakanlığı, 2020). Apart from that, a port tax is levied when a firm is exporting (TC Ticaret Bakanlığı, 2020). Hence, even if export-led growth is prioritized, exporting is not free of taxes and this seems to discourage potential exporter firms to export.

Based on the empirical results of this analysis, it was found out that the obstacle of corruption has a negative effect on the decision to export. The role of corruption as a discouraging factor to export is in line with (Olney, 2016). A recent approach by (Audretsch & Chowdhury, 2020) indicates that an improvement of institutional quality with respect to corruption improves firm internationalization by means of exporting. Regarding the specific macroeconomic context of North Cyprus economy, a recent report financed by the Friedrich Ebert Foundation highlights that the perception of corruption is widespread, and in particular, this widespread belief is oriented towards corruption in the allocation of credit and land (Gokcekus & Sonan, 2017). However, it is interesting to see that access to land does not play a role in the decision to export.

Furthermore, the results reveal that courts as an obstacle would impact the decision to export in a positive way. This result is in line with the contribution of (Anderson & Young, 2006), who find out that a weak legal framework would result in contracts that are not enforced; hence, an impediment in front of domestic trade occurs – and in our case, firms may escape from domestic trade by focusing on trade with foreign countries. Hence, problems associated with courts result in firms focusing on export instead of domestic trade. Does this mean that improving courts would reverse the decision to export? (Yoo, 2019) answers this question by "no", indicating that improving the legal framework would only change the composition of exports instead of reversing the decision to export.

One issue that is mentioned by (Flach & Gräf, 2020) is with regard to joining a trade agreement to foster innovation as a pre-condition for economic progress. The results reveal that firms active in the North Cyprus economy are facing political instability, and this motivates them to export rather than to focus on the domestic market. With the absence of any trade agreements, they choose to implement what a trade agreement brings as a benefit to competition: Export by escaping political instability in order to find a way to be more innovative.

However, this research also identifies a new channel that shapes the decision to export: The interaction between political instability and access to finance. Once this interaction occurs, it has a negative impact on the decision to export. To the knowledge of the author, this is a new channel introduced to the literature and has important implications: Political instability can be a triggering factor to switch from the domestic market to the foreign market, but once access to finance enters into this process, the decision to switch to the foreign market is not straightforward.

SOLUTIONS AND RECOMMENDATIONS

The results of this study reveal that Turkish Cypriot firms decide to export largely as a result of the weak legal and institutional conditions that the Turkish Cypriot economy is facing. A flat reading of this would imply that exporting firms are turning an unfavorable condition into a favorable one by enjoying the benefits of exporting, but the empirical observation that the interaction of the financial and institutional conditions would discourage them from export gives a different picture. Hence, access to finance and financial support for exporting firms should be isolated from political mechanisms. An important, and to the knowledge of the author, novel channel of interaction determining the firm export decision is identified therefore as the interaction between political instability and access to finance. Political instability itself affects all levels of firm-related decision-making processes; changing governments, changing government policies, changing bureaucratic staff, legal frameworks, and any possible channel of interaction where government should guarantee the basic conditions of exchange is endangered by political instability. Therefore, it is understandable that the firm may decide to sell its goods elsewhere to avoid the possible outcomes of political instability on its activities. In other words, political instability can act as a trigging factor for firm export decisions. This is also reflected in the analysis of (Bahri et al., 2020), which indicates a positive impact of corruption and political instability on exports. Nevertheless, there is a down side of it, as political instability together with access to finance may impact the export decision negatively.

For understanding this, it is important to relate to the context of political instability and access to finance. With regard to the macroeconomic context of the Turkish Cypriot economic activity, a leading role in access to finance is played by public banks (Kutlay, 2017; Şafaklı, 2002, 2006; Şafaklı & Özdeşer, 2002). Even though there are two public banks active in the Turkish Cypriot economy, their size in the banking sector is 32.7%, as significant as private banks (Kutlay, 2017). An important problem with regard to public banks' policies and attitudes towards customers is that their executive boards are appointed by the incumbent government (Şafaklı, 2006). One way to isolate access to finance mechanisms from political intervention is to establish a single agency free of political intervention that provides all kind of financial and technical support to firms. Such a single contact agency proves itself to be useful when supporting entrepreneurship (Erkut, 2016a), and exports are not an exception in that setup.

Another solution is regarding the role of tax rates which discourage firms to export. The role of corporate taxation has long been discussed in the literature, and found out to be negatively correlated with respect to firm export behavior. Nevertheless, in the specific context of the Turkish Cypriot economy, one of the impediments in exporting is with respect to the taxes associated with export – in addition to indirect exports being the only way to export to countries other than Turkey (or cross-border export to the southern part of the divide). Since indirect access to markets implies that an export via Turkey is associated with a further taxation, at least export-related taxes by Turkish Cypriot authorities should not be levied in order to reduce the discouraging effect of tax rates on export behavior.

More generalized solutions are associated with, first of all, the interaction between access to finance and political instability. Recent empirical evidence suggests that access to finance is more difficult for non-exporters than exporters (Wagner, 2019); however, the results from the study reveal that political instability may be a channel which influences firm access to finance, and as a result, firm export decision. Political instability may occur in many different forms. As one of the most recent microeconomic approaches focusing on political instability-export nexus, the approach by (Kapri, 2019) involves – among others – countries that went through prolonged periods of civil war. Hence, also political instability is a matter of definition. Whereas a pure isolation of access to finance from political instability would be an ideal-typical situation, policy makers need to rethink the channels of interaction between finance and political instability.

Second solution that can be addressed in a more generalized context is the role of tax rates in encouraging or discouraging firm decision to export. This is a long discussed topic in the literature, yet, little has been achieved on the question of the optimal taxation policy when it comes to exports. Recent empirical evidence by (Shi & Xu, 2020) highlights the misreporting behavior of Chinese firms to benefit from export tax refunds. The empirical results of this research indicate the negative impact of tax rates on firm export decision, but does not reveal what is needed to overcome this obstacle. Policy makers need to be creative about the role of taxation and export behavior, as this is very often open to manipulation.

A third issue can be highlighted regarding the role of weak or strong legal frameworks. The results indicate that a weak legal framework shifts the focus of the firms from the domestic market to foreign markets. As discussed previously, export behavior is not reversed when the legal framework becomes stronger; however, the composition of the exported goods change (Yoo, 2019). Therefore, for policy makers, a trade-off in policy making is either to focus on improving the legal framework for an overall better institutional quality, or, if this is difficult e.g. when it is combined with changing the constitution, focusing on the composition of goods which are exported due to the weak legal framework – and supporting these goods in particular. To summarize it, the trade-off is between improving the legal framework and improving the support for the particular composition of export goods under a weak legal framework.

FUTURE RESEARCH DIRECTIONS

One of the shortcomings of the article is with regard to its focus on a single point of time, with a restricted size of 120 firms for a single country. Therefore, the results should be interpreted with care. A possible extension would be to conduct a similar analysis with a panel data structure to observe the evolution of firm export decision, especially those mechanisms other than productivity which may explain firm export decisions. This can be analyzed in future research attempts. In addition, this research utilized secondary data to identify the possible channels of influence regarding export decisions. Future research may focus on a more detailed collection of data over a longer period of observation.

A second issue that can be relevant for future research is with regard to COVID-19 pandemics and how it has changed the perception of firms on their decision to export. By the time the chapter was written, a new survey on the economic influence of COVID-19 pandemics in North Cyprus was disseminated by the World Bank, hence, providing room for comparison and further analysis.

Third, this research attempted to explain firm decision based on the legal, financial and institutional frameworks. There is still a possibility that some factors not captured in the survey and in the empirical model may affect export decision of firms. By pointing out to these three limitations of this chapter, the author aims to highlight new avenues of research that can enhance the discussion around export development, which goes beyond the mere topic of productivity, as this topic seems to have a restricted explanatory power.

CONCLUSION

This research utilized the most recent Enterprise Survey data that was conducted for the first time for the Turkish Cypriot people. Based on the data and recent contributions on the decision to export, the research analyzed the role of legal, institutional and financial conditions on the firm decision to export by an empirical strategy of using probit regression and identifying marginal effects, where the decision to export was modelled as a binary variable. The results highlighted courts and political instability as obstacles that enable firm exports, tax rates and corruption as obstacles that disable firm exports. An interaction model on the role of access to finance was estimated, for which access to finance was found to be indirectly influencing export decisions through the political instability channel.

ACKNOWLEDGMENT

A preliminary draft of this chapter was presented in the session "Institutions and Trade" of the First Global Economic Policy Group Meeting organized by FernUniversität Hagen (Germany) and University of Westminster (UK) on 18 January 2021. I would like to thank the organizers for this opportunity and the participants for useful feedback. I would like to thank two anonymous referees and the editor for useful feedback as well.

REFERENCES

Adam, A., & Moutos, T. (2005). *Turkish Delight for Some, Cold Turkey for Others? The Effects of the EU-Turkey Customs Union*. CESifo Working Paper Series, 1550.

Anderson, J. E., & Young, L. (2006). Trade and Contract Enforcement. *Contributions to Economic Analysis & Policy*, *5*(1). Advance online publication. doi:10.2202/1538-0645.1574

Audretsch, D., & Chowdhury, F. (2020). Export Regulations, Credit Markets, and Corruption: Implications for Internationalization. *Academy of Management Proceedings*, *2020*(1), 10229. doi:10.5465/AMBPP.2020.10229abstract

Bahri, M., Sakka, O., & Kallal, R. (2020). The impact of corruption on the export intensity of SMEs in Tunisia: moderating effects of political instability and regulatory obstacles. *Journal of Entrepreneurship in Emerging Economies*. doi:10.1108/JEEE-03-2020-0055

Bernard, A. B., Jensen, J. B., Redding, S. J., & Schott, P. K. (2007). Firms in International Trade. *The Journal of Economic Perspectives*, *21*(3), 105–130. doi:10.1257/jep.21.3.105

Bilkey, W. J., & Tesar, G. (1977). The Export Behavior of Smaller-Sized Wisconsin Manufacturing Firms. *Journal of International Business Studies*, *8*(1), 93–98. doi:10.1057/palgrave.jibs.8490783

Chen, J., Sousa, C. M. P., & He, X. (2016). The determinants of export performance: A review of the literature 2006-2014. *International Marketing Review*, *33*(5), 626–670. doi:10.1108/IMR-10-2015-0212

Deb, R., Samalia, H. V., & Prusty, S. K. (2020). The role of informal competition in driving export propensity of emerging economy firms. *The International Journal of Sociology and Social Policy*, *40*(1/2), 184–203. doi:10.1108/IJSSP-06-2019-0131

Erkut, B. (2016a). Entrepreneurship and Economic Freedom: Do Objective and Subjective Data Reflect the Same Tendencies? *Entrepreneurial Business and Economics Review*, *4*(3), 11–26. doi:10.15678/EBER.2016.040302

Erkut, B. (2016b). Structural similarities of economies for innovation and competitiveness - a decision tree based approach. *Studia Oeconomica Posnaniensia*, *4*(5), 85–104. doi:10.18559/SOEP.2016.5.6

Ermolina, A. (2016). Business environment as the determinant of economic growth. *J. for International Business and Entrepreneurship Development*, *9*(4), 417. doi:10.1504/JIBED.2016.080020

Federici, D., & Parisi, V. (2012). *Corporate taxation and exports*. MPRA.

Flach, L., & Gräf, F. (2020). The impact of trade agreements on world export prices. *Review of International Economics*, *28*(1), 168–208. doi:10.1111/roie.12446

Flach, L., Irlacher, M., & Unger, F. (2019). *Corporate Taxes and Multi-Product Exporters: Theory and Evidence from Trade Dynamics*. CESifo Working Paper Series, 7809.

Fosu, A. K. (2003). Political Instability and Export Performance in Sub-Saharan Africa. *The Journal of Development Studies*, *39*(4), 68–83. doi:10.1080/713869426

Gokcekus, O., Henson, J., Nottebaum, D., & John, A. W.-S. (2012). Impediments to trade across the Green Line in Cyprus. *Journal of Peace Research*, *49*(6), 863–872. doi:10.1177/0022343312452286

Gokcekus, O., & Sonan, S. (2017). *Corruption Perceptions in North Cyprus: 2017 Report*. Academic Press.

Greene, W. H. (2012). *Econometric Analysis* (7th ed.). Pearson Education.

Kapri, K. (2019). Impact of political instability on firm-level export decisions. *International Review of Economics & Finance*, *59*, 98–105. doi:10.1016/j.iref.2018.08.008

Kaya, T., Erkut, B., & Thierbach, N. (2019). Entrepreneurial Intentions of Business and Economics Students in Germany and Cyprus: A Cross-Cultural Comparison. *Sustainability*, *11*(5), 1437. doi:10.3390u11051437

Koenig, P. (2009). Agglomeration and the export decisions of French firms. *Journal of Urban Economics*, *66*(3), 186–195. doi:10.1016/j.jue.2009.07.002

Kumarasamy, D., & Singh, P. (2018). Access to Finance, Financial Development and Firm Ability to Export: Experience from Asia-Pacific Countries. *Asian Economic Journal*, *32*(1), 15–38. doi:10.1111/asej.12140

Kutlay, K. (2017). Kuzey Kıbrıs'ta Banka Karlığını Etkileyen Faktörler: Ampirik bir Çalışma. *International Conference on "Scientific Cooperation for the Future in Economics and Administrative Sciences"*, 231–237.

Lileeva, A., & Trefler, D. (2010). Improved Access to Foreign Markets Raises Plant-Level Productivity… for Some Plants. *The Quarterly Journal of Economics*, *125*(3), 1051–1099. doi:10.1162/qjec.2010.125.3.1051

Manova, K. (2013). Credit constraints, heterogeneous firms, and international trade. *The Review of Economic Studies*, *80*(2), 711–744. doi:10.1093/restud/rds036

Melitz, M. J. (2003). The Impact of Trade on Intra-Industry Reallocations and Aggregate Industry Productivity. *Econometrica*, *71*(6), 1695–1725. doi:10.1111/1468-0262.00467

Movahedi, M., & Shahbazi, K. (2020). *Firms' export decisions: self-selection versus trial-and-error. Economics: The Open-Access, Open-Assessment E-Journal*. doi:10.5018/economics-ejournal.ja.2020-22

Muûls, M. (2015). Exporters and credit constraints. *Journal of International Economics*, *95*(2), 333–343. doi:10.1016/j.jinteco.2014.12.003

Olney, W. W. (2016). Impact of corruption on firm-level export decisions. *Economic Inquiry*, *54*(2), 1105–1127. doi:10.1111/ecin.12257

Şafaklı, O. V. (2002). KKTC'de Banka Krizleri açısından Kamu Finansmanının Etkinliği. *Uludağ Üniversitesi İktisadi ve İdari Bilimler Fakültesi Dergisi*, *21*(2), 65–84.

Şafaklı, O. V. (2006). KKTC'nin olası AB üyeliği karşısında Kamu Bankalarının Stratejik Analizi. *Ç.Ü. Sosyal Bilimler Enstitüsü Dergisi*, *15*(1), 313–332.

Şafaklı, O. V., & Özdeşer, H. (2002). An Analysis of the Cooperatives in the Turkish Republic Of Northern Cyprus in the Process of EU. *XVII. International Turkish Cooperative Congress on Globalization and Cooperatives*.

Shi, X., & Xu, Z. (2020). *Export Tax Refund and the Misreporting of Chinese Exporters*. Academic Press.

Siba, E., & Gebreeyesus, M. (2017). Learning to export and learning from exporting: The case of Ethiopian manufacturing. *Journal of African Economies*, *26*(1), 1–23. doi:10.1093/jae/ejw022

Singh, P., & Maiti, D. (2019). ICT, Access to Finance and Firm Exports: A Cross-Country Study. In D. Maiti, F. Castellacci, & A. Melchior (Eds.), *Digitalisation and Development: Issues for India and Beyond* (pp. 161–181). Springer.

Süreç, Y., & Eminer, F. (2019). *Rekabet Edebilirlik Raporu*. Academic Press.

The World Bank. (2016). *Turkish Cypriot Community: Workforce Development*. Author.

The World Bank. (2019). *World Bank Enterprise Survey for Turkish Cypriot Community*. enterprisesurveys.org.

TC Ticaret Bakanlığı. (2020). *Pazar Bilgileri*. Academic Press.

Ticaret Dairesi. (2019). *İhracat İstatistik Raporu*. Academic Press.

Turan Katircioglu, S. (2006). Causality between agriculture and economic growth in a small nation under political isolation. *International Journal of Social Economics*, *33*(4), 331–343. doi:10.1108/03068290610651643

Wagner, J. (2019). Access to Finance and Exports – Comparable Evidence for Small and Medium Enterprises from Industry and Services in 25 European Countries. *Open Economies Review*, *30*(4), 739–757. doi:10.100711079-019-09534-w

Wignaraja, G. (2013). Can SMEs participate in global production networks? In D. K. Elms & P. Low (Eds.), *Global value chains in a changing world* (pp. 279–312). World Trade Organization.

Yang, C.-H. (2018). Exports and innovation: The role of heterogeneity in exports. *Empirical Economics*, *55*(3), 1065–1087. doi:10.100700181-017-1312-8

Yoo, J. (2019). Better legal institutions: An intertemporal effect on export composition. *Economic Bulletin*, *39*(4), 1–8.

ADDITIONAL READING

Altınay, L., Bıçak, H. A., & Altınay, M. (2002). Economic Integration and the Tourism Industry of North Cyprus. *Tourism Economics*, *8*(3), 325–335. doi:10.5367/000000002101298151

Çavuşoğlu, B. (2016). Knowledge Economy and North Cyprus. *Procedia Economics and Finance*, *39*, 720–724. doi:10.1016/S2212-5671(16)30285-4

Çavuşoğlu, B., & Sağsan, M. (2016). Either Economize on Knowledge or Capitalize on Intellectuality: Educational Challenges for Economic Growth in the Turkish Republic of Northern Cyprus. *Turkish Librarianship*, *30*(2), 166–184.

Çelebi, A., & Özdeşer, H. (2014). Output Convergence of Exported Milk Products in Northern Cyprus. *International Journal of Economic Perspectives*, *8*(2).

Erkut, B. (2015). A Hung Parliament in the North: Outside Options after the 2003 Election en Route to the Annan Plan Referendum of 2004. *The Cyprus Review*, *27*(2), 105–122. https://cyprusreview.org/index.php/cr/article/download/49/19

Görgülü, M. E. (2016). The Effects of Isolation on the Turkish Republic of Northern Cyprus. *Journal of Business and Economics*, *7*(4), 249–258.

Maslakcı, A., Şeşen, H., & Sürücü, L. (2021). Multiculturalism, positive psychological capital and students' entrepreneurial intentions. *Education + Training*, *63*(4), 597–612. Advance online publication. doi:10.1108/ET-04-2020-0073

Nadiri, H., & Tümer, M. (2010). Influence of Ethnocentrism on Consumers' Intention to buy Dometsically Produced Goods. *Journal of Business Economics and Management*, *11*(3), 444–461. doi:10.3846/jbem.2010.22

Sharkey, T. W., Lim, J.-S., & Kim, K. I. (1989). Export Development and Perceived Export Barriers: An Empirical Analysis of Small Firms. *Management International Review*, *29*(2), 33–40.

Tanova, C. (2003). Firm size and recruitment: Staffing practices in small and large organisations in north Cyprus. *Career Development International*, *8*(2), 107–114. doi:10.1108/13620430310465534

KEY TERMS AND DEFINITIONS

Access to Finance: A firm's situation of being able to access financial support measures without any problems.

Enterprise Survey: A survey conducted by the World Bank with the aim of understanding the conditions of enterprising in different economies.

Export Development: A firm's attempts to sell its products to foreign markets, with the help of an enabling environment.

Indirect Tax: A tax that is collected by an intermediary to pay to government, with the consumer paying it indirectly as a part of the sale price.

Political Instability: The unstable structure of a government and its inclination to collapse in a short time due to unstable political structures.

Port Tax: A specific tax levied at ports.

Probit Regression: A type of regression analysis, in which the dependent variable is a binary outcome.

Chapter 7
A Literature Survey on Extensive and Intensive Margins in International Trade

Burcu Berke
Nigde Omer Halisdemir University, Turkey

ABSTRACT

Products and firms are homogeneous in traditional foreign trade theories; products show no horizontal or vertical differentiation. It is observed that growth in exports is only related to an increase in export quantity and that this is not decomposed into margins. Since Melitz's work, there has been an increase in studies that decompose the firms' heterogeneity and export growth in foreign trade into extensive and intensive margins. The concepts are addressed in the literature known as "new-new" foreign trade theories which include extensive margins, the number of exporting firms, the number of new trade partners, and the volume or variety of exported products. In brief, the growth of global trade is the result of new trade relations (extensive margin) or a rise in existing trade relations (intensive margin). As one of the rapidly developing trade theories in international economics, the main purpose of this study is to conduct a literature survey on the extensive and intensive margins of export growth.

INTRODUCTION

Recent literature on international economics focuses on the sources of trade growth. Economists divide export growth into two categories: extensive and intensive margins. "Extensive margin" is ending the export of previously exported goods, or exporting goods that were not previously exported. This margin commonly indicates that growth in exports stems from the change in diversity. On the other hand, the intensive margin explains the extent to which foreign trade grows or shrinks due to changes in currently traded goods (Gao, Whalley, & Ren, 2014). Therefore, foreign trade progresses over two different margins or is divided into these two margins. The first is the "intensive margin", which is the pre-existence of a bilateral trade relationship and its development over time. The second is an "extensive margin", which

DOI: 10.4018/978-1-7998-8314-2.ch007

is the start and subsequent growth of international trade between countries that did not trade with each other in the past or the termination of existing ones (Felbermayr, & Kohler, 2006).

Theoretically, since the differences in firm-level productivity is significant in foreign trade, incorporating a firm heterogeneity into foreign trade models means that "foreign trade is decomposed into an increase in the average exports of firms that were previously exporters ("intensive margin") and the number of exporters selling to other markets ("extensive margin")" (Dutt, Mihov, & Van Zandt, 2013). Margins can be expressed in the equations as follows:

$$\chi^{mn} \cong \chi_{EM}^{mn} + \chi_{IM}^{mn}$$

Here, it is seen that the growth of total exports from country *m* to country *n* is decomposed into extensive and intensive margins (*EM* and *IM*), or otherwise, their sum. The extensive margin can also be decomposed into price (or quality) and quantity (Hummels & Klenow, 2005; Kehoe & Ruhl, 2013). Efforts to decompose the two margins are usually specific to an industry or firm. Trade growth is driven by quantity, but it also means that, for sustainable growth, a country needs to allocate considerable amounts of capital, labor and natural resources to produce more than would be necessary. On the other hand, while trade growth is price driven and this price also reflects the quality of the product, such export growth may require more human capital and technological innovation to achieve sustainable growth. In these conditions, export growth is analysed in terms of extensive and intensive margins, quantity, price and variety (Bingzhan, 2011).

In traditional foreign trade theories, such as the models of Ricardian and Heckscher-Ohlin, products are homogeneous; there is no horizontal and vertical differentiation, and export growth is only based on an increase in quantity. In Krugman's (1979, 1980) new foreign trade theory, intra-industry trade product diversity is explained in the scope of choices and scale economies. In the new trade theory, export growth is based on the extensive margin since large economies will produce and export more goods under these conditions (Gao, Whalley & Ren, 2014).

In contrast to traditional theories and within the scope of new-new trade theories which assumes the existence of heterogeneous firms, Melitz (2003) mentioned the term "extensive margin" in foreign trade, which means that foreign trade grows with the emergence of new export firms, new trade partners, or otherwise an increase in the number of export firms. In new-new trade theories, the extensive margin may include the number of export firms, the number of new trading partners, and the number or variety of exported products. As a result, growth in world trade stems from new trade relations (extensive margin) or an increase in existing trade relations (intensive margin).

The main purpose of this study is to conduct a literature survey on the intensive and extensive margins of international trade. The following part of the study will provide an overview of selected theoretical and empirical studies on the subject.

BACKGROUND

Eaton and Kortum (2002), Melitz (2003) and Chaney (2005) initially examined the decrease of fixed and variable costs following the liberalisation of foreign trade and its effects on margins. The main idea of these studies was that when such costs decrease, "extensive" margins must rise in order for firms to increase their presence in the export market (Dutt, Mihov, & Van Zandt, 2013). Armington (1969) assumed that all countries produce and export some kind of good, and claimed that firms can grow by exporting more than just one export good ("intensive" margin). Drawing attention to the variety of exports from countries, Krugman (1981) noted that all countries export the same amount of goods per variety ("extensive" margin). In this context, Armington (1969) stated that exports increase as the economy grows, but these economies will not export a wider variety of goods. Krugman (1981) stated that production and exports will increase as the economy grows in monopolistic competitive models. As developers of one of the vertical differentiation models in foreign trade, Flam and Helpman (1987) drew attention to the quality dimension of foreign trade and emphasised that prosperous countries produce and export goods of superior quality.

Under these conditions, the price of domestic goods will be low in the world market because of the larger economies exporting various goods. On the other hand, larger economies may export a variety of goods to more countries or higher quality goods at higher prices ("variety" and "quality" margins may dominate) (Hummels and Klenow, 2005: 704, 705). Assuming that firms are heterogeneous and that the exports are at a fixed cost, Melitz (2003: 1695) initially stated that more firms will enter the export market as they become more productive. The same author also analysed the effects of intra-industry trade assuming that firms are heterogeneous. According to Melitz, foreign trade encourages productive firms to penetrate the export market, while relatively unproductive firms continue to produce only for the domestic market while the least productive, exit the market. As intra-industry trade expands, the more efficient firms tend to export more since the more productive firms attract more business.

The selected empirical studies generally emphasise "the role of extensive and intensive margins in foreign trade on export growth". Looking at Chaney (2005) and Manova (2008), it could be said that the authors agree on the extensive margins of exports, or that credit-constrained firms export less. However, they have contradicting opinions on the effects of credit constraints on intensive margins. Manova (2008) claimed that the existence of credit constraints would reduce export volumes, whereas Chaney (2005) argued that such a situation would not affect exports. Looking at studies that differentiate between intensive and extensive margins, Bernard et al. (2006) differentiated the growth of US exports at the firm level in the form of market entry and exit. The same authors defined "extensive margin" as firms entering and exiting the export market and "intensive margin" as changes in foreign sales achieved by export firms.

In this context, Hummels and Klenow (2005), who developed the work of Armington (1969) and Krugman (1981), distinguished between the diversity (extensive margin), quality (price) and quantity dimensions (intensive margin) of USA trade growth. In other words, in addition to the extensive margin, their work addressed an "intensive" margin that is divided into the factors of price and quantity. While the authors found that the major exporting countries export more diverse and higher quality goods, they also pointed out that, unlike labor-intensive economies, capital-intensive rich economies export more at higher prices and that most of the growth in exports are explained with the extensive margin. In other words, it is the higher quantities of each commodity that dominates the intensive margin, not higher unit prices. Consistent with the increase achieved in quality, richer countries export each good in higher quantities at higher prices. The authors also reported that diversity and quality are important factors in explaining foreign trade volumes.

On the other hand, in a study that investigated the development of world trade by distinguishing between final and intermediate goods, Yi (2003) found that, although trade costs are important, the intensive margin is related to fluctuations in the foreign trade volume which is based on vertical specialisation; Whereas, the extensive margin is related to the foreign trade of a certain input.

Felbermayr and Kohler (2006) claimed that the recognised "gravity" between trade flows and distance is related to the extensive margin, and observed that WTO membership increased foreign trade. According to the authors, while the number of exported products and the number of firms decreases with distance, an increase is observed in the intensive margin of average import or export values the firm receives per product.

In a study which decomposed real export growth for China, Amiti and Freund (2008) stated that the country has a comparative advantage in labor-intensive goods, and that improving specialisation is accompanied by export growth and thus export diversification is not important in export growth. In other words, China's export growth can be explained with the exports of existing products ("intensive margin") rather than new varieties ("extensive margin").

Reporting on the significant effects of monetary policy shocks on the extensive margin for the USA, Bergin and Corsetti (2008) claimed that new firms entering and exiting the market alter the transmission mechanisms of monetary policy (real and monetary shocks), or in other words, investment dynamics. Under these conditions, firms can become more capable of introducing new goods to the market by decreasing costs or increasing demand. Compared to the intensive margin, the welfare effects are more significant in the extensive margin. For example, given the entry costs to the market, a fall in the real interest rate as a result of the expansion of monetary policy encourages firms to invest and increases their profits and thus, encourages new firms to enter the market. However, when monetary policies are uncertain, the number of firms entering the market declines. In a sense, a stable monetary policy regulates the production levels of firms and their entry into the market. Thus, depending on the extent to which consumers and firms profit from the increasing variety of goods and intermediate inputs, the existence of an extensive margin magnifies the real effects of monetary policy.

Another aspect in international economics is the existence of "survival in foreign trade" theories and their links with margins. Some studies link trade margins to survival. In other words, there is also a line of literature that focuses on the duration of trade relations as a measure of intensive margins in particular. In this literature, export growth is divided into three components: The first is the creation of new markets and the trading of new products, the second is the continuity of trade relations and the third is the depth of these relations. The first component corresponds to the extensive margin as it measures increases in the number of export relations. The other two components correspond to the intensive margin because it identifies the depth of the existing trade relations between countries. A more comprehensive definition of the extensive margin would be: The first is exporting to a country that has not been traded with before, the second is exporting a new product that was previously not exported, and the third is the export of an existing product to a new destination market (Adelon and Kakinaka, 2018: 405, 406, 409).

Adelon and Kakinaka (2018) investigated the effects of extensive and intensive margins at the product level on export growth for Philippines, one of the fastest growing countries in South East Asia which mainly produces manufacturing industry products. The authors demonstrated that the weak export performance of the Philippines is due to the intensive margin, or otherwise, the role of survival and deepening in foreign trade. More specifically, their study found significant differences in the export performance of countries between Japan, the USA, China, Hong Kong and Korea, and their main trading partners including the ASEAN-5 and new importers (new ASEAN members). On the other hand, the extensive margin is still important in the export performance of the country because it diversifies the trade partners that the country exports to through new export relations. However, many of the new trade relations fail to contribute to long-term export growth due to their low trade values and short lifespans. In other words, only strong and deep new trade relations can have a significant impact on export growth. Ultimately, the ability of Philippines' long-term export relationships and new trade relations to contribute to total export growth depends on whether they survive in the long term. The reason for the country's weak export performance is that the intensive margin based on survival and deepening is weak. Since the trade relations of the country have a short lifespan, they fail to contribute to long-term export growth even if there is a diversification of trading partners over the extensive margin.

Traditional trade models generally attempt at answering the "who, when and why" of foreign trade, but fall short of inquiring "how long" trade relations last (Besedes and Prusa, 2006: 266, 267). In other words, the duration of foreign trade is generally overlooked in traditional models or it is assumed that it will last indefinitely once a trade relation is established. For example, in the H-O theorem, trade is based on differences in relative factor equipment and a foreign trade relation lasts as long as these differences exist. However, foreign trade dynamics and specialisation patterns may change over time. Market entry and exit can be important in trade. Therefore, traditional trade models cannot explain whether foreign trade is short or long term (Nitsch, 2009: 135). That said, some trade relationships are lasting or may export a product for several years. In practice, it is more common to observe short-term trade relations. "A country trades a product for some time before stopping. More than half of all trade relations last a one year, and approximately 80% lasts less than five years" (Besedes and Prusa, 2006: 267).

Another type of modelling that considers heterogeneity between products and countries is survival and time analysis in foreign trade. It is important whether some products have been imported repeatedly from a certain country over a relatively long period of time (Nitsch, 2009: 134). A few basic studies can be mentioned in this context. The literature on survival and duration in trade started with Besedes and Prusa (2006). Unlike the gravity models and trade patterns in trade, Besedes and Prusa (2006) studied the duration of US imports through survival analysis. In other words, the authors studied the duration that a country exports a product to the USA. In their study, the authors argued that trade is much more dynamic than believed, and that trade relations are generally very short-term. For example, "The average duration of exporting a product to the USA is very short, ranging from 2 to 4 years. If a country consecutively succeeds in exporting for a few years, it will be able to export its products in the long term" (p.266, 269). The same authors demonstrated that duration or continuity in work increases with the initial trade size. They also found that survival rates were higher for differentiated products compared to their homogeneous counterparts.

Gravity patterns in trade are successful in explaining trading patterns, so, they can also be important for the duration of trade. Trade relations tend to be longer lasting in cases of differentiated products, products with low substitution elasticity and bilateral trade (Nitsch, 2009: 135, 146). Emphasising the importance of duration and/or survival in trade relations and examining the survival time of importing a product from a specific country, Nitsch (2009) investigated the duration of Germany's foreign trade and found that survival in trade is affected by the product type and market structure. In the same study, Nitsch made classifications in terms of country, product and market characteristics. The duration of exporting a product to Germany (or, for Germany, the duration of importing a product) was longer from countries that are geographically close and similar (such as EU countries) and economically large (with high per capita income). The existence of trading pairs or bilateral trade, which has a large share in the German import market, prolongs the duration of trade and makes exit from the market difficult. While the duration of the trade or the hazard rates may increase, especially due to reciprocity or greater confidence in trade policies and increases in the real exchange rate of the foreign country, trade with more distant partners is shorter on average. In general, it is stated that most of the trade relations in German imports are very short lived. Consequently, it was found that while the duration of trade increases with trade value, the duration of a trade relations depends on the specific characteristics of the imported product as well as the nature of the import market.

SELECTED THEORETICAL AND EMPIRICAL STUDIES

In addition to the abovementioned basic publications, there are other studies highlighting the role of margins in international trade. Among them are: Helpman et al. (2008), Bernard et al. (2009), Mukerji (2009), Debaere and Mostashari (2010), Lawness (2010), Besedes and Prusa (2011), Bingzhan (2011), Coughlin and Well (2011), Foster, Poeschl and Stehrer (2011), Auray Eyquem and Poutineau (2012), Kehoe and Ruhl (2013), Markusen (2013), Dutt, Mihov and Van Zandt (2013), Chen (2013), Gao, Wholley and Ren (2014), Silva, Tenreyno and Wei (2014) and Kang (2018). In a study that decomposed the growth of world trade into extensive and intensive margins at the country level, Helpman et al. (2008) stated that the extensive margin indicates the trade growth of new trade relationships, while the intensive margin indicates trade growth in existing trade relations. The same authors also found that intensive margin trade growth is more important to overall trade growth.

Bernard et al. (2009) argued that extensive margins are the basis of changes in imports and exports among foreign trade partners. However, the authors also stated that the change in foreign trade over the period of one year was due to intensive margins. On the other hand, in a study investigating the behavior of US exports and imports during the 1997 Asian financial crisis, the authors found that while there were significant changes in the extensive margin during the crisis, the intensive margin largely explained the decline in exports and increase in imports.

Mukerji (2009) stated that foreign trade barriers hinder the diversity of goods by increasing costs. While there was a certain increase in traded goods already prior to the liberalisation of foreign trade (intensive margin), the trading of new goods increased post-liberalisation (extensive margin). Under these conditions, protectionism in foreign trade comes with a cost. Because, in a free trading structure, many existing goods will no longer be produced due to tariffs. Known as the Romer cost, this phenomenon is the negative welfare effect caused by goods no longer being produced due to foreign trade restrictions.

During their studies, which also considered countries that export to the USA, Debaere and Mostashari (2010) found that foreign trade liberalisation and tariff cuts increased extensive margins. In other words, moderate tariff cuts cause the extensive margin of foreign trade to expand and lead to growth in trade volumes. In a study focusing on the USA market, Lawless (2010) decomposed export growth into the amount of exporting firms (extensive margin) and average export sales (intensive margin), and found that foreign trade costs have a significant effect on the extensive margin (number of firms) yet only a limited effect on the intensive margin (sales per firm). Also, distance has a negative effect on both margins (and hence exports), and while only market size affects the intensive margin, the extensive margin is affected by factors such as language, geography, infrastructure, and other variables that get caught in import barriers.

Besedes and Prusa (2011) compared the export growth of countries based on their performance in the intensive and extensive margins. The authors elaborated on Melitz's (2003) model, in which exporters entered the market bearing sunk and fixed costs and included heterogeneous firms. According to the authors, a firm may enter the export market with inadequate information; however, although this firm can exit the market quickly after finding out about fixed costs, it is possible that this is delayed after the establishment of export relations. Unlike Hummels and Klenow (2005), who advocated the importance of extensive margin, Besedes and Prusa obtained results concerning intensive margins in long-term export growth, and noted the significance of factors like market entry, survival or export time and deepening in explanation of the differences in long-term export performance. They also divided export growth into three different situations: a) creating markets with new trading partners, b) survival or having permanent relationships, c) deepening existing trade relations (deepening of foreign trade relations decreases during weak economic times). Evaluating the effects of each channel on export growth, the authors found that the intensive margin is important for trade growth. In other words, since better survival means increased foreign trade relations, it contributes to the intensive margin; Whereas market entry affects the extensive margin. In conclusion, the authors found that developing countries are not as resilient as developed countries in export market survival and pointed to the importance of acquiring new trade partners for developing countries.

In contrast to other studies, Bingzhan (2011) decomposed trade growth into three margins and by categorising China's export growth into extensive margin, price, quantity or intensive margin, found that 70% of China's growing exports was due to "growth in quantity". In other words, China uses large amounts of capital, natural and cheap resources to achieve this level of export growth. Considering China's large workforce, the quantity-driven growth pattern is consistent with its comparative relative advantage. However, this quantity-based growth pattern causes extensive pollution of the environment as it requires vast amounts of natural resources. These factors will ultimately hinder sustainable growth. Since quantity-driven export growth is unsustainable in the long term, China should shift from quantity-based exports towards an extensive margin and quality-driven export growth. This is because product quality is important for a competitive structure for exports and internal growth.

Coughlin and Well (2011) argued that firms with larger ethnic networks can reduce the cost of becoming exporters or securing direct foreign investment. In a sense, ethnic networks will boost foreign trade flows by reducing information barriers. In addition, noting that the distance variable in foreign trade attraction models may be partial, the authors found that ethnic or informational networks increase foreign trade in intensive margins or that the flexibility of ethnic networks is positive. But in the extensive margin, this flexibility is ineffective, leading to the finding that ethnic networks do not increase trade. Ethnic networks increase exports in already existing trade relations. However, the authors found that there is no link between ethnic networks and entry into an export market.

Considering the effects of preferential trade agreements on increasing trade, Foster, Poeschl, and Stehrer (2011) investigated whether the significant effects of such agreements are based on a change in export diversity (extensive margin) or a change in the volume of available products (intensive margin). The study results show that exports respond positively to trade agreements between countries, whereas most of the increase in exports for large countries is due to the extensive margin (or an increase in the variety of goods traded).

In contrast to other studies, Auray, Eyquem, and Poutineau (2012) investigated the effects of European currency integration on the volatility of the extensive margin of foreign trade. In this study, the authors found that adopting a common currency (i.e. Euro) increased the volatility of the extensive margins of exports in most countries, however, the same margins reduced the volatility in Germany and Italy.

Estimating the effect of innovation (or number of patents) on exports, Chen (2013) decomposed this effect into extensive and intensive margins. Considering that innovation improves the export performance of countries, the author argued that innovation promotes the introduction of new products on the market and that each country expands its range of exported products or innovation increases the extensive margin. On the other hand, Chen also claimed that innovation both improves product quality or can increase productivity and exports, and reports that by increasing their intensive margins, each product leads to a greater export value. In other words, in literature, the extensive margin indicates the extent of exports or the number of products exported from a country, while the intensive margin indicates the depth of exports or the export value of each product from a country. Consequently, estimates indicate that innovation (or the number of patents) will increase the overall export performance of a country and will have a positive and significant effect on both margins, even if the effects are greater on the intensive margin. Splitting the intensive margin into price and quantity indicates that countries with more patents will export higher quantities of goods at higher prices. Innovation also improves the quality of exports. In addition, innovation has more pronounced effects in developing countries with lower gross domestic product per capita. Innovation increases the quality of exported products and stems from the higher intensive margin demand structure. In such countries, innovation also improves the welfare of exporters by increasing the extensive margin.

There is a positive relationship between the extensive margin and total foreign trade growth. In this respect, Keheo and Ruhl (2013) stated that while "extensive margin" is a major factor in the long-term growth of exports in developing countries, this is not the case for developed countries. In addition, the authors noted that foreign trade agreements, liberalisation and structural reforms had significant effects on the extensive margins, whereas periodic fluctuations did not. This study found that trade growth not only occurred in previously untraded goods, but also in goods traded in small quantities.

Markusen (2013) pointed to the extensive margin (or vertical specialisation) since foreign trade mainly consisted of previously untraded goods and services and that most of this new trade was in intermediate goods. The author noted that a growth in trade on the extensive margin might be the result of a decline in a country's trade costs. On the other hand, trade liberalisation can lead to the availability of some previously untraded goods and services or previously traded goods may become non-tradable in some countries. The main purpose of Markusen's study was to demonstrate foreign trade gains based on the growth in trade in the extensive margin. The basic condition of earning from foreign trade is that the global relative prices of the goods traded at the beginning remain the same. A country's increase in foreign trade in the extensive margin usually occurs following a decrease in trade costs. Under these conditions, the number of untraded goods decreases and firms producing such goods exit the market.

In a study investigating the effects of WTO/GATT membership on the intensive and extensive margins of foreign trade, Dutt, Mihov and Van Zandt (2013) claimed that WTO membership reduces the fixed costs of foreign trade rather than the variable costs, and that this increases the extensive margins of exports while having a decreasing effect on the intensive margin. Gao, Wholley, and Ren (2014) grouped China's export growth into three: extensive margin, quantity, and prices. The authors found that, because increasing income requires increasingly higher quality goods, China's export growth was increasingly dependent on price increases, while less on quantity increase. The extensive margin plays the least role in export growth. The same authors stated that there is a negative relationship between the extensive margin and the size of the countries. The extensive margin increases in smaller countries while it decreases in large countries such as China. This is because small countries experience a greater increase in product diversity when importing after trade liberalisation, as they start from a low extensive margin level. The authors stated that China's export growth was less affected by the 2008 global financial crisis compared to the rest of the world, and added that China's first reaction to better export conditions after the crisis was to drop prices and increase volumes or sales. The intensive margin contributes greater to export growth compared to the extensive margin.

Considering factors like distance, borders, colonies, common language, money, and religion, WTO membership and the existence of regional trade agreements, Silva, Tenreyno and Wei (2014) determined the effects of these variables on the extensive margin of foreign trade on a sectoral basis. Finally, Kang (2018) found that, the network of immigrants reduced fixed and variable costs for South Korea, and exports increased or had a positive effect on extensive (quantity of exported goods) and intensive (average value of exported goods) margins through trade-generating effects.

SOLUTIONS AND RECOMMENDATIONS

It is also important to include the effects of government policies into empirical studies i.e., subsidies to exporting firms, exempting small and medium-sized firms from tariffs and non-tariff barriers for specific periods, or spreading the baby industry thesis.

FUTURE RESEARCH DIRECTIONS

Despite the existence of comprehensive literature on the extensive and intensive margins of foreign trade, the literature on the link between survival and deepening and margins is still rather limited. It is expected that analyses on trade margins, survival and deepening will become more widespread with the help of new econometric techniques.

CONCLUSION

Products are homogeneous in traditional foreign trade theories, there is no horizontal and vertical differentiation, and export growth is assumed to be only based on quantity. In the horizontal intra-industry trade theory, although there are numerous product varieties horizontally, export growth can only happen by increasing product diversity because the prices are the same. In the vertical intra-industry trade theory, since products can be differentiated according to different quantities and prices, export growth can occur with increases in quality which is followed by an increase in product prices (Bingzhan, 2011).

This study shows that various factors (attraction, common religion, language, race, money, colony, WTO / GATT membership, number of innovations or patents, ethnic or informational networks, financial crises, trade barriers, trade liberalisation, etc.) play a role in increasing exports and decomposing them into extensive and intensive margins. An overview of the studies shows that extensive and intensive margins can be relatively effective to a greater or lesser degree in the growth of exports. With the emergence of new-new trade theories following Melitz (2003) and an increase in studies based on industry and firm specific data sets, it becomes important to decompose the heterogeneity of firms and products in the growth of trade at a global and national scale, the role of extensive and intensive margins, and more specifically, price, quantity and quality. In this context, extensive and intensive margins are being combined with the survival of firms and the deepening of exports in international trade theory. Therefore, this literature survey reconfirms the need for comprehensively addressing international trade theories based on both micro and macro data sets.

REFERENCES

Adelon, D. B. & Kakinaka, M. (2018). Extensive and intensive margins of exports: the case of the Philippines. *Asia Pacific Journal of Accounting and Economies, 25*(83-4), 404-418. doi:10.1080/16081625.2017.1293551

Amiti, M., & Freund, C. (2008). The anatomy of china's export growth. *World Bank Policy Research Working Paper*, *4628*(May), 1–26.

Armington, P. S. (1969). A theory of demand for products distinguished by place of production. *IMF Staff Papers*, *16*(1), 159–178. doi:10.2307/3866403

Auray, S., Eyquem, A., & Poutineau, J. C. (2012). The effect of a common currency on the volatility of the extensive margin of trade. *Journal of International Money and Finance*, *31*(5), 1156–1179. doi:10.1016/j.jimonfin.2011.12.016

Bergin, P. R., & Corsetti, G. (2008). The extensive margin and monetary policy. *Journal of Monetary Economics*, *55*(7), 1222–1237. doi:10.1016/j.jmoneco.2008.08.011

Bernard, A. B., Jensen, J. B., Redding, S. J., & Schott, P. K. (2009). The margins of US trade. *The American Economic Review*, *99*(2), 487–493. doi:10.1257/aer.99.2.487

Bernard, A. B., Jensen, J. B., & Schott, P. K. (2006). Trade costs, firms and productivity. *Journal of Monetary Economics*, *53*(5), 917–937. doi:10.1016/j.jmoneco.2006.05.001

Besedes, T., & Prusa, T. J. (2006). Ins, outs and the duration of trade. *The Canadian Journal of Economics. Revue Canadienne d'Economique*, *39*(1), 266–295. doi:10.1111/j.0008-4085.2006.00347.x

Besedes, T., & Prusa, T. J. (2011). The role of extensive and intensive margins and export growth. *Journal of Development Economics*, *96*(2), 371–379. doi:10.1016/j.jdeveco.2010.08.013

Bingzhan, S. (2011). Extensive margin, quantity and price in china's export growth. *China Economic Review*, *22*(2), 233–243. doi:10.1016/j.chieco.2011.01.007

Chaney, T. (2005). *Productivity overshooting: the dynamic impact of trade opening with heterogeneous firms*. Retrieved from https://www.researchgate.net/profile/Thomas-Chaney/publication/228961536_Productivity_Overshooting_The_Dynamic_Impact_of_Trade_Opening_with_Heterogeneous_Firms/links/0deec51c06bf8e653e000000/Productivity-Overshooting-The-Dynamic-Impact-of-Trade-Opening-with-Heterogeneous-Firms.pdf

Chen, W.C. (2013). The Extensive and intensive margins of exports: The race of innovation. *the World Economy, 36*(5), 607-635. doi:10.1111/twec.12032

Coughlin, C. C., & Well, H. J. (2011). Ethnic networks and trade: Intensive versus extensive margins. *Economics Letters*, *113*(1), 73–75. doi:10.1016/j.econlet.2011.05.023

Debaere, P., & Mostashari, S. (2010). Do tariffs matter for the extensive margin of international trade? An Empirical Analysis. *Journal of International Economics*, *81*(2), 163–169. doi:10.1016/j.jinteco.2010.03.005

Dutt, P., Mihov, I., & Van Zandt, T. (2013). The effect of WTO on the extensive and intensive margins of trade. *Journal of International Economics*, *91*(2), 204–219. doi:10.1016/j.jinteco.2013.08.001

Eaton, J., & Kortum, S. (2002). Technology, geography and trade. *Econometrica*, *70*(5), 1741–1779. doi:10.1111/1468-0262.00352

Felbermayr, G. J., & Kohler, W. (2006). Exploring the Intensive and extensive margins of world trade. *Review of World Economics*, *142*(4), 642–674. doi:10.100710290-006-0087-3

Flam, H., & Helpman, E. (1987). Vertical product differentiation and north-south trade. *The American Economic Review*, *77*(5), 810–822.

Foster, N., Poeschl, J., & Stchrer, R. (2011). The impact of preferential trade agreements on the margins of international trade. *Economic Systems*, *35*(1), 84–97. doi:10.1016/j.ecosys.2010.11.004

Gao, Y. J., Whalley, J., & Ren, Y. (2014). Decomposing China's export growth into extensive margin, export quality and quantity effects. *China Economic Review*, *29*, 19–26. doi:10.1016/j.chieco.2014.02.001

Helpman, E., Melitz, M., & Rubinstein, Y. (2008). Estimating trade flows: Trading partners and trading volumes. *The Quarterly Journal of Economics*, *123*(2), 441–487. doi:10.1162/qjec.2008.123.2.441

Hummels, D., & Klenow, P. J. (2005). The variety and quality of a nation's exports. *The American Economic Review*, *95*(3), 704–723. doi:10.1257/0002828054201396

Kang, K. (2018). The Effect of immigrants on the extensive and intensive margins of trade. *Applied Economics Letters*, *25*(2), 92–95. doi:10.1080/13504851.2017.1299092

Kehoe, T. J., & Ruhl, K. J. (2013). How Important is the new goods margin in international trade? *Journal of Political Economy*, *121*(2), 358–392. doi:10.1086/670272

Krugman, P. R. (1979). Increasing returns, monopolistic competition, and international trade. *Journal of International Economics*, *9*(4), 469–479. doi:10.1016/0022-1996(79)90017-5

Krugman, P. R. (1980). Scale Economies, product differentiation, and the pattern of trade. *The American Economic Review*, *70*(5), 950–959.

Krugman, P. R. (1981). Intraindustry specialization and the gains from trade. *Journal of Political Economy*, *89*(5), 959–973. doi:10.1086/261015

Lawless, M. (2010). Deconstructing gravity: Trade costs and extensive and intensive margins. *The Canadian Journal of Economics. Revue Canadienne d'Economique*, *43*(4), 1149–1172. doi:10.1111/j.1540-5982.2010.01609.x

Manova, K. (2008). Credit constraints, equity market liberalization and international trade. *Journal of International Economics*, *76*(1), 33–47. doi:10.1016/j.jinteco.2008.03.008

Markusen, J. R. (2013). Expansion of trade at the extensive margin: A general gains-from-trade result and illustrative examples. *Journal of International Economics*, *89*(1), 262–270. doi:10.1016/j.jinteco.2012.04.007

Melitz, M. J. (2003). The Impact of trade on intra-industry reallocations and aggregate industry productivity. *Econometrica, 71*(6), 1695–1725. doi:10.1111/1468-0262.00467

Mukerji, P. (2009). Trade liberalization and the extensive margin. *Scottish Journal of Political Economy, 56*(2), 141–166. doi:10.1111/j.1467-9485.2009.00478.x

Nitsch, V. (2009). Die another day: Duration in German import trade. *Review of World Economics, 145*(1), 133–154. doi:10.100710290-009-0008-3

Silva, J. M. C. S., Tenreyno, S., & Wei, K. (2014). Estimating the extensive margin of trade. *Journal of International Economics, 93*(1), 67–75. doi:10.1016/j.jinteco.2013.12.001

Yi, K. M. (2003). Can vertical specialization explain the growth of world trade? *Journal of Political Economy, 111*(1), 52–102. doi:10.1086/344805

ADDITIONAL READING

Alvarez, R., & Vergara, S. (2013). Trade exposure, survival and growth of small and medium-size firms. *International Review of Economics & Finance, 25*, 185–201. doi:10.1016/j.iref.2012.07.010

Baggs, J. (2005). Firm survival and exit in response to trade liberalization. *The Canadian Journal of Economics. Revue Canadienne d'Economique, 38*(4), 1364–1383. doi:10.1111/j.0008-4085.2005.00328.x

Chang, E. C. C., & Wu, W. C. (2016). Preferential trade aggrements, income inequality, and authoritarian survival. *Political Research Quarterly, 69*(2), 281–294. doi:10.1177/1065912916636688

Corcoles, D., Diaz-Mora, C., & Gandoy, R. (2015). Export survival in global production chains. *World Economy, 38*(10), 1526–1554. doi:10.1111/twec.12249

Dai, M., Harris, R., Lu, Y., & Lu, H. (2016). Exports and firm survival: Do trade regime and productivity matter? *Applied Economics Letters, 23*(6), 457–460. doi:10.1080/13504851.2015.1080800

Wagner, J. (2012). International trade and firm performance: A survey of empirical studies since 2006. *Review of World Economics, 148*(2), 235–267. doi:10.100710290-011-0116-8

KEY TERMS AND DEFINITIONS

Diversity and Trade Volume: Diversity refers to the diversity of products in the range of traded goods or making new products available to foreign trade partners on top of the existing ones. Foreign trade volume is the sum of export and import volumes. Diversity contributes to the extensive margin size of foreign trade.

Export Growth: The increase in the amount of world and / or country-specific exports.

Extensive Margin: The export of previously non-exported goods and the re-development or increase of trade between countries that previously did not trade with each other, and also the abandonment of existing ones. Export growth in this type of margin is usually due to an increase in product diversity.

Foreign Trade Barriers: Tariffs and quotas are foreign trade policy instruments implemented by countries to limit their imports. Tariffs reduce the demand for imported goods by rising prices of such goods. Quotas restrict the quantity of imported goods. The basic aim of both instruments is to reduce foreign trade deficits or to increase foreign trade balance by reducing or preventing imports.

Gravity: Foreign trade relations weaken with greater geographical distance between the countries, whereas foreign trade relations improve with closer proximity decreases or there is attraction.

Intensive Margin: The increase or decrease of foreign trade due to changes in traded goods. In this margin, there is a pre-existing foreign trade relation between countries which has been increasing over time.

New-New Trade Theories: Refers to the theories developed since the seminal work of Melitz (2003) and include the heterogeneity of firms and monopolistic competitive models. In this context, product and firm level analyses have gained considerable popularity.

Survival and Duration in Foreign Trade: Refers to the duration of foreign trade between countries. The longer a foreign trade relationship is maintained, the longer a country has survived in foreign trade. Time in foreign trade refers to the uninterrupted existence of a trade relationship between countries. In general, the Kaplan-Meier survival function is used for predictions in in the literature.

Traditional Trade Theories: In international economics, these theories include those starting from Adam Smith, Ricardo and Heckscher-Ohlin (H-O) factor proportions theorem and the new trade theories derived from it. In this context, there is a process extending from product period analysis to technological gap theorems.

Chapter 8
How the Global Financial Crisis and International Trade Affected Corporate Decisions?
International Evidence

Hasan Tekin
Karabuk University, Turkey

ABSTRACT

This chapter, first, draws an overview of the theoretical and conceptual framework of corporate decisions in the global financial crisis (GFC) context. Then, it shows the connectedness of corporate finance and international trade. Finally, employing a rich dataset, this chapter assesses the impact of international trade as well as the GFC on corporate financial decisions, particularly cash holdings, debt financing, and dividend payouts over the period 2002-2016. The findings show that international trade significantly affects corporate decisions. Firms with higher trade countries have higher debt level but lower cash and dividends across the globe. During the GFC, the positive impact of trade on debt shifts to negative. Also, trade has a positive effect on both cash and debt in the aftermath of the GFC. Taken together, international trade as an institutional setting influences corporate decisions and its role on cash, debt, and dividend differ during and after the GFC.

INTRODUCTION

Research on international trade has focused on the role of economies of scale and cross-country differences in productivity and factor endowments in predicting gains from trade and the pattern of aggregate trade flows according to comparative advantage. Additional insights have emerged from introducing firm heterogeneity in trade participation when there are fixed and variable trade costs. (Foley & Manova, 2015, p. 1)

Country-level factors may influence corporate finance decisions, which capture firm heterogeneity. Specifically, international trade has also an impact on corporate decisions as Foley & Manova (2015)

DOI: 10.4018/978-1-7998-8314-2.ch008

state. After the irrelevant proposals of Modigliani & Miller (1958, 1963), the literature of corporate finance literature grows to extend by examining financial crises, such as the 1997-1998 Asian Crisis, 2000 dot-com Crisis, the global financial crisis of 2007-2009 (GFC), 2010-2012 Eurozone Debt Crisis. Notably, the GFC has profoundly affected economics at both country-level and firm-level. However, the question of how the joint effect of the GFC and international trade on corporate decisions has not been sufficiently investigated by the literature yet, that is why this chapter intends to fill this gap in the literature.

To date, while some research has reviewed the literature on the relationship between international trade and corporate finance, no single study exists which empirically investigates this relationship in a financial crisis context.

The GFC originated firstly in the subprime mortgage market in the United States (US) in the second half of 2007, reached its peak worldwide following the collapse of Lehman Brothers in September 2008 and sustained its effect until June 2009 (Kahle & Stulz, 2013). The GFC has spread across trade links, international banks and particularly financial markets around the globe and influenced many economic sectors (Ahn et al., 2011; Berkmen et al., 2012). The GFC also affected firms across the globe, whereas other financial crises (1997-1998 Asian Crisis, 2010-2012 Eurozone Debt Crisis) only had impacts that were confined to companies or within specific regions (Mian & Sufi, 2015). Also, the GFC is also known as the Great Recession (Gertler & Gilchrist, 2018) because it has been the biggest recession since 1929, the Great Depression. Therefore, to understand the impact of the GFC on corporate decisions may open new insights new insights to realize what the world economy should project on the link between trade and corporate decisions in the aftermath of Covid-19.

Specifically, Foley & Manova (2015) review the emerging new literature regarding the association between international trade and corporate finance, but the empirical analyses of this literature remain untested. Therefore, this chapter empirically investigates the relationship between international trade and corporate decisions, cash, debt and dividend in particular by considering the role of the GFC in this relationship across the globe.

Specifically, this chapter first reviews the discussions in corporate finance literature in the context of the GFC by considering international trade and then empirically assesses the question of how the GFC and international trade affected corporate decisions employing the international data, including 82 countries, from 2002 to 2016.

Employing fixed effects, which overcome unobserved heterogeneity, the findings show that while trade is negatively related to cash holdings and dividend payouts, it is positively related to debt financing. The picture changes with the rise of the GFC. Specifically, though the positive impact of trade on debt financing gains significance from pre- to post-GFC but shifts to negative during the GFC. Next, the negative effect of trade on cash holdings before the GFC becomes positive after the GFC. Last, the role of trade on dividend payouts does not differ across subperiods. In sum, international trade has different effects on corporate decisions and these effects vary by the GFC owing to fluctuations in the trade mix that comprises export and import.

This chapter contributes to the literature in two ways. First, the role of trade on three specific corporate decisions, cash, debt and dividend is firstly assessed with the rich panel data set across the globe. Second, the joint impact of the post-GFC and trade on corporate finance may open new insights to understand what the world economy should project on the relationship between trade and corporate decisions after Covid-19.

The findings of this chapter also have several implications. First, managers should consider the role of trade on corporate decisions with the existence of financial crises. Next, investors should take into account trade volume and corporate policies of firms when and where to invest in. Then, policymakers should count enforcement of trade regulations. They may show tolerance on regulations during exogenous shocks like Covid-19. Finally, practitioners and researchers should consider the GFC as a milestone because of its destructive effect and imply for the Covid-19.

The rest of the chapter proceeds as follows: the section of controversies in the literature presents and evaluates the impact of the GFC on corporate decisions by showing the place of international trade on this equation. Then the research question is specified. Next, the section of methodology and data introduces panel methods, empirical models for this chapter and data set. After, the empirical results section presents and discusses the results of both univariate and multivariate analyses. Lastly, future research directions recommend the possible research, and the conclusion concludes the chapter.

BACKGROUND

Controversies in the Literature

International Trade and the Global Financial Crisis

Several papers examine the outcomes of the GFC for the real economy by discussing two main channels: trade channels and financial channels (Berkmen et al., 2012; D'Amato, 2020; Demirgüç-Kunt et al., 2020). Also, Berkmen et al. (2012, p. 44) point out other channels: underlying vulnerabilities and financial structure, and the overall policy framework.

With the rise of credit recession, developed markets have severely filled their demand from developing markets, which have a concentrated trade connection with developed markets. For example, since the GFC arose from the US, trade channels were more influenced by the shrinking of export to the US (Shikimi & Yamada, 2019). During the recession, trade channels reversely influenced borrowing, but they did not affect the investment policy and trade credit. Trade channels also have an impact on the credit policy of banks, not the financial decisions of firms (D'Amato, 2020). The literature employs trade openness, trade composition or trade direction to measure trade channels (Berkmen et al., 2012, p. 44).

Previous studies use financial openness, remittances' share, bank credits from developed markets and capital account constraints to estimate financial channels (Berkmen et al., 2012). Since the outset of the GFC in financial industries, the financial link between developed and developing countries has severely damaged. More recently, D'Amato (2020) shows that firms with lower cash and higher leverage minimized the drop in equity financing. Also, he finds that firms with lower cash accomplish the shortening the number of accounts receivables in the time of the GFC and its aftermath, whereas the GFC had a restricted effect on trade credit funding. Financially constrained firms and firms with lower cash provided liquidity from financially unconstrained firms and firms with higher cash as noted by Garcia-Appendini & Montoriol-Garriga (2013). Furthermore, cash holdings had had an impact on financial channels during the GFC. Notably, while smaller firms and firms with higher leverage opted to hold cash in a crisis and post-crisis periods, firms with lower leverage managed to raise their cash level (Shikimi & Yamada, 2019). Lastly, the financial channel reversely influenced the investment policy of firms with lower cash with the rise of the GFC.

Some emerging markets entered the crisis at risk, while others prepared for possible turbulences by benefiting from advantageous circumstances in the world market (Berkmen et al., 2012). The concentration of production in pre-GFC was raised to access external finance. Based on the external debt, the quick expansion of debt in developing countries has been encouraged across the globe. Several problems that are associated with balance sheets, currency devaluation, the reverse of cash flows and the crunch of credits originated at the outbreak of the crisis (D'Amato, 2020). Consequently, countries with complicated financial structures may have higher spillovers that are raised from financial channels.

The last channel is the power of the policy framework. Previous research measures this channel using variables capturing features of overall quality of institutions, fiscal and monetary policy and exchange rates (Berkmen et al., 2012). Countries with weaker monetary and fiscal positions, in pre-GFC, encountered higher output failures after the GFC (Chen et al., 2019). Countries with easily adjustable exchange rates are anticipated to control turbulences more quickly. Otherwise, higher losses in GDP arise with the inflexible exchange rate.

Cash Policy

Companies may increase their cash level when uncertainty arises. Song & Lee (2012) debate that firms hold more cash with the increase of cash flow risk. Opler et al. (1999) indicate that firms with higher cash flow volatility and growth raise their cash balances as supported by the precautionary motive. Cash holdings may be used as a hedging instrument when both information asymmetry and uncertainty rise as proven by the precautionary motive. Keynes (1936) argues that firms should save cash to mitigate difficulties when an exogenous shock arises. In a period of crisis, tightened and costly external finance forces firms to accumulate more cash. Consequently, firms substitute equity offerings, bond offerings and bank loans with cash holdings due to uncertainty (Song & Lee, 2012, p. 617). Besides, Shiau et al. (2018) show that Chinese and Taiwanese firms minimized their investment and raised their equities to increase their liquidity in the post-GFC as a response to the GFC. Hence, they take precaution for any uncertainty in future.

Agency costs and information asymmetry maintain their presence in imperfect markets. Thus, debt financing becomes quite challenging with the darkness of the GFC. Notably, following macroeconomic shocks, the precautionary motive proposes that financially constrained firms save more cash than unconstrained firms because of raised information asymmetry (Shiau et al., 2018; Tekin & Polat, 2020c). This case also affects the demand function for cash. Song & Lee (2012, p. 619) show that increased information asymmetry in the aftermath of turbulence influences the demand function for cash. Namely, the shift in East Asian firms' demand function for cash causes the holding of more cash of firms.

Debt Policy

While a positive association between uncertainty and asymmetric information occurs, the long-term debt substitutes with short-term debt as a result of an increase in information asymmetry during the turbulence. Furthermore, previous research argues that adverse selection and moral hazard as both types of information asymmetry are higher for smaller and private firms (D'Amato, 2020). Hence, in times of the credit supply shock, these firms face problems in accessing external finance due to its costs and making their investments.

While firms tend to raise the level of equity in a time of growth, they change their financing mix of debt and equity and decrease their borrowing when a credit recession arises. Previous research analyses the impact of the GFC on debt financing and they show mixed results. Some research shows a reverse relationship between the GFC and debt financing (Gonzalez, 2015; Zeitun et al., 2017; Van Hoang et al., 2018; Mimouni et al., 2019; D'Amato, 2020; Demirgüç-Kunt et al., 2020; Polat, 2020; Tekin & Polat, 2020d), whereas others demonstrate a positive association (Alves & Francisco, 2015; Daskalakis et al., 2017; Tekin & Polat, 2021a, 2021b).

Dividend Policy

Since dividend policy also depends on other financial linkages such as debt or investment, different scenarios may occur with an exogenous shock. Bliss et al. (2015, p. 522) make three predictions on dividends and repurchases to respond to the GFC. First, firms cut corporate payouts due to the rising costs of external finance. By employing the substitution form of payouts, the reduction in repurchases is more than that in dividends. Next, firms increase corporate payouts and drop cash holdings due to the reduction in demand for stocks. Thus, higher agency costs of liquidation negatively affect growth opportunities. Last, firms reduce corporate payouts by retaining more cash for further investment because of a keen rise in uncertainty. Bliss et al. (2015) demonstrate that the number of dividends (repurchases) nonpayers increased by 19% (37%) during the GFC. The fall in corporate payouts is replaced with an increase in cash holding or investment.

MAIN FOCUS OF THE CHAPTER

Research Question

Financial crises have significant influences on corporate financial behavior. When a financial crisis breaks, firms may take precautions by increasing borrowing, burning cash stocks or cutting dividends. To understand the impact of the GFC and international trade on corporate financial decisions, this study ask the research question as follows:

- How does international trade affect the policies of cash, debt and dividends before, during and after the GFC?

METHODOLOGY AND DATA

Methodology

The corporate finance literature largely utilizes methods of both cross-sectional and time-series called panel (longitudinal) data[1] (Lintner, 1956; Rajan & Zingales, 1995; La Porta et al., 2000; Frank & Goyal, 2009; Pinkowitz et al., 2016; Tekin, 2020b).

Panel data include three main static panel data methods:

1. **The Pooled Ordinary Least Squares (POLS)** [2],
2. **The Fixed Effects (FE)** [3],
3. **The Random Effects (RE)** [4].

Panel data includes group *i* and time *t*; so, FE or RE that is generally employed by more recent studies (Byrne & O'Connor, 2017; Chen et al., 2018; Tekin 2020a) may have more explanatory power than POLS. Since previous research commonly uses larger groups *i* and smaller time *t* (Fan et al. 2012; Oztekin 2015; Bates et al. 2018; Tekin & Polat, 2020b), FE is preferable to RE which can be demonstrated by some diagnostic tests.[5] However, if one of the right-hand side variables is time-invariant, RE is the proper method rather than FE (Seifert and Gonenc 2016, 2018). Specifically, leverage, short-term debt and cash holdings are continuous dependent variables and there is no time-invariant explanatory variable; therefore, FE may be the proper method for the static panel analyses in.

Empirical Strategy

Regarding the empirical strategy, three basic models are settled to assess the role of trade on cash, debt and dividend, respectively.

$$\begin{aligned} Cash_{ij,t} = {} & \beta_0 + \beta_1 Trade_{j,t} + \beta_2 Debt_{i,t} + \beta_3 Div_{i,t} + \beta_4 Size_{i,t} \\ & + \beta_5 Grow_{i,t} + \beta_6 Inv_{i,t} + \beta_7 Nwc_{i,t} + \beta_8 Cflow_{i,t} + \alpha_{ij} F_i + \alpha_t Y_t + \varepsilon_{ij,t} \end{aligned} \tag{1}$$

where, $Cash_{ij,t}$ is cash holdings for firm i and country j at time t, $Trade_{j,t}$ is trade for country j at time t, $Debt_{i,t}$ is debt financing for firm i at time t, $Div_{i,t}$ is dividend payout for firm i at time t, $Size_{i,t}$ is firm size for firm i at time t, $Grow_{i,t}$ is growth opportunities for firm i at time t, $Inv_{i,t}$ is investment for firm i at time t, $Nwc_{i,t}$ is net working capital for firm i at time t, $Cflow_{i,t}$ is cash flow for firm i at time t, αi is firm fixed effects, αt is year fixed effects and $\varepsilon ij,t$ is the error term.

$$\begin{aligned} Debt_{ij,t} = {} & \beta_0 + \beta_1 Trade_{j,t} + \beta_2 Cash_{i,t} + \beta_3 Div_{i,t} + \beta_4 Size_{i,t} + \beta_5 Grow_{i,t} \\ & + \beta_6 Prof_{i,t} + \beta_7 Tan_{i,t} + \beta_8 Tax_{i,t} + \beta_9 IMdebt_{i,t} + \alpha_{ij} F_i + \alpha_t Y_t + \varepsilon_{ij,t} \end{aligned} \tag{2}$$

where, $Debt_{ij,t}$ is debt financing for firm i and country j at time t, $Prof_{i,t}$ is profitability for firm i at time t, $Tan_{i,t}$ is tangibility for firm i at time t, $Tax_{i,t}$ is effective tax rate for firm i at time t and $IMdebt_{i,t}$ is industry median of debt for firm i at time t.

$$Div_{ij,t} = \beta_0 + \beta_1 Trade_{j,t} + \beta_2 Cash_{i,t} + \beta_3 Debt_{i,t} + \beta_4 Size_{i,t} + \beta_5 Grow_{i,t} + \sum Industry + \sum Year + v_{ij} + \varepsilon_{ij,t} \tag{3}$$

where, $Div_{ij,t}$ is dividend payouts for firm i and country j at time t, Σ*Industry* are set of dummies for industry, Σ*Year* are set of dummies for year and v_{ij} are controlling random effects for unobservable factors.

The full models that include interaction terms of Pre x Trade, Post x Trade and Crisis x Trade to investigate the joint impact of the GFC and international trade on cash, debt and dividend are as follows:

$$\begin{aligned} Cash_{ij,t} = {} & \beta_0 + \beta_1 Trade_{j,t} + \beta_2 \left(Pre_t x Trade_{j,t} \right) + \beta_3 \left(Post_t x Trade_{j,t} \right) + \beta_4 Debt_{i,t} + \beta_5 Div_{i,t} \\ & + \beta_6 Size_{i,t} + \beta_7 Grow_{i,t} + \beta_8 Inv_{i,t} + \beta_9 Nwc_{i,t} + \beta_{10} Cflow_{i,t} + \beta_{11} Pre_t + \beta_{12} Post_t + \alpha_{ij} F_i + \varepsilon \end{aligned} \tag{4}$$

where, $Pre_t xTrade_{k,t}$ is the interaction term of Pre and Trade, $Post_t xTrade_{j,t}$ is the interaction term of Post and Trade, Pre_t is the period dummy for pre-crisis and $Post_t$ is the period dummy for post-crisis.

$$\begin{aligned} Cash_{ij,t} &= \beta_0 + \beta_1 Trade_{j,t} + \beta_2\left(Crisis_t xTrade_{j,t}\right) + \beta_3 Debt_{i,t} + \beta_4 Div_{i,t} + \beta_5 Size_{i,t} \\ &+ \beta_6 Grow_{i,t} + \beta_7 Inv_{i,t} + \beta_8 Nwc_{i,t} + \beta_9 Cflow_{i,t} + \beta_{10} Crisis_t + \alpha_{ij} F_i + \varepsilon_{ij,t} \end{aligned} \tag{5}$$

where, $Crisis_t xTrade_{j,t}$ is the interaction term of Crisis and Trade and $Crisis_t$ is the period dummy for crisis.

$$\begin{aligned} Debt_{ij,t} &= \beta_0 + \beta_1 Trade_{j,t} + \beta_2\left(Pre_t xTrade_{j,t}\right) + \beta_3\left(Post_t xTrade_{j,t}\right) \\ &+ \beta_4 Cash_{i,t} + \beta_5 Div_{i,t} + \beta_6 Size_{i,t} + \beta_7 Grow_{i,t} + \beta_8 Prof_{i,t} + \beta_9 Tan_{i,t} \\ &+ \beta_{10} Tax_{i,t} + \beta_{11} IMdebt_{i,t} + \beta_{12} Pre_t + \beta_{13} Post_t + \alpha_{ij} F_i + \varepsilon_{ij,t} \end{aligned} \tag{6}$$

$$\begin{aligned} Debt_{ij,t} &= \beta_0 + \beta_1 Trade_{j,t} + \beta_2\left(Crisis_t xTrade_{j,t}\right) + \beta_3 Cash_{i,t} + \beta_4 Div_{i,t} + \beta_5 Size_{i,t} \\ &+ \beta_6 Grow_{i,t} + \beta_7 Prof_{i,t} + \beta_8 Tan_{i,t} + \beta_9 Tax_{i,t} + \beta_{10} IMdebt_{i,t} + \beta_{11} Pre_t + \alpha_{ij} F_i + \varepsilon_{ij,t} \end{aligned} \tag{7}$$

$$\begin{aligned} Div_{ij,t} &= \beta_0 + \beta_1 Trade_{j,t} + \beta_2\left(Pre_t xTrade_{j,t}\right) + \beta_3\left(Post_t xTrade_{j,t}\right) + \beta_4 Cash_{i,t} \\ &+ \beta_5 Debt_{i,t} + \beta_6 Size_{i,t} + \beta_7 Grow_{i,t} + \beta_8 Pre_t + \beta_9 Post_t + \sum Industry + v_{ij} + \varepsilon_{ij,t} \end{aligned} \tag{8}$$

$$\begin{aligned} Div_{ij,t} &= \beta_0 + \beta_1 Trade_{j,t} + \beta_2\left(Crisis_t xTrade_{j,t}\right) + \beta_3 Cash_{i,t} \\ &+ \beta_4 Debt_{i,t} + \beta_5 Size_{i,t} + \beta_6 Grow_{i,t} + \beta_7 Crisis_t + \sum Industry + v_{ij} + \varepsilon_{ij,t} \end{aligned} \tag{9}$$

Data

Since this chapter concentrates on the association between international trade and corporate finance, it includes both country- and firm-level variables. First, regarding country-level data, trade is obtained from the World Bank dividing by gross domestic product (GDP). Next, considering firm-level data, Worldscope data is retrieved from Datastream International database, which is useful to obtain either accounting or market data as hitherto carried out by recent research (Tekin, 2020a; Tekin & Polat, 2020a). The steps in the construction of the panel data as follows. First, non-financial firms are chosen excluding firms in the financial sector (banks, insurance firms, real estate firms and financial services) and the utility sector (electricity, gas, water and multi-utility firms), which have different accounting structures as conducted by recent research (Bates et al., 2018; Coldbeck & Ozkan, 2018). Then, all firms with any missing observations for any variable in the model during the sample period have been dropped.

The firms have been chosen for the period 2002-2016. These requirements result in 344,434 firm-years representing 33,803 sample firms across 82 countries.

Variables

Since this chapter aims to analyze the impact of trade on corporate decisions, cash holdings, debt financing and dividend payouts are dependent variables. The main explanatory variable is the trade that consists of export and import. By following the empirical literature, control explanatory variables are included in models.

Regarding control factors of corporate decisions, first, Rajan & Zingales (1995) determine the firm size, profitability, growth and tangibility as the baseline of debt financing. Frank & Goyal (2009) add the industry median of debt into the model. More recently, Tekin (2020c) specifies that effective tax rate, cash holdings and dividend payouts may affect debt financing. Therefore, this chapter includes these variables as controls of debt financing. Next, this chapter consists of the firm size, growth, dividend payouts, investment, net working capital and cash flows as control factors of cash holdings by following Opler et al. (1999). Last, Fama & French (2001) determine firm size, growth and profitability as main factors of dividend payouts, that is why this research includes these variables in addition to cash and debt as determinants of dividend payouts (Tekin & Polat, 2020b).

To understand the role of the GFC on corporate decisions, this chapter contains three period dummies which are pre (2002-2006), crisis (2007-2009) and post (2010-2016). Variable definitions are presented in Table 1.

Descriptive Statistics

Table 2 presents descriptive statistics for the entire period (2002-2016) and subperiods that are pre (2002-2006), crisis (2007-2009) and post (2010-2016). While the mean of dividend payouts decreases, that of cash holdings increases after the GFC. Since trade volumes rise with the high speed of globalization, trade increases despite the GFC over time.

The country list of the sample, observation numbers and the mean of cash, debt, dividend and trade across countries is presented in Table 3.

Correlation Matrix

Since the variance inflation factor (VIF) shows whether the data set face any multicollinearity issue, Table 4 indicates that all VIF values smaller than 5. Therefore, the entire period and subperiods do not suffer from the multicollinearity problem.

Table 1. Variable definitions

Variables	Symbols	Definitions
Cash ratio	Cash	Cash and short–term investments (WC02001) / Total assets (WC02999)
Debt ratio	Debt	Total debt (WC03255) / Total assets (WC02999)
Dividend ratio	Div	Cash dividends paid (WC04551) / Total assets (WC02999)
International trade	Trade	(Export + Import) / Gross domestic product (World Bank)
Firm size	Size	The log of total assets (WC02999)
Growth opportunities	Growth	[Total assets (WC02999) – Book value of equity (WC03501) + Market value of equity (WC08001)] / Total assets (WC02999)
Tangibility	Tan	Net property, plant and equipment (WC02501)/ Total assets (WC02999)
Profitability	Prof	Earnings before interest and tax (WC18191)/ Total assets (WC02999)
Effective tax rate	Tax	Total tax paid (WC01451)/ Total taxable income (WC01401)
Industry median debt	IMdebt	Industry median of total debt/ total assets by industry and year
Investment	Inv	Capital expenditures (WC04601) / Total assets (WC02999)
Net working capital	Nwc	[Current assets (WC02201) – Current liabilities (WC03101) – Cash and short-term investments (WC02001)] / Total assets (WC02999)
Cash flow	Cflow	[Total taxable income (WC01401) + Depreciation (WC01151)] / Total assets (WC02999)
Pre-crisis period	Pre	Dummy variable equals one for years 2002-2006, otherwise zero
Crisis period	Crisis	Dummy variable equals one for years 2007-2009, otherwise zero
Post-crisis period	Post	Dummy variable equals one for years 2010-2016, otherwise zero

Source: Worldscope

EMPIRICAL ANALYSES

Univariate Analyses

The whole sample is divided into high- and low-trade as above- and below-median of the trade by country and year (La Porta et al., 2000). Then, the means of all three corporate decisions across pre-crisis (2002-2006) and post-crisis (2010-2016) are presented in Table 5.

First, cash is lower for firms in high-trade countries. In other words, firms in high-trade countries hold less cash. However, since the rising importance of cash mainly during an exogenous shock, firms in high-trade countries increase their cash stocks more than those in low-trade countries.

Second, similar to cash, firms in high-trade countries have lower debt, but this picture differs from cash after the GFC. Specifically, while firms in high-trade countries drop their debt level, it is vice versa for those in low-trade countries.

Last, firms in high-trade countries pay out more dividends. Nevertheless, firms in both high- and low-trade countries decline their dividend payments in the aftermath of the GFC.

Overall, corporate decisions differ with the existence of trade and the GFC.

Table 2. Descriptive statistics

	Trade	Cash	Debt	Div	Size	Grow	Prof	Inv	Tan	Tax	Nwc	Cflow	IMdebt
2002-2016													
Mean	0.812	0.189	0.225	0.055	13.703	0.760	0.040	0.007	0.307	0.170	0.002	-0.046	0.170
SD	0.844	0.206	0.228	0.092	3.433	1.466	0.341	0.036	0.247	0.474	0.226	0.236	0.059
Minimum	0.207	0.000	0.000	0.000	4.762	0.088	-0.915	0.000	0.000	-3.073	-0.649	-0.823	0.001
Median	0.551	0.118	0.175	0.027	13.814	0.527	0.063	0.000	0.259	0.175	0.010	0.006	0.189
Maximum	4.426	0.940	1.000	0.897	31.502	20.876	0.951	0.477	0.977	3.361	0.863	0.933	0.315
2002-2006													
Mean	0.773	0.181	0.227	0.059	13.479	0.766	0.051	0.007	0.315	0.187	0.004	-0.039	0.177
SD	0.808	0.200	0.224	0.093	3.416	1.431	0.339	0.034	0.235	0.452	0.220	0.235	0.061
Minimum	0.207	0.000	0.000	0.000	4.762	0.088	-0.915	0.000	0.000	-3.073	-0.649	-0.823	0.003
Median	0.523	0.111	0.182	0.030	13.566	0.542	0.079	0.000	0.279	0.195	0.011	0.010	0.193
Maximum	4.254	0.940	1.000	0.897	25.118	20.876	0.951	0.477	0.977	3.361	0.863	0.933	0.315
2007-2009													
Mean	0.806	0.185	0.223	0.059	13.562	0.753	0.040	0.008	0.312	0.168	0.004	-0.050	0.164
SD	0.809	0.204	0.227	0.097	3.432	1.444	0.343	0.039	0.246	0.496	0.224	0.241	0.069
Minimum	0.221	0.000	0.000	0.000	4.762	0.088	-0.915	0.000	0.000	-3.073	-0.649	-0.823	0.001
Median	0.561	0.114	0.172	0.028	13.649	0.531	0.065	0.000	0.267	0.165	0.010	0.003	0.186
Maximum	4.373	0.940	1.000	0.897	31.502	20.876	0.951	0.477	0.977	3.361	0.863	0.933	0.295
2010-2016													
Mean	0.831	0.194	0.225	0.052	13.855	0.761	0.035	0.007	0.302	0.164	0.001	-0.048	0.170
SD	0.871	0.209	0.230	0.089	3.433	1.489	0.341	0.035	0.252	0.476	0.229	0.235	0.054
Minimum	0.207	0.000	0.000	0.000	4.762	0.088	-0.915	0.000	0.000	-3.073	-0.649	-0.823	0.006
Median	0.556	0.123	0.173	0.025	13.998	0.519	0.055	0.000	0.246	0.171	0.009	0.005	0.189
Maximum	4.426	0.940	1.000	0.897	26.284	20.876	0.951	0.477	0.977	3.361	0.863	0.933	0.281

Note. This table presents the mean, standard deviation (SD), minimum, median and maximum values of all variables across the whole sample period (2002-2016), pre-crisis period (2002-2006), crisis period (2007-2009) and post-crisis period (2010-2016).

Source: Worldscope

Multivariate Analyses

Table 6 answers the question of how does international trade affect cash, debt and dividend. While trade is negatively related to cash holdings and dividend payouts, trade is positively associated with debt financing. In model 1 and 2, firm- and year-FE are included in models. Hausman tests' results show that FE is preferable to RE. Besides, according to the LR test, RE is better than POLS, so model 3 is predicted by RE including industry- and year-FE.

Regarding the control variables of corporate decisions, first, the cash ratio is negatively related to debt, dividend, firm size, growth, networking capital and positively related to cash flow. However, investment has no impact on cash holdings.

Table 3. Sample composition and the mean of cash, debt, dividend, and trade by country

Country	N	Cash	Debt	Div	Trade	Country	N	Cash	Debt	Div	Trade
Australia	14,948	0.283	0.146	0.091	0.416	Malta	111	0.100	0.253	0.025	2.855
Austria	624	0.112	0.254	0.015	0.904	Mauritius	227	0.056	0.209	0.017	1.118
Bahrain	167	0.181	0.074	0.047	1.524	Mexico	1,225	0.094	0.255	0.056	0.570
Bangladesh	288	0.112	0.250	0.031	0.431	Montenegro	95	0.044	0.085	0.005	1.083
Belgium	1,041	0.138	0.244	0.065	1.430	Morocco	407	0.093	0.169	0.061	0.761
Bosnia	451	0.045	0.123	0.009	0.878	Netherlands	1,183	0.119	0.232	0.053	1.270
Brazil	2,584	0.123	0.301	0.056	0.247	New Zealand	1,197	0.124	0.236	0.058	0.579
Bulgaria	531	0.061	0.193	0.004	1.177	Nigeria	407	0.092	0.217	0.036	0.348
Canada	15,073	0.253	0.160	0.105	0.657	Norway	1,953	0.186	0.312	0.083	0.698
Chile	1,595	0.079	0.217	0.057	0.652	Oman	725	0.117	0.258	0.033	1.091
China	28,344	0.199	0.227	0.064	0.475	Pakistan	2,457	0.086	0.326	0.063	0.315
Colombia	281	0.062	0.142	0.021	0.369	Palestine	112	0.107	0.126	0.029	0.724
Croatia	546	0.081	0.214	0.008	0.839	Peru	657	0.121	0.287	0.194	0.462
Cyprus	544	0.087	0.314	0.007	1.168	Philippines	1,703	0.148	0.196	0.057	0.723
Czech Republic	80	0.079	0.249	0.008	1.259	Poland	3,982	0.114	0.182	0.063	0.852
Denmark	1,329	0.166	0.235	0.060	0.891	Portugal	548	0.069	0.374	0.014	0.689
Egypt	1,291	0.151	0.182	0.049	0.486	Qatar	208	0.164	0.203	0.04	0.941
Finland	1,525	0.138	0.267	0.058	0.722	Romania	1,063	0.098	0.153	0.011	0.730
France	6,816	0.167	0.212	0.048	0.547	Russia	2,867	0.098	0.257	0.056	0.501
Germany	6,738	0.172	0.204	0.059	0.703	Saudi Arabia	1,065	0.105	0.210	0.046	0.800
Greece	2,213	0.085	0.314	0.041	0.542	Serbia	202	0.060	0.175	0.006	0.835
Hong Kong	13,988	0.233	0.199	0.047	3.608	Singapore	7,423	0.198	0.209	0.053	3.670
Hungary	138	0.212	0.381	0.318	1.462	Slovakia	74	0.069	0.183	0.009	1.575
India	21,410	0.074	0.322	0.071	0.456	Slovenia	326	0.074	0.266	0.013	1.350
Indonesia	4,130	0.122	0.308	0.064	0.526	South Africa	2,856	0.134	0.183	0.065	0.570
Iraq	47	0.238	0.084	0.006	0.757	South Korea	19,346	0.164	0.245	0.055	0.814
Ireland	470	0.182	0.191	0.011	1.684	Spain	1,394	0.109	0.293	0.047	0.558
Israel	1,851	0.239	0.397	0.210	0.687	Sri Lanka	1,925	0.089	0.231	0.021	0.589
Italy	2,353	0.129	0.270	0.041	0.510	Sweden	4,155	0.198	0.176	0.039	0.822
Jamaica	87	0.178	0.097	0.046	0.878	Switzerland	2,094	0.183	0.208	0.019	1.039
Japan	44,841	0.202	0.220	0.036	0.266	Taiwan	18,343	0.219	0.198	0.049	1.270
Jordan	1,062	0.101	0.178	0.025	1.181	Thailand	6,036	0.112	0.279	0.062	1.229
Kazakhstan	86	0.089	0.309	0.039	0.731	Tunisia	344	0.155	0.229	0.033	0.997
Kenya	294	0.077	0.197	0.034	0.535	Turkey	3,076	0.098	0.225	0.020	0.491
Kuwait	840	0.164	0.185	0.033	0.953	UK	13,583	0.190	0.180	0.020	0.555
Latvia	241	0.068	0.170	0.008	1.113	Ukraine	89	0.062	0.179	0.013	0.998
Lebanon	10	0.940	0.219	0.521	0.898	US	49,168	0.230	0.265	0.058	0.262
Lithuania	232	0.058	0.263	0.025	1.337	Venezuela	148	0.100	0.125	0.026	0.504
Luxemburg	112	0.094	0.218	0.026	3.128	Vietnam	2,248	0.129	0.236	0.022	1.641
Macedonia	182	0.063	0.207	0.014	1.224	Zambia	103	0.101	0.163	0.062	0.699
Malaysia	9,826	0.144	0.201	0.046	1.697	Zimbabwe	100	0.072	0.089	0.019	0.762

Note. This table reports observation numbers (N) and the mean of cash. debt, dividend and trade across countries.

Source: Worldscope

Table 4. Correlation matrix

	Trade	Cash	Debt	Div	Size	Grow	Prof	Inv	Tan	Tax	Nwc	Cflow	VIF
2002-2016													
Cash	0.025												2.81
Debt	-0.042	-0.339											2.96
Div	-0.030	-0.069	0.046										1.21
Size	-0.038	-0.199	0.070	-0.046									1.33
Grow	-0.048	-0.026	0.320	-0.015	-0.207								1.35
Prof	-0.045	-0.736	0.797	0.093	0.149	0.265							2.83
Inv	-0.006	-0.057	0.001	-0.060	-0.056	0.169	0.034						1.08
Tan	-0.040	-0.398	0.215	0.372	0.119	-0.037	0.343	0.122					1.56
Tax	-0.046	-0.040	-0.027	-0.001	0.121	-0.037	0.009	-0.006	0.001				1.03
Nwc	0.040	-0.086	-0.390	-0.093	0.114	-0.311	-0.194	-0.010	-0.203	0.067			1.46
Cflow	0.065	-0.119	-0.203	-0.044	0.410	-0.250	-0.025	0.029	-0.009	0.136	0.372		1.43
IMdebt	0.037	-0.237	0.135	-0.041	0.205	-0.002	0.215	0.049	0.144	0.055	0.026	0.150	1.11
2002-2006													
Cash	-0.008												2.91
Debt	-0.040	-0.337											2.99
Div	-0.015	-0.067	0.052										1.23
Size	-0.084	-0.237	0.050	-0.055									1.41
Grow	-0.054	-0.027	0.315	-0.018	-0.220								1.35
Prof	-0.025	-0.739	0.809	0.082	0.155	0.264							2.88
Inv	-0.016	-0.042	-0.020	-0.056	-0.081	0.184	0.035						1.09
Tan	0.025	-0.407	0.218	0.378	0.171	-0.041	0.354	0.109					1.61
Tax	-0.070	-0.060	-0.033	-0.006	0.154	-0.047	0.014	-0.013	0.011				1.04
Nwc	0.062	-0.094	-0.401	-0.094	0.121	-0.311	-0.202	-0.003	-0.193	0.075			1.51
Cflow	0.078	-0.150	-0.207	-0.026	0.426	-0.266	-0.020	0.031	0.046	0.157	0.394		1.49
IMdebt	0.023	-0.273	0.140	-0.048	0.220	-0.007	0.238	0.032	0.186	0.071	0.018	0.150	1.14
2007-2009													
Cash	0.030												2.75
Debt	-0.057	-0.336											2.81
Div	-0.026	-0.068	0.050										1.24
Size	-0.030	-0.218	0.071	-0.038									1.34
Grow	-0.051	-0.022	0.342	-0.029	-0.211								1.36
Prof	-0.056	-0.727	0.798	0.092	0.163	0.273							2.75
Inv	-0.003	-0.059	0.008	-0.067	-0.044	0.142	0.035						1.08
Tan	-0.055	-0.390	0.204	0.393	0.129	-0.042	0.331	0.125					1.57
Tax	-0.042	-0.043	-0.024	-0.005	0.112	-0.039	0.012	-0.005	0.010				1.03
Nwc	0.047	-0.100	-0.379	-0.097	0.131	-0.328	-0.181	-0.011	-0.189	0.068			1.45
Cflow	0.094	-0.135	-0.199	-0.055	0.411	-0.254	-0.011	0.045	-0.002	0.132	0.372		1.43
IMdebt	0.060	-0.223	0.136	-0.087	0.224	0.002	0.210	0.047	0.062	0.050	0.048	0.170	1.12
2010-2016													
Cash	0.037												2.80
Debt	-0.037	-0.341											2.85
Div	-0.037	-0.070	0.039										1.19
Size	-0.025	-0.178	0.083	-0.035									1.31
Grow	-0.043	-0.026	0.313	-0.009	-0.197								1.35
Prof	-0.048	-0.737	0.790	0.097	0.146	0.263							2.84
Inv	-0.003	-0.063	0.008	-0.059	-0.050	0.176	0.034						1.09
Tan	-0.060	-0.396	0.218	0.362	0.096	-0.035	0.343	0.128					1.55
Tax	-0.037	-0.028	-0.026	0.002	0.114	-0.032	0.004	-0.003	-0.008				1.02
Nwc	0.027	-0.077	-0.390	-0.090	0.102	-0.303	-0.195	-0.012	-0.214	0.063			1.44
Cflow	0.047	-0.097	-0.203	-0.048	0.403	-0.240	-0.033	0.021	-0.038	0.129	0.361		1.40
IMdebt	0.037	-0.226	0.131	-0.013	0.195	-0.002	0.205	0.062	0.162	0.048	0.021	0.139	1.11

Note. This table presents the mean, standard deviation (SD), minimum, median and maximum values of all variables across the whole sample period (2002-2016), pre-crisis period (2002-2006), crisis period (2007-2009) and post-crisis period (2010-2016). Variance inflation factors (VIF) show whether the sample face multicollinearity problem in the last column. All VIF values smaller than 5, so there is no multicollinearity issue in the whole sample and subsamples.

Source: Worldscope

Table 5. Comparison of mean of corporate decisions across trade level

	Pre-crisis (2002-2006)	Post-crisis (2010-2016)	Post vs. Pre [t-stats]
Cash			
• High trade	0.169	0. 188	0.019 [17.93***]
• Low trade	0.193	0. 201	0.008 [6.18***]
• *Low vs. High* [t-stats]	0.024 [19.14***]	0.013 [13.88***]	
Debt			
• High trade	0.220	0. 211	–0.009 [–7.26***]
• Low trade	0.234	0. 239	0.005 [3.76***]
• *Low vs. High* [t-stats]	0.014 [9.85***]	0.028 [27.64***]	
Div			
• High trade	0.062	0.051	–0.011 [–21.32***]
• Low trade	0.056	0.053	–0.003 [–6.04***]
• *Low vs. High* [t-stats]	–0.006 –[9.38***]	0.002 [7.17***]	

Note. This table compares the mean of cash, debt and dividend across pre-crisis (2002-2006) and post-crisis (2010-2016) by trade level. Trade is divided into high- and low-trade above and below median of trade by year.

Source: Worldscope

Next, the debt ratio is positively associated with firm size, growth, profitability, tangibility, industry median of debt and negatively associated with cash, dividend and effective tax rate. Considering the sign and significance of coefficients of explanatory variables, trade-off theory is preferable to pecking order theory.

Last, the dividend ratio is adversely related to cash, firm size, growth but it is positively related to profitability.

Table 7 presents the results of the joint impact subperiods and trade on corporate decisions. First, the positive impact of trade on debt financing shifts to the negative, but the role of trade on cash and dividend does not change during the GFC. Second, the negative effect of trade on debt financing becomes positive from pre to post GFC. However, the adverse influence of trade on dividend does not differ by time. To conclude, while cash and debt policy vary with the presence of trade, dividend policy does not.

FUTURE RESEARCH DIRECTIONS

This chapter examines how international trade affected corporate decisions with the presence of the GFC as the turbulence time. Further research may shed new lights on literature by assessing the joint role of international trade and Covid-19, which is a recession time, on corporate financial decisions.

Table 6. International trade and corporate decisions

Variables	Cash (1)	Debt (2)	Div (3)
Trade	−0.000*	0.000***	−0.000***
	(0.000)	(0.000)	(0.000)
Cash		−0.628***	−0.036***
		(0.001)	(0.001)
Debt	−0.122***		0.013***
	(0.007)		(0.001)
Div	−0.188***	−0.030***	
	(0.004)	(0.004)	
Size	−0.025***	0.001**	−0.004***
	(0.001)	(0.000)	(0.000)
Grow	−0.003***	0.005***	−0.001***
	(0.001)	(0.001)	(0.000)
Prof		0.757***	
		(0.005)	
Tan		0.034***	
		(0.003)	
Inv	0.042		
	(0.026)		
Nwc	−0.127***		
	(0.004)		
Cflow	0.063***		
	(0.003)		
Tax		−0.002***	
		(0.000)	
IMdebt		0.085***	
		(0.010)	
Constant	0.494***	0.034***	0.117***
	(0.023)	(0.006)	(0.001)
Firm FE	YES	YES	NO
Industry FE	NO	NO	YES
Year FE	YES	YES	YES
Hausman test	4878.49***	466.03***	
LR test			11000***
Firms	33,803	35,678	35,900
Observations	344,434	367,465	374,247

Note. This table presents how does the international trade affect corporate decisions, cash, debt, and dividend, respectively. Variables defined in Table 1. Hausman test results confirm that Fixed effect is preferable than Random effect panel in columns 1 and 2. Also, Likelihood-ratio test result approves that Random effect panel Tobit model is better than Pooled OLS. *p<0.10, **p<0.05, ***p<0.01.

Table 7. The global financial crisis, international trade and corporate decisions

	Cash		Debt		Div	
	Pre/Post	Crisis	Pre/Post	Crisis	Pre/Post	Crisis
Variables	**(4)**	**(5)**	**(6)**	**(7)**	**(8)**	**(9)**
Trade	–0.000**	–0.000	0.000*	0.000***	–0.000	–0.000***
	(0.000)	(0.000)	(0.000)	(0.000)	(0.000)	(0.000)
Pre x Trade	–0.000***		0.000**		0.000	
	(0.000)		(0.000)		(0.000)	
Post x Trade	0.000**		0.000***		–0.000	
	(0.000)		(0.000)		(0.000)	
Crisis x Trade		0.000		–0.000***		–0.000
		(0.000)		(0.000)		(0.000)
Cash			–0.628***	–0.628***	–0.036***	–0.037***
			(0.008)	(0.001)	(0.001)	(0.001)
Debt	–0.122***	–0.127***			0.012***	0.013***
	(0.007)	(0.007)			(0.001)	(0.001)
Div	–0.189***	–0.192***	–0.031***	–0.031***		
	(0.004)	(0.004)	(0.004)	(0.004)		
Size	–0.025***	–0.021***	0.001***	0.002***	–0.004***	–0.005***
	(0.001)	(0.001)	(0.000)	(0.000)	(0.000)	(0.000)
Grow	–0.003***	–0.003***	0.005***	0.005***	–0.001***	–0.001***
	(0.001)	(0.001)	(0.001)	(0.001)	(0.000)	(0.000)
Prof			0.757***	0.757***		
			(0.005)	(0.005)		
Tan			0.034***	0.034***		
			(0.003)	(0.003)		
Inv	0.042	0.040				
	(0.026)	(0.026)				
Nwc	–0.127***	–0.129***				
	(0.004)	(0.004)				
Cflow	0.065***	0.061***				
	(0.003)	(0.003)				
Tax			–0.002***	–0.002***		
			(0.000)	(0.000)		
IMdebt			0.117***	0.113***		
			(0.009)	(0.010)		
Constant	0.591***	0.540***	0.027***	0.016***	0.121***	0.128***
	(0.013)	(0.012)	(0.006)	(0.005)	(0.001)	(0.001)
Firm FE	YES	YES	YES	YES	NO	NO
Industry FE	NO	NO	NO	NO	YES	YES
Period FE	YES	YES	YES	YES	YES	YES
Firms	33,803	33,803	33,803	33,803	33,803	33,803
Observations	344,434	344,434	344,434	344,434	344,434	344,434

Note. This table presents how do the international trade and the global financial crisis affect corporate decisions, cash, debt, and dividend, respectively. Variables defined in Table 1. *p<0.10, **p<0.05, ***p<0.01.

CONCLUSION

Since international trade affects firm heterogeneity in the context of corporate decisions, this chapter empirically tests this relationship and finds it differs with the existence of the GFC. Employing 344,434 firm-years from 82 countries for the period 2002-2016, the findings indicate that as trade is negatively related to cash holdings and dividend payouts, trade is positively associated with debt financing. However, the picture changes with the rise of the GFC. Especially, as the positive impact of trade on debt financing gains significance from pre- to post-GFC but changes to negative in time of the GFC. then, the negative effect of trade on cash holdings in pre-GFC becomes positive in post-GFC. Finally, the influence of trade on dividend payouts does not vary in subperiods. Overall, international trade has various impacts on corporate decisions and these impacts differ during the GFC due to variations in the trade that comprises of export and import.

This chapter contributes to the literature in some ways. First, the effect of trade on cash, debt and dividend is firstly investigated with the panel data set across the worldwide. Next, the joint influence of the post-GFC and trade on corporate decisions may open new insights to realize what the world economy should project on the relationship between trade and corporate decisions in the aftermath of Covid-19.

The implications of this chapter are manifold. First, managers should consider the impact of trade on corporate decisions with the presence of financial crises. Next, investors should take into account trade volume and corporate policies of firms when and where to invest in. After, policymakers should count implementation of trade regulations. They may show tolerance on regulations during exogenous shocks like Covid-19. Finally, practitioners and researchers should consider the GFC as a milestone due to its destructive effect and imply for the Covid-19.

ACKNOWLEDGMENT

This research received no specific grant from any funding agency in the public, commercial, or not-for-profit sectors.

REFERENCES

Ahn, J., Amiti, M., & Weinstein, D. E. (2011). Trade finance and the great trade collapse. *The American Economic Review*, *101*(3), 298–302. doi:10.1257/aer.101.3.298

Alves, P., & Francisco, P. (2015). The impact of institutional environment on the capital structure of firms during recent financial crises. *The Quarterly Review of Economics and Finance*, *57*, 129–146. doi:10.1016/j.qref.2014.12.001

Bates, T. W., Chang, C. H., & Chi, J. D. (2018). Why has the value of cash increased over time? *Journal of Financial and Quantitative Analysis*, *53*(2), 749–787. doi:10.1017/S002210901700117X

Berkmen, S. P., Gelos, G., Rennhack, R., & Walsh, J. P. (2012). The global financial crisis: Explaining cross-country differences in the output impact. *Journal of International Money and Finance*, *31*(1), 42–59. doi:10.1016/j.jimonfin.2011.11.002

Bliss, B. A., Cheng, Y., & Denis, D. J. (2015). Corporate payout, cash retention, and the supply of credit: Evidence from the 2008–2009 credit crisis. *Journal of Financial Economics*, *115*(3), 521–540. doi:10.1016/j.jfineco.2014.10.013

Byrne, J., & O'Connor, T. (2017). How do creditors respond to disclosure quality? Evidence from corporate dividend payouts. *Journal of International Financial Markets, Institutions and Money*, *49*, 154–172. doi:10.1016/j.intfin.2017.04.002

Chen, H. C., Chou, R. K., & Lu, C. L. (2018). Saving for a rainy day: Evidence from the 2000 dot-com crash and the 2008 credit crisis. *Journal of Corporate Finance*, *48*, 680–699. doi:10.1016/j.jcorpfin.2017.12.025

Chen, W., Mrkaic, M., & Nabar, M. (2019). The global economic recovery 10 years after the 2008 financial crisis. International Monetary Fund 19/83.

Coldbeck, B., & Ozkan, A. (2018). Comparison of adjustment speeds in target research and development and capital investment: What did the financial crisis of 2007 change? *Journal of Business Research*, *84*, 1–10. doi:10.1016/j.jbusres.2017.10.042

D'Amato, A. (2020). Capital structure, debt maturity, and financial crisis: Empirical evidence from SMEs. *Small Business Economics*, *55*(4), 919–941. doi:10.100711187-019-00165-6

Daskalakis, N., Balios, D., & Dalla, V. (2017). The behaviour of SMEs' capital structure determinants in different macroeconomic states. *Journal of Corporate Finance*, *46*, 248–260. doi:10.1016/j.jcorpfin.2017.07.005

Demirgüç-Kunt, A., Peria, M. S. M., & Tressel, T. (2020). The global financial crisis and the capital structure of firms: Was the impact more severe among SMEs and non-listed firms? *Journal of Corporate Finance*, *60*, 101514. doi:10.1016/j.jcorpfin.2019.101514

Foley, C. F., & Manova, K. (2015). *International trade, multinational activity, and corporate finance*. National Bureau of Economic Research, w20604.

Frank, M. Z., & Goyal, V. K. (2009). Capital structure decisions: Which factors are reliably important? *Financial Management*, *38*(1), 1–37. doi:10.1111/j.1755-053X.2009.01026.x

Garcia-Appendini, E., & Montoriol-Garriga, J. (2013). Firms as liquidity providers: Evidence from the 2007–2008 financial crisis. *Journal of Financial Economics*, *109*(1), 272–291. doi:10.1016/j.jfineco.2013.02.010

Gertler, M., & Gilchrist, S. (2018). What happened: Financial factors in the great recession. *The Journal of Economic Perspectives*, *32*(3), 3–30. doi:10.1257/jep.32.3.3

González, V. M. (2015). The financial crisis and corporate debt maturity: The role of banking structure. *Journal of Corporate Finance*, *35*, 310–328. doi:10.1016/j.jcorpfin.2015.10.002

Greene, W. H. (2012). *Econometric analysis* (7th ed.). Prentice-Hall International.

Keynes, J. M. (1936). *The general theory of employment, interest and money*. Macmillan Cambridge University Press.

La Porta, R., Lopez-de-Silanes, F., Shleifer, A., & Vishny, R. W. (2000). Agency problems and dividend policies around the world. *The Journal of Finance*, *55*(1), 1–33. doi:10.1111/0022-1082.00199

Lintner, J. (1956). Distribution of incomes of corporations among dividends, retained earnings, and taxes. *The American Economic Review*, *46*(2), 97–113.

Mian, A., & Sufi, A. (2015). *House of debt: How they (and you) caused the Great Recession, and how we can prevent it from happening again*. University of Chicago Press.

Mimouni, K., Temimi, A., Goaied, M., & Zeitun, R. (2019). The impact of liquidity on debt maturity after a financial crisis: Evidence from the Gulf Cooperation Council region. *Emerging Markets Finance & Trade*, *55*(1), 181–200. doi:10.1080/1540496X.2018.1425835

Opler, T., Pinkowitz, L., Stulz, R., & Williamson, R. (1999). The determinants and implications of corporate cash holdings. *Journal of Financial Economics*, *52*(1), 3–46. doi:10.1016/S0304-405X(99)00003-3

Pinkowitz, L., Stulz, R. M., & Williamson, R. (2016). Do US firms hold more cash than foreign firms do? *Review of Financial Studies*, *29*(2), 309–348. doi:10.1093/rfs/hhv064

Polat, A. Y. (2020). Borç vadesi ve finansal kriz: Türkiye örneği. *Erciyes Üniversitesi İktisadi ve İdari Bilimler Fakültesi Dergisi*, (1), 118–130. doi:10.18070/erciyesiibd.846318

Rajan, R. G., & Zingales, L. (1995). What do we know about capital structure? Some evidence from international data. *The Journal of Finance*, *50*(5), 1421–1460. doi:10.1111/j.1540-6261.1995.tb05184.x

Seifert, B., & Gonenc, H. (2016). Creditor rights, country governance, and corporate cash holdings. *Journal of International Financial Management & Accounting*, *27*(1), 65–90. doi:10.1111/jifm.12033

Seifert, B., & Gonenc, H. (2018). The effects of country and firm-level governance on cash management. *Journal of International Financial Markets, Institutions and Money*, *52*, 1–16. doi:10.1016/j.intfin.2017.12.001

Shiau, H. L., Chang, Y. H., & Yang, Y. J. (2018). The cash holdings and corporate investment surrounding financial crisis: The cases of China and Taiwan. *Chinese Economy*, *51*(2), 175–207. doi:10.1080/10971475.2018.1447833

Shikimi, M., & Yamada, K. (2019). Trade and financial channels as the transmission mechanism of the financial crisis. *International Review of Economics & Finance*, *63*, 364–381. doi:10.1016/j.iref.2019.04.008

Song, K., & Lee, Y. (2012). Long-term effects of a financial crisis: Evidence from cash holdings of East Asian firms. *Journal of Financial and Quantitative Analysis*, *47*(3), 617–641. doi:10.1017/S0022109012000142

Tekin, H. (2020a). Firm size and dividend policy of European firms: Evidence from financial crises. *Marmara Journal of European Studies*, *28*(1), 109–121.

Tekin, H. (2020b). How optimal cash changed by the global financial crisis? A multi-country analysis. *Economics and Business Letters*, *9*(2), 114–123. doi:10.17811/ebl.9.2.2020.114-123

Tekin, H. (2020c). Market differences and adjustment speed of debt, equity, and debt maturity. *Australian Journal of Management*. Advance online publication. doi:10.1177/0312896220968266

Tekin, H., & Polat, A. Y. (2020a). Agency theory: A review in finance. *Anemon: Journal of Social Sciences of Mus Alparslan University*, *8*(4), 1323–1329.

Tekin, H., & Polat, A. Y. (2020b). *Do market differences matter on dividend policy?* Borsa Istanbul Review. doi:10.1016/j.bir.2020.10.009

Tekin, H., & Polat, A. Y. (2020c). Is saving vital? Evidence from the financial crisis. *Economics and Business Letters*, *9*(2), 124–134. doi:10.17811/ebl.9.2.2020.124-134

Tekin, H., & Polat, A. Y. (2020d). The global financial crisis and capital structure decisions of Turkish SMEs: A review. *International Journal of Management Economics and Business*, *16*(3), 513–535. doi:10.17130/ijmeb.798509

Tekin, H., & Polat, A. Y. (2021a). Adjustment speed of debt maturity: Evidence from financial crises in East Asia. *Bulletin of Monetary Economics and Banking*, *24*(1), 71–92.

Tekin, H., & Polat, A. Y. (2021b). *Is leverage a substitute or outcome for governance? Evidence from financial crises.* International Journal of Emerging Markets. doi:10.1108/10.1108/IJOEM-03-2020-0297

Van Hoang, T. H., Gurău, C., Lahiani, A., & Seran, T. L. (2018). Do crises impact capital structure? A study of French micro-enterprises. *Small Business Economics*, *50*(1), 181–199. doi:10.100711187-017-9899-x

Zeitun, R., Temimi, A., & Mimouni, K. (2017). Do financial crises alter the dynamics of corporate capital structure? Evidence from GCC countries. *The Quarterly Review of Economics and Finance*, *63*, 21–33. doi:10.1016/j.qref.2016.05.004

ADDITIONAL READING

Azar, J. A., Kagy, J. F., & Schmalz, M. C. (2016). Can changes in the cost of carry explain the dynamics of corporate "cash" holdings? *Review of Financial Studies*, *29*(8), 2194–2240. doi:10.1093/rfs/hhw021

Bates, T. W., Kahle, K. M., & Stulz, R. M. (2009). Why do US firms hold so much more cash than they used to? *The Journal of Finance*, *64*(5), 1985–2021. doi:10.1111/j.1540-6261.2009.01492.x

Brealey, R. A., Myers, S. C., & Allen, F. (2014). *Principles of corporate finance* (11th ed.). McGraw-Hill Education.

Elsas, R., & Florysiak, D. (2015). Dynamic capital structure adjustment and the impact of fractional dependent variables. *Journal of Financial and Quantitative Analysis*, *50*(5), 1105–1133. doi:10.1017/S0022109015000496

Frank, M. Z., & Goyal, V. K. (2008). Trade-off and pecking order theories of debt. In B. E. Eckbo (Ed.), *Handbook of corporate finance: empirical corporate finance* (pp. 135–202). North-Holland. doi:10.1016/B978-0-444-53265-7.50004-4

Jensen, M. C. (1986). Agency cost of free cash flow, corporate finance and takeovers. *The American Economic Review*, *76*(2), 323–329.

Jensen, M. C., & Meckling, W. H. (1976). Theory of the firm: Managerial behavior, agency costs and ownership structure. *Journal of Financial Economics*, *3*(4), 305–360. doi:10.1016/0304-405X(76)90026-X

La Porta, R., Lopez-de-Silanes, F., Shleifer, A., & Vishny, R. W. (1997). Legal determinants of external finance. *The Journal of Finance*, *52*(3), 1131–1150. doi:10.1111/j.1540-6261.1997.tb02727.x

Ozkan, A. (2001). Determinants of capital structure and adjustment to long run target: Evidence from UK company panel data. *Journal of Business Finance & Accounting*, *28*(1-2), 175–198. doi:10.1111/1468-5957.00370

Wooldridge, J. M. (2002). *Econometric analysis of cross section and panel data*. MIT Press.

KEY TERMS AND DEFINITIONS

Agency Costs: Agency costs arise due to the separation of ownership and control in the company.

Bankruptcy Costs: Companies with higher debt may have higher bankruptcy costs. Thus, companies may prefer equity to debt.

Cash Holdings: Cash and short-term investments of companies are considered cash holdings.

Corporate Decisions: Companies have critical decisions like cash retention, debt-equity financing, dividend payouts, investment, and so on by determining their corporate policies.

Debt-Equity Financing: Companies balance their capital mix by increasing debt and decreasing equity, and vice versa.

Dividend Payouts: Companies pay out dividends to their shareholders by signaling their quality of firms.

Global Financial Crisis: The global financial crisis originated firstly in the subprime mortgage market in the United States (US) in the second half of 2007, reached its peak worldwide following the collapse of Lehman Brothers in September 2008 and sustained its effect until June 2009.

Information Asymmetry: Asymmetric information arises when managers have more information about the company's expectations, risks, and value than those outside the company.

International Trade: International trade is the trade of goods and services between different regions, which in many countries account for a large part of the gross domestic product.

Transaction Costs: Transaction costs occur when buying or selling goods and services.

ENDNOTES

1 The formulation of panel data is as follows: $y_{it} = \alpha_i + x'_{it}\beta + \varepsilon_{it}$ $(i=1, 2, ..., N \text{ and } t=1, 2, ..., T)$, (10) where y_{it} is a dependent variable, x'_{it} are explanatory variables, α_i contains an intercept and a set of group specific variables and ε_{it} is the error term. α_i and ε_{it} represent the unobserved factors (Greene, 2012, p. 182).

2 The formulation of Pooled Ordinary Least Squares–POLS is as follows: $y_{it} = \alpha + x'_{it}\beta + u_{it}$ $(i=1, 2, ..., N \text{ and } t=1, 2, ..., T)$, (11) α_i and ε_{it} are introduced by u_{it}. Though ε_{it} is not associated to explanatory variables, if α_i does, the heterogeneity bias occurs owing to the bias and inconsistency of the *POLS* (Greene, 2012, p. 183).

3 The formulation of Fixed Effect–FE is as follows: $y_{it} = \alpha_i + \gamma_t + x'_{it}\beta + \varepsilon_{it}$ *(i=1, 2, ..., N and t=1, 2, ..., T)*, (12) where α_i and γ_t present group- and time-dummy variables, respectively. α_i is unobserved and correlates with x_{it} results with a limited endogeneity. Neither α_i nor ε_{it} is related to x_{it} (Greene, 2012, p. 183).

4 The formulation of Random Effect–RE is as follows: $y_{it} = x_{'it}\beta + (\alpha_i + \varepsilon_{it})$ *(i=1, 2, ..., N and t=1, 2, ..., T)*, (13) The error term contains both α_i and ε_{it} . The serial correlation arises due the existence of α_i in each *T* and it can be solved by the *generalised least squares (GLS)* by using an advanced algebra (Greene, 2012, p. 183).

5 If the overidentification tests of Hausman and Arellano & Wooldridge are not rejected by regressing FE vs. RE, FE is the suitable model for the dataset.

Chapter 9
Financial Fragility and Its Impacts on International Trade and Economic Growth:
New Evidence From Fragile Five and Troubled Ten Countries

Ayberk Şeker
https://orcid.org/0000-0001-7750-6286
Bursa Technical University, Turkey

ABSTRACT

International trade cannot be considered separate from the current financial system in the context of imports and exports. In this context, the impact on international trade should be analyzed under the financial fragility hypothesis. This chapter aims to analyze the effects of financial fragility on Fragile Five and Troubled Ten countries' economic growth and trade strategies. In this direction, long-term relationships between variables are analyzed by Westerlund panel cointegration tests. According to the result of the panel cointegration tests, there are long-term relationships between exports, imports, gross domestic product, and financial fragility index. After determining the long-term relationships between variables, causality analyses have been carried out to reveal the direction of these relationships. According to Dumitrescu-Hurlin panel causality test results, there are bidirectional causality relationships between financial fragility index and export, import, and gross domestic product.

INTRODUCTION

International trade has a very important place in literature. Many models have been developed to analyze imports, exports and the trade balance. According to Mercantilists, the main purpose of international trade is to have foreign trade surplus. On the other hand, the theory of absolute advantages revealed by Adam Smith and the theory of comparative advantages developed by David Ricardo approach interna-

DOI: 10.4018/978-1-7998-8314-2.ch009

tional trade more complicated. The Heckscher-Ohlin Model focuses on natural resources, labor force and capital factors affecting net exports.

Along with the acceleration of globalization, economies of countries have become more open to global effects and thus more dependent on each other. Financial markets are at the top of the areas where this impact is felt the most. Associated with the internationalization of capital flows, financial markets have become very sensitive to foreign capital. In this context, countries have initiated liberalization processes in many areas, particularly financial markets, in order to attract more foreign capital, especially in the post-1980 period.

Fragility has been used in quite different meanings in disciplines that focus on different components of risk (Gnangnon, 2012; Naude et al., 2009). The concept of fragility usually consists of the vulnerability of economic units such as states or households. The fragility of these units manifests itself as the deterioration of the economy against economic crises and financial shocks (Andrews and Flores, 2008; Loayza and Raddatz, 2007). In summary, the definition of fragility differs according to the economic unit examined and according to which events these units may be under risk.

Financial fragility can be explained as a situation that is sensitive to the development of sudden shocks, which may occur in the markets and to show its effect on the economies of the country as a financial crisis on a large scale. While evaluating fragility in terms of the structure of the financial system, it is necessary to evaluate the crisis as the result of the interaction between fragility and some external shocks (Leviastuti, 2020; Allen & Gale, 2004). Financial liberalization is seen as an important factor increasing fragility. Financial fragility shows its effect as instability in the financial markets.

As a result of the global developments in economic integration, capital flows have reached the international level. Therefore, capital flows are exposed to the effects of current account deficit, exchange rate, foreign exchange reserves, public domestic debt stock, inflation, money supply and many other financial factors. In the context of imports and exports, international trade is also affected by variables such as a country's trade policies, trade barriers, current account deficit, exchange rate, foreign exchange reserves and inflation (Gopinath et al., 2020; Nwachukwu, 2019; Shousha, 2019; Itskhoki & Mukhin, 2017; Okore & Onoh, 2013; Radelet & Sachs, 2000). Financial crises is emerged in developing countries due to budget deficits, poor execution of exchange rate policies, international unexpected financial events, financial liberalization practices in inappropriate times and insufficient conditions and weakness of the domestic banking sector (Sachs et al., 1996). As the level of globalization increases and countries become more integrated with each other, their vulnerability to international financial crises increases. Accordingly, it is observed that global financial fluctuations have led to a break in the financial and macroeconomic structures of these countries (Neaime, 2016). These breakdowns can lead to economic crises due to the effects of important factors such as the increase in the current account deficit, fluctuations in exchange rates, the diminishing of foreign exchange reserves and the increase in inflation.

Minsky (1977), investigating the explanatory power of Keynesian Theory on capitalist economy in his study, argues that neoclassical theory is insufficient to explain the current financial system especially during crisis periods. Keynesian theory fails to explain financial crises that can occur periodically, and therefore the financial system should be considered unstable, unlike the neoclassical approach.

International trade cannot be considered separate from the current financial system in the context of imports and exports. In this context, the impact on international trade should be analyzed under the financial fragility hypothesis. According to Minsky, it is inevitable that sound financial structures turn into fragile financial structures over time in a capitalist economy. This situation arises from the change in expectations during the course of the conjuncture wave. According to Minsky, unless government expenditure compensates for the decline in investment spending, this is followed by decline in profitability and debt maintenance ability (Minsky, 1977; Rozmainsky & Rodionova; 2021). According to the financial fragility hypothesis, the most important intervention to compensate for financial crises is seen as state intervention. Moreover, Minsky indicates that the effectiveness of state intervention in the market has the effect of reducing the severity of business cycles. At this point, state intervention is shown as the only solution to financial fragility by Minsky (1977).

In this chapter, it is aimed to determine the effects of financial fragility on exports, imports and gross domestic product. In order to establish the international trade and financial fragility model for Fragile Five and Trouble Ten countries, exports, imports and financial fragility index in Fragile Five and Trouble Ten countries will be used as variables. Series are yearly between 2000 and 2019 in the analyzes. Financial fragility index is calculated by current account deficit, real effective exchange rate, foreign exchange reserve, inflation rate and money supply. In first, cross-sectional dependence test will be examined and then the stationarities of the variables are analyzed by means of second-generation panel unit root test. Later, the long-term relationships between variables will be analyzed via the Westerlund (2007) panel cointegration test. Afterwards, causality relationships between variables will be investigated using the Dumitrescu - Hurlin (2012) panel causality test. Fragile Five and Trouble Ten countries' trade strategies and economic growth and the impact of financial fragility on these variables are constituted the focus of this chapter. It is of great importance to reveal the effects of the financial fragility levels of countries on their international trade and economic growth in terms of establishing correct macroeconomic policies. Therefore, the findings to be obtained as a result of the study will provide important outputs for both the academic literature and policy makers.

BACKGROUND

Although the relationship between financial fragility, international trade and economic growth has been examined in the literature, the number of studies revealing the effects of financial fragility on international trade is very few. Accordingly, it is substantial to define financial fragility, which has significant effects on international trade and economic growth, and to determine the variables that compose this index.

There are many indicators used to measure fragility in the literature and these indicators play an important role in the definition of fragility. The definition of fragility, which differs according to the variables and indices used, is generally classified as financial and economic fragility (Mete et al., 2016).

Financial fragility occurs as a result of deterioration in financial instruments such as current account deficit, exchange rate, foreign exchange reserve, inflation and money supply in the macroeconomic balance (Ha et al., 2019; Andrianova & Demetriades, 2018; Cespedes et al., 2004). Financial fragility indicators, which are leading indicators against financial crises, provide important clues about the economic structure and its future. Minsky (1977) explained the financial fragility of an economy by distinguishing between a sound economy and a fragile economy. He stated that the economy has a fragile structure if the disruptions in the fulfillment of the economic obligations of the countries cause major changes in the economy and it cannot recover.

When the studies in the literature are examined, the financial fragility index created varies within the scope of the analyses. While more indicators are included in the financial fragility index in some studies, the financial fragility index is formed with narrower and specific indicators in a number of studies. The index revealing the causes of fragility is substantial because gross domestic product is not an indicator that fully reflects the development of developing countries. Because this situation does not reflect the structural and institutional weaknesses of these countries and the unfavorable situations in the economy (Gnangnon, 2012).

Briguglio (1995) based the fragility index on three components in his study. These components are determined as openness to external economic conditions, being an island country and distance and probability of natural disasters. Keen (1995) has tried to model Minsky's financial fragility hypothesis. The model included labor productivity, unemployment, wages, net investments, net profits, bank revenues and interest rates. According to the results of the analysis, a sound economy will either remain stable or shrink. Briguglio and Galea (2003) and Briguglio et al. (2009) constituted indexes that are more detailed by updating the fragility index in the forthcoming period. Variables of export intensity, export and import dependency added to these indexes. Svirydzenka (2016) suggests that indicators in the studies do not always contain the multidimensional aspects of financial development, offering nine indices that measure the efficiency, access and depth of financial markets and institutions.

As can be seen, many different financial fragility indexes have been created in the literature. In this chapter, the financial fragility index is calculated by taking into account the variables of current account deficit, real effective exchange rate, foreign exchange reserve, inflation and money supply. In this direction, long-term relationships and causality relationships between financial fragility index, international trade and GDP will be analyzed for Fragile Five and Trouble Ten countries in this chapter. Along with this chapter, significant contributions will be made to the literature by investigating the effects of financial fragility on international trade and gross domestic product.

MAIN FOCUS OF THE CHAPTER

The "Fragile Five" is a term revealed by Morgan Stanley in August 2013, because of that the developing countries in this group are unable to finance their economic growth expectations and become economies dependent on foreign investment. Turkey, Brazil, India, South Africa and Indonesia are located in Fragile Five countries group. Since 2015, these countries have experienced significant problems with the movement of capital from developing countries to developed countries. The movement of capital from developing countries to developed countries adversely affected not only the "Fragile Five" countries but also other developing countries. In this direction, Morgan Stanley has expanded the "Fragile Five" country group as a result of analysis and revealed the "Trouble Ten" countries. "Troubled Ten" countries asserted by Morgan Stanley are Taiwan, Singapore, Russia, Thailand, South Korea, Peru, South Africa, Chile, Colombia and Brazil (Chadwick, 2019).

It is observed that the economic growth momentum of China decreased with the decline in the export level in 2015. The decrease in demand in China's export market played an important role in this decline. In the face of this situation, China followed devaluation policies and developing countries in the global economy were adversely affected by these policies. Troubled Ten countries stand out among these countries, which have an important place in China's export market and are adversely affected by international capital movements (Gazel, 2016). In summary, Fragile Five and Troubled Ten countries are fragile economies that are rapidly affected by global economic conditions and capital movements.

As can be seen, fragility in country economies is directly related to macroeconomic and financial indicators. It is expected that the supply and demand conditions that direct international trade and trade relations that affect the economic growth rate will be in mutual interaction with the financial vulnerabilities of the countries in the global system. Accordingly, this chapter will examine the effects of financial fragility on international trade and economic growth, focusing on Fragile Five and Troubled Ten countries.

EMPIRICAL ANALYZES

The chapter aims to determine the impacts of financial fragility on export, import and gross domestic product in the Fragile Five and Trouble Ten countries. In order to constitute the research model in the chapter, it is used the data on financial fragility index, export, import and gross domestic product in Fragile Five and Trouble Ten countries. When considering the growth and trading strategies, it will focus on the impact of financial fragility on exports, imports and GDP in the Fragile Five and Trouble Ten countries.

The effects of financial fragility on international trade and gross domestic product of Fragile Five and Trouble Ten countries will be calculated with the mentioned model by using panel data analyses. Then, it will be determined policy recommendations about international trade and gross domestic product. Data on financial fragility index, export, import and gross domestic product are gained from the World Bank. Series are yearly between 2000 and 2019 in the analyzes. Due to the lack of data of Taiwan and Singapore, these countries could not be included in the analysis. Fragile Five and Troubled Ten countries list that is included in the analyses is located in Table 5 at Appendix. The variables used in the chapter is as follows:

$ln(fragility)_{it}$: Financial fragility index of Fragile Five and Trouble Ten countries
$ln(export)_{it}$: Exports of Fragile Five and Trouble Ten countries
$ln(import)_{it}$: Imports of Fragile Five and Trouble Ten countries
$ln(GDP)_{it}$: Gross domestic product of Fragile Five and Trouble Ten countries

According to this information, the panel times series models have been constituted for Fragile Five and Troubled Ten countries to find out the impacts of financial fragility on exports, imports and gross domestic product (1, 2, 3):

$$ln\left(export\right)_{it} = \beta_0 + \beta_1 ln\left(fragility\right)_{it} + \varepsilon_{it} \tag{1}$$

$$ln\left(import\right)_{it} = \beta_0 + \beta_1 ln\left(fragility\right)_{it} + \varepsilon_{it} \tag{2}$$

$$ln\left(GDP\right)_{it} = \beta_0 + \beta_1 ln\left(fragility\right)_{it} + \varepsilon_{it} \tag{3}$$

Firstly, cross-sectional dependence test was examined via Breusch and Pagan (1980), Pesaran (2004) and Pesaran et al. (2008) tests. Then, the stationarities of the variables were analyzed by means of second-generation panel unit root test (PESCADF) (Pesaran, 2007). Later, the long-term relationships between variables were analyzed using the Westerlund (2007) panel cointegration test. Thereafter, causality relationships between variables were investigated by the Dumitrescu - Hurlin (2012) panel causality test.

Calculation of Financial Fragility Index

First, the financial fragility index should be calculated in order to examine the effects of financial fragility on international trade and gross domestic product. The variables included in the index are standardized in order to calculate the financial fragility index. All observations (X) of each variable are standardized with "(X-μ)/σ" the formula. In other words, the observations of each variable subtract from the mean of the variable (μ) and divided by the standard deviation (σ) of the variable. The financial fragility index consists of the value of five variables included in the index, calculated by weighting equally. These five variables in the financial fragility index are current account deficit, real effective exchange rate, foreign exchange reserve, inflation and broad money supply. It shows that if the calculated financial fragility index increases, the crisis risk increases in the economy.

The current account deficit that is included in the financial fragility index has significant effects on a country's macroeconomic balances. Increasing current account imbalances cause trade deficits that may lead to foreign debt accumulation and loss of international competitiveness (Cespedes et al., 2004). Moreover, it is observed that exchange rate fluctuations have a significant impact on financial fragility, especially in countries whose exports depend on imports. This situation may cause both a decrease in foreign exchange reserves and a triggering of the current account deficit (Shousha, 2019; Itskhoki & Mukhin, 2017). Furthermore, money supply and inflation rates in the market also have significant effects on the financial and economic vulnerabilities of countries (Ha et al., 2019). Accordingly, current account deficit, exchange rates, foreign exchange reserves, inflation rates and money supply are included in the financial fragility index calculations within the scope of the study.

Cross-Sectional Dependence Test and Unit Root Analyses

The variables must be stationary in order to analyze the cointegration relation among the variables in panel time-series. Accordingly, stationary levels of variables should be ascertained. Before the unit root test, cross-sectional dependence must be examined on the variables. The first generation panel unit root estimations do not take into account the cross-sectional dependence of the simultaneous error terms. It has been remarked in the literature that not considering cross-sectional dependence may create important distortions in panel unit root analyzes. It can reveal results that are more accurate in the event that an analysis considers cross-sectional dependence. Hence, it is implemented by Breusch and Pagan (1980) (4), Pesaran (2004) (5,6) and Pesaran et al. (2008) (8) tests to panel time series in order to examine for cross-sectional dependence.

$$LM = T\sum_{0=1}^{N-1}\sum_{J=0+1}^{N} P_{ij}^{2} \sim X_{\frac{N(N-1)}{2}}^{2} \tag{4}$$

$$CD = \sqrt{\frac{2T}{N(N-1)}}\left(\sum_{i=1}^{N-1}\sum_{j=i+1}^{N} P_{ij}\right) \sim N(0,1) \tag{5}$$

$$CD_{LM} = \sqrt{\frac{1}{N(N-1)}} \sum_{i=1}^{N-1} \sum_{j=i+1}^{N} P_{ij} \left(T\rho_{ij}^2 - 1 \right) \sim N(0,1) \tag{6}$$

$$LM_{adj} = \sqrt{\frac{2}{N(N-1)}} \sum_{i=1}^{N-1} \sum_{j=i+1}^{N} \frac{(T-k)P_{ij}^2 - \mu_{Tij}}{\vartheta_{Tij}} \sim N(0,1) \tag{7}$$

Table 1. Results of cross-sectional dependence

Variables	CD Test	Statistic	Probability
ln(fragility)	LM	516.413	0.000
	CD	16.066	0.000
	CD_{LM}	43.994	0.000
	LM_{adj}	43.705	0.000
ln(export)	LM	1045.429	0.000
	CD	32.329	0.000
	CD_{LM}	94.434	0.000
	LM_{adj}	94.144	0.000
ln(import)	LM	1049.091	0.000
	CD	32.385	0.000
	CD_{LM}	94.783	0.000
	LM_{adj}	94.493	0.000
ln(GDP)	LM	994.096	0.000
	CD	31.513	0.000
	CD_{LM}	89.539	0.000
	LM_{adj}	89.249	0.000

According to Table 1, results show that the null hypothesis that ascribes to cross-sectional independence, is rejected for financial fragility index, export, import and gross domestic product variables. In this direction, it is determined that there is cross-sectional dependence in all panel time series. Because of that cross-sectional section dependence is influenced by the asymptotic properties of the first-generation unit root tests, it is need to analyze the variables via second-generation unit root tests, which take into account the correlation of the panel data series (Şeker, 2020). Second-generation unit root test results are shown in Table 2. CADF test statistic is as follows (8,9):

$$y_{it} = (1-\varphi)_{\mu_i} + \varphi_i y_{i,t-1} + u_{it} \tag{8}$$

$$CIPS = N^{-1}\sum_{i=1}^{N} CADF_i \tag{9}$$

Table 2. Pesaran's CADF panel unit root test results

Variables	Level		First Difference	
	T-Bar Stat.		T-Bar Stat.	
	C	C+T	C	C+T
ln(fragility)	-1.839	-1.835	-3.509***	-3.741***
ln(export)	-1.904	-2.235	-2.771***	-2.824**
ln(import)	-2.051	-2.339	-2.761***	-3.004***
ln(GDP)	-1.966	-2.301	-2.923***	-2.832**

Note: "C" represents constant term, "C + T" stands for constant and trend. ***, **, and * indicate significance at 1%, 5% and 10% respectively.

The second-generation panel unit root test results indicate that the variables have unit root in their levels (Pesaran, 2007). This result shows that relationships among the Fragile Five and Trouble Ten countries as actors in the market are affected mutually (Giannetti, 2015: 551). However, there is no unit root in the first differences of variables. In other words, it is seen that all variables are stationary in the first differences of the series [I(1)]. After unit root tests are performed, co-integration analyses will apply to ascertain long-term relationships between the variables.

Westerlund Panel Cointegration Analysis

Westerlund (2007) cointegration analysis investigates the long-term relationship among the variables. Due to the determination of cross sectional dependence in series, it was decided to perform Westerlund panel cointegration analysis that is one of the second-generation panel cointegration tests. This cointegration analysis provides four panel cointegration tests based upon the error correction model in order to examine the cointegration relationship between panel data. The existence of the cointegration relationship is evaluated by examining whether each unit has its own error correction (Tatoğlu, 2013: 239). Westerlund panel cointegration test results of equation 1, equation 2 and equation 3 are indicated in Table 3. Westerlund (2007) cointegration test calculates test statistics using the model below (10):

$$\Delta y_{it} = \delta_i' d_t + \alpha_i y_{i,t-j} + \lambda_i' x_{i,t-1} + \sum_{j=0}^{p_i} \gamma_{ij} \Delta x_{i,t-j} + \sum_{j=1}^{p_i} \alpha_{ij} \Delta y_{i,t-j} + e_{it} \tag{10}$$

Westerlund panel cointegration analysis results show that h_0 hypothesis has been rejected at 1% and 10% significance level in both models. In other words, the cointegration relation is ascertained between panel data series in equation 1 and the long-term relationship of the panel series is confirmed. Moreover, h_0 hypothesis has been rejected at 1%, 5% and 10% significance levels in the constant and constant-trend model in equation 2 and 3. According to statistics, there are cointegration relations among panel data series in equation 2 and 3. When the results are evaluated, it has been determined that there are long-term relationships between financial fragility and exports, imports and gross domestic product. These

Table 3. Westerlund panel cointegration test results

	Cointegration Tests	Constant Model	Constant and Trend Model
		Test Statistics	
Equation (1)	G_τ	-3.617***	-4.273***
	G_a	-8.634	-10.168
	P_τ	-7.453***	-7.416
	P_a	-9.055***	-11.418*
Equation (2)	G_τ	-3.306***	-4.133***
	G_a	-7.918	-8.768
	P_τ	-6.281*	-6.462
	P_a	-7.094**	-9.329
Equation (3)	G_τ	-4.376***	-6.289***
	G_a	-9.462*	-15.540**
	P_τ	-6.667**	-7.573
	P_a	-7.392**	-13.249***

Note: ***, **, and * indicate significance at 1%, 5% and 10% respectively.

results reveal that financial fragility has long-term effects on international trade and economic growth. Therefore, it has been determined that countries should take into account their financial fragility levels while creating macroeconomic policies.

Dumitrescu - Hurlin Panel Causality Analysis

It is employed Dumitrescu - Hurlin (2012) panel causality test in order to causality relationships among the variables. Dumitrescu - Hurlin (2012) assert the hypothesis that although there is no homogeneity of Granger causality relationship, it cannot be rejected causality relationship in at least one cross-section. In this direction, Dumitrescu - Hurlin (2012) panel causality test is performed considering the cross-sectional dependence.

Results of Dumitrescu - Hurlin (2012) of panel causality test are shown in Table 4. Dumitrescu - Hurlin panel causality test model (11) is as follows (Dumitrescu and Hurlin, 2012: 1457):

$$Y_{i,t} = a_i + \sum_{k=1}^{k} Y_i^{(k)} Y_{i,t-k} + \sum_{k=1}^{k} \beta_i^{(k)} X_{i,t-k} + e_{i,t} \tag{11}$$

Panel causality test results show that there are bidirectional causality relationships from financial fragility index to exports, imports and gross domestic product of Fragile Five and Trouble Ten countries. Considering the results, it is seen that the financial fragility levels of Fragile Five and Trouble Ten countries have important impacts on exports, imports and gross domestic product of these countries. Accordingly, it is revealed that Fragile Five and Trouble Ten countries have to take into account financial fragility in the economy while macroeconomic policies are constituted.

Table 4. Results of Dumitrescu - Hurlin panel causality test

Causality Direction	Z^{HNC}, *N, T*	Z^{HNC}, *N*
ln(fragility) ¿ ln(export)	3.019***	4.193***
ln(export) ¿ ln(fragility)	3.586***	4.917***
ln(fragility) ¿ ln(import)	6.082***	8.106***
ln(import) ¿ ln(fragility)	4.161***	5.651***
ln(fragility) ¿ ln(GDP)	4.918***	6.619***
ln(GDP) ¿ ln(fragility)	3.447***	4.739***

Note: ***, **, and * indicate significance at 1%, 5% and 10% respectively.

SOLUTIONS AND RECOMMENDATIONS

Financial fragility has caused significant problems in international trade and economic growth prospects. Financial vulnerabilities affect negatively not only in the gross domestic product, but also has caused important problems in supply and demand in international trade.

Achieving sustainable international trade and economic growth depends on keeping the macroeconomic indicators that constitute financial fragility in balance. Accordingly, countries with fragile economies should pay attention to macroeconomic indicators such as current account deficit, exchange rate, foreign exchange reserves, inflation and money supply. The high level of current account deficit causes countries to have balance of payment deficits continuously and this may cause problems such as borrowing or loss of foreign exchange reserves. Besides, countries becoming a closed to global economic system can experience inflation problems in the economy. Increasing commodity prices can adversely affect the production and consumption processes due to inflation. Accordingly, it is required that countries constitute their exchange rate and monetary policies correctly.

It is a well-known fact that countries must have a sound financial and economic structure in order to gain competitive advantage in international trade. Accordingly, it is seen that countries with financial balance will not have problems in financing their international trade and production. In addition, exports should not be dependent on imports for countries not to have problems in their financial balance. Otherwise, an increase in exports of countries enhances its imports, which will make the country financially more fragile. Therefore, countries need to improve their production infrastructures and technologies in order to reduce the dependence of exports on imports. As a result, countries require to strengthen their financial structures through macroeconomic policies in order to increase their international trade volumes and achieve economic growth.

FUTURE RESEARCH DIRECTIONS

Nowadays, the effects of financial fragility on international trade and economic growth are felt more than the economic crises that occurred in the past, due to the increasing level of globalization. The interdependence of countries has increased because of that globalization has reached the highest point, hence important problems have arisen in the economies of countries due to the financial fragility.

Countries should increase their production levels and their international trade volumes in order to exist in international competition. In this direction, it is need to implement the correct macroeconomic policies and incentive systems in order to prevent financial fragility.

In line with the above information and data, it is substantial to investigate what macroeconomic policies need to be formulated to prevent financial fragility in the academic literature. Empirical studies will be important to determine the financial steps to be taken in order to solve the problems in international trade finance and to realize economic growth expectations. Accordingly, the economic policies that should be implemented in order to reduce the current account deficit, sufficient foreign exchange reserves, stabilizing the exchange rate and inflation should be discussed in detail.

CONCLUSION

This chapter examines the effect of financial fragility of Fragile Five and Troubled Ten countries in terms of international trade and economic growth prospects. Therefore, the chapter contributes to theoretical and empirical literature of financial fragility, international trade and economic growth because of that the effects of financial fragility on international trade and gross domestic product are clearly revealed.

Long-term relations among financial fragility index, exports and gross domestic product of Fragile Five and Troubled Ten countries are examined via Westerlund panel cointegration method in the chapter. Westerlund panel cointegration method permits estimating long-term relationships between the variables. Moreover, the causality relationship between the variables is analyzed via Dumitrescu-Hurlin panel causality methods in the chapter. These empirical approaches provide new perspectives to test relationships between the financial fragility index, exports and gross domestic product.

First, Westerlund panel cointegration analysis is implemented to determine the long-term relations between the variables. In accordance with the results, it has been ascertained that there is a long-term relationship among financial fragility index, exports, imports and gross domestic product. Thus, it has been clearly demonstrated that financial fragility has long-term effects on international trade and gross domestic product. Therefore, these results support the hypothesis that the effects of financial fragility can be mitigated by applying correct policies in the economy and keeping macroeconomic indicators in balance. Otherwise, it is expected that the long-term effects of financial fragility on international trade and economic growth will create an environment of instability and uncertainty (Pitterle et al., 2015).

According to results of Dumitrescu-Hurlin panel causality analysis, there are bidirectional causality relationships between financial fragility index and both exports, imports and gross domestic product in Fragile Five and Troubled Ten countries. As a result of the causality analysis, it is proved that the mutual interaction between financial fragility and both international trade and economic growth expectations, due to the fragile economic and financial structures of the developing countries is considered within the scope of the study. Results of the analysis performed in accordance with the research hypothesis indicates that the development of sound macroeconomic and financial policies will improve the international trade and economic growth performances of Fragile Five and Troubled Ten countries.

REFERENCES

Allen, F., & Gale, D. (2004). Financial fragility, liquidity, and asset prices. *Journal of the European Economic Association*, *2*(6), 1015–1048. doi:10.1162/JEEA.2004.2.6.1015

Andrews, C., & Flores, M. (2008). Improving food crisis responses in fragile states. *UNUWIDER Research Paper, 42*, 1-16.

Andrianova, S., & Demetriades, P. O. (2018). Financial development and financial fragility: Two sides of the same coin? *Comparative Economic Studies*, *60*(1), 54–68. doi:10.105741294-017-0047-z

Breusch, T. S., & Pagan, A. R. (1980). The Lagrange multiplier test and its applications to model specification in econometrics. *The Review of Economic Studies*, *47*(1), 239–253. doi:10.2307/2297111

Briguglio, L., Cordina, G., Farragia, N., & Vella, S. (2009). Economic vulnarability and resilience: Concepts and measurement. *Oxford Development Studies*, *37*(3), 229–247. doi:10.1080/13600810903089893

Briguglio, L., & Galea, W. (2003). Updating and augmenting the economic vulnerability index. Occasional paper, Islands and Small States Institute of the University of Malta.

Cespedes, L. F., Chang, R., & Velasco, A. (2004). Balance sheets and exchange rate policy. *The American Economic Review*, *94*(4), 1183–1193. doi:10.1257/0002828042002589

Chadwick, M. G. (2019). Dependence of the "Fragile Five" and "Troubled Ten" emerging market financial systems on US monetary policy and monetary policy uncertainty. *Research in International Business and Finance*, *49*, 251–268. doi:10.1016/j.ribaf.2019.04.002

Dumitrecsu, E. I., & Hurlin, C. (2012). Testing for Granger non-causality in heterogeneous panels. *Economic Modelling*, *29*(4), 1450–1460. doi:10.1016/j.econmod.2012.02.014

Gazel, S. (2016). Finansal gelişme ve ekonomik büyüme ilişkisi: 1990-2014 yılları zordaki onlu ülkeler uygulaması. *Business and Economics Research Journal*, *7*(3), 39–52. doi:10.20409/berj.2016321807

Giannetti, C. (2015). Unit roots and the dynamics of market shares: An analysis using an Italian banking micro- panel. *Empirical Economics*, *48*(2), 537–555. doi:10.100700181-013-0795-1

Gnangnon, K. (2012). Does structural economic vulnerability matter for public indebtedness in developing countries. *Serie Etudes Et Documents Du Cerdi*, *36*, 1–34.

Gopinath, G., Boz, E., Casas, C., Díez, F. J., Gourinchas, P. O., & Plagborg-Møller, M. (2020). Dominant currency paradigm. *The American Economic Review*, *110*(3), 677–719. doi:10.1257/aer.20171201

Ha, J., Stocker, M. M., & Yilmazkuday, H. (2019). *Inflation and exchange rate pass-through*. Policy Research Working Paper WPS 8780.

Itskhoki, O., & Mukhin, D. (2017). *Exchange Rate Disconnect in General Equilibrium*. NBER Working Paper 23401, National Bureau of Economic Research.

Keen, S. (1995). Finance and economic breakdown: Modeling Minsky's "financial instability hypothesis". *Journal of Post Keynesian Economics*, *17*(4), 607–635. doi:10.1080/01603477.1995.11490053

Leviastuti, A. (2020). Does the ease of starting a new business affect country's financial vulnerability? Evidence from eight European economies. *Jurnal Teknik Industri*, *22*(2), 123–132. doi:10.9744/jti.22.2.123-132

Loayza, N. V., & Raddatz, C. (2007). The structural determinants of external vulnerability. *The World Bank Economic Review*, *21*(3), 359–387. doi:10.1093/wber/lhm018

Mete, M., Pekmez, G., & Kıyançiçek, C. (2016). Effect of 2008 financial crisis on fragile eight: Theoretical review. *Electronic Journal of Social Sciences*, *15*(57), 689–709.

Minsky, H. P. (1977). The financial instability hypothesis: An interpretation of Keynes and an alternative to "standard" theory. *The Challenge (Karachi)*, *20*(1), 20–27. doi:10.1080/05775132.1977.11470296

Naude, M., Santos-Paulino, W., & Mcgillivary, A. (2009). *Vulnerability in developing countries*. United Nations University Press.

Neaime, S. (2016). Financial crises and contagion vulnerability of MENA stock markets. *Emerging Markets Review*, *27*, 14–35. doi:10.1016/j.ememar.2016.03.002

Nwachukwu, T. (2019). A global financial crises and international trade – the impact on Nigerian exports. *International Journal of Economics and Financial Management*, *4*(4), 1–19.

Okore, O. A., & Onoh, J. O. (2013). The impact of capital account liberalization on economic growth in Nigeria. *European Journal of Business and Management*, *5*(2), 34–40.

Pesaran, M. H. (2004). *General diagnostic tests for cross section dependence in panels*. IZA Discussion Paper No. 1240.

Pesaran, M. H. (2007). A simple panel unit root test in the presence of cross section dependence. *Journal of Applied Econometrics*, *22*(2), 265–312. doi:10.1002/jae.951

Pesaran, M. H., Ullah, A., & Yamagata, T. (2008). A bias-adjusted LM test of error cross-section independence. *The Econometrics Journal*, *11*(1), 105–127. doi:10.1111/j.1368-423X.2007.00227.x

Pitterle, I., Haufler, F., & Hong, P. (2015). Assessing emerging markets' vulnerability to financial crisis. *Journal of Policy Modeling*, *37*(3), 484–500. doi:10.1016/j.jpolmod.2015.03.010

Radelet, S., & Sachs, J. (2000). The onset of the East Asian financial crisis. In P. Krugman (Ed.), *Currency crises* (pp. 105–162). University of Chicago Press.

Rozmainsky, I., & Rodionova, T. (2021). The financial fragility hypothesis and the debt crisis in Italy in the 2010s. *Terra Economicus*, *19*(1), 6–16. doi:10.18522/2073-6606-2021-19-1-6-16

Sachs, J., Tornell, A., & Velasco, A. (1996). Financial crises in emerging markets: The lessons from 1995. Paper no. w5576, National Bureau of Economic Research. doi:10.3386/w5576

Şeker, A. (2020). The impacts of liner shipping connectivity and economic growth on international trade case of European countries and Turkey. In G. Ç. Ceyhun (Ed.), *Handbook of research on the applications of international transportation and logistics for world trade* (pp. 139–150). IGI Global. doi:10.4018/978-1-7998-1397-2.ch008

Shousha, S. (2019). *The dollar and emerging market economies: Financial vulnerabilities meet the international trade system.* International Finance Discussion Papers 1258.

Svirydzenka, K. (2016). Introducing a new broad-based index of financial development. *IMF Working Papers, 16*, 1.

Tatoğlu, F. Y. (2013). *İleri Panel Veri Analizi*. Beta Yayıncılık.

Westerlund, J. (2007). Testing for error correction in panel data. *Oxford Bulletin of Economics and Statistics*, *69*(6), 709–748. doi:10.1111/j.1468-0084.2007.00477.x

ADDITIONAL READING

Ampudia, M., Vlokhoven, H., & Zochowski, D. (2016). Financial fragility of Euro area household. *Journal of Financial Stability*, *27*, 250–261. doi:10.1016/j.jfs.2016.02.003

Andrianova, S., & Demetriades, P. O. (2018). Financial development and financial fragility: Two sides of the same coin? *Comparative Economic Studies*, *60*(1), 54–68. doi:10.105741294-017-0047-z

Argitis, G., & Nikolaidi, M. (2014). The financial fragility and the crisis of the Greek government sector. *International Review of Applied Economics*, *28*(3), 274–292. doi:10.1080/02692171.2013.858667

Brunetti, E., Giarda, E., & Torricelli, C. (2015). Is financial fragility a matter of illiquidity? An appraisal for Italian households. *Review of Income and Wealth*, *62*(4), 628–649. doi:10.1111/roiw.12189

Dasgupta, Z. (2020). Economic slowdown and financial fragility the structural malaise of India's growth process. *Economic and Political Weekly*, *55*(13), 46–53.

Daud, S. N. M., Marzuki, A., Ahmad, N., & Kefeli, Z. (2019). Financial vulnerability and its determinants: Survey evidence from Malaysian households. *Emerging Markets Finance & Trade*, *55*(9), 1991–2003. doi:10.1080/1540496X.2018.1511421

Emmons, W. R., & Noeth, B. J. (2013). Economic vulnerability and financial fragility. *Review - Federal Reserve Bank of St. Louis*, *95*(5), 361–388. doi:10.20955/r.95.361-388

Kim, Y. I., Kim, H. C., & Yoo, J. H. (2016). Household over-indebtedness and financial vulnerability in Korea: Evidence from credit bureau data. *KDI Journal of Economic Policy*, *38*(3), 53–77. doi:10.23895/kdijep.2016.38.3.53

Neaime, S. (2016). Financial crises and contagion vulnerability of MENA stock markets. *Emerging Markets Review*, *27*, 14–35. doi:10.1016/j.ememar.2016.03.002

Vitali, S., Battiston, S., & Gallegati, M. (2016). Financial fragility and distress propagation in a network of regions. *Journal of Economic Dynamics & Control*, *62*, 56–75. doi:10.1016/j.jedc.2015.10.003

KEY TERMS AND DEFINITIONS

Financial Fragility: Can be explained as a situation that is sensitive to the development of sudden shocks, which may occur in the markets and to show its effect on the economies of the country as a financial crisis on a large scale.

Fragile Five Countries: Is a term revealed by Morgan Stanley in August 2013, because of that the developing countries in this group are unable to finance their economic growth expectations and become economies dependent on foreign investment. Turkey, Brazil, India, South Africa and Indonesia are located in Fragile Five countries group.

Troubled Ten Countries: Describe that Morgan Stanley has expanded the "Fragile Five" country group as a result of analysis and revealed the "Trouble Ten" countries in 2015. "Troubled Ten" countries asserted by Morgan Stanley are Taiwan, Singapore, Russia, Thailand, South Korea, Peru, South Africa, Chile, Colombia and Brazil.

APPENDIX

Table 5. Fragile five and troubled ten countries

Fragile Five Countries	Troubled Ten Countries
Brazil	Brazil
India	Chile
Indonesia	Colombia
South Africa	Peru
Turkey	Russia
	Singapore
	South Africa
	South Korea
	Taiwan
	Thailand

Chapter 10
The Future of Trade Fairs After the COVID-19 Pandemic

Mehmet Sami Süygün
https://orcid.org/0000-0002-3928-7438
Tarsus University, Turkey

ABSTRACT

Globalization has made the whole world a common market for businesses by removing the commercial borders between countries. Increased competition in the global market has pushed businesses that want to operate in this arena to implement new strategies. As a promotion activity, fairs have been the most important assistant of the companies that want to internationalize over the years. Although the concept of fair organizations has changed with the effect of digitalization in the historical process, fairs still continue their main function of bringing buyers and sellers together. The subject of this chapter is how virtual fairs, which have increased their importance in marketing activities with the pandemic, will affect the future of trade fairs. In this context, the history of the fairs, their place and importance in international marketing, virtual fairs, and the impact of the COVID-19 pandemic on the future of international fairs will be discussed.

INTRODUCTION

It is clear from the marketing literature that trade fairs are one of the significant marketing communication tools. Marketing communications are all promotional elements of the marketing mix including communication between its target audiences and an organization on all matters affecting marketing performance (Broderick and Pickton, 2005: 4). Marketing communication is a component of a business's marketing mix, and the tools it uses can be divided into five categories: direct marketing, advertising, personal selling, sales promotion and public relations (Kotler, 1999: 272). Each category contains specific promotional tools used to communicate with consumers. Of these primary tools; other communication methods are derived, such as lobbying, product placement, sponsorship, facility visits, events, in-store and merchandising activities, conferences, websites and trade shows, customer magazines (Kimmel, 2005: 156). According to Broderick and Pickton (2005: 675), Kotler (1999: 272), Smith *et al.* (2004:

DOI: 10.4018/978-1-7998-8314-2.ch010

61), trade fairs are included in promotional tools such as sales promotion and personal selling. Gopalakrishna and Lillien (2012: 226), expressed fairs as a tool to improve the sales of various products and differentiated them from personal selling by bringing current and potential customers to the seller rather than bringing the seller to the consumer.

Trade shows are ideal for introducing a company's range of products to potential distributors and new customers and have long been widely used by both incumbent firms and newcomers. The changing nature of the Business to Business (B2B) landscape for both supplier and buyer is altering the nature of the traditional trade fair environment, largely driven by the technological revolution (Gopalakrishna ve Lillien, 2012: 240). As a new trend in the field of trade fairs, virtual fairs offer a new environment where users can communicate and interact anywhere at anytime. A virtual trade fair is a type of virtual event where exhibitors and visitors connect to interact and exchange information through the virtual environment, irrespective of geographical location (Gottlieb and Bianchi, 2017: 17). The Covid-19 pandemic has deeply affected the fair industry, just as education, tourism and many other fields. According to UFI, The Global Association of the Exhibition Industry, revenues of the global industry dropped by 68% in 2020 comparing with 2019 (UFI Media Release, 2021). According to the results of the research conducted by 450 fair organizers from 24 countries in 2020, the rate of those who said that virtual fairs will replace physical fairs after the pandemic remained at 14%, while the rate of those who stated that there would be a shift to hybrid events with more digital elements was 80% (UFI 26 th Baramoter, 2021: 17). Similar to the effect of the Covid-19 pandemic on e-commerce, distance education and flexible working, it is likely that it will accelerate the digital transformation of fair organizations.

The research topic of this section is how the Covid-19 Pandemic will affect the future of virtual fairs, whose history goes back much further. In this context, the concepts of trade and fair and virtual trade fair, the history of fairs, the place and importance of fairs in international marketing, the advantages and disadvantages of physical and virtual fairs, and the impact of the Covid-19 Pandemic on the future of international fairs will be discussed.

BACKGROUND

New technologies and digitalization have been very effective in marketing activities as in every field. Digital marketing, which can be described as succeeding marketing goals by applying technology, data and digital media (Chaffey and Chadwick, 2019: 11), has also transformed the components of the marketing communication mix (ibid., 30). Public relations, market research, advertising, sponsorship, exhibitions and trade shows, direct marketing, packaging, sales promotion and personal selling are also used online in marketing communication. In the beginning, the trade fair industry used the internet only as a marketing tool with which it could interact with the market (Li, 2010: 273), but later the industry discovered the flexibility of virtual trade fairs and encouraged their use as a marketing communication tool (Gottlieb and Bianchi, 2016: 18). Previous research has addressed trade fairs' role in communication and interaction of businesses with their customers (Rosson and Seringhaus, 1995; Blythe, 2010; Sarmento and Farhangmehr, 2015; Hansen, 2000; Siemieniako and Gębarowski, 2017), impact on internationalization (Kalafsky and Gress, 2013; Solberg, 1991; Seringhaus and Rosson, 2000; Monreal and Weiss, 2019), impact on the diffusion of innovation (Pöllmann, 2013; Bathelt, 2017; Chlodnicki *et al.*, 2011; Ahola, 2012; Zhu *et al.*, 2020), features of being sectoral clusters (Maskell *et al.*, 2004; Power and Jansson, 2008; Bathelt and Schuldt, 2008; Ramírez-Pasillas, 2010; Li, 2014). Studies dealing with the role of new virtual communication technologies in trade fairs, trends and virtual trade fairs (Lee-Kelly *et al.*, 2004; Çavuşoğlu, 2006; Geigenmüller, 2010; Bathelt and Schuldt, 2010; Sharda *et al.*, 2012; Pecherskaya *et al.*, 2019; Barbini, 2003; Gottlieb & Bianchi, 2016; Vik *et al.*, 2018; Sarmento and Simões, 2019; Edge *et al.*, 2020) are less common. It is thought that the future of trade fairs should be handled more within the scope of the changes caused by the pandemic. Although there are studies that address the impact of the pandemic on the economy (Bulin and Tenie, 2020; Fernandes, 2020; Bauer and Weber; 2020; Saini *et al.*, 2020; Mohapatra *et al.*, 2020), including trade fairs (Adams, 2020; Shereni *et al.*, 2021; Hu and Olivieri, 2021), there are not many (Nikitina, 2021; Gajjar and Parmar, 2020; Vogel and Ajoudani, 2020) academic studies dealing with physical and virtual trade fairs. In this way, this study might contribute to the literature by focusing on how the existing trend on virtual trade fairs will be affected with the Covid-19 Pandemic also by discussing the past studies.

Trade Fairs in Physical and Virtual Platforms

Trade fairs, which were also percieved as trade shows, exhibits, expositions, conventions or scientific/ technical conferences, were essentially the coming together of a whole industry at a specific location and time (Situma, 2012: 221). A trade fair has been defined as an assisting marketing event in the form of an exhibition, exposition or bazaar. It occurs at periodically recurring intervals, usually once a year. It has predetermined working hours ranging from one day to several weeks. Its purpose is to disseminate information on the goods and services of exhibitors who have rented spaces or stands that are clustered, properly distributed and separated from each other within a certain structure to potential buyers (Banting & Blenkhorn, 1974: 286). In simple terms, trade fairs are opportunities for retailers to view and sample the offerings of wholesalers, manufacturers and ancillary service providers (Laing and Frost, 2017: 9). There were two different kinds of trade fairs. First type was the business-to-business trade shows. The audience of this type of trade fairs were the wholesalers and retailers and this type of trade shows have the aim of pushing products through the distribution channel. Second type was consumer trade shows which were targeted the general public and were designed to stimulate end-user demand (Sarmento and Simoes, 2018: 154; Situma, 2012: 221). Palumbo and Herbig (2002: 95), mentioned two types of trade fairs, vertical and horizontal. A horizontal show displays an extensive diversity of products. The Hamburg Fair in Germany is an example of such an event, displaying both consumer and industrial products. A vertical fair is product-specific; it may be limited to certain products such as medical products, computers, or electronics.

Fairs, like markets, are as old as market economies. The periodicity of the fairs has been the decisive difference between the two, while the market is continuous. Fairs are generally held once or twice a year (Carreras and Torra, 2005: 3). This temporary society has all the challenges and opportunities of more permanent societies (Krugman *et al.*, 2006: 2). Therefore they have been essential sales and communication tools all over the world for many centuries. Historically, trade fairs date back to the era when trade mostly took place in marketplaces. It is possible to trace the origin of trade fairs back to biblical times. However, especially since the 16th century, trade fairs have been the main means of reaching potential customers and promoting products. The London World's Fair, which took place in 1851, was the first truly modern trade event. The purpose of the fair was to promote the commercial activities of British companies in the international market (Palumbo and Herbig, 2002: 96). There had been Universal Exhibitions also in Paris (1855, 1867, 1878, 1889), New York (1853), Munich (1854), Porto (1865), Wien (1873), Lyon (1873), Philadelphia (1873), Sydney (1879), Melbourne (1880), Amsterdam (1883), New

Figure 1. 2009 Interfood & Drink Sofia Trade Fair
Source: Taken by the author

Orleans (1885), Antwerp (1885), Brussels (1888), Barcelona (1888), Chicago (1895) (Carreras and Torra, 2005: 8). In the 19th century, universal trade fairs were also held in countries such as China, India and Russia. Today, many trade fairs with very different contents continue to be held in different parts of the world. Anuga Trade Fair for Food and Beverages, China Fisheries & Seafood Expo, International Gift & Decoration Fair, Footwear Show New York Expo, Guangzhou International Lighting Exhibition, SIAL Paris Food Industry are a few examples of trade fairs. Figure 1 presents a visual from of the 2009 Interfood & Drink Fair held in Sofia, the capital of Bulgaria.

At trade fairs, one can sell manufactured or represented products, find services and products to buy and investigate the status of competitors and competition in the market. Testing receptivity of products, observing customer behavior, obtaining agents and distributors, distributing promotional material, networking with colleagues, capturing leads and keeping on top of the competition are the opportunities presented by trade shows besides attaining sales orders (Palumbo and Herbig, 2002: 94). Kalafsky and Gress (2013: 305), mention the advantages of trade fairs as the opportunity of sellers to access a large number of potential buyers, measure customer reactions to their products, develop business relationships, and display their products. According to Appleyard (2006: 11), effective selling consists of 60 percent of listening, 30 percent of presentation, and 10 percent of completion. A trade show includes all the components of an effective sale and therefore offers an opportunity for direct selling. The listening has to be executed through the wholly artificial means of market research through direct mail and advertising. An advertisement has to take an attitude that best fits the majority of the target audience, neglecting any intend to fulfil individual needs. On a fair booth, individual attention can be given to each visitor and their particular needs can be met with an individualized solution. The relationship between buyers and sellers at trade shows goes far beyond traditional buying behavior. Therefore, trade fairs are an important tool for the interaction of companies and relationship marketing (Sarmento and Simoes, 2018:1786).

Trade fairs and exhibitions have been changed from the rudimentary ones to the most professional ones in time. In the past, to sell and buy products was the most important goals of trade show. But nowadays exhibiting companies in trade fairs have much more wide objectives (Rehak, 2008: 11). Originally, trade shows developed as specialised fairs where buyers could examine samples and place sales orders for delivery at a later date. Generally, they were held regularly hereby becoming fixed in the business calendar and were held either at central trading cities or in regions which specialised in manufacturing certain products. In the 20th century, fairs became far more prominent as places to showcase the latest industry trends and where industry participants come together to develop network and relationships with business (Laing and Frost, 2017: 10). Despite the prominence of communication and information technologies in daily work routines, personal contact between people remains a distinctive tool for exchanging information, solving problems and developing relationships (Bathelt and Schuldt, 2010: 1958). However, a number of reasons, like increasing technological opportunities, cost and time savings, new trends and pandemic, support other approaches. Within this scope, in addition to face-to-face interaction and physical coexistence, interest in virtual interaction forms has increased in recent years. According to Bartle (2004: 3), vitual means "that which isn't, having the form or effect of that which is" and virtual worlds are places where dreams meet reality. As the need for physical presence erodes and intimacy becomes less of an issue, forms of virtual interaction such as the dynamic network, virtual company, virtual team, virtual communities and virtual fair are emerging. The new notion of the "virtual fairs" emerged as a result of the excess demand for physical exhibitions. This approach appeared from the Association of Exhibition Organisers and clear the way for farseeing businesses that see the Internet as an alternative platform (Lee-Kelley *et al.*, 2004: 634). The first virtual fairground experience in the historical process was realized with the design of the "Avatars98" conference area. This experience includes designs for spaces as well as "discussion pods" and showroom booths that the database interface will automatically create for speakers and attendees (Damer, 2008: 99).

A virtual trade fair is a kind of virtual event, where exhibitors and visitors come together through the virtual environment to interact and exchange information irrespective of geographic location (Gottlieb and Bianchi, 2017: 17). A characteristic virtual trade fair usually includes a virtual showroom where users enter by registering. Exhibitors can create virtual booths to display their goods or present their services, just like at a physical trade show. In virtual fairs, exhibitors can present their products to potential customers around the world without having to visit them personally (Remolar *et al.*, 2015: 4562). In both cases it is important to ensure that the stand is visited. Some online events such as online conferences, webinars, training, and competitions can be organized to increase the traffic in virtual fairs, similar to support activities such as traditional dance shows, catering and competitions, which are held to increase the interest in the fair area and in particular the stand area in physical fairs.

In Figure 2, the visual of Shoedex 2020 Shoes, Bags and Leather Accessories Fair, the first virtual fair of Turkey, held on 1-3 June 2020 is presented. The Virtual Fair was opened under the auspices of the Ministry of Trade, under the coordination of the Turkish Exporters Assembly, in cooperation with the Aegean Leather and Leather Products Exporters' Association and IZFAŞ, with the participation of 31 Turkish shoe and saddlery exporters and 250 importers from 35 countries.

Figure 2. Shoedex 2020 SHOES, BAGS and LEATHER ACCESSORIES FAIR
Source: www.eib.org.tr

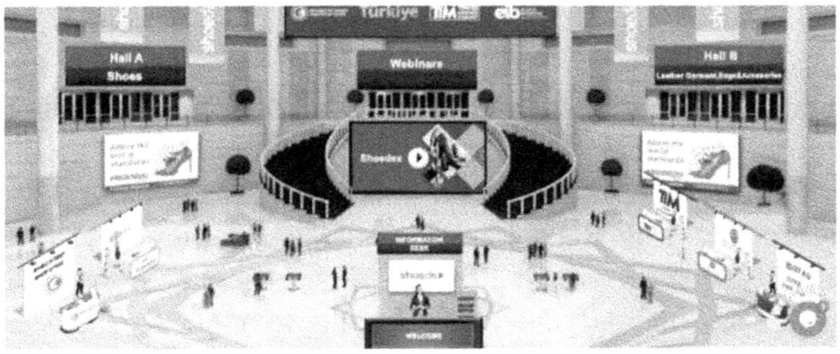

Physical Trade Fairs vs. Virtual Trade Fairs

Trade fairs are events that can take place on physical platforms where exhibitors interact in person, or on virtual environments where exhibitors interact through computer-mediated forms. Both platforms have some advantages and disadvantages.

The most important advantage of physical fairs is that they allow face-to-face communication. Bathelt and Schuldt (2010: 1957), underlined the importance of temporary face-to-face contact in creating and expanding knowledge. Trade show visits are important "learning trips" that help industrial buyers solve their business problems with creative thinking. Emotional stimuli are very effective in acquiring knowledge and physical fairs allow this. For example, physical fairs allow fashion designers to touch garment fabric samples. Thus, by touching fabrics, they can collect information that is not accessible to the eye, such as softness or temperature (Rinallo *et al.*, 2010: 253). This also applies to the senses of taste and smell. Thanks to these features, physical fairs offer significant advantages for exhibitors from many sectors.

Physical fairs have some disadvantages such as limited geographical access due to distance, limited visiting opportunities with opening and closing hours, and entrance fees (Sharda *et al.*, 2012: 51). Stand rental and design costs are high in international fairs. For this reason, it often forms a significant part of a company's sales budget. In addition, exhibitions consume resources with time and manpower requirements in the design, manufacture, transportation and assembly of the stands. And there are also costs such as participants' accommodation, travel and daily living expenses (Lee *et al.*, 2004: 635).

In the beginning, the low cost nature of the internet was the main driving factor for the development of virtual fairs. International participants can attend virtual fairs with very little expense. This is the main reason for the popularity of virtual fairs, which allows companies to save on budget. (Remolar *et al.*, 2015: 4562). Although budget savings are seen as the most important advantage of virtual fairs, it may not meet the expectations that are overly hopeful. A successful virtual trade show process is closely linked to the Customer Relationship Management (CRM) process as well as physical and organizational resources. Therefore, turning to virtual fairs instead of physical fairs may not always mean reducing costs. Sometimes it can mean a redistribution of costs. Another reason virtual trade fairs stand out from the top advantages is that they make it easy for a firm to serve its entire market. Virtual events are open to participants from all over the world, even in different time zones. Moreover, it does not include the difficulties caused by distance and travel routes. (Geigenmüller, 2010: 286). Virtual events help maintain communication between participants in different time zones. And increases the efficiency of knowledge transfer between exhibitors and visitors. The opportunity for participants to access virtual fairs at anytime and anywhere offers a significant advantage. Based on in-depth interview data with managers who have attended virtual trade fairs before, Gottlieb and Bianchi (2016), grouped the perceived benefits of participation in virtual trade fairs compared to physical trade fairs under three themes. First, it is one of the ways to communicate with current and potential stakeholders. Second, it provides access to new markets in a cost-effective manner, while providing additional opportunities to increase revenues with the remainder of the budget. Third, it helps organizations raise their brand image and collect more and more systematically information from the market through the data flow they provide. Limited delegate registration data is captured at conventional trade shows, however with virtual trade shows, considerable delegate information is captured and stored online including workshop attendances, chatroom conversations, promotional material tracking and sharing (Edge *et al.*, 2020: 6). This provides an advantage for customer relationship management.

The most important disadvantage of virtual fairs is that they do not have such an important feature as addressing the senses that they offer face-to-face communication. According to Sarmento and Simoes (2018: 1795), At physical trade fairs, the senses and emotions are at the forefront. Physical fairs offer participants an unforgettable experience fueled by the senses and emotions. A virtual environment cannot replace this platform that feeds on human emotions. While visitor behavior at physical trade fairs cannot be characterized by "fun and emotions", this is not to deny that exhibitors can have fun or experience unforgettable moments at the fair (Rinallo *et al.*, 2010: 253). Virtual fairs ignore the features of an exhibition such as escaping from the office environment, seeing and being seen by exhibitors and visitors, being held every year. These details prevent it from being a special event to look forward to, savor and remember later (Appleyard, 2006: 226). Virtual fairs have also been investigated in terms of their impact on the components of the marketing mix. Lee-Kelley *et al.* (2004), examined the attitudes of Middle Eastern exhibition organizers towards the use of virtual fairs. The study findings pointed to the potential of virtual fairs in terms of components of the marketing mix. The study concluded that although virtual fairs do not provide a strong environment for the location component, they offer a beneficial environment in terms of product, promotion and price, which are other marketing mix components. According to the results of the study, it was stated that the weaker environment of the virtual fairs for the place component may be due to the fact that they are only used to convey information rather than allowing the distribution of goods. Bathelt and Schuldt (2010: 1961), investigated the similarities and differences between physical and virtual fairs using the classification scheme consisting of global co-presence, face to face interaction, observation, focused communities, multiplex meetings and relationships components. Advantages of physical fairs are; high accessibility of exhibitors, strong communication with facial expressions, gestures and facial expressions, observation of the reactions of participants, high-quality professional environment, direct/credible feedback mechanisms. Advantages of virtual fairs are; high availability independent of time and place, strong goal orientation, observation of websites and web activities, quick information transfer.

Future of Trade Fairs

In 2018, 5 million exhibitors took part in approximately 32,000 exhibitions held in more than 180 countries and 303 million people visited. Exhibitions generated more than $136.9 billion in direct expenditure by visitors, exhibitors and additional related expenditures. Exhibitions supported 1.3 million direct jobs worldwide and generated a direct GDP of $81.1 billion. After taking into account indirect and induced effects, exhibitions contributed $325 billion in total output, 3.2 million jobs, and $197.5 billion in GDP to the global economy in 2018. The total GDP of $197.5 billion supported by the global exhibition sector makes this sector larger than the economies of countries such as Hungary, Kuwait, Sri Lanka and Ecuador, placing it in 56th place worldwide. (UFI, 2019: 6).

As can be seen from the Figure 3, the revenues of the global trade fair industry fell by 68% in 2020 compared to 2019. A total of 224 billion USD of output related to the fair was not produced. 2.4 million direct or indirect jobs were affected. Business agreements of 370 billion USD between the exhibitors could not be signed due to the Covid-19 Pandemic.

Figure 3. Covid-19 economic damage on exhibitions globally
Source: ufi.org/research

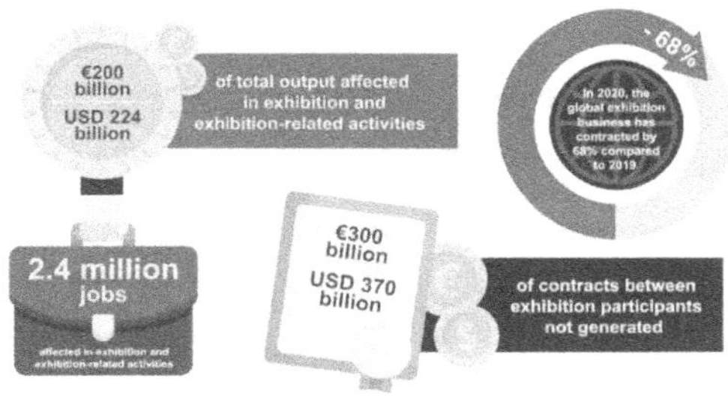

This global crisis has affected many countries. Germany, one of the countries with the largest share in fair revenues, is one of them. More than 70% of the 368 exhibitions scheduled to take place in Germany in 2020 had to be canceled by the organizers or postponed to 2021 and 2022. In the same period, approximately 50 digital events took place (www.auma.de/en). Events such as live music and cinema, along with fairs, experienced the most dramatic revenue decline in its history in 2020, with a decrease of 64% compared to 2019. Moreover, these revenues are not expected to return to pre-pandemic levels until 2024 (PWC, 2020: 6).

What made 2020 different from 2019 in terms of trade fairs was undoubtedly the global pandemic as an environmental factor. In addition technological, political, legal, social and economic factors at macro level and visitors, exhibitors, trade fair companies, governmental institutions, business system partners, associations and other stakeholders at micro level also have an impact on trade fairs, as presented in Figure 4.

Like the pandemic, sustainability is one of the environmental factors affecting trade fairs. Virtual fairs have much smaller carbon footprints than their physical equivalents. Sustainability, combined with Covid-19 may increase the reluctance to travel, so events, at least in the short term, may become more local rather than big international gatherings. It may also mean that event products are broken down to smaller molecular audiences (Peck, 2021: 9). Technologies such as the internet, web conferencing, video conferencing, simulations, and virtual reality have an impact on the future of trade fairs. However, sometimes, as in the covid-19 pandemic, one factor can increase the influence of the other factor. Although virtual fairs have existed for decades, their development has accelerated with the effect of the pandemic and it has started to be talked about more in the future of trade fairs. Just like the impact of the pandemic on e-commerce and distance education. The economic effects of the pandemic have also

Figure 4. Factors affecting trade shows
Source: Kirchgeorg et al., 2010: 304

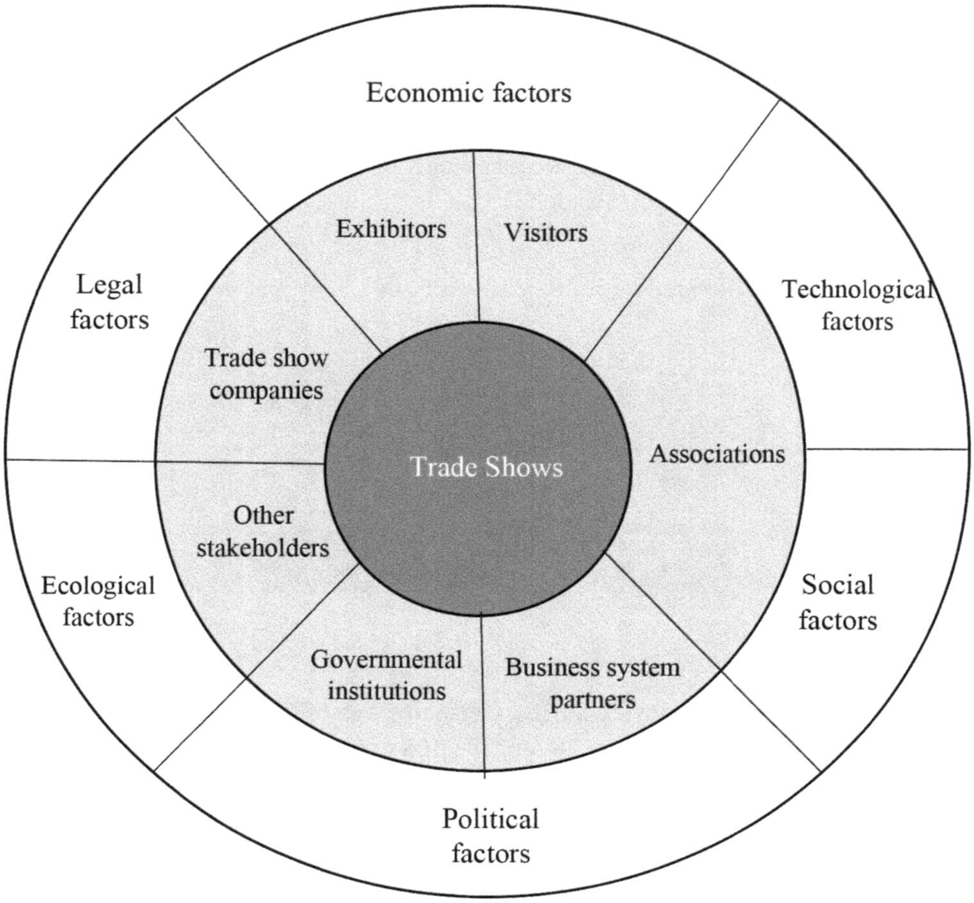

affected policy makers, and virtual fairs have also been added to the scope of government support, which was mainly given to physical fairs in the past. Undoubtedly, this situation is in favor of virtual fairs. For instance, before pandemic there are supports for participation in international domestic trade fairs and participation in international fairs and exhibitions in Turkey (Süygün, 2019: 37) but not for virtual fairs. After the pandemic, in January 2021, the Turkish government announced a virtual fair support. In order to encourage the participation to international virtual fairs which are approved by the Ministry of Trade, the expenses, related to the participation and organization to the virtual fairs are supported at 50% and up to $50,000 per activity. Such practices are also widespread in different countries. The Covid-19 Pandemic has accelerated and strengthened this trend. The US government offers companies the opportunity to promote their products and services to potential buyers and stakeholders in a foreign market through virtual environments (www.trade.gov/virtual-fair). Previously, the Singapore goverment did not provide support for virtual trade fairs. Under the budget 2021 enhancements, the goverment now supports the expenses incurred to participate in approved virtual trade fairs (KPMG, 2021: 3). The German Federal Ministry of Economic Cooperation and Development supports German and European companies in opening new supply markets and connecting with manufacturers at virtual meetings and trade fairs (IPD, 2020: 1).

Despite many factors that can affect the future of trade fairs, the most prominent one is undoubtedly the virtual fairs that use the blessings offered by technology. The post-pandemic situation of virtual fairs, which is the most mentioned in the future of fairs, arouses the curiosity of practitioners. The 26th UFI Global Exhibition Barometer (2021: 16) conducted a survey to explore industry views on the future of trade fairs after the Covid-19 Pandemic. The survey data consists of the responses of 457 participating companies from 64 countries in two separate periods, June 2020 and December 2020. As the same question was asked 6 months ago, the comparisons allow identifying trends.

- 64% (57% 6 months ago) stated that the Covid-19 Pandemic has revealed the importance of face-to-face events and therefore the industry will recover quickly after the pandemic
- 63% (57% 6 months ago) stated that they believe there will be fewer international physical fairs in the post-pandemic period and that physical fairs will be held with fewer participants
- 80% (82% 6 months ago) of the companies stated that they think that digital items will come to the fore more in the post-pandemic period and there will be a tendency towards hybrid events.
- Only 14% (17% 6 months ago) stated that they believed that physical activities will be replaced by virtual activities.

In another study conducted on 103 marketing executives with physical and virtual trade fair experience, 93% of respondents stated that they transferred their budgets to virtual fairs during the Covid-19 Pandemic. However, in the same research, only 10.7% of the participants stated that they would prefer a virtual event to a physical fair (SalesRoads, 2021: 7).

The results of these extremely comprehensive surveys provide insight into the future of trade fairs. It seems more likely that hybrid fairs will increase their weight rather than physical fairs giving way to virtual fairs.

CONCLUSION AND RECOMMENDATIONS

In the past, the best way to communicate with customers and gather information about rival products and new trends was to attend trade fairs. Thanks to technology, everything is much easier now. It takes a few minutes to share product information and images. Moreover, with applications such as simulation technology and virtual reality, these sharing have become much more realistic.

With new technologies, trendy forms of media are competing for an increased share of the marketing budget. For example, the budget spent on developing the website or to participate a virtual fair also puts pressure on the physical fair budget. According to Appleyard (2006: 226), in most cases, of course, it's not an 'either/or' situation, it's about reaching the right cost-effectiveness balance. Therefore, various marketing activities continue to be carried out together. From the practitioners' point of view, virtual trade fairs complement rather than replacing physical fairs, as they do not offer a substitute for face-to-face interaction (Geigenmüller, 2010: 286). There will be physical events that are the anchor events for the industry to get together with communities to meet face to face, but there will be the addition of digital events as communities want to learn and share information and content all the year (Sedky, 2021: 4). In a hybrid event, online attendees from all over the world can join the event live. Increased reach with virtual joins backed by physical attendance allows more guests to attend events. In this way, events become more innovative, contribute to the protection of the environment and increase their effectiveness.

The Covid-19 Pandemic, the biggest pandemic of the 21st century, has had devastating effects on nearly all areas of economic activity. The volume, size and scope of events, especially international ones, make them more vulnerable to the Covid-19 Pandemic (Mohanty *et al.*, 2020: 3). As an event, fairs have also been adversely affected by the covid-19 pandemic, as they both bring crowds together and require contact services such as transportation and accommodation. According to UFI, global fair industry revenues for 2020 dropped by 68%, compared to 2019 (UFI Media Release, 2021).

While the concept of virtual technologies emerged in the early 1960s (Stone, 1993:167), the first virtual fair work took place in the 1990s (Damer, 2008: 99). Despite their existence since the 90s, it is a matter of curiosity whether virtual fairs, which have increased their weight on the agenda of companies and governments, especially with the covid-19 pandemic, can replace physical fairs in the future. The future of virtual fairs will likely depend on virtual fair systems evolving technologically to offer greater value propositions for exhibitors and visitors (Gottlieb and Bianchi, 2016: 17). To achieve this, some improvements can be made by taking advantage of the feedback from the post-pandemic experiences. Providing more information to both participants and visitors about using virtual fair technology, finding ways that will appeal to the senses, evaluating better the potential they offer for customer relations management will contribute to the spread of virtual fairs in the future. However, it does not seem easy for virtual fairs to meet and replace the advantages of physical fairs such as touching, seeing, feeling and socializing, which arise from the fact that human beings are social beings. In some fairs, as in the case of tourism and employment, digital media can be used more heavily. And virtual fairs can be a complementary element to ensure that visitors who cannot come to the physical fair for any reason participate in the fair. Virtual fairs will be an integral part of fairs, but the main focus will continue to be physical fairs, at least in the near future.

FUTURE RESEARCH DIRECTIONS

The current situation and future of physical and virtual trade fairs before and after the pandemic are conceptually discussed by using various studies in the literature. On the other hand, it is suggested that this study, which is based on secondary data, should be reshaped by research based on first hand data. It is also recommended that a new research based on conceptual and field applications specific to the hybrid fairs proposed within the scope of this study should be conducted. It is thought that studies can be realized on participants in different regions in order to measure different behavioral patterns towards the change of the future of fairs.

LIMITATIONS

The findings of this theoretical study based on secondary data. It is possible to talk about two difficulties in accessing secondary data. The first is that there has not been much study yet on the impact of Covid-19 Pandemic, which was declared as a pandemic in March 2020, on trade fairs. Secondly, since the pandemic is not over yet, there is not enough data both from the literature and from the field on how the sector will react after the pandemic. In this context, the study aims to examine the future of fairs by considering the possible effects of the Covid-19 Pandemic with the available data.

ACKNOWLEDGMENT

This research received no specific grant from any funding agency in the public, commercial, or not-for-profit sectors.

REFERENCES

Adams, R. (2020). Despite the absence of trade fairs, chemours, merck, schlenk shepherd showcase their new products. *Focus on Pigments*, *2020*(7), 1–2. doi:10.1016/j.fop.2020.08.001

Ahola, E. K. (2012). Towards an understanding of the role of trade fairs as facilitators of consumer creativity. *Journal of Marketing Communications*, *18*(5), 321–333. doi:10.1080/13527266.2010.528587

Appleyard, J. (2006). *How to exhibit at trade fairs: the complete guide to making your company's next exhibition enormously rewarding*. How To Books.

Banting, P. M., & Blenkhorn, D. L. (1974). The role of industrial trade shows. *Industrial Marketing Management*, *3*(5), 285–295. doi:10.1016/0019-8501(74)90004-2

Barbini, F. M. (2003). Innovative Trade Fairs for Incubating Virtual Enterprises. In *Working Conference on Virtual Enterprises* (pp. 543-550). Springer.

Bartle, R. A. (2004). *Designing virtual worlds*. New Riders.

Bathelt, H. (2017). Trade fairs and innovation. In *The Elgar companion to innovation and knowledge creation*. Edward Elgar Publishing. doi:10.4337/9781782548522.00042

Bathelt, H., & Schuldt, N. (2008). Between luminaires and meat grinders: International trade fairs as temporary clusters. *Regional Studies*, *42*(6), 853–868. doi:10.1080/00343400701543298

Bathelt, H., & Schuldt, N. (2010). International trade fairs and global buzz, Part I: Ecology of global buzz. *European Planning Studies*, *18*(12), 1957–1974. doi:10.1080/09654313.2010.515815

Bauer, A., & Weber, E. (2020). COVID-19: How much unemployment was caused by the shutdown in Germany? *Applied Economics Letters*, 1–6. doi:10.1080/13504851.2020.1789544

Blythe, J. (2010). Trade fairs as communication: A new model. *Journal of Business and Industrial Marketing*.

Broderick, A., & Pickton, D. (2005). *Integrated marketing communications*. Pearson Education UK.

Bulin, D., & Tenie, I. P. (2020). Preliminary assessment of the COVID-19 pandemic impact on the tourism industry. *Global Economic Observer*, *8*(1), 41–46.

Carreras, A., & Torra Fernández, L. (2005). *Why did modern trade fairs appear?* Universitat Pompeu Fabra.

Çavuşoğlu, M. (2006). A Research on the Problems of Virtual Fairs and the Advantages of E-Commerce in Turkey and in the World. *İstanbul Üniversitesi İşletme Fakültesi Dergisi, 35*(2).

Chaffey, D., & Ellis-Chadwick, F. (2019). Digital Marketing. Academic Press.

Chlodnicki, M., Leszczyński, G., & Zieliński, M. (2011). Trade fairs—A tool for the spread of innovation. In *4th International Conference for Entrepreneurship, Innovation and Regional Development*. National Center for Development of Innovation and Entrepreneurial Learning.

Damer, B. (2008). Meeting in the ether: A brief history of virtual worlds as a medium for user-created events. *Artifact, 2*(2), 94–107. doi:10.1080/17493460903020877

Edge, M., Ghosh, S., & Liang, Y. (2020). *The Evolution of Virtual Trade Shows: A Literature Review from the UK Medical Device Industry*. European Marketing Academy.

Ege İhracatçı Birlikleri. (2021). *Aegean Exporters Union*. Retrieved from https://www.eib.org.tr/en/

Fernandes, N. (2020). *Economic effects of coronavirus outbreak (COVID-19) on the world economy*. IESE Business School Working Paper, No. WP-1240-E.

Gajjar, A., & Parmar, B. J. (2020). The Impact of COVID-19 on Event Management Industry in India. *Global Journal of Management and Business Research*, 37–43. doi:10.34257/GJMBRFVOL20IS2PG37

Geigenmüller, A. (2010). The role of virtual trade fairs in relationship value creation. *Journal of Business and Industrial Marketing, 25*(4), 284–292. doi:10.1108/08858621011038243

Gopalakrishna, S., & Lilien, G. L. (2012). Trade shows in the business marketing communications mix. In *Handbook of business-to-business marketing*. Edward Elgar Publishing. doi:10.4337/9781781002445.00022

Gottlieb, U., & Bianchi, C. (2017). Virtual trade shows: Exhibitors' perspectives on virtual marketing capability requirements. *Electronic Commerce Research and Applications, 21*, 17–26. doi:10.1016/j.elerap.2016.12.004

Hansen, K. (2000). From selling to relationship marketing at international trade fairs. *Journal of Convention & Exhibition Management, 2*(1), 37–53. doi:10.1300/J143v02n01_03

Hu, L., & Olivieri, M. (2021). How to Leverage Digital Marketing in B2B: A Study on Italian SMEs During the Covid-19 Outbreak. In *Digital Marketing & eCommerce Conference* (pp. 112–120). Springer. doi:10.1007/978-3-030-76520-0_12

International Trade Administration of the US. (2021). Retrieved from https://www.trade.gov/virtual-fair

IPD. (2020 November). Retrieved from Press Release, https://www.importpromotiondesk.com/fileadmin/user_upload/Publikationen/pressemitteilungen/201124_IPD_Press_Release_Virtual_Matchmaking.pdf

Kalafsky, R. V., & Gress, D. R. (2013). Trade Fairs as an Export Marketing and Research Strategy: Results from a Study of K orean Advanced Machinery Firms. *Geographical Research, 51*(3), 304–317. doi:10.1111/1745-5871.12019

Kimmel, A. J. (Ed.). (2005). *Marketing communication: New approaches, technologies, and styles*. Oxford University Press on Demand.

Kirchgeorg, M., Jung, K., & Klante, O. (2010). The future of trade shows: Insights from a scenario analysis. *Journal of Business and Industrial Marketing*, *25*(4), 301–312. doi:10.1108/08858621011038261

Kotler, P. (1999). *Marketing Management: The Millennium Edition*. Prentice Hall.

Kotler, P., & Armstrong, G. (2007). *Principles of Marketing* (12th ed.). Academic Press.

KPMG. (2021, April). *Incentive Snippets*. Retrieved from https://assets.kpmg/content/dam/kpmg/sg/pdf/2021/04/Incentive-Snippets-Issue-16.pdf

Krugman, C., & Wright, R. R. (2006). *Global Meetings and Exhibitions* (Vol. 28). Wiley.

Laing, J. H., & Frost, W. (2017). Journeys of well-being: Women's travel narratives of transformation and self-discovery in Italy. *Tourism Management*, *62*, 110–119. doi:10.1016/j.tourman.2017.04.004

Lee-Kelly, L., David, G., & Nada, F. A.-S. (2004). Virtual Exhibitions: An Ex-ploratory Study of Middle East Exhibi-tors' Dispositions. *International Marketing Review*, *21*(6), 634–643. doi:10.1108/02651330410568051

Li, L. Y. (2010). Antecedents and effect of internet implementation for trade shows. J.Bus. Indus. *Market*, *25*(4), 272–283.

Li, P. F. (2014). Global temporary networks of clusters: Structures and dynamics of trade fairs in Asian economies. *Journal of Economic Geography*, *14*(5), 995–1021. doi:10.1093/jeg/lbu009

Maskell, P., Bathelt, H., & Malmberg, A. (2004). *Temporary clusters and knowledge creation: the effects of international trade fairs, conventions and other professional gatherings*. Academic Press.

Mohanty, P., Dhoundiyal, H., & Choudhury, R. (2020). *Events Tourism in the Eye of the COVID-19 Storm: Impacts and Implications* (1st ed.). Apple Academic Press.

Mohapatra, S., Priyanka, V., Mohapatra, S., Kohli, I., & Mishra, R. K. (2020). Impact Of Corona Virus Covid-19 On the Global Economy. *International Journal of Agricultural and Statistics Sciences*, *16*(2), 771–778.

Monreal-Pérez, J., & Geldres-Weiss, V. V. (2019). *A configurational approach to the impact of trade fairs and trade missions on firm export activity*. BRQ Business Research Quarterly. doi:10.1016/j.brq.2018.11.001

Nikitina, O. (2021). Convention and Exhibition Industry: Digitalization and Strategic Leadership During the COVID-19 Crisis and After the Pandemic. In *1st International Scientific Conference "Legal Regulation of the Digital Economy and Digital Relations: Problems and Prospects of Development" (LARDER 2020)* (pp. 215-220). Atlantis Press.

Palumbo, F., & Herbig, P. A. (2002). Trade shows and fairs: An important part of the international promotion mix. *Journal of Promotion Management*, *8*(1), 93–108. doi:10.1300/J057v08n01_09

Pecherskaya, M. D., Mamatkulov, S. I., & Butanov, H. T. (2019). Virtual Fairs as A Modern Tool of Marketing. *Acta of Turin Polytechnic University in Tashkent*, *9*(3), 25–27.

Peck Isobel. (2021). *The Fix, A Monthly Vei Digital Digest*. Retrieved from https://cd100848-2bdf-4893-9b66-4304140e139e.filesusr.com/ugd/538ca9_e5bd224c59df40848c60f6bed902c3b5.pdf

Pöllmann, M. P. (2013). *Process definition for innovation in trade fairs* (Doctoral dissertation). Edinburgh Napier University.

Power, D., & Jansson, J. (2008). Cyclical clusters in global circuits: Overlapping spaces in furniture trade fairs. *Economic Geography*, *84*(4), 423–448. doi:10.1111/j.1944-8287.2008.00003.x

PWC. (2020). *Perspectives from the Global Entertainment & Media Outlook 2020–2024*. Retrieved from https://www.pwc.com/gx/en/entertainment-media/outlook-2020/perspectives.pdf

Ramírez-Pasillas, M. (2010). International trade fairs as amplifiers of permanent and temporary proximities in clusters. *Entrepreneurship and Regional Development*, *22*(2), 155–187. doi:10.1080/08985620902815106

Řehák, A. (2008). *Analysis of perspective trends in trade fairs*. Univerzita Tomáše Bati ve Zlíně.

Remolar, I., Garcés, A., Rebollo, C., Chover, M., Quirós, R., & Gumbau, J. (2015). Developing a virtual trade fair using an agent-oriented approach. *Multimedia Tools and Applications*, *74*(13), 4561–4582. doi:10.100711042-013-1822-0

Republic of Turkey Ministry of Trade. (2021). Retrieved from https://ticaret.gov.tr/destekler/ihracat-destekleri/pazara-giriste-dijital-faaliyetlerin-desteklenmesi

Rinallo, D., Borghini, S., & Golfetto, F. (2010). Exploring visitor experiences at trade shows. *Journal of Business and Industrial Marketing*, *25*(4), 249–258. doi:10.1108/08858621011038207

Rosson, P. J., & Seringhaus, F. R. (1995). Visitor and exhibitor interaction at industrial trade fairs. *Journal of Business Research*, *32*(1), 81–90. doi:10.1016/0148-2963(94)00012-4

Saini, S., Bansal, A., & Sadhana, R. K. (2020). A study on the impact of corona virus (Covid-19) on the global food industry. *International Journal in Management and Social Science*, *8*(6).

SalesRoads. (2021). *White Paper, The State Of Trade Show Lead Generation*. Retrieved from https://salesroads.com/resource/trade-show-lead-gen/

Sarmento, M., Farhangmehr, M., & Simões, C. (2015). A relationship marketing perspective to trade fairs: Insights from participants. *Journal of Business and Industrial Marketing*, *30*(5), 584–593. doi:10.1108/JBIM-01-2013-0024

Sarmento, M., & Simões, C. (2019). Trade fairs as engagement platforms: The interplay between physical and virtual touch points. *European Journal of Marketing*, *53*(9), 1782–1807. doi:10.1108/EJM-10-2017-0791

Sedky Herve. (2021). *The Fix, A Monthly Vei Digital Digest*. Retrieved from https://cd100848-2bdf-4893-9b66-4304140e139e.filesusr.com/ugd/538ca9_e5bd224c59df40848c60f6bed902c3b5.pdf

Seringhaus, F. H., & Rosson, P. J. (2000, Apr.). Exhibitors at international trade fairs: The influence of export support. *LTA*.

Sharda, R., Sikolia, D., Thomas, J., & Sambasivan, R. (2012). A Design Science Approach to Virtual World Implementation of Trade Fairs. Pacific Asia. *Journal of the Association for Information Systems*, *4*(2), 4.

Shereni, N. C., Ncube, F. N., & Mazhande, P. (2021). Exhibitors' preference at trade fairs: The case of Zimbabwe International Trade Fair (ZITF). *Journal of Convention & Event Tourism*, 1–21. doi:10.1080/15470148.2021.1893241

Siemieniako, D., & Gębarowski, M. (2017). B2B trade fairs and promise management as a relationship marketing concept. *Journal of Customer Behaviour*, *16*(3), 237–261. doi:10.1362/147539217X15071081721116

Situma, S. P. (2012). The effectiveness of trade shows and exhibitions as organizational marketing tool (analysis of selected companies in Mombasa). *International Journal of Business and Social Science*, *3*(22), 219–230.

Smith, T. M., Gopalakrishna, S., & Smith, P. M. (2004). The complementary effect of trade shows on personal selling. *International Journal of Research in Marketing*, *21*(1), 61–76. doi:10.1016/j.ijresmar.2003.04.003

Solberg, C. A. (1991). Export promotion and trade fairs in Norway: are there better ways? *International Perspectives on Trade Promotion and Assistance*, 119-125.

Stone, R. J. (1993). Virtual reality: toys or tools of the trade? In *Aslib Proceedings*. MCB UP Ltd. doi:10.1108/eb051321

Süygün, S. (2019). Promotion Of International Trade. In Dynamics of Globalization at the Crossroads of Economics (pp. 35-43). Peter Lang GmbH, Internationaler Verlag der Wissenschaften.

UFI. (2019). *Global Economic Impact of Exhibitions, 2019 Edition*. Retrieved from https://www.ufi.org/wp-content/uploads/2019/04/Global-Economic-Impact-of-Exhibitions_b.pdf

UFI. (2021). *Media Release*. Retrieved from https://www.ufi.org/wp-content/uploads/2021/02/MR_UFI-releases-figures-stating-the-impact-of-COVID-19_4february2021.pdf

UFI. (2021). *Global Exhibition Barometer, 26th edition*. Retrieved from https://www.ufi.org/wp-content/uploads/2021/01/26th_UFI_Global_Barometer_january_2021.pdf

Vik, Å. S., Nørbech, B. C., & Jeske, D. (2018). Virtual career fairs: Perspectives from Norwegian recruiters and exhibitors. *Future Internet*, *10*(2), 19. doi:10.3390/fi10020019

Vogel, J., & Ajoudani, A. (2020). Virtual Conferences in Times of COVID-19: Embracing the Potential. *IEEE Robotics & Automation Magazine*, *27*(3), 19–19. doi:10.1109/MRA.2020.3008838

Zhu, Y. W., Bathelt, H., & Zeng, G. (2020). Are trade fairs relevant for local innovation knowledge networks? Evidence from Shanghai equipment manufacturing. *Regional Studies*, *54*(9), 1250–1261. doi:10.1080/00343404.2019.1695046

ADDITIONAL READING

Bathelt, H., Golfetto, F., & Rinallo, D. (2014). *Trade shows in the globalizing knowledge economy*. OUP Oxford. doi:10.1093/acprof:oso/9780199643080.001.0001

Egwuenu, A. S., Chiyem, I. R., & Olannye, A. P. (2019). Trade Fairs And Marketing Performance. *Nigerian Journal of Management Sciences*, *7*(1).

Golfetto, F., & Rinallo, D. (2015). The evolution of trade show systems: Lessons from Europe. In *Temporary Knowledge Ecologies*. Edward Elgar Publishing. doi:10.4337/9781782548096.00009

Herbig, P., O'Hara, B., & Palumbo, F. A. (1998). Trade show: Who, what, why. *Marketing Intelligence & Planning*, *16*(7), 425–435. doi:10.1108/02634509810244444

Leszczyński, G., & Zieliński, M. (2011). T*he Role of Trade Fairs in Sales: Trends and Research Propositions*. In Global Sales Science Conference, University of Bocconi, Mediolan.

Mruk, H., Jerzyk, E., Stefańska, M., Stefański, R., & Nestorowicz, R. (2015). Fair Trade: Trends for the Future. In Fair Trade in CSR Strategy of Global Retailers (pp. 175-197). Palgrave Macmillan. doi:10.1057/9781137389046_7

Proszowska, A. (2018). Coopetition in the operating of the trade fairs market. *International Journal of Contemporary Management*, *17*(1), 217–232. doi:10.4467/24498939IJCM.18.012.8391

Tafesse, W., & Skallerud, K. (2015). Towards an exchange view of trade fairs. *Journal of Business and Industrial Marketing*, *30*(7), 795–804. doi:10.1108/JBIM-05-2014-0090

KEY TERMS AND DEFINITIONS

Cluster: It is the sustainable organized activities of companies and supporting institutions in a certain geographical region, in a certain sector, in order to achieve the goals they have determined with a common mind.

Consumer Relationship Management (CRM): It is a marketing approach that provides long-term relationships with customers by taking into account their wishes and needs.

COVID-19: Covid-19 is an infectious disease caused by a newly discovered coronavirus.

Digitalization: Digitalization is the process of transferring accessible information into a digital environment that can be read by a computer.

Gross Domestic Product (GDP): GDP is the total market value of all the finished goods and services produced within a country's borders in a specific time.

Hybrid Events: Events that offer both face-to-face and virtual experiences simultaneously.

Marketing Mix: Marketing mix is the use of product, place, promotion, and price concepts to carry out marketing activities in the best way.

Chapter 11
Upgrading the Global Value Chains After COVID-19:
Some Policy Implications

Osman Seraceddin Sesliokuyucu
https://orcid.org/0000-0001-6539-0992
Suleyman Demirel University, Turkey

ABSTRACT

The COVID-19 pandemic-related economic lockdowns and restrictions have caused socio-economic uncertainties in the world since 2020. The pandemic-induced economic shocks affected world trade, especially the reactions in fragile markets. As a result of the strict rules taken by the countries, the decrease in the supply of intermediate goods inputs used in industries worldwide, supply shock has caused global supply chains and economic problems to spread through supply chains. Due to the increase in demand exceeding the current supply and production capacity, the fragmented production system, which spread throughout the world, led to the risks related to global value chains (GVC). In this context, discussion of the uplift processes within the chain, which expresses the upgrading perspective, has come to the fore again. The solutions in chains, which are applied by industries in the pandemic process, emphasize the importance of backward and forward linkages in the chain.

INTRODUCTION

The high rate of product fragmentation between industries and countries, integration of existing trading structure, processes related to production coordination such as Foreign Direct Investment (FDI), and infrastructure services has turned into a complex structure that has not been seen in previous periods in the World. The COVID-19 pandemic related economic lockdowns and restrictions caused socio-economic uncertainties in the World since March 2020. The pandemic-induced economic shocks affected World trade, especially the reactions in fragile markets. As a result of the strict rules taken by the countries, the decrease in the supply of intermediate goods inputs used in industries worldwide; supply shock has caused global supply chains and economic problems to spread through supply chains. Pandemic process,

DOI: 10.4018/978-1-7998-8314-2.ch011

considering cost optimization, just-in-time production, and minimum stock keeping practices by firms, has revealed the sensitivity of international supply chains to such shocks. The process affects almost all countries in the world economically. Also, when outages occur in countries that are key suppliers of intermediate inputs, this effect will cover all firms in their supply chains (Gopinath, 2020).

The activities within the Global Value Chains (GVC), which is defined as a whole of activities and where all activities from product development to disposal after use are carried out by different locations and businesses, have also led to the negative impact of the activities within the GVC. Compared to traditional trade, GVC, fragmentation of manufacturing processes and individual task specialization in global locations have shifted the focus of competition from industries to tasks in manufacturing processes. GVC has the potential to develop and enhance the world economy through the management of fragmented value chains, global business problems, and forward-backward links. GVC is actively demonstrating its impact on economies by leading to productivity growth, competitiveness, international trade, and the rise of industries and countries along the value chain. GVC analyzes to local producers; provides important information on how to improve production processes, achieve stability and high quality, and speed up return processes (Humphrey and Schmitz, 2002).

The GVC analyzes are investigated the global industries from two different perspectives: top-down and bottom-up (Gereffi and Fernandez-Stark, 2016). The basic concept for a top-down view is "governance", which examines the organization of global industries by connecting GVC leading firms and various supplier networks, while the main concept for a bottom-up view is "upgrading", which emphasizes the strategies countries, regions, and firms use to maintain or improve their position in the global economy. (Gereffi, 2014). Upgrading processes, which means the integration of developing countries with deeper links to the world economy and their increasing activities within the GVC and transition to higher value-added production processes within the chain; provides an important motivation for increasing competitive pressures and maximizing profits. The upgrading process means moving from existing production activities to higher value-added activities (Milberg and Winkler, 2013) can occur in different forms: Reorganizing production processes to obtain more valuable outputs (Product Upgrading), increase the unit value by moving to more complex product lines (Process Upgrading), increase the content of skills by decreasing or increasing functions (Functional Upgrading) or transition to new productive activities (Upgrading in the Chain). Upgrading processes lead to the emergence of economic development for nations and development in many social, cultural, political, and environmental areas. Upgrading which is an important point in the transition to high profitability affects the competitiveness of firms in the national economy and contributes significantly to their transition from local to global (Humphrey and Schmitz, 2002). Forward GVC participation means the export of the products by the other countries and the sale by the other country and Backward GVC participation means countries' import into the chain by importing intermediate inputs in the production of products (OECD, 2013).

The emergence of the GVC has opened up new avenues for development and industrialization. Developing countries are now able to participate in existing supply chains instead of establishing complete chains domestically, and their increasing degree of expertise frees them from the need to develop different competitive tasks, leading them to reveal their comparative advantages. Also, GVC participation can be a tool for developed countries to revitalize their slow growth and lead to economic and social development on average (Kummritz et al., 2017). Due to the increase in demand exceeding the current supply and production capacity, the fragmented production system, which spread throughout the world during the COVID-19 epidemic, led to the risks related to GVC more clearly. Especially, the shortage of medical equipment and products emerged as a result of the countries being dependent on imports and brought some problems such as export restrictions and bid wars. The continuation of similar problems with shipping delays and restrictions that emerged because of individual countries' measures led to the need to re-evaluate complex value chains and submit new policy recommendations. While governmental solutions to the COVID-19 issue raised transportation and communication expenses, border closures and border inspections increased transportation delays. Port closures and changes in port rules, such as restrictions on crew changes, wreaked havoc on shipping networks, resulting in a shortage of capacity where it was most needed. Different factors, such as ship operators who respond to a sharp drop in transportation demand by restricting supply to avoid a drop in transportation costs, and air cargo firms that have seen an increase in costs due to travel restrictions, have all contributed to the issue of international production segmentation becoming brought to the forefront of this process. As a result, many policymakers and analysts advocate interventions in favor of reorganizing value chains to reduce fundamental goods country's dependence and increase value chain robustness, and these discontents frequently support the return of manufacturing activities to national borders and the return of overseas activities to traditionally industrialized countries (Bacchetta et al., 2021).

Discussion of the upgrading processes within the chain, which expresses the upgrading perspective, has come to the fore again. The effective solutions put forward by countries operating in higher value-added production processes, especially in overcoming the shortage of medical equipment and products, emphasize the importance of backward and forward linkages in the chain. In this context, this chapter aims to provide a view about GVC and the upgrading process-based in the COVID-19 era. In line with this purpose, first section is about background about general information on GVC and upgrading processes, and in the second section of the chapter GVC and upgrading processes in times of crisis will be presented. In the following sections, the changes that occurred in the context of GVC and upgrading before and after the COVID-19 process are evaluated and suggestions will be presented.

BACKGROUND

Global Value Chains

The main ideas of classical international trade theories, the foundations of which were laid two centuries ago by David Ricardo, continued their influence from Hecksher-Ohlin to Samuelson. The basic propositions of this approach likewise continued until the 1970s (Inomata, 2017):

- Markets are in perfect competition and producers are constantly operating at constant returns to scale.
- An industry involved in trade consists of homogeneous producers.
- Nations only trade in final products, and each product is produced solely through the factors of production of the exporting country.

The first proposition of classical theories began to be criticized in the 1970s and 1980s with studies suggesting the new trade theory approach. The main feature of the approach pioneered by Krugman (1979; 1980) and popularized by Helpman and Krugman (1985); firms expand their fields by entering new markets and increase their production scales thanks to the expanding markets. This approach, which emphasizes the existence of international trade under imperfect competition, is the first approach that provides a reasonable explanation for the spread of intra-industry trade between countries with similar technologies and factors (Yüksel and Sarıdoğan, 2011; Inomata, 2017).

The evolution of international trade theories generally stems from the need to bridge the gap between newly discovered phenomena and the predictions of existing models. The source of criticism for the second general proposition of classical theories is (Grubel and Lloyd, 1971)'s empirical findings on intra-industry trade. Studies by Grubel and Lloyd as well as Bernard and Jensen (1999) and Bernard et al., (1995) reveal the heterogeneous structure in firm productivity between exporting and non-exporting firms in a particular industry, which is revealed by examining the data on a firm basis. It was seen as an important criticism brought on the assumption of the classical approach. The approach, which was later expanded by Melitz (2003) within the scope of new-new trade theories, takes into account the endogenous selection mechanism of the firm in entering or exiting the market by making the assumption of a fixed cost in entering export activities, and thus brings the assumption that heterogeneous firms can coexist in an industry.

Changes for third overall argument of the classical theory is still ongoing. These approaches, which are directly related to the development line of the literature on GVC, have become more prominent as a result of the separation of production processes into certain sections, especially as a result of the development of transportation modes and radical changes in information and communication technologies. Seperated departments are mostly located across national borders. These transnational settlements often lead to the most efficient distribution of tasks. Approaches that address not only the movement of final products, but also the movements of tasks and the added values created by these tasks, which constitute the main subject of the ongoing literature today, try to carry the criticisms of classical theories to a more explanatory ground (Inomata, 2017).

The GVC approach (as cited in Milberg and Winkler, 2010), which started with the transition of developing countries from import substitution strategies to export-oriented development strategies in the 1980s, has been determined in the literature different concepts; "global production sharing" (Yeats, 1998), "international compartmentalization" (Jones and Kierzkowski, 1988), "vertical specialization" (Hummels et al., 2001), "multistage production" (Dixit and Grossman, 1982), "subcontracting", "offshoring" and "outsourcing". All of these different definitions have been associated with the increasing importance of vertical manufacturing or commercial chains across countries (De Backer and Yamano, 2011). The most basic point where the concept of GVC differs from other theories is the diversity of intellectual resources in this field, that is, the number of explanations brought through different perspectives. The initial theories of the literature on the international fragmentation of production (Feenstra and Hanson, 1996; Campa and Goldberg, 1997); segregation (Baldwin, 2006) and trade in task (Grossman and Rossi-Hansberg, 2006) theories followed.

The changing global supply and value chain structures, with results such as the distribution of production processes to different countries and the fact that each country becomes a player in the value chain, has resulted in an increase in outsource and offshore activities, resulting in a more complex international trade structure and therefore its measurements. The fact that multinational firms move their production processes to different locations more intensively and try to optimize their production processes in these positioning processes ensures that the actors in the less developed and developing markets are also actively involved in world trade. The increasing integration of global supply chains has led to the interconnection of almost all countries around the world by a network of resources (Klassen and Whybark, 1994). The countries that make up the value chains and the networks created by the firms in these countries make decisions that affect not only their own structures, abilities and results, but also other representatives with whom they interact. These decisions are considered as the determinant of organizational processes on behalf of all the actors forming the chain (Inomata, 2017).

GVC, which is a sociologically based approach, primarily focuses on the coordination of firm activities and considers the creation and transfer of value within the system, unlike Porter's value chain concept, which is concerned with how to renew firm strategies. Therefore, the GVC approach is not considered as a global extension of Porter's value chain approach in terms of scope and motivation. GVC is generally evaluated the firm's a wide spectrum covering all activities such as production, distribution, sales and marketing, R&D and innovation. Therefore, besides the cost reduction advantages, other motivations such as entry into emerging markets and access to strategic assets and foreign information make GVC work (De Backer and Yamano, 2011).

The GVC approach emphasizes that in many applications clustered producers do not sell to open markets and that the links of segregated retailers and local producers of chains depend on the management of strong leading firms. GVC provides local manufacturers with the opportunity to learn ideas from global manufacturers on how to improve their production processes, achieve stability and high quality, and increase responsiveness. GVC analysis also deals with how global production and distribution systems are organized. This organization includes transactions between many firms that are constantly repeated. Important questions for this coordination can be addressed as follows (Humphrey and Schmitz, 2002):

- The question of ***what to produce*** involves the design of the product's broad and detailed features.
- The question on ***how to produce*** involves the description of the production process.
- The ***physical product flow*** question includes how much will be produced and how the product will flow through the chain.

In the GVC approach, which aims to explain the trajectory of a product's path from design and to production, retail sale and final consumption (Leslie and Reimer, 1999), the questioned point is the entirety of a good and/or service. The main analytical focus is on how goods and/or services are coordinated and how economic value is distributed among the participants in the chain (Neilson and Pritchard, 2010). There are 6 (six) basic dimensions explored by Gereffi (1996, 1999) for the GVC methodology, which was formulated since the mid-90s and started to gain popularity:

1. GVC Input-Output Structure
2. Geographical Coverage
3. Governance Structure
4. Local Institutional Context
5. Industry Stakeholders
6. Upgrading in the Chain

Three of these dimensions (GVC Input-Output Structure, Geographical Coverage, and chain upgrading) are considered global, while the other three are considered local dimensions. The GVC approach analyzes the global economy from these two opposing points. Governance of GVC plays a key role for the global perspective, while upgrading in the chain is important for the local dimension (Gereffi and Fernandez-Stark, 2016).

Upgrading in Global Value Chains

Advancement through GVC or orientation to higher-value activities has gained importance in development and job creation in the global economy, where competition remains intense and production becomes fragmented and geographically dispersed (Gereffi and Fernandez-Stark, 2016). Upgrading as a concept is defined as the transition process of economic actors (nations, firms, workers) from low-value activities to relatively higher-value activities in global production networks (Gereffi et al., 2005). Various mixes of government policies, institutions, firm strategies, technologies, and employee skills are associated with upgrading success.

With GVC, economic development is increasingly associated with "economic upgrading" or "industrial upgrading". Accordingly, firms tend to move towards high value-added activities in the production chain of certain commodities. These activities include increasing productivity and skills through training, mechanization, and acquaintance with new technologies (Milberg and Winkler, 2013).

Humphrey and Schmitz (2002) stated in their study that the increase in GVC occurs in four different ways:

1. **Product Upgrading** refers to the joining of the actors to the chain as a result of reorganizing the production systems or switching to superior technologies, making them more effective in the transformation of inputs into outputs. This upgrading process may arise from changing product structures and requirements as a result of consumer preferences. Product upgrading processes (Mitchell et al., 2009) led by leading buyers (large market chains, countries or other institutions) cause manufacturers to stay competitive and continue on their way.
2. **Process Upgrading** refers to increase unit value by moving to more sophisticated product lines. it is usually due to competition within or between chains. Manufacturers have to respond to existing pressures to reduce costs per unit in production in order to stay in the market.
3. **Functional Upgrading** refers to the change of position of actors in GVC by acquiring new functions or reducing existing functions by increasing all skill content of activities (Humprey and Schmitz, 2002). This upgrading results in the transition to relatively higher value-added processes in the combination of functions within the chain. Functional upgrading can occur in two different ways: elimination of intermediaries and acquisition of new productive capacities. While the first of these causes the structure of the value chain to be changed; the second one leads to more value-added positions by staying within the same value (Vysin, 2017). The best example in terms of functional upgrading is the textile industry value chain that exists between many different Asian countries. Developing countries in this chain are changing their positions by differentiating their functions (Gereffi, 1999).
4. **Cross-Industry (Chain) Upgrading** refers to the transition of firms in chains to new productive activities. Cross-industry upgrading; It emerges as a result of the actors switching to another product or a niche service as a result of obtaining the necessary information (Ponte, 2008). Firms may encounter barriers to entry in their inter-sectoral movements in order to maintain their existence by moving towards more profitable chains. However, shifting existing skills to similar areas and mastering the processes in the chain can reduce these obstacles (Mitchell et al., 2009; Guerrieri and Pietrobelli, 2004).

In addition to these four different upgrading processes, Fernandez-Stark et al. (2014) added two different types of upgrading to the GVC literature. The first of the types of upgrading considered; ***value chain entry***, which refers to the first time firms participate in national, regional or global value chains. This form of upgrading is one of the most difficult renewal decisions. It connects backward links in which firms in an industry (domestic or foreign) begin to supply tradable inputs and/or services for firms (usually Multinationals) located in the country and already placed in a separate GVC. ***Market upgrading***, which involves moving to more sophisticated markets that require adapting to new and more rigorous standards or larger markets that need larger scale production and price accessibility, has been considered as another upgrading model.

Based on the input-output structure of the value chain and the institutional framework of each country, upgrading models varies by industry and country. Certain sectors necessitate a linear upgrading, and governments must develop competence in one area of the value chain before progressing to the next. (Gereffi and Fernandez-Stark, 2016). Apart from the major problems linked to the economic upgrading of the chain's participants, there are certain challenges with GVC's upgrading. The "smile curve," which comprises procedures used for chains that were originally accessible in the computer sector, depicts the approach to the transition of actors from basic activities linked to activities in the chain to more sophisticated and greater value-added processes. (Shih, 1996) (Figure 1).

Figure 1. Smile curve

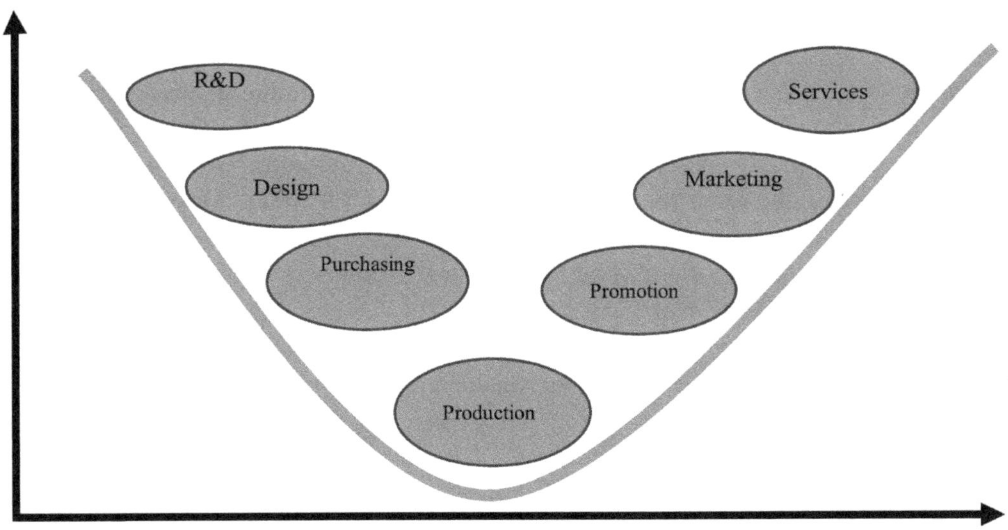

In Figure 1 The X-axis is shown the actors in the value chain and the Y-axis is shown the added value increase of each activity. While the Smile Curve is generally used in firm-based studies, it is also considered as a descriptive measurement method for studies at the country level. The basic questions (Ye et al., 2015) to be answered in Smile Curves, where value-added activities are shown gradually, are given below:

1. What is the relationship between developed and developing countries in the value creation and distribution process in GVC?
2. Does the GVC get deeper or flatter on curves?
3. Are developing countries in the low value creation part of GVC?
4. What policies enable countries to maintain their competitiveness in GVC?
5. How can developing countries successfully integrate GVC and move from low value-added activities to high value-added activities in the chain?

Answering these questions better and more clearly is also important for the design of effective development strategies, industrial policies and international governance (Ye et al., 2015).

It is considered that the forms of upgrading that are largely discussed in the GVC literature are linked to economic indicators, i.e., economic upgrading. Recent research has found that social and environmental variables have a two-way link with GVC growth. The upgrading processes expand the scope of Corporate Social Responsibility (CSR) by focusing not only on efforts to improve working conditions of global firms, but also on other non-corporate measures initiated by NGOs and governments. Less relevant is whether a particular measure of CSR is effective and "under what conditions" upgrading is more likely and how it relates to economic development (Barrientos et al., 2011).

While the studies in the literature discussed on the factors likely to affect the ability of countries to upgrading in the GVC are mainly based on case studies, there are only a few recent studies with econometric models (Engel and Taglioni, 2017). Kummritz et al. (2016), using the value added produced by certain sectors as a measure of economic growth, and measures of backward and forward GVC participation (foreign value added in exports by third countries and domestic added value in re-exports) to identify national characteristics that may be associated with economic improvement through GVC participation. in the study where he tested the effect; They discussed the GVC approach on the econometric basis, addressing infrastructure, connectivity, investment and trade policy, business environment and institutions, financial and labor markets, skills and training, innovation and product standards, as well as labor, social and environmental standards. The findings of the study revealed that general GVC integration increases the domestic added value of a country. In addition, it has been concluded that firms that maintain commercial relations with the actors in the GVC have significant effects on their revenues. Connectivity, training and skills, and compliance with standards are critical for countries selling to KDZ. The researchers concluded that the policy areas considered to be important in economic development in GVC have the expected impact.

GVC AND CRISES

GVC and 2008-2009 Financial Crisis

The biggest global recession of the twenty-first century has been seen as the economic tension, which started with the bursting of the housing bubble that emerged in the USA in 2007, spread rapidly to the rest of the world through finance and trade channels. It has been defined as a structural crisis, also called the "Globalization Crisis". The Asian crisis at the end of the 90s and the 2008-2009 Economic Crisis revealed that the size of the new globalization wave changed and passed from commercial markets to financial markets. While most of the crises have regional effects in the world, which has witnessed various financial crises in the past 30 years, the high commercial and financial imbalances in the 2008-09 crisis brought along liquidity problems along with the demand collapse. The division of production, which is one of the most important factors in the global perception of this crisis, has also revealed the complex structure of globalization (Cattaneo et al., 2010).

Figure 2. 1975-2019 trade and trade in services in world economy
Source: (Worldbank-Databank, 2021)

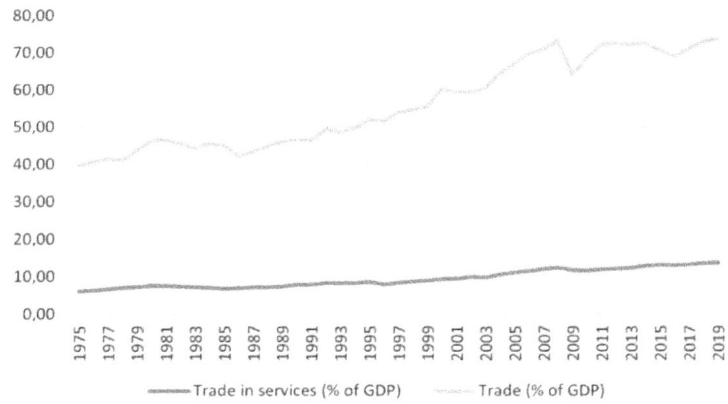

As the impact of the economic crisis on world trade started to become more evident, there were decreases in trade volumes. According to the World Trade Organization (WTO; Gereffi and Fernandez-Stark, 2010), while the world trade volume decreased by more than 12% in 2009, the decline in the services sector remained relatively low. The main reason for the sharp decrease in trade volume compared to previous periods was first shown as the sharp contraction in demand across the world and in the regions. The increase in the trade volume, which showed an expansion in the initial stages, was reduced by the lack of financing in foreign trade and the contraction of intermediate goods trade in GVC. The existence of trade between countries, that is, the fact that basically all countries in the world are connected by trade networks, had a significant impact on the international spread of the crisis. The transition of developing countries from import substitution industrialization to export-led growth strategies has led to greater foreign dependency and more sensitivity to external shocks. The fact that the export rate, which was 10% in the 1970s, increased to 33% in low and middle-income countries in 2007, reveals the impact of the global crises on these countries. The rising dependency on exports increased from 3% to 43% for China in the period 1970-2007, and the same increase has also increased in developing countries such as Argentina, India, Mexico and Korea, and these countries have increased their share in world goods trade and become more fragile in times of crisis. (Milberg and Winkler, 2010; Gereffi and Fernandez-Stark, 2010).

The increase in national and regional connections around the world since the mid-1980s, and this increase until before the 2008-09 crisis was accompanied by a growth of twice the GDP in international trade and a significant increase in the organization of production stages. Trade changes and reforms in China and different Asian countries have led to the differentiation of roles and commercial connections in world trade. While these processes, which led to the formation of strong regional value chains, led to rapid growth in developing countries, they were also effective in reducing the income gap between countries. The international disintegration of all stages, activities and tasks related to production and the development of GVC accordingly led to the deepening of the effects of the crisis. (World Bank, 2019). GAZ, which lost its effect in the situation that emerged after the 2008-09 crisis, faced the cessation of activities due to the decrease in the elasticity of GDP in world trade (Antràs, 2020). While the problems encountered in countries and sectors that were more deeply integrated into international trade during and after the crisis were at a higher level (Baldwin, 2009), it revealed the high impact of GVC in spreading economic shocks on a global scale due to its cyclical nature (Di Stefano, 2021).

The studies discussed in the literature after the crisis reflect different perspectives. The findings of the study, in which the global input-output tables were analyzed, showed that international trade fell more than the world GDP at the beginning of the crisis. The main reason for this situation is the demand uncertainty arising from the fact that firms do not place their orders as in normal periods and use their parts and stocks. At the same time, the protectionist tendencies that emerged as a result of the measures taken by the countries caused the uncertainties and costs in the production chains to increase. The high level of integration of emerging markets in the pre-crisis period and the inclusion of new countries in this integration process were influential in the stabilization of GVC after a while. In addition, the continuing decrease in transportation and communication costs was seen as another factor. The softening of commercial policies, which pose great obstacles to trade and investment, has emerged as another factor in balancing GVC. In this process, non-tariff barriers began to fall quite rapidly, and manufacturing taxes also decreased significantly (Ciglioli et al., 2021).

In this process, economic development was increasingly associated with "economic upgrading" or "industrial upgrading" in GVC and required firms to move to higher value-added activities along the production chain of a particular good. This development has led to increased productivity and skills through mechanization and the introduction of new technologies. In addition, compliance with existing corporate strategies by establishing close links with leading firms and improvements in the manufacturing industry have brought about qualitative changes as firms move from part production or assembly to design and more integrated production, fully integrated production, and original brand design (Milberg and Winkler, 2010).

GVC and Upgrading in Pre- and Post-COVID-19 Period

Developing as a response to the increasing competition conditions in local and global markets, GVC continues its development on the basis of coordinating activities and actors in different production locations under the leadership of multinational firms operating in the global order (Gölgeci, Yildiz and Andersson, 2020). Multinational firms basically act within the framework of three purposes. The first of these is to manage the limited rationality between the parties by dealing with the information asymmetries and information processing capabilities of the actors in their systems. The second is to manage limited reliability by mitigating risks in the efforts of the actors with whom they interact to fulfill open-ended or incomplete contracts. Finally, they aim to create an organizational context by supporting both product and service innovation and skill development through interaction between actors (Kano et al., 2020). With the effect of globalization and developing technology, multinational firms have gained the opportunity to act more effectively and in wider geographies in their value chain activities. However, the complex structure that emerged alongside the simplifying conditions brought along problems such as strategic management and determination of spatial distributions.

Figure 3. World trade and production since 2019 (Jan. 2019 = 100)
Source: CPB world trade Monitor.

As a result of the increasing integration in the international context, as in the 2008-09 crisis, the problem of the rapid spread of the impact of the possible crises and the higher impact has emerged. After the worldwide pandemic crisis, the transformations in product and service trade brought dramatic results. GVC, which regressed after the 2008-09 crisis but continued to recover and expand after a while, was effective in spreading the effects of the pandemic process as a chain, since it constitutes almost half of world trade. In Figure 3, it is seen that world trade and industrial production have shrunk significantly on a monthly basis as of the end of 2019. It can be stated that the most important factors in this sharp decline are the production stoppages in many locations and the deadlocks that hinder the operation of value chains (Ciglioli et al., 2021).

Due to the fact that globalization and the pandemic are intertwined due to widespread production networks and integration processes, it has caused the nature of the world economy to deteriorate. In addition to these effects, the fact that international human mobility has come to a standstill due to both individual measures and government restrictions has contributed to the increase of this effect (Antras et al., 2020). In the study, in which the developments in world trade were evaluated according to the size and characteristics of the ships, Cerdiero et al. (2020) offered a different perspective on the decline in trade. In the study, in which the signals emitted by global ships on a daily basis are used; It was observed that world trade made a Double Bottom in February, April and May 2020. By October 2020, it was revealed that world trade entered a stronger recovery period than world GDP. In this context, the results of the study mean that the recovery processes are fast in GVC processes, which are directly related to world trade by nature. These developments regarding maritime transport activities, which are used extensively in production activities spread around the world, show that the negative developments experienced in the beginning of the COVID-19 process can be tolerated with the rapid recovery process.

The COVID-19 epidemic, which caused the risks related to segmented production processes managed around the world to be seen more clearly, brought with it the necessity of interventions for the reorganization of value chains in order to limit the dependence on imports in basic goods and increase the durability of the chains. The process, which was already existing before the pandemic process and was compatible with the targets such as shifting the production processes to the main country and reviving industrial policies, significantly affected the decisions taken in the national and international arena (Bacchetta et al., 2021). Basically, GVC, which is associated with international trade, investment and finance at the ***macro level***; national and regional economies at a ***medium (meso) level*** and communities and workers at a ***micro level***, provides a framework for analysis of supply chains of pandemic products (Gereffi, 2020). The main considerations regarding this framework are presented below:

- **Globally operating industries have governance structures**. GVC determines the performance requirements (such as price, quality, delivery schedules) for the actors scattered in different locations in line with the strategies of the leading firms.
- **There are business divisions that specialize in global supply chains.** Actors in global chains, which are divided into specific business divisions, produce specific components and end products that increase the efficiency of the chain. Failure to produce and source diversification in the products produced may endanger the entire chain.
- **Chains whose geography may change over time**; they can be affected by multiple factors such as country conditions, firm strategies, technology changes or government policies (Gereffi and Wu, 2020).
- **The value created between the chains is unevenly distributed**. The highest values created within chains are created by pre-production (such as R&D, Design) and post-production (such as marketing, branding) services (Fernandez-Stark and Gereffi, 2019).
- **Policies implemented by national governments can place significant pressures on leading firms in chains.** Ongoing economic pressures such as the 2008-2009 global recession and the recently revived economic nationalism processes will continue to have an impact after the pandemic process.

Studies in the literature in the context of GVC in the early and later stages of COVID-19 offer some assumptions that the current global epidemic will not sow the seeds of an intensified deglobalization phase of the current global epidemic, even if it returns to pre-COVID-19 levels in the short-to-medium term. In this direction, approaches to the recovery process in the airline industry, which have an important role in connecting nations and re-accelerating globalization, are also among the approaches that shape the process. The forecast for the shape of the industry after the crisis indicates that the recovery will take a long time, at least in the short-medium term. The fact that international travel will inevitably be less preferred by passengers on social distance and psychological basis in the coming periods causes it to be seen as an important obstacle to the return of international mobility (Ciglioli et al., 2021). It is stated that annual values related to air cargo transportation are effective in the participation of GVC, especially for the transportation of light in cargo and heavy in cost products. In the results of the report prepared by Shepherd (2016), which deals with the relationship between air transport and GVC; It has been found that countries with high airline efficiency are more involved in global production networks and their more presence in these processes leads to economic growth and expansion. The prolongation of the recovery process in the airline industry is one of the factors that will directly and indirectly affect the world economy and trade. In line with these evaluations, it is one of the possible scenarios for new locations to operate in chains other than existing locations, as a result of minimizing the interaction between the actors within the GVC. When evaluated in general; logistics operations are based not only on the effectiveness of the logistics infrastructure, but also on the regulatory framework in the target country. Direct shipping requirements (preventing goods from being shipped from third countries), requirements to pass through a specific customs port, and restrictive air, sea or land transport regulations increase exporters' shipping costs. Technical measures, such as administrative procedures, determination of applicable duties related to customs formalities and import permits, causing cumbersome operation; leads to increased costs of transportation and customs procedures. The fact that more than one limit will be exceeded for the products that are subject to trade in GVC causes these costs to increase exponentially. The cumulative effect of such barriers increases costs, not only in monetary terms but also in delayed delivery (OECD, 2013).

These developments bring advantages and disadvantages for the enterprises that continue to take place in the GVC. Problems that arise in international travel will lead to a decrease in trade and chain links between overseas or non-border countries and will bring advantages in the process in countries that are closer to each other and have border neighbors. It is important to reduce the barriers to trade and market entry in these processes, which will enable countries that carry out their activities in GVC through lower value-added products to enter the chains in the context of more active and higher value-added products. In the course of its development, GVC has also changed the perspective on traditional trade barriers, such as tariffs, regarding cost reduction. In the new studies discussed, it is stated that restrictions on trade, reducing supply chain barriers for services related to management, transportation and communication infrastructure will have more impact on GDP and trade growth than the complete elimination of tariffs (Kummritz et al., 2017). Removing barriers to the supply chain can increase GDP by about 5 percent and trade by 5 percent, compared to an increase of between 1% and 10% if all tariff costs are removed (WEF, 2013). Developing countries, on the other hand, can be the main beneficiaries of these trade facilitations. However, transportation costs remain the main barrier for developing country suppliers to join, establish or upgrade in GVC (OECD, 2013).

Influenced by the increasing FDI (Foreign Direct Investment) rates and the human capital structure of countries with the commercial liberalization movements that have emerged around the world since the 1980s, GVC is in line with the skills of domestic firms in adopting new or more advanced technologies from outside investors. has led to a state of acceptance and development that offers In particular, the existence of a high and medium skilled workforce, which is called a skilled workforce, is important in the adoption and application of these technologies. Studies in the literature show that employees with better education and skills have an impact on both their wages and the profitability of firms that offer FDI to the country (Blalock and Gertler, 2009; Girma and Wakelin, 2007). However, in addition to these findings, there are also studies in the literature stating that there are negative effects on behalf of domestic small firms (Sinani and Meyer, 2004). This negative effect evolves as the problems that may arise due to foreign investors paying more to the skilled workforce may negatively affect competition (Farole and Winkler, 2014). When this situation is evaluated in terms of GVC participation in the COVID-19 period; It can be stated that the presence of innovative firms in the country and the quality of human capital owned by these firms will ensure higher levels of participation.

The labor potential of nations is a variable that positively affects GVC participation and upgrading. However, strict policies on employees in the current workforce lead to a decrease in productivity and adversely affect investments from abroad. ***Labor Freedom***, which is one of the political indicators in countries; states that there should be movements in line with the free market economy rather than the union rights of the employees. This requirement is an approach to regulating the productivity and efficiency of the labor market. Heavy trade union rights on the workforce is an approach that punishes both employers and the workforce. In addition to these restrictions on labor force, the ability of domestic consumers to operate as buyers and/or sellers in international markets is a situation faced by many governments. While policy makers implement some measures, they also bring with them significant obstacles both in domestic ***Commercial Freedom*** and ***Financial Freedom***. Restrictions on trade freedom can manifest in the form of tariffs, export taxes, trade quotas, or outright trade bans. However, trade restrictions also take different forms, particularly the form of regulatory barriers to health or safety. The degree to which the state hinders the free movement of foreign trade has a direct impact on individuals' ability to pursue their economic goals and maximize their productivity and welfare. In addition to commercial restrictions, financial restrictions also cause the market to operate under restricted movements. A financial system that does not work well will create barriers for actors to spend, save or invest (Farole and Winkler, 2014). When evaluated in general, the restriction of freedoms within the system will create negative effects on the domestic market and lead to a decrease in communication with international markets. This situation will negatively affect the participation of GVC in the periods after as well as in the pre-COVID-19 period. ***Political Stability***, which is an important variable that affects the commercial structures of countries both in micro and macro terms and prevents them from attracting investments from the international market, is also among the factors that will be effective in this process. Especially during periods of political instability; International trade agreements, regime changes, etc. cause international investors to stay away from the domestic market. Basically, situations such as lack of confidence in the market, uncertainty and volatility in prices also affect investments negatively (Rotunno and Vezina, 2012). From these perspectives, it can be stated that the political uncertainties experienced in the countries during the post-COVID-19 recovery processes will directly and/or indirectly affect the GVC participation by affecting the FDI coming into the country.

FUTURE RESEARCH DIRECTIONS

GVC processes consists of many different infrastructures apart from upgrading (governance etc.). The expansion of the dimensions examined and the regions and/or countries discussed in the evaluations regarding these processes is important for the picture that will emerge after the pandemic. From the perspective of GVC, the future studies will focus on intangible assets (such as human capital), services that have become more important in the context of high technologies embedded in the production and delivery processes, and areas such as institutional arrangements and intellectual property rights will bring about a better understanding and analysis of the process. Improving the learning processes of existing and/or new firms, encouraging them to be innovative and removing the obstacles in front of them are also seen as facilitating factors in the solution process. These approaches, which are important in terms of encouraging upgrading processes between and within the sectors, will enable the creation of macro, meso and micro advantages in an increasingly competitive environment.

Evaluating the upgrading processes, which play an important role in the market differentiation and product and/or service diversification of the firms, from different perspectives in the context of industries and regions will move to higher value-added processes and will pave the way for both the activities in the chain and the developments in the field of activity of the firms. It will eliminate the differences between locations with different characteristics in terms of innovation and knowledge production. Upgrading processes will also trigger systemic transformations by changing roles in terms of learning and innovation through increased connections. Bringing new perspectives from different dimensions to the issue in the upgrading processes, which will reduce the impact of increasing government policies in many areas from trade policies to local innovations, increases the importance of future studies.

CONCLUSION

The expectations regarding the world economy and trade structure, which entered an unprecedented economic crisis with the pandemic epidemic, are that the effects of this crisis cannot be resolved in the short-medium term. The production segmentation, which further expanded the scope of the economic crisis in the world, caused different countries and regions to be significantly affected by this crisis. However, with this effect, it is obvious that the foundations of recovery in the post-crisis period will be through these networks. Governments and businesses are forced to transition to a different production strategy when demand is suddenly doubled or more. In this view, it is implausible to believe that a country can retain and sustain an industry with the necessary production capacity during a crisis. When opposed to isolated and silo-based tactics, anticipation, preparedness, and international cooperation can provide superior results (Miroudot, 2020).

At the global level, the perception of GVC and the measures to be taken against possible risks should be clarified. Making the mobility of global trade traceable through developing technology will enable to be prepared for possible risks and to solve problems faster in the short and long term. At the national level, increasing different supply connections will contribute to maintaining the supply-demand balance in times of crisis by reducing the risks regarding foreign dependency. At the same time, measures taken at the national level will lead to long-term advantages for businesses that have different connections to global networks. Diversifying supply chains and increasing connections will enable businesses to become more agile by increasing their mobility in possible crisis.

In this context, it will be more possible to measure and discuss the effect of GVC activities in the post-pandemic recovery process more accurately through data on the world economy. The statistical data that will emerge in the following processes will show the table and map of the situation more clearly. Besides the pandemic; economic, political and social issues within and between countries can also be expressed as the determinants of this recovery process. The activities in the chain, which should be evaluated as a whole, will be shaped by these determinants.

REFERENCES

Antràs, P. (2020). Conceptual Aspects of Global Value Chains. *The World Bank Economic Review*, *34*(3), 551–574. doi:10.1093/wber/lhaa006

Antràs, P., Redding, S. J., & Rossi-Hansberg, E. (2020). Globalization and pandemics (No. w27840). National Bureau of Economic Research.

Bacchetta, M., Bekkers, E., Piermartini, R., Rubinova, S., Stolzenburg, V., & Xu, A. (2021). *COVID-19 and global value chains: A discussion of arguments on value chain organization and the role of the WTO* (No. ERSD-2021-3). WTO Staff Working Paper.

Baldwin, R. (2009). The great trade collapse: What caused it and what does it mean? *The great trade collapse: Causes, consequences and prospects, 100*(105), 1.

Baldwin, R. E. (2006). *Globalisation: the great unbundling(s)*. Economic Council of Finland.

Barrientos, S., Gereffi, G., & Rossi, A. (2011). Economic and social upgrading in global production networks: A new paradigm for a changing world. *International Labour Review, 150*(3-4), 319–340. doi:10.1111/j.1564-913X.2011.00119.x

Barrientos, S., & Smith, S. (2007). Do workers benefit from ethical trade? Assessing codes of labour practice in global production systems. *Third World Quarterly, 28*(4), 713–729. doi:10.1080/01436590701336580

Bernard, A. B., & Jensen, J. B. (1999). *Exporting and productivity* (No. w7135). National Bureau of Economic Research.

Bernard, A. B., Jensen, J. B., & Lawrence, R. Z. (1995). Exporters, jobs, and wages in US manufacturing: 1976-1987. *Brookings papers on economic activity. Microeconomics, 1995*, 67–119.

Blalock, G., & Gertler, P. J. (2009). How firm capabilities affect who benefits from foreign technology. *Journal of Development Economics, 90*(2), 192–199. doi:10.1016/j.jdeveco.2008.11.011

Campa, J., & Goldberg, L. S. (1997). The evolving external orientation of manufacturing industries: evidence from four countries (No. w5919). National Bureau of Economic Research.

Cattaneo, O., Gereffi, G., & Staritz, C. (2010). *Global Value Chains in a Postcrisis World: A Development Perspective*. World Bank Publications. doi:10.1596/978-0-8213-8499-2

Cerdeiro, D. A., Komaromi, A., Liu, Y., & Saeed, M. (2020). World seaborne trade in real time: A proof of concept for building AIS-based nowcasts from scratch (No. 20/57). International Monetary Fund.

Ciglioli, S., Giovannetti, G., Marvasi, E., & Vivoli, A. (2021). (Forthcoming). The Resilience of Global Value Chains during the Covid-19 pandemic: The case of Italy. *Economia Italiana. Editrice Minerva Bancaria.*

De BackerK.YamanoN. (2011). International comparative evidence on global value chains. SSRN 2179937. doi:10.2139srn.2179937

Di Stefano, E. (2021). COVID-19 and Global Value Chains: The Ongoing Debate. *Bank of Italy Occasional Paper*, (618).

Dixit, A. K., & Grossman, G. M. (1982). Trade and protection with multistage production. *The Review of Economic Studies, 49*(4), 583–594. doi:10.2307/2297288

Elliott, K. A., & Freeman, R. B. (2003). *Can labor standards improve under globalization?* Peterson Institute Press.

Engel, J., & Taglioni, D. (2017). The middle-income trap and upgrading along global value chains. *Global Value Chain Report*, 119-139.

Farole, T., & Winkler, D. (2014). The Role of Mediating Factors for FDI Spillovers in Developing Countries: Evidence from a Global Dataset. *Making foreign direct investment work for Sub-Saharan Africa: Local spillovers and competitiveness in global value chains, 59.*

Feenstra, R. C., & Hanson, G. H. (1996). Globalization, outsourcing, and wage inequality (No. w5424). National Bureau of Economic Research.

Fernandez-Stark, K., Bamber, P., & Gereffi, G. (2014). Global value chains in Latin America: A development perspective for upgrading. Global value chains and world trade: Prospects and challenges for Latin America, 79-106.

Fernandez-Stark, K., & Gereffi, G. (2019). Global value chain analysis: a primer. In *Handbook on Global Value Chains*. Edward Elgar Publishing. doi:10.4337/9781788113779.00008

Gereffi, G. (1996). Global commodity chains: New forms of coordination and control among nations and firms in international industries. *Competition & Change*, *1*(4), 427–439. doi:10.1177/102452949600100406

Gereffi, G. (1999). International trade and industrial upgrading in the apparel commodity chain. *Journal of International Economics*, *48*(1), 37–70. doi:10.1016/S0022-1996(98)00075-0

Gereffi, G. (2014). Global value chains in a post-Washington Consensus world. *Review of International Political Economy*, *21*(1), 9–37. doi:10.1080/09692290.2012.756414

Gereffi, G. (2020). What does the COVID-19 pandemic teach us about global value chains? The case of medical supplies. *Journal of International Business Policy*, *3*(3), 287–301. doi:10.105742214-020-00062-w

Gereffi, G., & Fernandez-Stark, K. (2010). *The offshore services value chain: developing countries and the crisis*. The World Bank. doi:10.1596/1813-9450-5262

Gereffi, G., & Fernandez-Stark, K. (2016). *Global value analysis: a primer* (2nd ed.). Center on Globalization Gobernance & Competitiveness.

Gereffi, G., Humphrey, J., & Sturgeon, T. (2005). The governance of global value chains. *Review of International Political Economy*, *12*(1), 78–104. doi:10.1080/09692290500049805

Gereffi, G., & Wu, X. (2020). Global Value Chains, Industrial Hubs, and Economic Development in the Twenty-first Century. In The Oxford Handbook of Industrial Hubs and Economic Development. OUP.

Girma, S., & Wakelin, K. (2007). Local productivity spillovers from foreign direct investment in the UK electronics industry. *Regional Science and Urban Economics*, *37*(3), 399–412. doi:10.1016/j.regsciurbeco.2006.11.006

Golgeci, I., Yildiz, H. E., & Andersson, U. R. (2020). The rising tensions between efficiency and resilience in global value chains in the post-COVID-19 world. *Transnational Corporations Journal, 27*(2).

Gopinath, G. (2020). The great lockdown: Worst economic downturn since the great depression. *IMF Blog, 14*.

Grossman, G. M., & Rossi-Hansberg, E. (2008). Trading tasks: A simple theory of offshoring. *The American Economic Review*, *98*(5), 1978–1997. doi:10.1257/aer.98.5.1978

Grubel, H. G., & Lloyd, P. J. (1971). The empirical measurement of intra-industry trade. *The Economic Record*, *47*(4), 494–517. doi:10.1111/j.1475-4932.1971.tb00772.x

Guerrieri, P., & Pietrobelli, C. (2004). Industrial districts' evolution and technological regimes: Italy and Taiwan. *Technovation*, *24*(11), 899–914. doi:10.1016/S0166-4972(03)00048-8

Helpman, E., & Krugman, P. R. (1985). *Market structure and foreign trade: Increasing returns, imperfect competition, and the international economy*. MIT Press.

Hummels, D., Ishii, J., & Yi, K. M. (2001). The nature and growth of vertical specialization in world trade. *Journal of International Economics*, *54*(1), 75–96. doi:10.1016/S0022-1996(00)00093-3

Humphrey, J., & Schmitz, H. (2002). How does insertion in global value chains affect upgrading in industrial clusters? *Regional Studies*, *36*(9), 1017–1027. doi:10.1080/0034340022000022198

Inomata, S. (2017). *Analytical frameworks for global value chains: An overview.* Global Value Chain Development Report.

Jones, R. W., & Kierzkowski, H. (1988). *The Role of Services in Production and International Trade: A Theoretical Framework*. The Institute for Research on Public Policy.

Kano, L., Tsang, E. W., & Yeung, H. W. C. (2020). Global value chains: A review of the multi-disciplinary literature. *Journal of International Business Studies*, *51*(4), 1–46. doi:10.105741267-020-00304-2

Klassen, R. D., & Whybark, D. C. (1994). Barriers to the management of international operations. *Journal of Operations Management*, *11*(4), 385–396. doi:10.1016/S0272-6963(97)90006-1

Krugman, P. (1980). Scale economies, product differentiation, and the pattern of trade. *The American Economic Review*, *70*(5), 950–959.

Krugman, P. R. (1979). Increasing returns, monopolistic competition, and international trade. *Journal of International Economics*, *9*(4), 469–479. doi:10.1016/0022-1996(79)90017-5

Kummritz, V., Taglioni, D., & Winkler, D. (2017). *Economic upgrading through global value chain participation: which policies increase the value added gains?* The World Bank. doi:10.1596/1813-9450-8007

Leslie, D., & Reimer, S. (1999). Spatializing commodity chains. *Progress in Human Geography*, *23*(3), 401–420. doi:10.1177/030913259902300304

Melitz, M. J. (2003). The impact of trade on intra-industry reallocations and aggregate industry productivity. *Econometrica*, *71*(6), 1695–1725. doi:10.1111/1468-0262.00467

Milberg, W., & Winkler, D. (2010). Trade, crisis, and recovery: restructuring global value chains. *Global value chains in a postcrisis world: A development perspective*, 23-72.

Milberg, W., & Winkler, D. (2013). *Outsourcing Economics: Global Value Chains in Capitalist Development*. Cambridge University Press. doi:10.1017/CBO9781139208772

Miroudot, S. (2020). Resilience versus robustness in global value chains: Some policy implications. *COVID-19 and trade policy: Why turning inward won't work*, 117-130.

Mitchell, J., Keane, J., & Coles, C. (2009). *Trading up: How a value chain approach can benefit the rural poor. COPLA Global*. Overseas Development Institute.

Neilsno, J., & Pritchard, B. (2010). Fairness and ethicality in their place: The regional dynamics of fair trade and ethical sourcing agendas in the plantation districts of South India. *Environment & Planning A*, *42*(8), 1833–1851. doi:10.1068/a4260

OECD. (2013). *OECD Economic Outlook, Volume 2013 Issue 1*. OECD Publishing. . doi:10.1787/eco_outlook-v2013-1-en

Pegler, L., & Knorringa, P. (2007). *Integrating labour issues in global value chain analysis: Exploring implications for labour research and unions. In Trade union responses to globalisation: A review by the Global Unions Research Network*. ILO.

Ponte, S. (2008). Developing a vertical dimension to chronic poverty research: Some lessons from global value chain analysis. *Chronic Poverty Research Centre Working paper*, (111).

Rotunno, L., & Vézina, P. L. (2012). Chinese networks and tariff evasion. *World Economy*, *35*(12), 1772–1794. doi:10.1111/j.1467-9701.2012.01452.x

Shepherd, B. (2016). Infrastructure, trade facilitation, and network connectivity in Sub-Saharan Africa. *Journal of African Trade*, *3*(1-2), 1–22. doi:10.1016/j.joat.2017.05.001

Shih, S. (1996). *Me-Too is Not My Style: Challenge Difficulties, Break through Bottlenecks, Create Values*. The Acer Foundation.

Sinani, E., & Meyer, K. E. (2004). Spillovers of technology transfer from FDI: The case of Estonia. *Journal of Comparative Economics*, *32*(3), 445–466. doi:10.1016/j.jce.2004.03.002

Vysin, M. (2017). *The role of development cooperation for upgrading in Uganda's organic fruit value chain* (Doctoral dissertation). Uniwien.

World Bank. (2019). *World development report 2020: Trading for development in the age of global value chains*. The World Bank.

Ye, M., Meng, B., & Wei, S. J. (2015). Measuring smile curves in global value chains (No. 530). Institute of Developing Economies, Japan External Trade Organization (JETRO).

Yeats, A. J. (1998). *What can be expected from African regional trade arrangements? Some empirical evidence*. Some Empirical Evidence (November 1998). World Bank Policy Research Working Paper, (2004).

Yüksel, E., & Saridoğan, E. (2011). Uluslararası Ticaret Teorileri ve Paul R. Krugman'ın Katkıları. *Öneri Dergisi, 9*(35), 199-206.

ADDITIONAL READING

Gereffi, G. (2020). What does the COVID-19 pandemic teach us about global value chains? The case of medical supplies. *Journal of International Business Policy*, *3*(3), 287–301. doi:10.105742214-020-00062-w

KEY TERMS AND DEFINITIONS

Backward Linkages: It refers to the backward connections of the actors involved in the GVC.

COVID-19: It is the abbreviation used for the virus that has been struggling during the pandemic process that has affected the whole world since the beginning of 2020.

Forward Linkages: It refers to the forward connections of the actors involved in the GVC.

Global Value Chains: It defines the processes that are spread all over the world and include all the stages from the first stage of production to the after consumption of all the actors involved in the production processes.

Governance in Global Value Chains: It is the process that includes the relationships and interactions between the leading firms and other actors in the GVC.

Multi-National Firms: Businesses operating in different regions and/or locations outside of their main operating countries.

Upgrading in Global Value Chains: It means that the actors in the GVC move from low value-added production processes to higher value-added production processes.

Chapter 12
The Effect of COVID-19 on the Spanish Wine Industry

Bartolomé Marco-Lajara
https://orcid.org/0000-0001-8811-9118
University of Alicante, Spain

Pedro Seva-Larrosa
University of Alicante, Spain

Lorena Ruiz-Fernández
https://orcid.org/0000-0001-8894-9701
University of Alicante, Spain

Javier Martínez-Falcó
https://orcid.org/0000-0001-9004-5816
University of Alicante, Spain

ABSTRACT

The Spanish wine sector has not remained unaffected by the impact of COVID-19. This research aims to analyse the impact of COVID-19 on the Spanish wine sector, quantifying a phenomenon on which there is no academic literature, because although the impact of the pandemic on the wine sector has been studied at a general level, it has not been analysed in the Spanish case. An exploratory approach was adopted for the research in order to analyse the behaviour of the variables that measure the degree of commercialisation of Spanish wine in both the domestic and foreign markets. In addition, the research gathers and quantifies the measures carried out by the Spanish government to help the wine sector overcome the current crisis.

DOI: 10.4018/978-1-7998-8314-2.ch012

INTRODUCTION

A global pandemic is not a new scenario for humankind, as there are several precedents of pandemics throughout human history that have affected human activities and global economic growth. Humanity is currently facing COVID-19, an infectious disease caused by the Severe Acute Respiratory Syndrome Coronavirus 2 (SARS-CoV-2) that was first detected in Wuhan, capital of China's Hubei province, in late 2019.

Coronavirus disease has been classified as a global pandemic (WHO, 2020) with almost 3,013,280 deaths worldwide and 140,858,072 million infections, according to data provided by Johns Hopkins University as of 20 April 2021 and is described by the International Labour Organization (ILO) as "the most serious crisis since World War II" (ILO, 2020). As far as Spain is concerned, as of 20 April 2021, the number of infected people is 3,410,199 while the number of deaths stands at 76,981 according to data provided by the Spanish Ministry of Health.

Although wine is one of the most widely consumed beverages in the world (Gutiérrez-Escobar et al., 2021), the pandemic has had a devastating effect on the wine industry since its inception by decreasing global wine revenues by 14% by 2020 (Lu, 2020). Alongside the devastating effects of the pandemic on the wine industry are other crises, such as the damage caused by climate change and the outbreak of bushfires in some of the world's major wine-producing regions. Thus, while the French region of Burgundy had its earliest harvest season in history in 2020, California experienced four of the five biggest fires in the last two decades and Australia's 2019-2020 bushfire season was the fifth deadliest in the country's history (Canavati et al., 2020).

In this context, the Spanish wine industry has not remained unaffected by the impact of the COVID-19. Spain is a world reference in the wine sector, ranking first in the world in terms of surface area and export volume, as well as third in terms of production (OIV, 2020), which highlights the economic weight of the wine industry in the Iberian country. However, due to the coronavirus outbreak, Spanish wineries are facing unprecedented adversity in their business. Following the declaration of the state of emergency by the Spanish Government on 14 March 2020, the main sources of impact for the wine industry stemmed from the temporary closure of establishments in the hotel, restaurant and catering sector (Horeca), as well as the cancellation of events due to mobility restrictions. During the 99 days of the Spanish state of emergency, which ended on 21 June, there was no wine consumption linked to the flow of tourism, as no travel between Autonomous Communities was allowed, nor was the arrival of foreign tourists. As a result, wineries and specialised retail outlets have started to develop and implement the online services and home deliveries, increasing online sales considerably (AFI, 2020).

The main focus of the chapter is on analysing the impact of COVID-19 on the Spanish wine industry, describing and quantifying a phenomenon on which there is no academic literature, since although the impact of the pandemic on the wine industry has been studied at a general level, it has not been analysed for the Spanish case. The wine industry generates a Gross Domestic Product (GDP) of more than 23,700 million euros in Spain, equivalent to 2.2% of the Spanish GDP, providing more than 427,700 jobs and representing 2.4% of Spanish employment (AFI, 2020). However, despite the importance of the wine industry for the Iberian country, the effect of COVID-19 on this industry has not been analysed. In this way, the research aims to fill this gap in the academic literature.

An exploratory approach was adopted for the research, in order to analyse the behaviour of the variables that measure the degree of commercialisation of Spanish wine in both the domestic and foreign markets. The research gathers and quantifies the measures carried out by the Spanish government to help the wine industry overcome the current crisis. Therefore, the findings of this research are therefore of particular interest to the academic community, as well as to companies and professionals in the wine and agricultural sector, as they improve the current knowledge of the Spanish wine industry in a context of unprecedented instability for the sector due to the coronavirus. In addition, the research serves to identify the different strategies through which Spanish wineries can cope with the crisis caused by the pandemic.

This paper is structured as follows. First, after this brief introduction, section 2 presents the theoretical framework, providing a theoretical review of the literature on the effect of COVID-19 in different industries, with special emphasis on the wine industry. Section 3 explains the methodology followed in the empirical part to address the different objectives. Section 4 presents the main results obtained in the research. Section 5 discusses the solutions and recommendations given to the wine industry to overcome the current crisis derived from the coronavirus. Section 6 discusses future lines of research. Finally, section 7 presents the conclusions obtained from the work, highlighting the most relevant contributions.

THEORETICAL BACKGROUND

The rapid spread of the coronavirus has generated an unprecedented production of knowledge with the aim of ending the current pandemic, leading to a collective scientific effort in the form of a multitude of papers and resources of all kinds. In this context, the effectiveness of the scientific communication and publication system is being put to the test (Kupferschmidt, 2020).

From the thematic point of view of scientific production, there has been a notable orientation towards research on epidemiological and virological topics (Chahrour et al., 2020). However, it is essential to know the effect of the pandemic on different industries so that both organizations and government decision makers can make the right choices, since, in the current time of uncertainty, the knowledge generated around this issue can be decisive in dealing with COVID-19. For this reason, in addition to virological and epidemiological research, there is a new stream of research focused on determining the impact of the pandemic on different sectors of the economy. Table 1 reflects this new trend, as it shows the abundant research indexed in the Web of Science database[1] that addresses the effect of COVID-19 on different industries. Furthermore, as well as showing the incipient interest in this topic, it highlights the scarcity of academic literature focusing on the wine industry, as only two studies exist and they address the effect on the Australian and Italian cases. Due to the scarcity of academic literature on the effect of COVID-19 on the wine industry and, in particular, on the Spanish industry, it was decided to fill this gap in the literature with the purpose of providing new knowledge to both academics and professionals in the industry.

The impact of the pandemic on the air transport, shipping and tourism industries has mostly been studied using a global approach, as research addressing the impact of Covid-19 on these industries tries to quantify the impact at the global level rather than at the country level. This may be due to the idiosyncrasies of these industries, as their survival and growth depend to a large extent on the free mobility of people, goods and capital. In contrast, the impact of the pandemic on the food, energy and hospitality industries has mostly been analysed at country level, which may be due to the cultural, gastronomic and raw material heterogeneity of each country.

Table 1. Scientific articles addressing the impact of coronaviruses on different industries

Authors	Industry	Journal
Maneenop & Kotcharin (2020)	Airline	Journal of air transport management
Abu-Rayash & Dincer (2020)	Airline	Energy Research & Social Science
Van Senten et al. (2021)	Aquaculture	Applied Economic Perspectives and Policy
Waiho (2020)	Aquaculture	Aquaculture Reports
Thatcher et al. (2020)	Education	Journal of Risk and Financial Management
Tamrat (2021)	Education	Studies in Higher Education
Wang et al. (2021)	Energy	International Journal of Green Energy
Pradhan et al. (2020)	Energy	Energy Sources
Song et al. (2020)	Energy	Environmental Geochemistry and Health
Lechtenberg (2020)	Energy	ZKG International
Gray (2020)	Food	Canadian Journal of Agricultural Economics
Wittwer & Anderson (2020)	Food	Wine & Viticulture Journal
Çakır et al. (2020)	Food	Applied Economic Perspectives and Policy
Brewin (2020)	Food	Canadian Journal of Agricultural Economics
Höhler & Lansink (2020)	Food	Agribusiness
Telukdarie et al. (2020)	Food	Sustainability
Hailu (2020)	Food	Canadian Journal of Agricultural Economics
Adnan & Nordin (2020)	Food	Environment, development and sustainability
Solomon et al. (2020)	Food	Sugar Tech
McEwan et al. (2020)	Food	Canadian Journal of Agricultural
Morton (2020)	Food	World development
Hossain (2020)	Food	Journal of Agricultural Sciences
Bressan et al. (2021)	Food	International Journal of Entrepreneurial Behavior & Research
Patel (2020).	Healthcare	Journal of Advanced Oral Research
Kanna & Rajasekaran (2020)	Healthcare	Journal of Hand and Microsurgery
Roy et al. (2020)	Hospitality	Anatolia
Yang et al. (2020)	Hospitality	International Journal of Contemporary Hospitality Management
Sama et al. (2020)	Insurance	Home Health Care Management & Practice
Babuna et al. (2020)	Insurance	International journal of environmental research and public health
Davies et al. (2020)	Leisure	Animals
Drewes et al. (2021)	Leisure	Soccer & Society
Notteboom et al. (2021)	Shipping	Maritime Economics & Logistics
Yazir et al. (2020)	Shipping	International Maritime Health
Gössling (2021)	Tourism	Journal of Sustainable Tourism
Foo et al. (2020)	Tourism	Current Issues in Tourism
Karagiannis & Metaxas (2020)	Tourism	Sustainability
Hong et al. (2020)	Tourism	International Journal of Environmental Research and Public Health
Jaipuria et al. (2020)	Tourism	Tourism Recreation Research
Gil-Alana & Poza (2020)	Tourism	Tourism Economics
Almeida & Silva (2020)	Tourism	Advances in Hospitality and Tourism Research
Sharma & Nicolau (2020)	Tourism	Annals of tourism research
Tiwari et al. (2020)	Tourism	Journal of Teaching in Travel & Tourism
Lu & Zheng (2020)	Tourism	Current Issues in Tourism
Seraphin & Dosquet (2020)	Tourism	Worldwide Hospitality and Tourism Themes
Rahmanov et al. (2020)	Tourism	Marketing and Management of Innovations
Altuntas & Gok (2021)	Tourism	International Journal of Hospitality Management

Source: Own elaboration

Likewise, it is possible to state that all industries have been affected by the pandemic. However, the magnitude of the consequences has not been uniform for all of them. The consequences have been particularly devastating for the service sector. As far as the hospitality industry is concerned, some restaurants have limited their seating capacity, while others have closed their facilities altogether due to government orders or to preserve liquidity once restrictions are lifted (Roy et al., 2020). Those with the necessary financial resources have been quick to switch to home delivery services (Yang et al., 2020), but as the health crisis drags on, the hospitality industry is seeking financial support and advice from states to help them weather the crisis.

In terms of the tourism industry, the effects of the pandemic are seriously affecting the development of tourism activities worldwide (Gössling, 2021), especially in those countries where there is a higher contribution of tourism to GDP, such as Mexico, Spain and Italy (WEF, 2019). The literature reviewed shows the negative impact of COVID-19 on different business models belonging to the tourism industry among which cruise tourism (Lu & Zheng, 2020), education tourism (Tiwari et al. 2020), wine tourism (Karagiannis & Metaxas, 2020) sustainable tourism (Almeida & Silva, 2020) or B&B tourism (Hong et al., 2020) can be highlighted. Mountain and second home tourism (Seraphin & Dosquet, 2020), on the other hand, proves to be more resilient by acting as a placebo effect of previous tourism models.

The measures put in place by the different states to restrict the mobility of citizens have not only led to a significant reduction in tourist demand, but have also caused massive flight cancellations by the world's major airlines (Almeida & Silva, 2020). In fact, the airline industry was one of the first to be affected by the event, as the disease is easily transmitted from person to person (Maneenop & Kotcharin, 2020). The shipping industry, for its part, has also been negatively affected by the pandemic, with a 4.76% drop in freight rates during 2020 in the container shipping segment, since sudden drops in consumer demand have an immediate impact on shipping activity levels and port operations (Notteboom et al., 2021).

On the secondary sector side, there is a predominance of scientific production analysing the effect of the pandemic on the energy industry. The energy industry has not remained oblivious to the effect of COVID-19, generating a major impact especially on renewable energies (Song et al., 2020). Developing countries such as India and China aimed to increase their renewable energy capacity by 2022, but growth has largely stalled as a result of the pandemic (Song et al., 2020; Pradhan et al., 2020). The commissioning of new solar and wind power plants slowed in 2020 and is expected to slow by almost 10% during 2021, with Brazil, Mexico and South Africa being the most affected by renewable energy projects, as installation processes are in the contracting phase (Pradhan et al., 2020).

As far as the primary sector is concerned, agriculture and the food industry have suffered to a lesser extent from the impacts of the pandemic (Gray, 2020). This is largely because people have continued to consume and store food during state-decreed confinements. However, both agriculture and the food industry have been affected by spillover impacts. The literature reviewed discusses such indirect effects on various foods such as fruit and vegetables (Çakır et al., 2020), cereals (Brewin, 2020), rice (Adnan & Nordin, 2020), sugar (Solomon et al., 2020) and pork (McEwan et al., 2020). From the demand side, both have been affected by the panic of people stockpiling more food than necessary, raising concerns about shortages of foods such as sterilised milk, pasta, rice and canned food (Yazir et al., 2020). On the supply side, COVID-19 has caused a supply shock due to reduced worker mobility, transport delays and limited availability of some raw materials (Höhler & Lansink, 2020). As a result, governments have taken various measures to ensure the proper functioning of food supply chains (Morton, 2020).

In terms of wine consumption, sales have been affected not only by the temporary drop in expected revenues, but also by the measures of social distancing and self-isolation that have led, as explained above, to the closure of restaurants, as well as to the decline in travel and tourism. In this regard, the work of Wittwer & Anderson (2020) and Bressan et al. (2021) deserve special consideration, as they analyse the effect of the pandemic on the Australian and Italian wine industry respectively. Both studies show a decline in wine sales in their respective countries during 2020. They argue that this is largely due to the effect of the pandemic and the fact that wine is a minority beverage in the one major economy that has not fallen into recession: China. They also point out that wine producers who are highly dependent on visits to wineries for sales are those where the decline in wine sales is most severe, and the situation could be further exacerbated if they do not develop their e-commerce capabilities. In addition, those wineries that lack liquidity may be particularly vulnerable, as they may be forced to close or sell to a more viable winemaker with more money. However, this will be less likely the faster the economic recovery after COVID-19.

Another possibility to understand the effect of Covid-19 on the wine industry is to look at past crises and their effect on the wine industry. On the one hand, from a health point of view, it is possible to highlight the Spanish flu pandemic in 1918. During this period, wine prices fell by more than 25%, recovering from the fall in 1921 (Dimson et al., 2015). However, except for the health situation, the context was very different. The year 1918 marked the end of the Great War, the wine market was much less globalised than it is today, the political situation was extremely unstable and economic conditions were marked by rising inflation (Cardebat et al., 2020). On the other hand, from a forest fire point of view, it is possible to point out that forest fires have increased in frequency and severity in some of the main wine producing regions of the world and are becoming increasingly difficult to contain (Ferrer-Lorenzo et al., 2019).

Alongside these developments, the wine sector has recently been threatened by other events such as tariffs imposed by the Trump Administration and Brexit. On the one hand, the tariffs imposed by the Trump Administration have been particularly worrying for Spanish still wines, i.e. non-sparkling and non-generous wines (Villaécija, 2019). Moreover, the fact that they were imposed on some countries (France, Germany, United Kingdom and Spain) and not on others (Italy, Portugal and others) has been particularly damaging, affecting Spanish exports in one of its key markets (Haro, 2020). Regarding Brexit, the Trade and Cooperation Agreement reached in extremis on 24 December 2020 between the European Union (EU) and the United Kingdom was a clear relief for the Spanish and European wine sector, as it avoided the imposition of tariffs or export quotas on EU member countries (Daniel, 2021). Therefore, the post-Brexit agreement has benefited the Spanish wine industry, preventing goods and merchandise, including wine, from being regulated by the general framework of the World Trade Organization (WTO), which applies an average tariff of 3% (López, 2021).

Likewise, the decline in winery sales since the beginning of the outbreak has caused a domino effect on the revenues of several other sectors linked to the wine industry, notably non-profit organisations and wine co-operatives (Canavati et al., 2020). DeYoung (2020) through his research shows how non-profit wine organisations have deemed it as necessary to move from not-for-profit business models to social enterprise models, as non-profit organisations in the wine industry can alleviate the difficult financial challenges caused by the pandemic by diversifying their sources of income. For the Spanish case, Fuentes-Fernandez (2020) analysed the Grandes Vinos cooperative, which launched a campaign to raise more than 250,000 euros to finance the development of the vaccine and support the wine industry after the onset of the pandemic. Grandes Vinos benefited from its previous experience in fundraising for charitable causes in collaboration with other organisations. Thanks to its relational capital, as well as its previous experience with social projects, Grandes Vinos understood COVID-19 as a commitment to support society and the wine industry. Thus, companies can improve their economic performance while at the same time helping the territory in which they are located. This underlines that the future development of the wine industry depends to a large extent on its willingness to find creative ways to address the threats caused by past and future crises (Canavati et al., 2020).

METHODOLOGY

The research is conducted under a quantitative approach with an exploratory scope, as the research addresses a current topic on which there is no previous academic literature. Likewise, a non-experimental design is adopted, which implies that no modifications have been made to the independent variables and the conditions observed are those present in the natural context (García-Fernández & Cordero-Borjas, 2010).

In terms of information sources, secondary information has been used to carry out the research, as in an age where large amounts of data are collected and archived, the ability to use and interpret existing data is becoming increasingly important (Andrews et al., 2012). Thus, as Hakim (1982) points out, the analysis of a topic through the review of secondary sources generates additional and different knowledge.

Data from the consumption panel of the Spanish Ministry of Agriculture, Fisheries and Food (Spanish acronym, MAPA) are used to analyse household wine consumption. The aim of the Ministry of Agriculture, Fisheries and Food's consumption panel is to find out the direct demand for food in Spanish households, by systematically collecting and analysing information on what Spaniards buy for consumption at home. In addition, the data provided by the MAPA has also made it possible to identify and quantify the economic amount of aid provided by the Spanish state to overcome the current crisis. For the analysis of consumption in the Horeca sector and exports, data from the Spanish Wine Interprofessional Organisation (Spanish acronym, OIVE) and the Spanish Wine Market Observatory (Spanish acronym, OEMV) are used. Finally, for sales through wine clubs and the Internet, data from the Spanish Wine Federation (Spanish acronym, FEV) are used.

ANALYSIS AND RESULTS

Commercialization of Spanish Wine in the Domestic Market

The Horeca sector has been one of the most affected by the pandemic, which, as a consequence, has had repercussions on the wine industry, as it represents a third of Spanish wine sales. Thus, in terms of employment, the activities that make up this sector are in the top 3 of those that have had to resort to the Record of Temporary Employment Regulation (Spanish acronym, ERTE) to cope with the adverse economic context.

Figure 1 shows the 15 sectors of activity most affected by ERTEs in 2020. As can be seen, food and beverage services (31.95%), accommodation services (14.75%) and retail trade (7.47%) were the most affected by the pandemic in terms of employment in 2020, as they were the sectors in which the most requests for ERTEs were made as a result of the economic instability caused by the pandemic. Thus, out of every 100 workers covered by the ERTE during 2020, 31 were in the catering sector and 14 in accommodation services, highlighting the tough situation experienced by both sectors.

Figure 1. Main sectors (top-15) affected by ERTE in Spain in 2020
Source: Own elaboration based on data from the Ministry of Labour and Social Economy

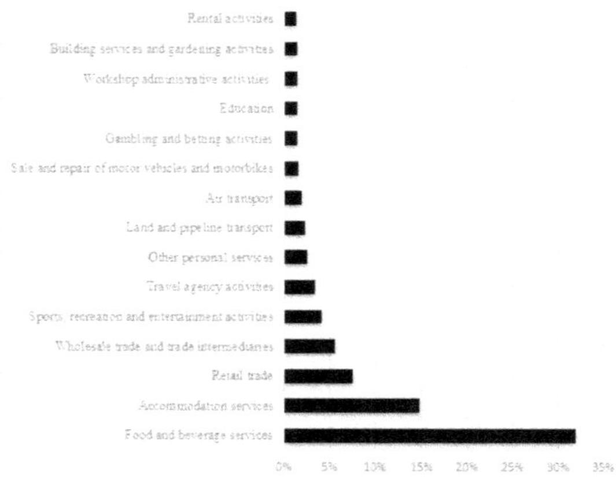

It is also important to note the negative effect of the pandemic on the entertainment sector (4.05%), as it is one of the sectors in which companies have made most use of ERTEs. The effect of the virus on the entertainment industry directly affects wine consumption, as wine is a social act, being linked in many occasions to celebrations and special events.

However, some of the extra-domestic consumption of wine moved into the domestic sphere of households. As can be seen in Figure 2, following the closure of hotel and catering establishments, in April and May 2020 there was a sharp increase in wine consumption by Spanish households of around 61.15% and 46.39% respectively compared to the same month of the previous year, according to MAPA data. Moreover, from March 2020, coinciding with the state of alarm decree, monthly wine consumption by Spanish households is higher than in the previous year in all the months analysed, since from that month onwards the year-on-year rates of monthly consumption for 2020 are positive.

Figure 2. Evolution of monthly wine consumption by Spanish households
Source: Own elaboration based on MAPA

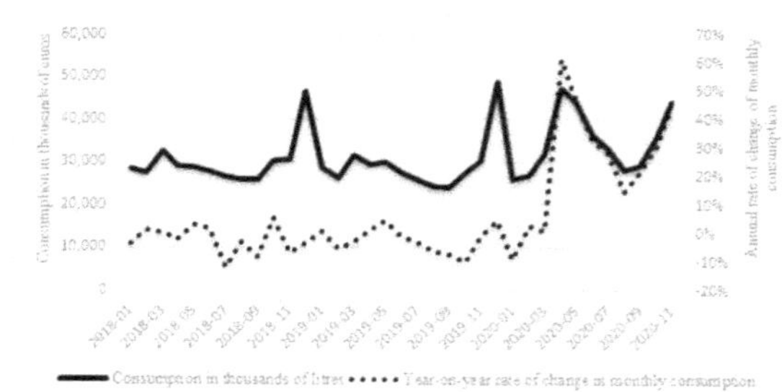

Likewise, during the 99 days of the state of alarm in Spain (which ended on 21 June), during which travel between Autonomous Communities was not permitted, nor was the arrival of foreign tourists, there was no consumption of wine linked to the flow of tourism and in the months immediately following the end of the state of emergency, tourist inflows were limited. In this regard, it should be noted that the fall in the number of foreign tourists visiting Spain for leisure and holiday purposes reached 64.00% year-on-year in March 2020, with no arrivals recorded in April and May, according to data from the INE (see Figure 3). Furthermore, following the end of the state of emergency in June 2020, powers were decentralised to the autonomous communities, each of which has introduced mobility restrictions that continue to hinder the entry of tourists and, as a result, the recovery of wine tourism.

Figure 3. Number of international tourists visiting Spain for leisure purposes in 2020 (Millions of tourists)
Source: Own elaboration based on INE data

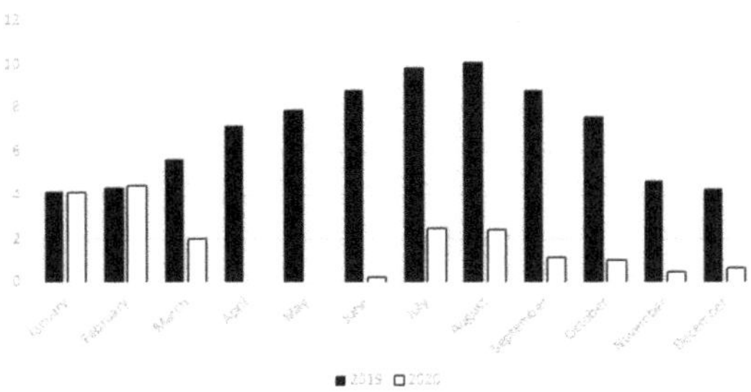

Figure 4 shows wine consumption in Spain through the different marketing channels. As can be seen, there is a drop in total wine consumption in 2020 compared to 2019, with a year-on-year fall of 3.76%. However, only the Horeca channel experienced a decrease in consumption, as wine consumption increased in all other channels. On the one hand, wine consumption in households rose sharply by 19.2% in 2020 compared to the previous year. On the other hand, consumption through the Horeca channel, experienced an unusual reduction in 2020, with the lowest consumption values in the last decade, from 295 million litres in 2019 to 151 million litres in 2020, a reduction of 48.8%. Regarding the rest of the channels, it is possible to observe that there was a notable increase in consumption, with an increase of 10.52% in 2020 compared to the previous year.

Figure 4. Wine consumption in Spain through different channels (Million litres)
Source: Own elaboration based on MAPA, OIVE and OEMV data.

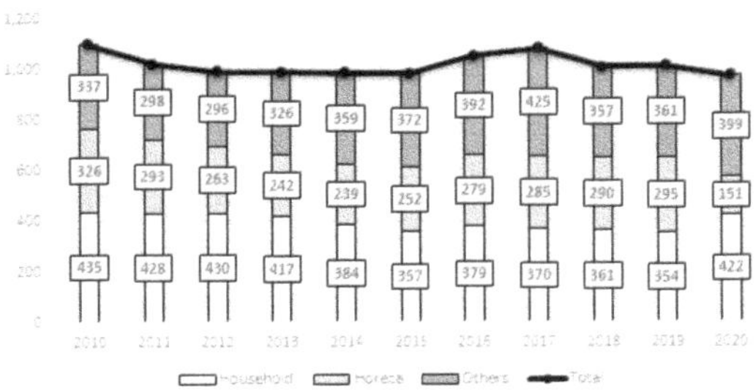

Within the "other" group, the rise in wine sales through the online channel stands out. According to a study carried out by the FEV, Spanish wineries increased their online sales by 161% between February and July 2020. Given the remarkable increase through this channel, some Regulatory Councils have set up digital platforms to facilitate online sales of the wineries in their demarcation. However, it should be noted that although the increase is significant and positive for the wine sector, the online channel represents a very small percentage of the sales made by the wineries, around 1% on average.

Commercialization of Spanish Wine in Foreign Market

The impact of the pandemic on the sales made by wineries has crossed borders, affecting exports. In this sense, wineries have had to deal with incidents in their sales abroad, mainly due to the temporary closure of hotel and catering establishments in other countries. However, the variability in the historical series of monthly export flows of wine products makes it difficult to quantify the specific impact of COVID-19 on exports, since these are also conditioned by other factors such as stock management or the level of abundance of harvests, among others. Figure 5 shows how the value of Spanish exports of wine products reached a three-year low in the months of April and May 2020, standing at 202.4 million euros in the latter month.

Figure 5. Monthly evolution of Spanish wine exports 2018 - 2020 (million euros)
Source: Own elaboration based on OEMV

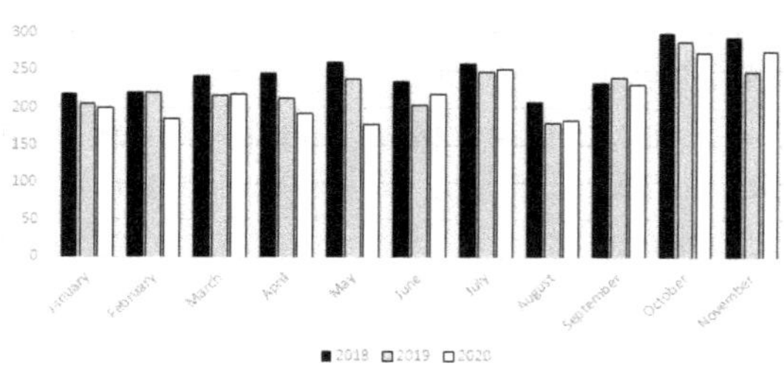

Figure 6 shows the evolution of exports from 2018 to 2020. From December October 2019 to January 2020 there is a sharp drop in wine exports, both in terms of volume and value, with a total reduction in 2020 compared to the previous year of 11.26%% of exports in terms of value and 13.78% of exports in terms of volume. However, from February 2020 exports stabilise and although there are ups and downs, it is possible to point to a growth trend. Moreover, from August 2020, the difference between the monetary value and the value in volume is increasing, leading to an increase in the euro per litre of wine exported from that month onwards, reaching €1.37/litre in November 2020. Thus, as export barriers have not increased considerably, exports have been able to continue their normal course. In contrast, the barriers imposed on tourism have led to a drastic reduction in tourism, to the detriment of the Spanish wine industry, as shown in Figure 3.

Figure 6. Spanish wine exports (2018-2020)
Source: Own elaboration based on OIVE and OEMV data

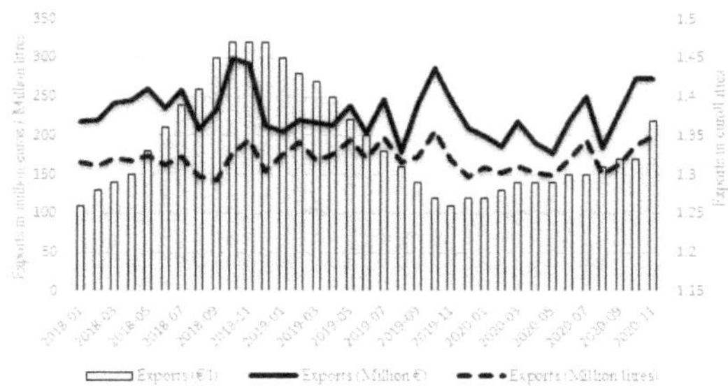

Extraordinary Measures Taken by the Spanish Government in the Wine Sector to Deal With the COVID-19 Crisis

On June 11, 2020, Royal Decree 557/2020, of June 9, 2020, came into force in Spain, adopting extraordinary measures in the wine sector to address the crisis caused by the COVID-19 pandemic. These measures have been crisis distillation, private storage and green harvesting, which aim to balance the markets, i.e., to offset wine supply and demand. Specifically, the measures aim to achieve the distillation of 2 million hectoliters of wine, the storage of 2.25 million hectoliters and the introduction of green harvesting with a budget of 10 million euros.

On the one hand, forced distillation consists of distilling and converting part of the wine into alcohol, thus taking it off the market. This measure is used at very specific moments and always with the authorisation of the administrations. The action, planned for 2 million hectolitres of wine, defines separate quotas for wines with protected designation of origin (PDO) and for other wines, with 0.5 million hl for the former and 1.5 million hl for the latter, with aid amounts respectively of 40 and 30 euros per hectolitre. Moreover, in order to ensure that all wine-growing areas can benefit from the aid, additional aid is foreseen when the distance to the distillery is more than 150 kilometres. Thus, the beneficiaries of this aid are authorised distillers of wine products who process wine into alcohol, who must pay the amount of the aid plus the full transport surcharge, net of distillation costs, to the supplier of the wine. In addition, although the resulting alcohol cannot be used for consumption, it may end up being used to make hydro-alcoholic gel or other sanitary uses, and there are currently various proposals in this direction as a result of the great demand (Cacho-Borrás, 2021). Therefore, wineries, distilleries and society all benefit from this aid. Table 2 shows the origin of the wines included in the application to benefit from the measure for both wines with PDO and other wines.

On the other hand, the private storage aid, planned for 2.25 million hectolitres, is aimed exclusively at wines with PDO, with the recovery of the market, are expected to resume both their price and their sales rhythm. Private storage is, therefore, a tool for the mismatch between wine supply and demand, as it encourages wine to remain at a standstill until it improves in price. The amount of the aid is 0.027 €/hl of wine and day of storage, for a period of 180 days for all wines, which can be extended to 270 or 360 days in the case of reds. Table 3 shows the regional breakdown of aid requested for private storage for both PDO wines and other wines.

Table 2. The regional breakdown for the measure based on crisis distillation

Autonomous Community	Crisis distillation			
	Wines with PDO		Other wines	
	Volume (hl) Applications	Amount (€)	Volume (hl) Applications	Amount (€)
Andalusia	18,865.0	392,392.5	29,142.5	602,008.6
Aragon	75,575.0	1571,962.0	250.0	5,164.3
Castile-La Mancha	350,263.5	7,285,490.6	1,809,875.6	37,387,348.4
Castile and Leon	61,325.7	1,275,578.0	3,111.0	64,265.2
Catalonia	89,589.0	1,863,455.0	7,403.8	152,944.1
Extremadura	50,977.5	1,060,334.6	287,812.0	5,945,451.4
Madrid	588.8	12,247.0	338.0	6,982.2
Murcia	15,550.0	323,440.4	1,740.0	35,943.9
Navarra	12,420.0	258,346.7	1,225.2	25,310.5
La Rioja	1,000.0	20,800.0	970.0	20,037.6
Valencian Community	293,574.4	6,106,357.1	47,100.0	972,964.1
Total	969,729.2	20,170,404.2	2,188,968.1	45,218,420.7

Source: Own elaboration based on MAPA

Table 3. The regional breakdown for the measure based on private storage

Autonomous Community	Private storage			
	Wines with PDO		Wines with PGI	
	Volume (hl)	Amount (€)	Volume (hl)	Amount (€)
Andalusia	69,226.8	336,715.0	1,230.0	8,967.0
Aragon	83,638.9	585,033.6	0.0	0.0
Balearic Islands	4,849.6	29,530.4	1,458.2	8,464.8
Canary Islands	1,837.9	10,461.3	0.0	0.0
Castilla La Mancha	263,071.7	2,339,325.0	136,104.2	865,635.4
Castile and Leon	133,078.5	892,303.8	17,774.1	134,816.3
Catalonia	407,596.2	2,089,688.6	2,000.0	9,720.0
Extremadura	10,087.2	54,710.9	23,068.3	118,217.6
Galicia	11,976.5	67,382.8	0.0	0.0
Madrid	768.7	5,620.3	0.0	0.0
Murcia	43,123.0	384,646.9	0.0	0.0
Navarre	119,113.8	895,224.6	0.0	0.0
Basque Country	261,919.5	1,837,782.2	749.5	3,642.5
La Rioja	608,563.1	5,142,004.1	0.0	0.0
Valencian Community	48,763.5	370,534.9	0.0	0.0
Total	2,067,615.5	15,040,965.0	182,384.4	1,149,463.8

Source: Own elaboration based on MAPA

Lastly, aid for green harvesting was proposed for a maximum amount of 10 million euros for the 2020 harvest of complete plots of land under PDOs. Green harvesting is a viticulture practice that consists of removing a quantity of grapes from a given vineyard when it has not yet reached ripeness, thus reducing its productive potential and favouring the elimination of surpluses. The grapes are harvested exclusively by hand and the harvested bunches of grapes are left on the land of the plot itself for biodegradation and can even be buried on the plot itself (Díez, 2020). The objective of green harvesting is to compensate economically and to increase the quality of the grapes, as the cost of elimination per hectolitre is lower than if it were a processed or semi-processed product. Moreover, using this method also prevents more vines from being uprooted than necessary, which means that in future years with better sales forecasts, production can continue as usual without the risk of a surplus. Table 4 shows the regional breakdown of aid requested for green harvesting.

Table 4. The regional breakdown for the measure based on green harvesting

Autonomous Community	Green harvesting	
	Hectares requested	**Total aid accepted (€)**
Andalusia	21.0	19,677.0
Aragon	41.3	26,640.7
Balearic Islands	112.5	176,773.9
Castile-La Mancha	2,311.3	1,659,759.0
Castile and Leon	1,743.7	2,851,267.2
Catalonia	2,231.5	2,374,325.4
Extremadura	669.0	340,312.4
Galicia	4.7	15,976.5
Madrid	57.9	23,975.5
Murcia	568.6	323,269.7
Navarra	155.7	149,384.0
Basque Country	43.2	84,382.8
La Rioja	632.8	971,131.7
Valencian Community	1,409.1	983,123.6
Total	10,002.9	10,000,000.0

Source: Own elaboration based on MAPA

SOLUTIONS AND RECOMMENDATIONS

In view of the impact of COVID-19 on the Spanish wine industry, the Spanish government published Royal Decree 557/2020 of 9 June, adopting extraordinary measures in the wine industry. These referred, as already mentioned, to the implementation of aid for crisis distillation, as well as measures aimed at storage and green harvesting in order to rebalance the market from the supply side. However, the wine sector's Designations of Origin (DOs) are expecting 2021 to be even tougher than the previous year, due to the impact of the pandemic, and are calling on the Government to provide more funds for aid programmes, according to the Spanish Conference of Wine Regulatory Councils (Spanish acronym, CECRV).

Thus, the CECRV recalls that quality wines have been the most affected by the crisis associated with the coronavirus, as their sales depend to a greater extent on the on-trade and tourism (Alcántara, 2020). Against this backdrop, the results of this research suggest that the future for the recovery of the Spanish wine industry lies in boosting online sales, food channels and exports to compensate for the decline in the Horeca channel. Likewise, resilience must be the key capacity of Spanish wineries, since in a sector that is mainly made up of small family businesses, they must be able to develop and strengthen their capacity to adapt to turbulent environments and to search for new markets.

FUTURE RESEARCH DIRECTIONS

Despite the contributions made, it is also possible to establish certain limitations of the work. In this sense, the most important limitation refers to the data used, as they are secondary data. To overcome this limitation, as a future line of research authors would like to ask wineries directly about the effects of the pandemic on their economic situation, as well as their opinion about the different measures that the Spanish government has developed to improve the situation of wine companies. In parallel, authors want to investigate whether wineries with PDO have been less affected in terms of sales by COVID-19 or whether, on the contrary, the appellation has had no effect on the impact caused by the pandemic.

CONCLUSION

The results of this research are of particular interest to the academic community, as well as to companies and professionals in the wine and agricultural sectors, as they improve current knowledge of the Spanish wine industry in a context of unprecedented instability for the sector because of the coronavirus. This research also contributes to improving the understanding of the the economic distribution of the measures implemented by the Spanish government to alleviate the effects of the pandemic. In this way, the research aims to fill a gap in the literature, as the effect of COVID-19 on the Spanish wine industry has not been addressed.

Regarding the marketing of Spanish wine in the domestic market, the sharp reduction in wine consumption through the Horeca channel deserves special attention. After the Spanish government declared a state of emergency on 14 March, hotels and restaurants were closed as a preventive measure against the accelerated spread of the coronavirus, which meant the closure of one of the most important strategic channels for the commercialisation of wine, representing a third of wine sales in the Iberian country. As a result, wine consumption in this channel fell from 295 million litres of wine in 2019 to 151 million litres in 2020, a year-on-year decrease of 48.80%. Furthermore, it should be borne in mind that, although the first state of emergency ended on 21 June 2020, powers in terms of preventive measures were subsequently transferred to the autonomous communities, which have applied strict restrictions that have made it impossible in many cases for hotels and restaurants to open, so there are few expectations of growth in wine consumption through the Horeca channel by 2021. It is also important to point out that during the 99 days of the state of alarm in Spain, during which travel between Autonomous Communities and the arrival of foreign tourists were not allowed, there was no wine consumption linked to the flow of tourists, and subsequently, the influx of tourists has been limited, which has had a considerable detrimental effect on wine tourism in Spain.

On the other hand, Household wine consumption experienced a notable increase, from 354 million litres of wine consumed in 2019 to 422 million litres in 2020, a rise in relative terms of 19.2%. This increase can be explained by the shift of food and beverage consumption from restaurants to households, as the population has been unable to go to bars and restaurants as a result of mobility restrictions. Alongside this fact, the outbreak of the pandemic brought with it public concern about a possible absenteeism crisis, causing the population to stockpile more food and beverages than necessary. In addition, Spanish wineries increased their online sales by 161% between February and July 2020, representing one of the best ways to sell wines while complying with health restrictions. Thus, although the online channel represents a very small percentage of the sales made by wineries, around 1% on average, it is good news for the wine sector as well as an opportunity to start diversifying the wine distribution channels available to wineries. However, it should be noted that the reduction in consumption in the Horeca channel (-48.80%) has not been offset by the increase in consumption in Spanish households (+19.2%) and in other channels (10.52%), including online.

As far as wine sales abroad are concerned, wineries have had to cope with some impact on their foreign sales, as Spanish exports of wine products reached a three-year low in the months of April and May 2020, with a reduction in exports in 2020 compared to the previous year of 11.26% in terms of value and 13.78%% in terms of volume. Nevertheless, the variability of the historical series of monthly wine product export flows makes it difficult to quantify the specific impact of COVID-19 on exports, as these are also conditioned by other factors such as stock management or the level of abundance of harvests, among others. Likewise, the fall in exports is not only explained by the COVID-19 effect, but also by other important events such as Brexit or the tariffs imposed by the US administration.

With regard to the extraordinary measures carried out by the Spanish government to mitigate the effect of the coronavirus, it is worth highlighting the implementation of three measures that have enabled the granting of subsidies to the wine sector amounting to 91,579,254€, these are: crisis distillation, private storage and green harvesting. The three measures are essentially aimed at balancing wine supply and demand, as well as providing economic support to the sector in the wake of an unprecedented crisis. However, wine industry professionals consider that this aid has not been sufficient and, in a way, has not benefited wine with PDO (Alfonso, 2020). Therefore, from the point of view of wine professionals, the distribution and focus of these funds must be reoriented so that they fall on those products that are suffering the most from the effects of this crisis, quality wines, as they are the most damaged by the current crisis, both due to the closure of the Horeca channel and to the fall in tourism.

ACKNOWLEDGMENT

This research received no specific grant from any funding agency in the public, commercial, or not-for-profit sectors.

REFERENCES

Abu-Rayash, A., & Dincer, I. (2020). Analysis of mobility trends during the COVID-19 coronavirus pandemic: Exploring the impacts on global aviation and travel in selected cities. *Energy Research & Social Science*, *68*(101693), 1–9. PMID:32839706

Adnan, N., & Nordin, S. (2020). How COVID 19 effect Malaysian paddy industry? Adoption of green fertilizer a potential resolution. *Environment, Development and Sustainability*, 1–41. PMID:33020694

AFI. (2020). *Importancia económica y social del sector vitivinícola en España.* Interprofesional del vino de España.

Alcántara, C. (2020). *El vino regional aguanta el envite de la crisis: los caldos resisten, las bodegas se reinventan.* https://murciaplaza.com/el-vino-regional-aguanta-el-envite-de-la-crisis-los-caldos-resisten-las-bodegas-se-reinventan

Alfonso, M. (2020). *Las ayudas al vino para paliar el covid-19, insuficientes.* https://www.lavozdegalicia.es/noticia/somosagro/2020/07/17/ayudas-vino-paliar-covid-19-insuficientes/00031594999615702422745.htm

Almeida, F., & Silva, O. (2020). The Impact of COVID-19 on Tourism Sustainability: Evidence from Portugal. *Advances in Hospitality and Tourism Research*, *8*(2), 440–446.

Altuntas, F., & Gok, M. S. (2021). The effect of COVID-19 pandemic on domestic tourism: A DEMATEL method analysis on quarantine decisions. *International Journal of Hospitality Management*, *92*(102719), 1–9. doi:10.1016/j.ijhm.2020.102719 PMID:33519015

Andrews, L., Higgins, A., Andrews, M., & Lalor, J. (2012). Classic grounded theory to analyse secondary data: Reality and reflections. *The Grounded Theory Review*, *11*(1), 12–26.

Ayati, N., Saiyarsarai, P., & Nikfar, S. (2020). Short and long term impacts of COVID-19 on the pharmaceutical sector. *Daru: Journal of Faculty of Pharmacy, Tehran University of Medical Sciences*, *28*(2), 799–805. doi:10.100740199-020-00358-5 PMID:32617864

Babuna, P., Yang, X., Gyilbag, A., Awudi, D., Ngmenbelle, D., & Bian, D. (2020). The impact of Covid-19 on the insurance industry. *International Journal of Environmental Research and Public Health*, *17*(16), 5766. doi:10.3390/ijerph17165766 PMID:32784978

Baicu, C., Gârdan, I., Gârdan, D., & Epuran, G. (2020). The impact of COVID-19 on consumer behavior in retail banking. Evidence from Romania. *Management & Marketing. Challenges for the Knowledge Society*, *15*(1), 534–556. doi:10.2478/mmcks-2020-0031

Bressan, A., Alonso, A., & Kok, S. (2021). Confronting the unprecedented: Micro and small businesses in the age of coronavirus disease 2019. *International Journal of Entrepreneurial Behaviour & Research*, *27*(3), 799–820. doi:10.1108/IJEBR-09-2020-0602

Brewin, D. (2020). The impact of COVID-19 on the grains and oilseeds sector. *Canadian Journal of Agricultural Economics*, *68*(2), 185–188. doi:10.1111/cjag.12239

Cacho-Borrás, A. (2021). *¿Qué es y para qué se pide una destilación de crisis?* https://cadenaser.com/emisora/2021/02/06/ser_ciudad_real/1612604141_866560.html

Çakır, M., Li, Q., & Yang, X. (2020). COVID-19 and Fresh Produce Markets in the United States and China. *Applied Economic Perspectives and Policy*, *43*(1), 341–354. doi:10.1002/aepp.13136

Canavati, S., Bauman, M., & Wilson, D. (2020). The Wine Industry & the COVID-19 Pandemic. *Wine Business Journal*, *4*(2), 1–4.

CardebatJ.MassetP.WeisskopfJ. (2020). COVID-19: What is Next for the Market for Fine Wines? *Available at* SSRN 3636317. doi:10.2139srn.3636317

Chahrour, M., Assi, S., Bejjani, M., Nasrallah, A., Salhab, H., Fares, M., & Khachfe, H. (2020). A bibliometric analysis of COVID-19 research activity: A call for increased output. *Cureus*, *12*(3), 1–7. doi:10.7759/cureus.7357 PMID:32328369

Davies, E., McConn-Palfreyman, W., Williams, J., & Lovell, G. (2020). The Impact of COVID-19 on Staff Working Practices in UK Horseracing. *Animals (Basel)*, *10*(11), 1–18. doi:10.3390/ani10112003 PMID:33143200

DeYoung, H. (2020). Napa Green: Funding Nonprofit Social Ventures In Crisis. *Wine Business Journal*, *4*(2), 54–83.

Díez, L. (2020). *Reticencias en Rioja a la vendimia en verde: «Es preferible guardar la uva»*. https://nuevecuatrouno.com/2020/06/21/ayudas-vendimia-verde-rioja-insuficiente-plazos-escasos/

Dimson, E., Rousseau, P., & Spaenjers, C. (2015). The price of wine. *Journal of Financial Economics*, *118*(2), 431–449. doi:10.1016/j.jfineco.2015.08.005

Doraiswamy, S., Abraham, A., Mamtani, R., & Cheema, S. (2020). Use of Telehealth During the COVID-19 Pandemic: Scoping Review. *Journal of Medical Internet Research*, *22*(12), 1–15. doi:10.2196/24087 PMID:33147166

Drewes, M., Daumann, F., & Follert, F. (2021). Exploring the sports economic impact of COVID-19 on professional soccer. *Soccer and Society*, *22*(1-2), 125–137. doi:10.1080/14660970.2020.1802256

Foo, L., Chin, M., Tan, K., & Phuah, K. (2020). The impact of COVID-19 on tourism industry in Malaysia. *Current Issues in Tourism*, 1–5. doi:10.1080/13683500.2020.1777951

Fuentes-Fernández, R. (2020). Grandes Vinos: The "Over the Rainbow" initiative & corporate philanthropy during a tragedy. *Wine Business Journal*, 82-93.

García-Fernández, F., & Cordero-Borjas, A. (2010). Proceso de gestión del conocimiento en Carabobo (Venezuela) y Tamaulipas (México). *Pensamiento & Gestión*, *28*, 132–154.

Gil-Alana, L., & Poza, C. (2020). The impact of COVID-19 on the Spanish tourism sector. *Tourism Economics*, 1–8.

Gössling, S. (2021). Tourism, technology and ICT: A critical review of affordances and concessions. *Journal of Sustainable Tourism*, *29*(5), 733–750. doi:10.1080/09669582.2021.1873353

Gray, R. (2020). Agriculture, transportation, and the COVID-19 crisis. *Canadian Journal of Agricultural Economics*, *68*(2), 239–243. doi:10.1111/cjag.12235

Gutiérrez-Escobar, R., Aliaño-González, M. J., & Cantos-Villar, E. (2021). Wine Polyphenol Content and Its Influence on Wine Quality and Properties: A Review. *Molecules (Basel, Switzerland)*, *26*(3), 718. doi:10.3390/molecules26030718 PMID:33573150

Hailu, G. (2020). Economic thoughts on COVID-19 for Canadian food processors. *Canadian Journal of Agricultural Economics*, *68*(2), 163–169. doi:10.1111/cjag.12241

Hakim, C. (1982). *Secondary analysis in social research: A guide to data sources and methods with examples*. Allen and Unwin/Unwin Hyman.

Haro, J. (2020). *Los aranceles de Trump dejan a España en desventaja ante otros socios de la UE*. https://www.eleconomista.es/economia/noticias/10720845/08/20/Los-aranceles-de-Trumpdejan-a-Espana-en-desventaja-ante-otros-socios-de-la-UE.html

Höhler, J., & Lansink, A. (2020). Measuring in the impact of COVID-19 on stock prices and profits in the food supply chain. *Agribusiness*, *37*(1), 171–186. doi:10.1002/agr.21678 PMID:33362339

Hong, Y., Cai, G., Mo, Z., Gao, W., Xu, L., Jiang, Y., & Jiang, J. (2020). The impact of COVID-19 on tourist satisfaction with B&B in Zhejiang, China: An importance–performance analysis. *International Journal of Environmental Research and Public Health*, *17*(10), 3747. doi:10.3390/ijerph17103747 PMID:32466326

Hossain, S. (2020). Impacts of COVID-19 on the agri-food sector: Food security policies of Asian productivity organization members. *Journal of Agricultural Sciences*, *15*(2), 116–132. doi:10.4038/jas.v15i2.8794

ILO. (2020). *ILO Monitor: COVID-19 and the World of Work*. https://www.ilo.org/wcmsp5/groups/public/dgreports/dcomm/documents/briefingnote/wcms_738753.pdf

Jaipuria, S., Parida, R., & Ray, P. (2020). The impact of COVID-19 on tourism sector in India. *Tourism Recreation Research*, 1–16.

Kanna, R., & Rajasekaran, S. (2020). The Impact of COVID-19 on Future Orthopaedic Practice. *Journal of Hand and Microsurgery*, *2*, 44–120.

Karagiannis, D., & Metaxas, T. (2020). Sustainable Wine Tourism Development: Case Studies from the Greek Region of Peloponnese. *Sustainability*, *12*(12), 5223. doi:10.3390u12125223

Kupferschmidt, K. (2020). Preprints bring 'firehose' of outbreak data. *Science*, *367*(6481), 963–964. doi:10.1126cience.367.6481.963 PMID:32108094

Lechtenberg, D. (2020). The impact of Covid-19 on the alternative fuels industry. *ZKG International*, *73*(7-8), 24–27.

López, A. (2021). *Alivio en el sector vitivinícola español por el Acuerdo post-Brexit entre la UE y el Reino Unido*. http://www.sevi.net/es/3582/2000/15837/Alivio-en-el-sector-vitivin%C3%ADcola-espa%C3%B1ol-por-el-Acuerdo-post-Brexit-entre-la-UE-y-el-Reino-Unido.htm

Lu, Y. (2020, Dec.). Wine report 2020. *Statista Consumer Market Outlook.*

Lu, Y., & Zheng, Q. (2020). Twitter public sentiment dynamics on cruise tourism during the COVID-19 pandemic. *Current Issues in Tourism, 24*(7), 892–898. doi:10.1080/13683500.2020.1843607

Maneenop, S., & Kotcharin, S. (2020). The impacts of COVID-19 on the global airline industry: An event study approach. *Journal of Air Transport Management, 89*(101920), 1–6. PMID:32874021

McDermaid, M., & Newton, S. (2020). Paradise Ridge Winery: Can a tragedy strengthen a brand? *Wine Business Journal, 4*(2), 5–28.

McEwan, K., Marchand, L., Shang, M., & Bucknell, D. (2020). Potential implications of COVID-19 on the Canadian pork industry. *Canadian Journal of Agricultural Economics, 68*(2), 201–206. doi:10.1111/cjag.12236

Morton, J. (2020). On the susceptibility and vulnerability of agricultural value chains to COVID-19. *World Development, 136*(105132), 1–4. PMID:32836692

Notteboom, T., Pallis, T., & Rodrigue, J. (2021). Disruptions and resilience in global container shipping and ports: The COVID-19 pandemic versus the 2008–2009 financial crisis. *Maritime Economics & Logistics*, 1–32.

OIV. (2020). *Estadísticas*. https://www.oiv.int/es/statistiques/recherche

Patel, N. (2020). Impact on dental economics and dental healthcare utilization in COVID-19: An exploratory study. *Journal of Advanced Oral Research, 11*(2), 128–136. doi:10.1177/2320206820941365

Pradhan, S., Ghose, D., & Shabbiruddin. (2020). Present and future impact of COVID-19 in the renewable energy sector: A case study on India. *Energy Sources. Part A, Recovery, Utilization, and Environmental Effects*, 1–11. doi:10.1080/15567036.2020.1801902

Rafael, D. (2021). *Más impuestos al vino y pérdida de competitividad, riesgos de la era post Brexit para el sector agroalimentario*. https://www.eleconomista.es/empresas-finanzas/agro/noticias/10997429/01/21/Mas-impuestos-al-vino-y-perdida-de-competitividad-riesgos-de-la-era-post-Brexit-para-el-sector-agroalimentario.html

Rahmanov, F., Aliyeva, R., Rosokhata, A., & Letunovska, N. (2020). Tourism management in Azerbaijan under sustainable development: Impact of COVID-19. *Marketing and Management of Innovations, 3*(3), 195–207. doi:10.21272/mmi.2020.3-14

Roy, H., Gupta, V., Faroque, A., & Patel, A. (2020). The impact of COVID-19 on the foodservice industry in Vancouver, British Columbia, Canada. *Anatolia, 32*(1), 157–160. doi:10.1080/13032917.2020.1857803

Sama, S., Quinn, M., Galligan, C., Karlsson, N., Gore, R., Kriebel, D., & Lindberg, J. (2020). Impacts of the COVID-19 Pandemic on Home Health and Home Care Agency Managers, Clients, and Aides: A Cross-Sectional Survey, March to June, 2020. *Home Health Care Management & Practice, 33*(2), 125–129. doi:10.1177/1084822320980415

Seraphin, H., & Dosquet, F. (2020). Mountain tourism and second home tourism as post COVID-19 lockdown placebo? *Worldwide Hospitality and Tourism Themes, 12*(4), 485–500. doi:10.1108/WHATT-05-2020-0027

Sharma, A., & Nicolau, J. (2020). An open market valuation of the effects of COVID-19 on the travel and tourism industry. *Annals of Tourism Research*, *83*(102990), 1–4. PMID:32834220

Solomon, S., Rao, G. P., & Swapna, M. (2020). Impact of COVID-19 on Indian sugar industry. *Sugar Tech*, *22*(4), 547–551. doi:10.100712355-020-00846-7 PMID:32837056

Song, Y., Liu, T., Li, Y., & Ye, B. (2020). The influence of COVID-19 on grid parity of China's photovoltaic industry. *Environmental Geochemistry and Health*, 1–16. doi:10.100710653-020-00701-4 PMID:32857234

Tamrat, W. (2021). Enduring the impacts of COVID-19: Experiences of the private higher education sector in Ethiopia. *Studies in Higher Education*, *46*(1), 59–74. doi:10.1080/03075079.2020.1859690

Telukdarie, A., Munsamy, M., & Mohlala, P. (2020). Analysis of the Impact of COVID-19 on the Food and Beverages Manufacturing Sector. *Sustainability*, *12*(22), 9331. doi:10.3390u12229331

Thatcher, A., Zhang, M., Todoroski, H., Chau, A., Wang, J., & Liang, G. (2020). Predicting the Impact of COVID-19 on Australian Universities. *Journal of Risk and Financial Management*, *13*(9), 1–20. doi:10.3390/jrfm13090188

Tiwari, P., Séraphin, H., & Chowdhary, N. (2020). Impacts of COVID-19 on tourism education: Analysis and perspectives. *Journal of Teaching in Travel & Tourism*, 1–26. doi:10.1080/15313220.2020.1850392

Van Senten, J., Engle, C., & Smith, M. (2021). Effects of COVID-19 on US aquaculture farms. *Applied Economic Perspectives and Policy*, 1–13.

Villaécija, R. (2019). *Los aranceles de Trump amenazan a España: 400 millones en aceite y 300 en vino.* https://www.elmundo.es/economia/macroeconomia/2019/10/03/5d95bf0621efa04e508b457f.html

Waiho, K., Fazhan, H., Ishak, S., Kasan, N., Liew, H., Norainy, M., & Ikhwanuddin, M. (2020). Potential impacts of COVID-19 on the aquaculture sector of Malaysia and its coping strategies. *Aquaculture Reports*, *18*(100450), 1–6. doi:10.1016/j.aqrep.2020.100450

Wang, Q., Chen, D., & Chang, C. (2021). The impact of COVID-19 on stock prices of solar enterprises: A comprehensive evidence based on the government response and confirmed cases. *International Journal of Green Energy*, *18*(5), 443–456. doi:10.1080/15435075.2020.1865367

WEF. (2019). *The travel & tourism competitiveness report 2019-travel and tourism at a tipping point.* http://www3.weforum.org/docs/WEF_TTCR_2019.pdf

WHO. (2020). *Coronavirus disease (COVID-19) Pandemic.* World health Organization. https://www.who.int/emergencies/diseases/novel-coronavirus-2019

Wittwer, G., & Anderson, K. (2020). COVID-19 and global beverage markets: Impacts on Australian wine industry. *Wine & Viticulture Journal*, *35*(3), 61–66.

Yang, Y., Liu, H., & Chen, X. (2020). COVID-19 and restaurant demand: Early effects of the pandemic and stay-at- home orders. *International Journal of Contemporary Hospitality Management*, *13*(12), 3809–3834. doi:10.1108/IJCHM-06-2020-0504

Yazir, D., Şahin, B., Yip, T., & Tseng, P. (2020). Effects of COVID-19 on maritime industry: A review. *International Maritime Health*, *71*(4), 253–264. doi:10.5603/IMH.2020.0044 PMID:33394490

ADDITIONAL READING

Bardají, I., Estavillo, J., & Iráizoz, B. (2014). Export performance: Insights on the Spanish wine industry. *European Journal of International Management*, *8*(4), 392–414. doi:10.1504/EJIM.2014.062969

Ferrer-Lorenzo, J., Maza-Rubio, M., & Abella-Garcés, S. (2019). Business model and performance in the Spanish wine industry. *Journal of Wine Research*, *30*(1), 31–47. doi:10.1080/09571264.2019.1573358

Fischer, C., & Gil-Alana, L. A. (2009). The nature of the relationship between international tourism and international trade: The case of German imports of Spanish wine. *Applied Economics*, *41*(11), 1345–1359. doi:10.1080/00036840601019349

Herrero-Hernández, E., Andrades, M., Álvarez-Martín, A., Pose-Juan, E., Rodríguez-Cruz, M. S., & Sánchez-Martín, M. J. (2013). Occurrence of pesticides and some of their degradation products in waters in a Spanish wine region. *Journal of Hydrology (Amsterdam)*, *486*, 234–245. doi:10.1016/j.jhydrol.2013.01.025

Martínez-Carrión, J., & Medina-Albaladejo, F. (2010). Change and development in the Spanish wine sector, 1950–2009. *Journal of Wine Research*, *21*(1), 77–95. doi:10.1080/09571264.2010.495856

Maylín-Aguilar, C., & Montoro-Sánchez, Á. (2020). The Industry Life Cycle in an Economic Downturn: Lessons from Firm's Behavior in Spain, 2007–2012. *Journal of Business Cycle Research*, 1-30.

Morrison, A., & Rabellotti, R. (2017). Gradual catch up and enduring leadership in the global wine industry. *Research Policy*, *46*(2), 417–430. doi:10.1016/j.respol.2016.09.007

Pradana, M., Pérez-Luñ, A., & Fuentes-Blasco, M. (2019). Revisiting measure of absorptive capacity: Applying the scales in spanish wine industry. *Journal of Management Information and Decision Sciences*, *22*(4), 515–526.

KEY TERMS AND DEFINITIONS

Crisis Distillation: It consists of the distillation of part of the wine to convert it into alcohol, thus removing it from the market. It is used at very specific moments and always with the authorization of the administrations.

Green Harvesting: Refers to the destruction of grape clusters while they are still immature, thus reducing the yield of the area in question to zero.

Horeca: A distribution channel for food that is characterized by the preparation and marketing of food and beverages that have been purchased in advance.

Private Storage: The measure consists of withdrawing part of the products from the market by applying an aid to store them in warehouses.

Protected Designation of Origin: A distinction whose purpose is to identify a product originating from a specific place, whose quality is fundamentally due to a particular geographical environment, with the natural and human factors inherent to it.

Record of Temporary Employment Regulation: A temporary authorization for a company to suspend one or more employment contracts for a determined period of time. That is to say, to dispense for a period of time of its employees being exempted from paying them.

Wine Tourism: It consists of getting to know in depth and from the inside, the whole world of wine: issues of the wineries, vineyards, winemaking, history, etc.

ENDNOTE

1 The last consultation was held on April 20, 2021.

Chapter 13
Impact of COVID-19 on International Trade:
New Evidence From Economic Sectors

Reenu Kumari
Meerut Institute of Engineering and Technology, Meerut, India

Ashwani Sharma
Meerut Institute of Engineering and Technology, Meerut, India

ABSTRACT

All the countries are facing serious problems affecting their economic growth. In 2020, many countries faced negative GDP per capita growth due to the coronavirus pandemic. Therefore, this chapter investigates how coronavirus (COVID-19) affected international trade (IT) and how this changed over time. Secondly, the authors analyzed how international trade collapsed. Thirdly, the chapter highlights the negative effects of COVID-19 on international trade including economic sectors. Furthermore, it discussed the opportunities and forthcoming policies and what kinds of actions have been taken by the government bodies.

INTRODUCTION

Since 1990's, Trade has raised income by 24% worldwide, 50% for the poorest 40% of the population. The World Bank helps those countries who have suffered from employment, poverty, education, and infrastructure and provides a path for the access to international markets. Trade plays a significant role in the economic growth that reduces poverty, provides job opportunities, and makes better business relations between two different kinds of countries (including developing and developed countries). With the help of Trade reduce the obstacles between developed and developing countries, these obstacles include deter the accessibly in international market, ambiguous regulatory and administrative environment, political environment etc. Although, after globalization still all the developing countries are not experiencing the benefits of international trade due to climate change, culture changes, political change

DOI: 10.4018/978-1-7998-8314-2.ch013

and technological changes. With the help of table 1 and figure 1 reveal that World import and export and import& export value index (2000=100) were increased during 2001-2005, 2006-2010, 2011-2016 but during 2016-2018 import as well as export were in decline.

Table 1. World imports and exports (2000-2018)

World	Average (2001-2005)	Average (2006-2010)	Average (2011-2016)	Average (2016-2018)
Import value index (2000 = 100)	123.589003	214.056424	276.169981	270.498911
Export value index (2000 = 100)	124.0503021	217.589578	283.296701	275.14651

Sources: World Bank, 2019

Figure 1. World imports and exports (2000-2018)
Sources: World Bank, 2019
Note: 1 represents year 2001-05, 2 represents 2006-10, 3 represents 2011-16, and 4 represents 2016-2018.

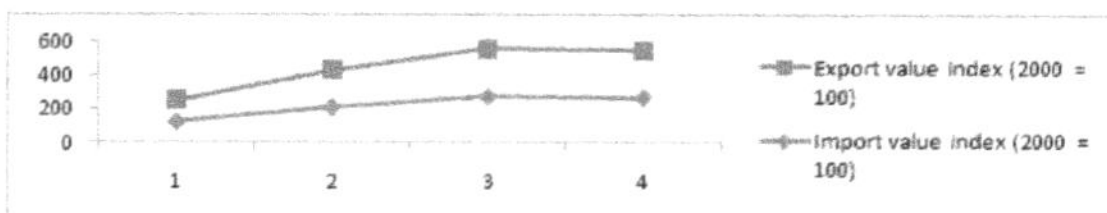

In 2019 and 2020, international trade will continue to decline in Developed and developing countries due to covid-19. Although, Infectious diseases are not new kind of diseases in the world as we saw covid 19 because in history people has also faced this type of diseases like SARS (2003), plague (2007), H1N1 (2009), cholera (1917), Ebola (2014), and MERS-Cov (2014). Although initially it was seen in China (Huang et al., 2020; Wu et al., 2020) and later it was spread in developed countries (US & Russia) and later in South-East Asian (Gruszczynski, 2020). Policy makers believed this disease could be controlled as previous diseases were controlled such as SARS. But this has not happened in most developing countries (SEA countries) and still they are facing the problem of Covid-19. It may be due to various factors like politics, availability of natural resources, government rules and regulations etc. This epidemic situation has extended to other areas (sectors) of the world and finally the World Health Organization (WHO) was announced as a pandemic.

Thus, COVID-19 continues to hit throughout the world, including health of the people, living standard, supply chain, economic growth etc. Now the question rose: how to win from this big battle and how to recover from the economic loss (including imports and exports). Although, George et al., (2010), Anaeto and Chioma, (2007) revealed that the economic impact of SARS, H1N1, avian influenza has varied from country to country and depends on how to deal with the disease. As compared with the situation in 2003, both have downfall trends of international trade but in 2003 the world international trade recovered on a large scale. Moreover, most of the studies (Siu and Wong 2004; Hai et al. 2004; Hanna and Huang 2004) analyzed the economic impacts of SARS. The spread of COVID-19 has shocked the world economy, suspending business exercises and forcing people to remain at home. As per gauges, the COVID-19 emergency left 25 million jobless in Pakistan pushing millions towards yearning and neediness. Areas like the travel industry, security exchanges, diversion and fabrication are the most noticeably awful hits.

The worldwide economy projection is 2.4% to 2.9% while China's financial conjecture has been minimized from 6.1% to 4.9% (OECD 2020). It has in the long run prompted and decreased in utilization, disturbed the store network and interfered with absolute creation level universally. Therefore, this stun in worldwide monetary exercises can be isolated into the interest and supply-side. Its consolidated impacts remember to succumb to GDP development rate, swapping scale deterioration, ascend in the expansion rate, ascend in joblessness, wage slice, financial and social palliative measures, fall in loan fee (Ataguba, 2020). Moreover, it has influenced organizations across the globe as they have closed down activities and it is influencing endless individuals who are laid off because of the impact of the pandemic.

BACKGROUND

Some authors Dun & Bradstreet, (2020); Bai et al., (2020); Sohrabi et al., (2020); Lai et al., (2020), found that there is no doubt Covid-19 upset the life of human beings as well as the global supply chain. The Covid-19 pandemic situation also negatively affects the demand of the commodity because of demand shock in 2019-2020. Due to the negatively affected supply and demand, the side effects reflect the plunging GDP which is estimated by 0.2 percent in India and GDP could reach 4.8 percent. For the upcoming year, 2021 estimated GDP to reduce by 0.5 percent and reached 6 percent. Work along supply chains may likewise turn into a limitation as the infection spreads. In the end of the 2020, almost all sectors are going to start or reopen but in the month of March 2021, again lockdown came so effects of COVID-19on the international trade (import and export) found negative (WTO, 2021). Most of the academic researchers (Bonadio et al., 2020; Baker et al., 2020; Eichenbaum et al., 2020) focused in this area but still this area required more lighting.

Therefore, our chapter tried to make three distinct contributions in existing literature. Firstly, to analyze how international trade collapsed by Covid-19 we have taken different sectors. Secondly, to analyze the effects of Covid-19 on international trade (including agriculture sector, manufacturing sector and service sector). Then, find out challenges in international trade during & post Covid-19 and opportunities for international trade. The last section discussed the forthcoming policies and necessary actions taken by the government.

MAIN FOCUS OF THE CHAPTER

International Trade Collapsed by Covid 19

World economy has affected negatively not just because of COVID-19 while consequences are depending on the various factors such as normal behavior changes such as peoples evading public transport or movement from one place to other places and shopping centers interruption of supply, narrow policy adoption in world financial market conditions, shifted purchasing pattern by the public, stochastic market share price and commodity prices and lose confidence level (Fernandes, 2020). March 2020 OECD Interim Economic Outlook, global GDP almost 13 percent decline in first half of 2020 due to the Covid -19 has negatively affected the corporate debt and management of sovereign. Misleading corporate debts in any country is a clear need to keep trade flowing (including demand and supply of goods and services) because trade is essential to save the lives of the people and livelihoods. But, it is possible to reduce the export and import restriction; maintain supply chain, and cooperation from different countries. This kind of challenge is faced when trade tensions exist in any country. Figure 2 shows Spain (ESP) was highly affected by the irregular chain of international trade and further followed by France (FRA), Italy (ITA), Great Britain and Northern Ireland (GBR), Russia (RUS), etc. During lockdown tariff increases among the major traders, no significant support by the government and inefficiency of workers due to infection by covid-19.

Figure 2. Output collapse during first half of 2020
Projected change in GDP at constant prices between 2019Q4 and 2020Q2 (per cent)
Source: OECD, 2020

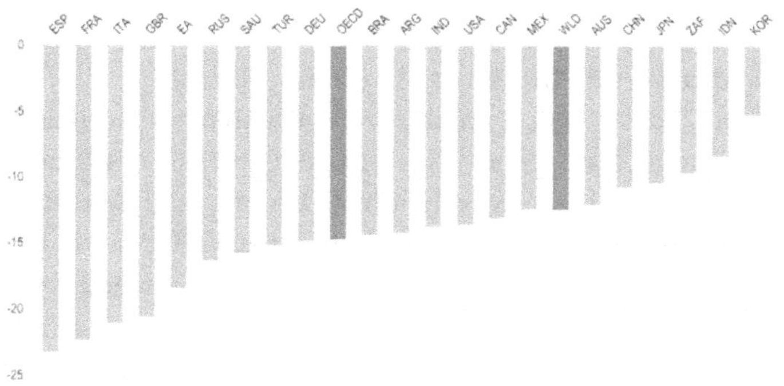

Table 2. Exports and imports (2018-2020) including selected some countries

Group/country	Volume of exports			Volume of imports		
	2018	2019	2020a	2018	2019	2020a
World	3.1	-0.5	-8.8	3.8	-0.4	-8.5
Developed Countries *of which*	2.6	0.0	-12.0	2.5	0.1	-10.5
Japan	2.6	-1.6	-9.2	3.1	0.9	-4.4
United States	4.2	-0.5	-12.1	5.2	-0.3	-9.1
Euro area	1.9	-0.2	-13.3	2.2	0.0	-12.2
Developing Countries *of which:*	3.8	-1.1	-4.7	5.7	-1.2	-5.6
China	5.4	0.5	-4.4	6.9	-0.4	-2.0
Asia (excl. China)	3.7	-1.8	-4.4	6.9	-2.3	-6.6
Latin America	3.0	0.5	-8.7	4.8	-1.6	-12.0
Africa and Middle East	1.0	-3.9	-3.1	0.6	-0.2	-2.0

Source: UNCTAD secretariat calculations based on CPB *World Trade Monitor*, July 2020.
Note:
a Percentage change between the average for the period January to May 2020 and January to May 2019.

(Percentage change over previous year)

Figure 3 and Figure 4 show annual average import and export growth rate in Africa, America, Europe, Asia and Oceania. In 2018, merchandise trade volume was 2.9% growth and in 2019 merchandise trade volume declined 0.1% as compared to previous year. World GDP growth declined 2.9% in comparison to the previous year (2018) and slowed to 2.3% in 2019. The US $ value of merchandise trade declined year after year, dropping 3% US$ 18.89 trillion in 2019. The district displaying the biggest drop in the volume of its fares was the euro territory, which additionally showed the biggest withdrawal in the volume of imports. As far as concerns are concerned, regardless of being the nation previously hit by the COVID-19 pandemic, China just saw a generally moderate decrease in its volume of imports. UNCTAD exchange current projects and unrestricted economy product value record demonstrate that worldwide exchange esteems and costs have been adversely affected since the primary quarter of 2020 by the COVID-19 flare-up. The plunge is relied upon to quicken during the second quarter of the year. Imports and tolls of clinical things added up to about $2 trillion, including intra-EU exchange (import and export), which tended to generally 5% of complete globe item trade 2019; Defensive supplies used in the fight against Coronavirus pull in a typical duty of 11.5% and go as high as 27% in specific countries

Figure 3. Exports annual average growth rate
Source: UNCTAD, 2020

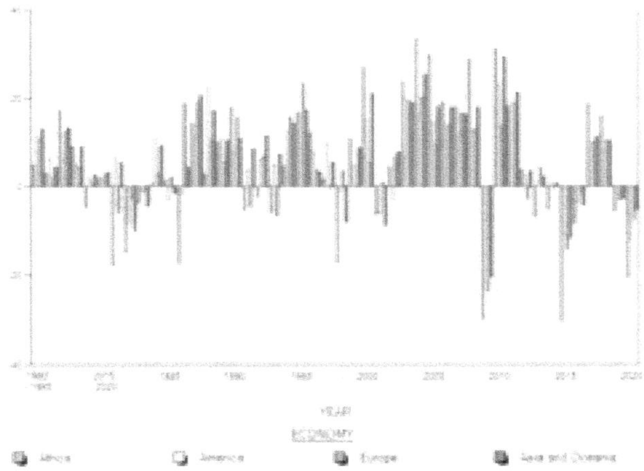

Figure 4. Imports annual average growth rate
Source: UNCTAD, 2020

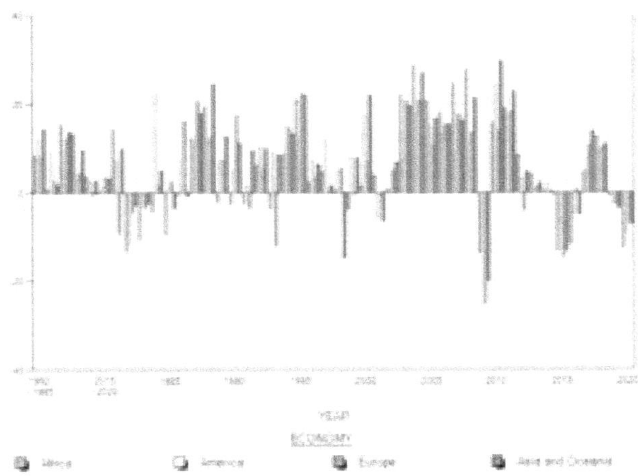

Table 3 reveals that trade clinical things which have been depicted as fundamental and in outrageous lack during the Corona virus emergency amounted to about US$ 597 billion each of 2019, addressing 1.7% of hard and fast world item trade. The ten greatest giving economies addressed pretty much 3/4 of supreme world admissions of the things while the ten greatest buyers addressed roughly 66% of world imports.

Table 3. Trade in medical goods (medical imports) in different countries

Country	Total imports		Medical imports	Share of total medical imports			
	Value	Share of imports of all products	Share of world imports	Medical equipment	Medical supplies	Medicines	Personal protective products
	(US$ billion)	(%)	(%)	(%)	(%)	(%)	(%)
World	1 011.3	6	100	14	17	56	13
1. United States	193.1	8	19	16	16	59	10
2. Germany	86.7	7	9	12	18	57	13
3. China	65.0	3	6	23	15	46	16
4. Belgium	56.6	13	6	8	12	75	5
5. Netherlands	52.7	8	5	16	20	55	8
6. Japan	44.8	6	4	16	16	56	13
7. United Kingdom	41.1	6	4	11	15	62	12
8. France	40.5	6	4	12	20	53	15
9. Italy	37.1	8	4	9	15	66	9
10. Switzerland	36.9	13	4	6	9	80	5

Source: WTO, 2020

EFFECTS OF COVID 19 ON INTERNATIONAL TRADE

In this section, majorly three economic sectors are included (Agriculture, manufacturing & servicing) that were highly affected by the covid 19. Very rarely found that covid 19 have a positive effect on international trade, so here only the negative effects of covid 19 on international trade are considered.

Negative Effect on Agriculture Sector

The primary important sectors for human progress is agriculture and is associated to food security (Abdelhedi and Zouari, 2020; Kogo et al.,2020; Lopez-Ridaura et al., 2019). This essential area is vital for any economy according to different perspectives like, share in GDP, employment and foreign exchange earning etc. According to World Bank, (2016) found that adults labor made a living through agriculture. Agriculture sector is not only the process of farming and cultivation, it connects farm production to final consumer and COVID-19 has affected all the processes in agricultural activities. When there is an outbreak of infectious disease, there is also an increase in hunger and malnutrition (Burgui, 2020; Sar et al.,2010). Moreover, it seems to affect the food production system and food value chain. The adverse consequence of pandemic on supply and demand for food may lead food security in danger (Siche R, 2020). There are some precautionary actions have taken by many countries to manage the speed of infection such as home quarantine, travel restrictions and business shutdown and as the disease increases then situation became more worsen that caused labor shortage for the harvest, create difficulties in front of the farmers to bring their product to market. Because of these activities taken by many countries World Product exchange is accepted to decline by 13% to 22% (WTO, 2020). The Food and Agriculture Organization (FAO, 2020a) states that COVID-2019 was affecting agriculture in two significant aspects: the supply and demand for food. These two aspects are directly related to food security, so food security is also at risk (as cited in Siche, 2020).. Similarly, it also affects international trade due to a sudden change in consumption patterns triggered by the measures put in place.

Hence, the objective to find the negative effect on the agriculture sector is to analyze the relationships between agriculture Supply and demand as import and export data of first quarter of 2019 vs. 2020, March 2019 vs. 2020 and April 2019 to. 2020 how these relationships are being affected by events related to the disease of COVID-19 shown in Figure 5 and Figure 6.

Figure 5. Agricultural exports by region percentage change
Source: WTO Secretariat estimates

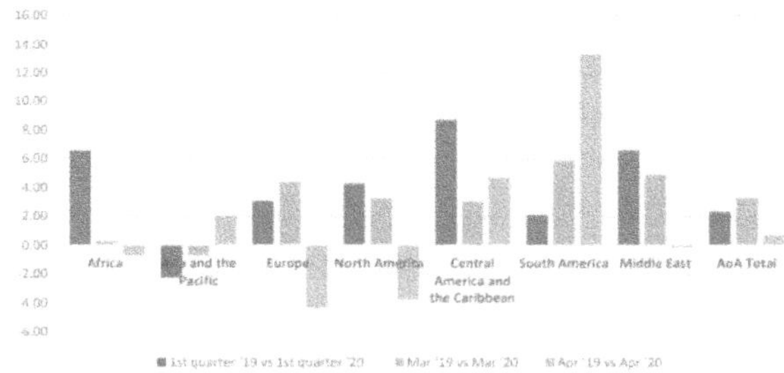

Figure 6. Agricultural imports by region percentage change
Source: WTO Secretariat estimates

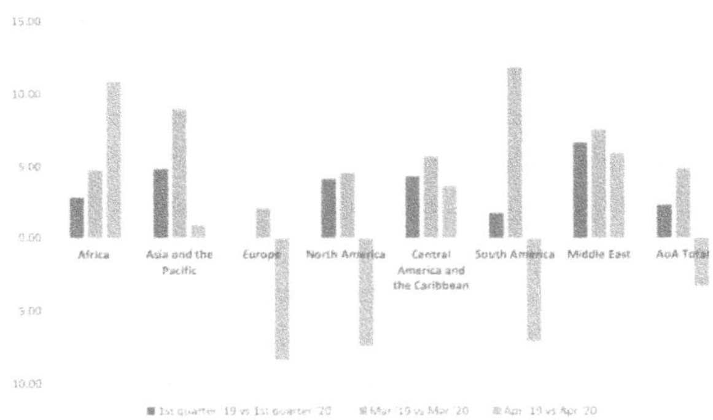

As also according to the WTO 2020 Secretariat has published a new information in the report of covid-19 and agriculture: a story of resilience, the demand for certain agricultural products which are prepared by many agriculture crops (e.g., oils, resins, fibers, clothing, energy, cosmetics, and plastics) dropped significantly, while increasing for others eatable and home consumable agriculture products reflecting initial panic purchasing and increased home-based consumption. In April 2020, exports dropped also for several food products, strikingly for higher-esteem items, such as fresh produce, dairy and meat, which are generally more dependent on deals to restaurants, schools and the travel industry area than to families. Also, high-esteem transient items moved via air were hit more enthusiastically by the abrupt breakdown in air traveler traffic, which reduced airship cargo limits and raised cost.

Negative Effect on Manufacturing Sector

The international production and supply chain system was disrupted due to covid 19 pandemic. The COVID-19 pandemic has broken the greater part of transportation connections and conveyance systems between providers, production facilities and customers. During the early disease spread of the pandemic, suspects are suggested to the medical hospitals for detachment, finding, and to analyze the infection rate of infection and for this there is huge demand of medical utilities as thermal scanners, ventilators, face masks, sanitizers, PPE, and essential food items and medical utilities will was overcome the sales of other manufacturing products which was produced less due to low demand like Automobile products, public transport, and textile products Similarly, Failure of supplies and uncertainty in raw material supply, Impacting ability to ship and receive products on time due to short- ages and logistics bottlenecks (Kuma, Luthra,Mangla,Kazançoglu,2020)

According to the assessment by UNCTAD, the Covid-19 flare-up could cause worldwide FDI to contract by 5%-15%, in light of the ruin in collecting territory joined with the creation line conclusion. The antagonistic results of Covid-19 on FDI adventures are needed to be high in the energy, vehicle, and transporter endeavors. In light of the diseases of Covid-19 across the globe, the producers of the auto, substance, equipment, and plane are going up against worries concerning the openness of unrefined material. In the equipment territory, mobile phones and client contraptions associations have begun decline in progress exercises and conceded the introduction of new things joined with the Coronavirus scene, which in this way has encroached upon the stock of parts. The worldwide manufacturing development which was at that point decelerating in 2019 because of the exchange strains among predominant economies is required to decrease because of financial disturbances set off by Covid-19.

The examination on the impact of Covid-19 on the overall amassing industry is requested into vehicle, food and drink, compound, mechanical assembly, electrical and contraptions, metal, flight, drug and clinical stuff, and others. The equipment business is all things considered basically impacted as a result of the Covid-19 pandemic, as China addresses practically 85% of the total worth of parts utilized in PDAs and practically 75% by virtue of TVs. Each essential section, for instance, printed circuit sheets, versatile introductions, Driven chips, memory, open cell TV sheets, and capacitors are imported from China. By far most of the Chinese creation lines were shut down because of the Covid pandemic. Appropriately, in January 2020, Chinese venders have extended part costs by right around 2-3% infeasible from insufficiency of arrangements as a result of plant conclusion. Thus, it has unfavorably impacted the equipment delivering region across the globe.

Table 4 shows that how driving organizations changes underway interaction and techniques, and standard working systems to keep up the assembling cycle however that can't assist with conquering the pandemic impact on assembling area Due to the COVID-19, the majority of the worldwide or nearby assembling ventures (auto, transport, drug, food, and so on) need to restore their creation limit and crude material sourcing. As indicated by UNCTAD gauges, the most influenced areas incorporate accuracy instruments, apparatus, car and correspondence gear.

Table 4. World's leading manufacturing companies affected by COVID-19

Companies	Industry
Ford	Automobile manufacturing
Tesla	Automobile manufacturing
Airbus	Aircraft manufacturing
Zara	Fashion
Bacardi	Alcohol
Gucci	Apparel
Indian Ordnance Factory	Defence

Source: World Economic Forum, 2020b

Negative Effect on Service Sector

The service sector includes industries such as tourism, food, healthcare, transport, education and media and culture industries etc. and these were also highly affected by COVID -19 Pandemic. During a pandemic, individuals have been told to remain at home, and individuals have consequently moved in the direction of diversion, instruction, and social exercises, which has, thusly, over-burden real time and other online services.

Transportation sector is the significant sector that influenced by lock down during Covid 19 pandemic and interruption in vehicle movement system directly affected the service sector that is crucial for all micro, small and medium enterprise that is called MSME for the world and which is more dedicated for market demand.(Bouey, 2020). The loss of media income is also about USD10 billion due to media closer and the expense was not minimized due to reporting and coverage and news and information (Hall, 2020). Similarly during several social distancing and lockdown circumstances, 79.7% of the workforce of human articulations, redirection, and news sources lost their positions or were put on obliged leave in the United Kingdom (Mangan, 2020).Hospitality industry was also no far from pandemic effect as make survival became challenging by adopting that innovative precautionary strategies and maintain the customer trust related to safety (Vasiljeva et al, 2020). As other service sector, education industries plays very important and valuable role for learner and this pandemic disrupted learning for more than 107 billion learner in the world. Organizations and schools' terminations have brought about numerous and various difficulties, for example, physical and mental wellbeing risks, highly job losses, salary deductions, income losses, families in custody, quarantine (Olingo, 2020).

During this Covid pandemic, the pressure on associations has changed from moving individuals to keeping a center transportation framework practical with a skeleton group to ensure the proceeding with development of cargo and basic representatives. In pre-COVID-multiple times, innovation and IT was never utilized in transport. Way finding through pilots is a relatively old idea, yet utilizing it to keep social separation will be a creative thought. Establishment of the outside booth to handle packed circumstances is additionally set up, and a large number of these have carried out touch-less screens. Individuals' development observation can restrict the spread of COVID-19; however, it might raise security issues (Hutchinson, 2020).

The services like hotels, restaurants, tour operators and travel agencies, which are under the international tour and travel industry has seemingly been the hardest hit by the emergency up until this point, given that mobility restrictions and border closures halted the movement of tourists abroad

The decrease in stock exchange coming about because of the financial stoppage is adding to a lessening in related service exchanges, like the worldwide oceanic vehicle of cargo. Furthermore, mobility restrictions on people are also affecting cross-border freight transport services.

OPPORTUNITIES FOR INTERNATIONAL TRADE POST COVID 19

Recollect that varieties in the volume of exchange streams will in general be more unpredictable than changes in genuine yield. This is especially the case during times of financial emergency. Looking back to the global financial crisis, worldwide yield saw a constriction of 1.3 percent in 2009, while the volume of world exchange enrolled a fall of 12.6 percent (CPB, 2020). Notwithstanding, the effect of the covid-19 pandemic on exchange volumes goes past the sharp constriction in financial development and request experienced because of the covid-19 flare-up. It incorporates the interruptions experienced in transport connections and supply chains across the globe as governments presented extreme limitations with an end goal to stem the infection's spread. Such limitations incorporate the shutting down of ports and boundaries, requirements on air travel (affecting the vehicle of merchandise by means of airship cargo), just as postponements in traditional handling (especially applicable for the exchange of short-lived merchandise). Similarly, the appropriation of exchange boundaries by various nations, especially concerning sending out limitations on clinical supplies and food items, has served to additionally push down exchange volumes.

Figure 7. Forecasting of world merchandise trade volume, 2015Q1-2022Q4
Source: WTO and UNCTAD for trade data: WTO for forecasts.

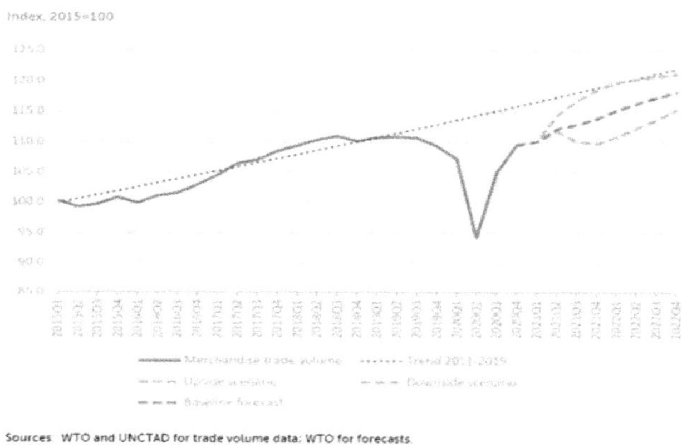

World merchandise trade volume is expected to increase by 8.0% in 2021 in the wake of falling 5.3% in 2020, a more modest decrease than recently assessed. Trade development will probably ease back to 4.0% in 2022, with the absolute volume of worldwide trade staying beneath the pre-pandemic pattern. World GDP at market trade rates should increase by 5.1% in 2021 and 3.8% in 2022, subsequent to shrinking by 3.8% in 2020. Product exchange ostensible dollar terms fell in 2020 by 7% while business administration's sends declined by 20%. (WTO & UNCTAD 2020)

SOLUTIONS AND RECOMMENDATIONS

In this section discuss the course of actions which is taken by the government during a pandemic situation. Post for other policy briefs in this course of action that will look even more significantly into unequivocal issues. Approaching Briefs include: Trade help, Government support, Global Value Chains for major work and items trade.

Trade Facilitation: If the government expanded the exchange offices then regardless of extensive vulnerability support up the trust in exchange and worldwide market by improving straightforwardness. Straightforward data will advance the sound public arrangement and worldwide co-activity to keep exchange streaming. Despite the fact that it is a troublesome undertaking to give straightforward data about the exchange, the OECD is sharing data on global exchange and nation activities towards

Coronavirus with the assistance of WTO so these activities help support in approach creators managing the monetary emergency or other pandemic circumstance. Additionally, in the agribusiness field, our yearly Monitoring and Evaluation of Agricultural strategies help to follow and survey the effect of nation measure comparable to agri food creation and exchange reaction to COVID-19.

Government Support: Second most significant advance ought to be government backing to keep worldwide stockpile chains going, particularly for fundamentals (counting including food items, clinical supplies and ICT labor and products. Despite the fact that, we began to have a number of difficulties keeping these stock chains. For instance, cancelation of traveler trips because of a boycott during Coronavirus. Just the pressing delivery of fundamental merchandise has risen, bringing about the expansions in the cost of air payload as analyzed from the past cost. Significant transportation ports revealed yearly drops in freight between 10 to 20 percent in February (Baschuk, 2020). At the time the illness struck, tremendous measures of movement holders were in Chinese ports, and cutoff points on their improvement have actuated a come up short on that has seen the cost of compartments climb (a portion of the time generally), with stream on impacts to the detriment of weight, including food things. Lockdowns are in addition impacting the accessibility of work to dump ships at ports (extremely in nations where this is less robotized) or brought costs up considering expanded shielding systems for laborers. Much more generally speaking, all stock chains are being affected by the need to guarantee extra flourishing and security endeavors for all people in the creation association (which affect expenses and time). Cutoff centers around flexibility of individuals and lockdowns are affecting a game plan of exchange measures, from certified appraisals of items for SPS, to testing and statement for TBT, to changing how threatening to unloading evaluations are driven. These are adding to the time and expenses of generally exchanging things that matter. They will require coordinated activity among governments – and with the private domain – to discover answers for the decided objectives affecting the capacity to get significant things where they are required most.

Global Value Chains for trade: - Obligations on clinical items crucial for combating Coronavirus (for instance a couple of countries keep up obligations of up to 10 percent on Corona virus test units) (Baldwin and Evenett, 2020) as different countries have viably done. It deduces working with accreditation strategy to permit new things to be exchanged as quickly as time permits and guaranteeing that particular necessities are science-based and don't superfluously limit exchange. At long last, it proposes improved exchange help to keep things moving as speedy as could be expected – including perceiving key activities expected to guarantee smooth practices structures with kept human intervention

In like manner, there are different unavoidable expenses in the current pandemic; significantly more motivation to stay away from practices that add to costs for dealers and clients. Administrator among these is the need to keep away from passing on limits on fundamental items, such as clinical gear and, particularly, food things. Right now, more than 60 countries have restricted sections of pivotal items and consistently development and food things.

CONCLUSION

The main aim of this chapter is to present early proof for the effects of COVID-19 on international trade. Discuss about the history of COVID-19and how it is spread in the world. Additionally, we investigated which countries are most affected by COVID-19and most affected trade among 186 countries in the year of 2020. Although, based on WHO, report December 2020 we found the ten most affected countries including America, India, Brazil, Russia, France, UK, Italy, Turkey, Spain, and Argentina by covid 19. From the second section of this chapter, we found that international trade collapsed by COVID-19 but consequences are depend on the various factors such as normal behavior changes such as peoples evading public transport or movement from one place to other places and shopping centers interruption of supply, narrow policy adoption in world financial market conditions, shifted purchasing pattern by the public, stochastic market share price and commodity prices and lose confidence level. Moreover, section 3 analyzed negative effects on agriculture, manufacturing and services sector. The agriculture sector is well-working worldwide in the food esteem chain but due to the pandemic situation this sector is helpless against interruptions in this key area. An unexpected absence of versatility across borders and inside nations has caused work deficiencies in nations that are dependent on occasional traveler labourers in the agri-food area, which, thusly, has influenced food accessibility and costs worldwide. The worldwide manufacturing development which was at that point decelerating in 2019 because of the exchange strains among predominant economies is required to decrease because of financial disturbances set off by COVID-19.

Trade development will probably ease back to 4.0% in 2022, with the absolute volume of worldwide trade staying beneath the pre-pandemic pattern. In the last section of this chapter discussed which types of actions have been taken by the government during COVID-19. Post for other policy briefs in this course of action that will look even more significantly into unequivocal issues. Approaching Briefs include: Trade help, Government support, Global Value Chains for major work and items trade.

After going through the literature, we found some recommendations and suggestions for the government and policy makers, consumers, traders, exporters, importers etc. At the time of pandemic situation, the health department is the most important department in the world so the government should relax the import and export restrictions on essential goods, such as medicines, medical equipment, & food products. If the government will be engaged in removing export restrictions and then buyers, firms, individuals, countries engage in the handling of panic buying or hoarding so there is a risk of a pandemic situation will come under control.

In the area of agriculture, manufacturing and service sectors, we lost seasonal workers for the planting and harvesting, logistic restraints, technical measures, facilities of travel and tourism. Although, overall supply chain has disrupted due to pandemic situation, therefore, government should need to invest urgently in boosting production capacity, with the help of private investors, regional and global markets investment. Moreover, the government has taken a more decision regarding how to increase the overall global supply of essential medical supplies for the fighting against the COVID-19such as vaccines, masks, oxygen gas cylinders, hospitals, beds, etc. Although some governments (America, Russia, Turkey, China) have taken fast decisions regarding how to win from this pandemic situation, some counties (Southeast Asian countries) are lacking.

On the basis of some government reports COVID-19will come again as a third way of coronavirus. Although the government is also aware about this expected fact, governments rightly are concerned to protect their own populations as well as economic growth. In the world, developing countries are not able to produce their own products (including medical, daily uses, equipment's, machinery etc.) due to the limited financial budget. So, for these countries, the governments of developed countries should take initiatives to integrate under developing countries in the progression. These countries have sufficient manufacturing capacity but due to the lack of labour efficiency, mobility restrictions, technology unawareness not properly utilized. Collaboration is necessary to avoid further appreciation in ongoing trading strains. Therefore, collaboration between the developed and developing countries ensures that we can remove this problem and reach about to win from this situation.

If the government should commit not impose new and heavy tariffs or trade restrictive measures because it does not correct the time period to impose additional costs on firms and consumers through traffic. Due to the covid crisis already consumers, manufacturers, wholesalers etc faced extra burden regarding additional costs on the goods & services.

Limitations of the Study with the Future Direction

This study has its own boundaries in terms of data used because this chapter considered only the conceptual facts, figures, and tables & ignored the empirical work. For the improvement of this chapter work further, we can consider empirical work which applies some econometric model, techniques and based on some micro and macro-economic variables (including interest rate, infrastructure, trade openness, investor interest, inflation, rule of laws, exchange rate) related to international trade.

REFERENCES

Abdelhedi, I. T., & Zouari, S. Z. (2020). Agriculture and Food Security in North Africa: A Theoretical and Empirical Approach. *Journal of the Knowledge Economy*, *11*(1), 193–210. doi:10.100713132-018-0528-y

Anaeto, M., & Chioma, G. (2007). Avian influenza in Nigeria: Suggestions for eradication. *International Journal of Poultry Science*, *6*(5), 67–371. doi:10.3923/ijps.2007.367.371

Arndt, C., & Lewis, J. D. (2001). The HIV/AIDS pandemic in South Africa: Sectoral impacts and unemployment. *Journal of International Development*, *13*(4), 427–449. doi:10.1002/jid.796

Bai, Y., Yao, L., Wei, T., Tian, F., Jin, D. Y., Chen, L., & Wang, M. (2020). Presumed asymptomatic carrier transmission of COVID-19. *Journal of the American Medical Association*, *323*(14), 1406–1407. doi:10.1001/jama.2020.2565 PMID:32083643

Baker, S. R., Bloom, N., Davis, S. J., & Terry, S. J. (2020). *Covid-induced economic uncertainty (No. w26983)*. National Bureau of Economic Research. doi:10.3386/w26983

Baldwin, R., & Freeman, R. (2021). *Trade conflict in the age of COVID-19*. VoxEU. org.

Baldwin, R., & Tomiura, E. (2020). Thinking ahead about the trade impact of COVID-1 *Economics in the Time of COVID-19, 59.*

Bermejo, A. (2004). HIV/AIDS in Africa: International responses to the pandemic. *New Economy*, *11*(3), 164–169. doi:10.1111/j.1468-0041.2004.00357.x

Bonadio, B., Huo, Z., Levchenko, A. A., & Pandalai-Nayar, N. (2020). *Global supply chains in the pandemic (No. w27224)*. National Bureau of Economic Research. doi:10.3386/w27224

Bouey, J. (2020). *Assessment of COVID-19's impact on small and medium-sized enterprises: Implications from China*. RAND Corporation. doi:10.7249/CT524

Burgui, D. (2020). *Coronavirus: How action against hunger is responding to the pandemic*. Available in: https://www.actionagainsthunger.org/story/coronavirus-how-action-against-hunger-responding-pandemic

Curran, E. (2020). Urgent Demand for Medical Equipment is Making Air Cargo Fees "Absolutely Crazy". *Bloomberg*. https://www.bloomberg.com/news/articles/2020-03-30/-absolutely-crazy-air-cargo-fees-highlight-supply-chain-squeeze

Eichenbaum, M. S., Rebelo, S., & Trabandt, M. (2020). *The macroeconomics of epidemics (No. w26882)*. National Bureau of Economic Research. doi:10.3386/w26882

Evenett, S. J. (2020). Sicken thy neighbour: The initial trade policy response to COVID-19. *World Economy*, *43*(4), 828–839. doi:10.1111/twec.12954

FAO - Food and Agriculture Organization. (2020a). *Q&A: COVID-19 pandemic - impact on food and agriculture*. Available in: http://www.fao.org/2019-ncov/q-and-a/en/

FernandesN. (2020). *Economic effects of coronavirus outbreak (COVID-19) on the world economy*. Available at SSRN 3557504. doi:10.2139srn.3557504

Gruszczynski, L. (2020). The COVID-19 pandemic and international trade: Temporary turbulence or paradigm shift? *European Journal of Risk Regulation*, *11*(2), 337–342. doi:10.1017/err.2020.29

Guan, W. J., Ni, Z. Y., Hu, Y., Liang, W. H., Ou, C. Q., He, J. X., Liu, L., Shan, H., Lei, C., Hui, D. S. C., Du, B., Li, L., Zeng, G., Yuen, K.-Y., Chen, R., Tang, C., Wang, T., Chen, P., Xiang, J., ... Zhong, N. S. (2020). Clinical characteristics of corona virus disease 2019 in China. *The New England Journal of Medicine*, *382*(18), 1708–1720. doi:10.1056/NEJMoa2002032 PMID:32109013

Hall, S. (2020). *This is How COVID-19 is Affecting the Music Industry. World Economic Forum*. Available online at: https://www.weforum.org/agenda/2020/05/this-is-how-covid-19-is-affecting-the-music-industry/

Hanna, D., & Huang, Y. (2004). The impact of SARS on Asian economies. *Asian Economic Papers*, *3*(1), 102–112. doi:10.1162/1535351041747978

Hutchinson, A. (2020). *More nations are looking to use cell phone data to track the COVID-19 outbreak, raising privacy concerns*. Social Media Today.

Kumar, A., Luthra, S., Mangla, S. K., & Kazançoğlu, Y. (2020). COVID-19 impact on sustainable production and operations management. *Sustainable Operations and Computers*, *1*, 1–7.

Lai, C. C., Shih, T. P., Ko, W. C., Tang, H. J., & Hsueh, P. R. (2020). Severe acute respiratory syndrome coronavirus 2 (SARS-CoV-2) and coronavirus disease-2019 (COVID-19): The epidemic and the challenges. *International Journal of Antimicrobial Agents*, *55*(3), 105924.

Mangan, D. (2020). Covid-19 and labour law in the United Kingdom. *Eur. Lab. Law J.*, *11*, 332–346. doi:10.1177/2031952520934583

McKibbin, W., & Fernando, R. (2020). The economic impact of COVID-19. *Economics in the Time of, COVID-19*, 45.

Olingo Allan. (2020). *Economy hit hard as services slow down; Daily Nation*. Nation Media Group.

Pramiyanti, A., Mayangsari, I. D., Nuraeni, R., & Firdaus, Y. D. (2020). Public perception on transparency and trust in government information released during the COVID-19 pandemic. *Asian Journal for Public Opinion Research*, *8*(3), 351–376.

Sar, T. T., Aernan, P. T., & Houmsou, R. S. (2010). H1N1 Influenza Epidemic: Public Health Implications for Nigeria. *International Journal of Virology*, *6*, 1–6.

Siche, R. (2020). What is the impact of COVID-19 disease on agriculture? *Scientia Agropecuaria*, *11*, 3–6.

Siu, A., & Wong, Y. R. (2004). Economic impact of SARS: The case of Hong Kong. *Asian Economic Papers*, *3*(1), 62–83.

Sohrabi, C., Alsafi, Z., O'neill, N., Khan, M., Kerwan, A., Al-Jabir, A., ... Agha, R. (2020). World Health Organization declares global emergency: A review of the 2019 novel coronavirus (COVID-19). *International Journal of Surgery, 76*, 71-76.

Statistics, A. B. O. (2020). *Jobs by Industry Sub-division*. Available online at: https://www.abs.gov.au/statistics/labour/employment-and-unemployment/labour-force-australia-detailed-quarterly/latest-release

Tramontana, A. R., George, B., Hurt, A. C., Doyle, J. S., Langan, K., Reid, A. B., ... Slavin, M. (2010). Oseltamivir resistance in adult oncology and hematology patients infected with pandemic (H1N1) 2009 virus, Australia. *Emerging Infectious Diseases*, *16*(7), 1068.

Vasiljeva, M., Neskorodieva, I., Ponkratov, V., Kuznetsov, N., Ivlev, V., Ivleva, M., Maramygin, M., & Zekiy, A. A. (2020). Predictive Model for Assessing the Impact of the COVID-19 Pandemic on the Economies of Some Eastern European Countries. *J. Open Innov. Technol. Mark. Complex, 6*, 92.

World Health Organization. (2020a). *Corona virus disease (COVID-19): situation report, 165*. WHO.

World Health Organization. (2020b). *Corona virus disease (COVID-19): situation report, 114*. WHO.

World Health Organization. (2020c). *Corona virus disease (COVID-19): situation report, 198*. WHO.

WTO. (2020). *Covid-19 and Agriculture: A Story of Resilience, Information Note*. https://www.wto.org/english/news_e/news20_e/agri_27aug20_e.htm

WTO. (2021a). *World Trade Primed for Strong but Uneven Recovery after COVID-19 pandemic shock*. https://www.wto.org/english/news_e/pres21_e/pr876_e.htm

WTO. (2021b). https://www.wto.org/english/tratop_e/covid19_e/agric_report_e.pdf

WTO. (2021c). https://www.wto.org/english/tratop_e/covid19_e/covid19_e.htm

WTO. (2021d). https://www.wto.org/english/tratop_e/covid19_e/trade_related_goods_measure_e.htm

WTO. (2020). *Trade shows signs of rebound from COVID-19, recovery still uncertain*. Press release. https://www.wto.org/english/ news_e/pres20_e/pr862_e.htm

Wu, A., Peng, Y., Huang, B., Ding, X., Wang, X., Niu, P., & Jiang, T. (2020). Genome composition and divergence of the novel coronavirus (2019-nCoV) originating in China. *Cell Host & Microbe*, *27*(3), 325–328.

Wu, Y., Xu, X., Chen, Z., Duan, J., Hashimoto, K., Yang, L., & Yang, C. (2020). Nervous system involvement after infection with COVID-19 and other coronaviruses. *Brain, Behavior, and Immunity*, *87*, 18–22.

Compilation of References

Abdal, A., & Ferreira, D. M. (2021). Deglobalization, Globalization, and the Pandemic: Current Impasses of the Capitalist World-Economy. *Journal of World-systems Research*, *27*(1), 202–230. doi:10.5195/jwsr.2021.1028

Abdelhedi, I. T., & Zouari, S. Z. (2020). Agriculture and Food Security in North Africa: A Theoretical and Empirical Approach. *Journal of the Knowledge Economy*, *11*(1), 193–210. doi:10.100713132-018-0528-y

Abu-Rayash, A., & Dincer, I. (2020). Analysis of mobility trends during the COVID-19 coronavirus pandemic: Exploring the impacts on global aviation and travel in selected cities. *Energy Research & Social Science*, *68*(101693), 1–9. PMID:32839706

Adam, A., & Moutos, T. (2005). *Turkish Delight for Some, Cold Turkey for Others? The Effects of the EU-Turkey Customs Union*. CESifo Working Paper Series, 1550.

Adams, R. (2020). Despite the absence of trade fairs, chemours, merck, schlenk shepherd showcase their new products. *Focus on Pigments*, *2020*(7), 1–2. doi:10.1016/j.fop.2020.08.001

Adelon, D. B. & Kakinaka, M. (2018). Extensive and intensive margins of exports: the case of the Philippines. *Asia Pacific Journal of Accounting and Economies, 25*(83-4), 404-418. doi:10.1080/16081625.2017.1293551

Adnan, N., & Nordin, S. (2020). How COVID 19 effect Malaysian paddy industry? Adoption of green fertilizer a potential resolution. *Environment, Development and Sustainability*, 1–41. PMID:33020694

AFI. (2020). *Importancia económica y social del sector vitivinícola en España.* Interprofesional del vino de España.

Aguilera, R., Ciravegna, L., Cuervo-Cazurra, A., & González-Pérez, M. (2017). Multilatinas and the internationalization of Latin American firms. *Journal of World Business*, *52*(4), 447–460. doi:10.1016/j.jwb.2017.05.006

Aguinis, H., Villamor, I., Lazzarini, S. G., Vassolo, R. S., Amorós, J. E., & Allen, D. G. (2020). Conducting management research in Latin America: Why and what's in it for you? *Journal of Management*, *46*(5), 615–636. doi:10.1177/0149206320901581

Ahn, J., Amiti, M., & Weinstein, D. E. (2011). Trade finance and the great trade collapse. *The American Economic Review*, *101*(3), 298–302. doi:10.1257/aer.101.3.298

Ahola, E. K. (2012). Towards an understanding of the role of trade fairs as facilitators of consumer creativity. *Journal of Marketing Communications*, *18*(5), 321–333. doi:10.1080/13527266.2010.528587

Alam, M. S., & Paramati, S. R. (2016). The impact of tourism on income inequality in developing economies: Does Kuznets curve hypothesis exist? *Annals of Tourism Research*, *61*, 111–126. doi:10.1016/j.annals.2016.09.008

Al-Awadhi, A. M., Alsaifi, K., Al-Awadhi, A., & Alhammadi, S. (2020). Death and contagious infectious diseases: Impact of the COVID-19 virus on stock market returns. *Journal of Behavioral and Experimental Finance*, *27*, 100326. Advance online publication. doi:10.1016/j.jbef.2020.100326 PMID:32292707

Albertoni, N., & Wise, C. (2021). International trade norms in the age of Covid-19 nationalism on the rise? *Fudan Journal of the Humanities and Social Sciences*, *14*(1), 41–66. doi:10.100740647-020-00288-1

Alcántara, C. (2020). *El vino regional aguanta el envite de la crisis: los caldos resisten, las bodegas se reinventan.* https://murciaplaza.com/el-vino-regional-aguanta-el-envite-de-la-crisis-los-caldos-resisten-las-bodegas-se-reinventan

Alfonso, M. (2020). *Las ayudas al vino para paliar el covid-19, insuficientes.* https://www.lavozdegalicia.es/noticia/somosagro/2020/07/17/ayudas-vino-paliar-covid-19-insuficientes/00031594999615702422745.htm

Allen, F., & Gale, D. (2004). Financial fragility, liquidity, and asset prices. *Journal of the European Economic Association*, *2*(6), 1015–1048. doi:10.1162/JEEA.2004.2.6.1015

Almeida, F., & Silva, O. (2020). The Impact of COVID-19 on Tourism Sustainability: Evidence from Portugal. *Advances in Hospitality and Tourism Research*, *8*(2), 440–446.

Altuntas, F., & Gok, M. S. (2021). The effect of COVID-19 pandemic on domestic tourism: A DEMATEL method analysis on quarantine decisions. *International Journal of Hospitality Management*, *92*(102719), 1–9. doi:10.1016/j.ijhm.2020.102719 PMID:33519015

Alves, P., & Francisco, P. (2015). The impact of institutional environment on the capital structure of firms during recent financial crises. *The Quarterly Review of Economics and Finance*, *57*, 129–146. doi:10.1016/j.qref.2014.12.001

Amiti, M., & Freund, C. (2008). The anatomy of china's export growth. *World Bank Policy Research Working Paper*, *4628*(May), 1–26.

Anaeto, M., & Chioma, G. (2007). Avian influenza in Nigeria: Suggestions for eradication. *International Journal of Poultry Science*, *6*(5), 67–371. doi:10.3923/ijps.2007.367.371

Anderson, J. E., & Young, L. (2006). Trade and Contract Enforcement. *Contributions to Economic Analysis & Policy*, *5*(1). Advance online publication. doi:10.2202/1538-0645.1574

Andrews, C., & Flores, M. (2008). Improving food crisis responses in fragile states. *UNUWIDER Research Paper, 42*, 1-16.

Andrews, L., Higgins, A., Andrews, M., & Lalor, J. (2012). Classic grounded theory to analyse secondary data: Reality and reflections. *The Grounded Theory Review*, *11*(1), 12–26.

Andrianova, S., & Demetriades, P. O. (2018). Financial development and financial fragility: Two sides of the same coin? *Comparative Economic Studies*, *60*(1), 54–68. doi:10.105741294-017-0047-z

Antràs, P., Redding, S. J., & Rossi-Hansberg, E. (2020). Globalization and pandemics (No. w27840). National Bureau of Economic Research.

Antràs, P. (2020). Conceptual Aspects of Global Value Chains. *The World Bank Economic Review*, *34*(3), 551–574. doi:10.1093/wber/lhaa006

Appleyard, J. (2006). *How to exhibit at trade fairs: the complete guide to making your company's next exhibition enormously rewarding*. How To Books.

Aquino Rodríguez, C. (2015). El Perú en la Alianza del Pacífico: Cómo poder aprovechar este acuerdo para relacionarnos más con Asia. *Pensamiento Crítico*, *20*(2), 7–23. doi:10.15381/pc.v20i2.11800

Arango, M. (2006). *Evolución y crisis del sistema financiero colombiano. Serie estudios y perspectivas. 11*. CEPAL.

Ariza-Ricaldi, P., López-Lira, A., & Giraldo-Mejía, W. (2019). SME Internationalization in Latin America: Evidence from Mexico and Peru. In Regional Integration in Latin America (pp. 99-111). Emerald Publishing Limited. doi:10.1108/978-1-78973-159-020191008

Armington, P. S. (1969). A theory of demand for products distinguished by place of production. *IMF Staff Papers*, *16*(1), 159–178. doi:10.2307/3866403

Arndt, C., & Lewis, J. D. (2001). The HIV/AIDS pandemic in South Africa: Sectoral impacts and unemployment. *Journal of International Development*, *13*(4), 427–449. doi:10.1002/jid.796

Ashraf, B. N. (2020a). Stock markets' reaction to COVID-19: Cases or fatalities? *Research in International Business and Finance*, *54*, 101249. Advance online publication. doi:10.1016/j.ribaf.2020.101249 PMID:34170989

Assaf, A. G., & Tsionas, M. (2018). The estimation and decomposition of tourism productivity. *Tourism Management*, *65*, 131–142. doi:10.1016/j.tourman.2017.09.004

Audretsch, D., & Chowdhury, F. (2020). Export Regulations, Credit Markets, and Corruption: Implications for Internationalization. *Academy of Management Proceedings*, *2020*(1), 10229. doi:10.5465/AMBPP.2020.10229abstract

Auray, S., Eyquem, A., & Poutineau, J. C. (2012). The effect of a common currency on the volatility of the extensive margin of trade. *Journal of International Money and Finance*, *31*(5), 1156–1179. doi:10.1016/j.jimonfin.2011.12.016

Ayati, N., Saiyarsarai, P., & Nikfar, S. (2020). Short and long term impacts of COVID-19 on the pharmaceutical sector. *Daru: Journal of Faculty of Pharmacy, Tehran University of Medical Sciences*, *28*(2), 799–805. doi:10.100740199-020-00358-5 PMID:32617864

Azimli, A. (2020). The impact of COVID-19 on the degree of dependence and structure of risk-return relationship: A quantile regression approach. *Finance Research Letters*, *36*, 101648. Advance online publication. doi:10.1016/j.frl.2020.101648 PMID:32837368

Babuna, P., Yang, X., Gyilbag, A., Awudi, D., Ngmenbelle, D., & Bian, D. (2020). The impact of Covid-19 on the insurance industry. *International Journal of Environmental Research and Public Health*, *17*(16), 5766. doi:10.3390/ijerph17165766 PMID:32784978

Bacchetta, M., Bekkers, E., Piermartini, R., Rubinova, S., Stolzenburg, V., & Xu, A. (2021). *COVID-19 and global value chains: A discussion of arguments on value chain organization and the role of the WTO* (No. ERSD-2021-3). WTO Staff Working Paper.

Badshah, I. U. (2013). Quantile regression analysis of the asymmetric return-volatility relation. *Journal of Futures Markets*, *33*(3), 235–265. doi:10.1002/fut.21551

Bahri, M., Sakka, O., & Kallal, R. (2020). The impact of corruption on the export intensity of SMEs in Tunisia: moderating effects of political instability and regulatory obstacles. *Journal of Entrepreneurship in Emerging Economies*. doi:10.1108/JEEE-03-2020-0055

Baicu, C., Gârdan, I., Gârdan, D., & Epuran, G. (2020). The impact of COVID-19 on consumer behavior in retail banking. Evidence from Romania. *Management & Marketing. Challenges for the Knowledge Society*, *15*(1), 534–556. doi:10.2478/mmcks-2020-0031

Bai, Y., Yao, L., Wei, T., Tian, F., Jin, D. Y., Chen, L., & Wang, M. (2020). Presumed asymptomatic carrier transmission of COVID-19. *Journal of the American Medical Association*, *323*(14), 1406–1407. doi:10.1001/jama.2020.2565 PMID:32083643

Baker, S. R., Bloom, N., Davis, S. J., Kost, K., Sammon, M., & Viratyosin, T. (2020). The unprecedented stock market reaction to COVID-19. *Review of Asset Pricing Studies*, *10*(4), 742–758. doi:10.1093/rapstu/raaa008

Baker, S. R., Bloom, N., Davis, S. J., & Terry, S. J. (2020). *Covid-induced economic uncertainty (No. w26983)*. National Bureau of Economic Research. doi:10.3386/w26983

Balassa, B. (1974). Types of Economic Integration. *Proceedings of Fouth World Congress of the Integrational Economic Association.*

Balcilar, M., Bonato, M., Demirer, R., & Gupta, R. (2018). Geopolitical risks and stock market dynamics of the BRICS. *Economic Systems*, *42*(2), 295–306. doi:10.1016/j.ecosys.2017.05.008

Baldwin, R. (2009). The great trade collapse: What caused it and what does it mean? *The great trade collapse: Causes, consequences and prospects, 100*(105), 1.

Baldwin, R. E. (2006). *Globalisation: the great unbundling(s).* Economic Council of Finland.

Baldwin, R., & Freeman, R. (2021). *Trade conflict in the age of COVID-19.* VoxEU. org.

Baldwin, R., & Lopez-Gonzalez, J. (2013). *Supply-chain trade: A portrait of global patterns and several testable hypotheses.* NBER Working Papers, 18957. National Bureau of Economic Research.

Baldwin, R., & Tomiura, E. (2020). Thinking ahead about the trade impact of COVID-1 *Economics in the Time of COVID-19, 59.*

Banco Central de Chile. (2010). *Cuentas Nacionales de Chile 2003-2009.* Author.

Banco Central de Chile. (2021). *Anuario Cuentas Nacionales 2020.* Author.

Banco de México. (1996). *Trade data.* https://www.banxico.org.mx/SieInternet/consultarDirectorioInternetAction.do?sector=1&accion=consultarDirectorioCuadros&locale=es

Banting, P. M., & Blenkhorn, D. L. (1974). The role of industrial trade shows. *Industrial Marketing Management*, *3*(5), 285–295. doi:10.1016/0019-8501(74)90004-2

Barbini, F. M. (2003). Innovative Trade Fairs for Incubating Virtual Enterprises. In *Working Conference on Virtual Enterprises* (pp. 543-550). Springer.

Barrientos, S., Gereffi, G., & Rossi, A. (2011). Economic and social upgrading in global production networks: A new paradigm for a changing world. *International Labour Review*, *150*(3-4), 319–340. doi:10.1111/j.1564-913X.2011.00119.x

Barrientos, S., & Smith, S. (2007). Do workers benefit from ethical trade? Assessing codes of labour practice in global production systems. *Third World Quarterly*, *28*(4), 713–729. doi:10.1080/01436590701336580

Barrios, S. (2003). Foreign Direct Investment, Competition and Industrial Development in the Host Country. *European Economic Review*, (49), 1761–1784.

Bartle, R. A. (2004). *Designing virtual worlds*. New Riders.

Bates, T. W., Chang, C. H., & Chi, J. D. (2018). Why has the value of cash increased over time? *Journal of Financial and Quantitative Analysis*, *53*(2), 749–787. doi:10.1017/S002210901700117X

Bathelt, H. (2017). Trade fairs and innovation. In *The Elgar companion to innovation and knowledge creation*. Edward Elgar Publishing. doi:10.4337/9781782548522.00042

Bathelt, H., & Schuldt, N. (2008). Between luminaires and meat grinders: International trade fairs as temporary clusters. *Regional Studies*, *42*(6), 853–868. doi:10.1080/00343400701543298

Bathelt, H., & Schuldt, N. (2010). International trade fairs and global buzz, Part I: Ecology of global buzz. *European Planning Studies*, *18*(12), 1957–1974. doi:10.1080/09654313.2010.515815

Bauer, A., & Weber, E. (2020). COVID-19: How much unemployment was caused by the shutdown in Germany? *Applied Economics Letters*, 1–6. doi:10.1080/13504851.2020.1789544

Bauman, Z. (2015). *La globalización, consecuencias humanas*. Ciudad de México: FCE.

Baur, D. G. (2013). The structure and degree of dependence: A quantile regression approach. *Journal of Banking & Finance*, *37*(3), 786–798. doi:10.1016/j.jbankfin.2012.10.015

Beaverstock, J. V., Smith, R. G., & Taylor, P. J. (2000). World-City Network: A New Metageography? *Annals of the Association of American Geographers*, *90*(1), 123–134. doi:10.1111/0004-5608.00188

Beck, K. (2020). What drives international trade? Robust analysis for the European Union. *Journal of International Students*, *13*(3), 68–84. doi:10.14254/2071-8330.2020/13-3/5

Bello, W. (2004). Deglobalization: Ideas for a New World Economy. Zed Books.

Bello, W. (2013). *Capitalism's Last Stand? Deglobalization in the Age of Austerity*. Zed Books. doi:10.5040/9781350218895

Beltrán, L. N., & Ferrer, H. E. (2016). Alianza Pacífico: Una perspectiva geopolítica y económica. *Dimensión Empresarial*, *14*(1), 79–94.

Bergin, P. R., & Corsetti, G. (2008). The extensive margin and monetary policy. *Journal of Monetary Economics*, *55*(7), 1222–1237. doi:10.1016/j.jmoneco.2008.08.011

Berkmen, S. P., Gelos, G., Rennhack, R., & Walsh, J. P. (2012). The global financial crisis: Explaining cross-country differences in the output impact. *Journal of International Money and Finance*, *31*(1), 42–59. doi:10.1016/j.jimonfin.2011.11.002

Bermejo, A. (2004). HIV/AIDS in Africa: International responses to the pandemic. *New Economy*, *11*(3), 164–169. doi:10.1111/j.1468-0041.2004.00357.x

Bernard, A. B., & Jensen, J. B. (1999). *Exporting and productivity* (No. w7135). National Bureau of Economic Research.

Bernard, A. B., Jensen, J. B., & Lawrence, R. Z. (1995). Exporters, jobs, and wages in US manufacturing: 1976-1987. *Brookings papers on economic activity. Microeconomics*, *1995*, 67–119.

Bernard, A. B., Jensen, J. B., Redding, S. J., & Schott, P. K. (2007). Firms in International Trade. *The Journal of Economic Perspectives*, *21*(3), 105–130. doi:10.1257/jep.21.3.105

Bernard, A. B., Jensen, J. B., Redding, S. J., & Schott, P. K. (2009). The margins of US trade. *The American Economic Review*, *99*(2), 487–493. doi:10.1257/aer.99.2.487

Bernard, A. B., Jensen, J. B., & Schott, P. K. (2006). Trade costs, firms and productivity. *Journal of Monetary Economics*, *53*(5), 917–937. doi:10.1016/j.jmoneco.2006.05.001

Berry, A. (1998). The Impact of Globalization and the Information in Latin America. In A. S. Bhalla (Ed.), *Globalization, Growth and Marginalization*. Macmillan Press. doi:10.1007/978-1-349-26675-3_4

Berstein, S., & Marcel, M. (2019). *Sistema Financiero en Chile: Lecciones de la Historia Reciente*. Banco Central de Chile. https://www.bcentral.cl/documents/33528/133323/dpe67.pdf/08b40379-9553-fac0-f077-8ad5083f6a7f?t=1573269248660

Bértola, L., & Ocampo, J. (2012). Latin America's debt crisis and "lost decade". In *The Economic Development of Latin America since Independence*. Oxford University Press. https://sas-space.sas.ac.uk/6500/1/Bertola%20and%20Ocampo%20paper.pdf

Besedes, T., & Prusa, T. J. (2006). Ins, outs and the duration of trade. *The Canadian Journal of Economics. Revue Canadienne d'Economique*, *39*(1), 266–295. doi:10.1111/j.0008-4085.2006.00347.x

Besedes, T., & Prusa, T. J. (2011). The role of extensive and intensive margins and export growth. *Journal of Development Economics*, *96*(2), 371–379. doi:10.1016/j.jdeveco.2010.08.013

Bevir, M. (2009). *Key Concepts in Governance*. SAGE Publications Inc. https://sk.sagepub.com/books/key-concepts-in-governance

Bhagwati, J. (2004). In Defence of Globalization. Oxford University Press.

Bhalla, S. (2002). *Imagine There's no Country: Poverty, Inequality, and Growth in the Ear of Globalization*. Institute for International Economics.

Bilkey, W. J., & Tesar, G. (1977). The Export Behavior of Smaller-Sized Wisconsin Manufacturing Firms. *Journal of International Business Studies*, *8*(1), 93–98. doi:10.1057/palgrave.jibs.8490783

Bingzhan, S. (2011). Extensive margin, quantity and price in china's export growth. *China Economic Review*, *22*(2), 233–243. doi:10.1016/j.chieco.2011.01.007

Blalock, G., & Gertler, P. J. (2009). How firm capabilities affect who benefits from foreign technology. *Journal of Development Economics*, *90*(2), 192–199. doi:10.1016/j.jdeveco.2008.11.011

Bliss, B. A., Cheng, Y., & Denis, D. J. (2015). Corporate payout, cash retention, and the supply of credit: Evidence from the 2008–2009 credit crisis. *Journal of Financial Economics*, *115*(3), 521–540. doi:10.1016/j.jfineco.2014.10.013

Blythe, J. (2010). Trade fairs as communication: A new model. *Journal of Business and Industrial Marketing*.

Bonadio, B., Huo, Z., Levchenko, A. A., & Pandalai-Nayar, N. (2020). *Global supply chains in the pandemic (No. w27224)*. National Bureau of Economic Research. doi:10.3386/w27224

Bora, D., & Basistha, D. (2020). The outbreak of COVID-19 pandemic and its impact on stock market volatility: Evidence from a worst-affected economy. *Journal of Public Affairs*. Advance online publication. doi:10.1002/pa.2623 PMID:33786019

Bouey, J. (2020). *Assessment of COVID-19's impact on small and medium-sized enterprises: Implications from China*. RAND Corporation. doi:10.7249/CT524

Bressan, A., Alonso, A., & Kok, S. (2021). Confronting the unprecedented: Micro and small businesses in the age of coronavirus disease 2019. *International Journal of Entrepreneurial Behaviour & Research*, *27*(3), 799–820. doi:10.1108/IJEBR-09-2020-0602

Breusch, T. S., & Pagan, A. R. (1980). The Lagrange multiplier test and its applications to model specification in econometrics. *The Review of Economic Studies*, *47*(1), 239–253. doi:10.2307/2297111

Brewin, D. (2020). The impact of COVID-19 on the grains and oilseeds sector. *Canadian Journal of Agricultural Economics*, *68*(2), 185–188. doi:10.1111/cjag.12239

Briguglio, L., & Galea, W. (2003). Updating and augmenting the economic vulnerability index. Occasional paper, Islands and Small States Institute of the University of Malta.

Briguglio, L., Cordina, G., Farragia, N., & Vella, S. (2009). Economic vulnarability and resilience: Concepts and measurement. *Oxford Development Studies*, *37*(3), 229–247. doi:10.1080/13600810903089893

Broderick, A., & Pickton, D. (2005). *Integrated marketing communications*. Pearson Education UK.

Brohman, J. (1996). *Popular Development, Rethinking the Theory and Practice of Development.* Backwell Publishers.

Broll, U., & Jauer, J. (2014). *How international trade is affected by the financial crisis: the gravity trade equation* (No. 03/14). Dresden Discussion Paper Series in Economics.

Brown. (2002). *The Effects of Multinational Production on Wages and Working Conditions in Developing Countries.* Research Seminar in International Economics, Discussion Paper No. 484, Michigan University.

Bulin, D., & Tenie, I. P. (2020). Preliminary assessment of the COVID-19 pandemic impact on the tourism industry. *Global Economic Observer, 8*(1), 41–46.

Burgui, D. (2020). *Coronavirus: How action against hunger is responding to the pandemic.* Available in: https://www.actionagainsthunger.org/story/coronavirus-how-action-against-hunger-responding-pandemic

Byrne, J., & O'Connor, T. (2017). How do creditors respond to disclosure quality? Evidence from corporate dividend payouts. *Journal of International Financial Markets, Institutions and Money, 49,* 154–172. doi:10.1016/j.intfin.2017.04.002

Caballero Argáez, C. (2019). Una visión retrospectiva de dos crisis financieras de los últimos cuarenta años en Colombia. *Revista Desarrollo y Sociedad, 82*(82), 133–165. doi:10.13043/dys.82.5

Caballero, C., & Machado, G. (2020). De la crisis de 'fin de siglo' a la del 'coronavirus'. La economía colombiana en el siglo XXI. *Coyuntura Económica: Investigación Económica y Social, 50,* 15–74.

Cacho-Borrás, A. (2021). *¿Qué es y para qué se pide una destilación de crisis?* https://cadenaser.com/emisora/2021/02/06/ser_ciudad_real/1612604141_866560.html

Çakır, M., Li, Q., & Yang, X. (2020). COVID-19 and Fresh Produce Markets in the United States and China. *Applied Economic Perspectives and Policy, 43*(1), 341–354. doi:10.1002/aepp.13136

Caldara, D., & Iacoviello, M. (2018). *Measuring geopolitical risk.* FRB International Finance Discussion Paper, (1222).

Calderón, C., & Caire, G. (2012). Génesis y desarrollo de la crisis macroeconómica de 1995. In C. Calderón & V. M. Cuevas (Eds.), *Macroeconomía abierta en América Latina: teoría y evidencia.* EON.

Calderon, C., & Hernández, L. (2017). Integración económica, crisis económicas y ciclos económicos en México. *Contaduría y Administración, 62*(1), 64–84. doi:10.1016/j.cya.2016.10.001

Campa, J., & Goldberg, L. S. (1997). The evolving external orientation of manufacturing industries: evidence from four countries (No. w5919). National Bureau of Economic Research.

Canavati, S., Bauman, M., & Wilson, D. (2020). The Wine Industry & the COVID-19 Pandemic. *Wine Business Journal, 4*(2), 1–4.

Caporale, G. M., Costamagna, R., & Rossini, G. (2016). Competitive devaluations in commodity-based economies: Colombia and the Pacific Alliance group. *CESifo Working Paper Series,* 5907.

Carare, A., & Stone, M. R. (2003). *Inflation targeting regimes.* IMF Working Papers, 03/9. International Monetary Fund.

CardebatJ.MassetP.WeisskopfJ. (2020). COVID-19: What is Next for the Market for Fine Wines? *Available at* SSRN 3636317. doi:10.2139srn.3636317

Cárdenas, M., & Martínez, H. (2020). *COVID-19 in Colombia: Impact and Policy Responses.* Center for Global Development. https://www.cgdev.org/publication/covid-19-colombia-impact-and-policy-responses

Cardona-ArenasC. D.Serna-GómezH. M. (2020). COVID-19 and oil prices: Effects on the Colombian peso exchange rate. doi:10.2139srn.3567942

Carreras, A., & Torra Fernández, L. (2005). *Why did modern trade fairs appear?* Universitat Pompeu Fabra.

Castañeda, J. (2000 January 7). *La Crisis Colombiana. El Tiempo.* https://www.eltiempo.com/archivo/documento/MAM-1295359

Cattaneo, O., Gereffi, G., & Staritz, C. (2010). *Global Value Chains in a Postcrisis World: A Development Perspective.* World Bank Publications. doi:10.1596/978-0-8213-8499-2

Çavuşoğlu, M. (2006). A Research on the Problems of Virtual Fairs and the Advantages of E-Commerce in Turkey and in the World. *İstanbul Üniversitesi İşletme Fakültesi Dergisi, 35*(2).

CEPAL. (2002). *Globalización y desarrollo.* Recuperado el 10 de julio de 2018 de https://repositorio.cepal.org/bitstream/handle/11362/2724/2

Cerdeiro, D. A., Komaromi, A., Liu, Y., & Saeed, M. (2020). World seaborne trade in real time: A proof of concept for building AIS-based nowcasts from scratch (No. 20/57). International Monetary Fund.

Cespedes, L. F., Chang, R., & Velasco, A. (2004). Balance sheets and exchange rate policy. *The American Economic Review, 94*(4), 1183–1193. doi:10.1257/0002828042002589

Chadwick, M. G. (2019). Dependence of the "Fragile Five" and "Troubled Ten" emerging market financial systems on US monetary policy and monetary policy uncertainty. *Research in International Business and Finance, 49*, 251–268. doi:10.1016/j.ribaf.2019.04.002

Chaffey, D., & Ellis-Chadwick, F. (2019). Digital Marketing. Academic Press.

Chahrour, M., Assi, S., Bejjani, M., Nasrallah, A., Salhab, H., Fares, M., & Khachfe, H. (2020). A bibliometric analysis of COVID-19 research activity: A call for increased output. *Cureus, 12*(3), 1–7. doi:10.7759/cureus.7357 PMID:32328369

Champion, M. Y. (2001). Nationalization and privatization in Peru: Socio-economic images in perpetual conflict? *Journal of Socio-Economics, 30*(6), 517–532. doi:10.1016/S1053-5357(01)00128-7

Chaney, T. (2005). *Productivity overshooting: the dynamic impact of trade opening with heterogeneous firms.* Retrieved from https://www.researchgate.net/profile/Thomas-Chaney/publication/228961536_Productivity_Overshooting_The_Dynamic_Impact_of_Trade_Opening_with_Heterogeneous_Firms/links/0deec51c06bf8e653e000000/Productivity-Overshooting-The-Dynamic-Impact-of-Trade-Opening-with-Heterogeneous-Firms.pdf

Chaves-García, C. A. (2018). Aproximación teórica y conceptual para el análisis de la Alianza del Pacífico. *Desafíos, 30*(1). doi:10.12804/revistas.urosario.edu.co/desafios/a.5775

Chen, W., Mrkaic, M., & Nabar, M. (2019). The global economic recovery 10 years after the 2008 financial crisis. International Monetary Fund 19/83.

Chen, W.C. (2013). The Extensive and intensive margins of exports: The race of innovation. *the World Economy, 36*(5), 607-635. doi:10.1111/twec.12032

Chen, H. C., Chou, R. K., & Lu, C. L. (2018). Saving for a rainy day: Evidence from the 2000 dot-com crash and the 2008 credit crisis. *Journal of Corporate Finance, 48*, 680–699. doi:10.1016/j.jcorpfin.2017.12.025

Chen, J., Sousa, C. M. P., & He, X. (2016). The determinants of export performance: A review of the literature 2006-2014. *International Marketing Review, 33*(5), 626–670. doi:10.1108/IMR-10-2015-0212

Chlodnicki, M., Leszczyński, G., & Zieliński, M. (2011). Trade fairs—A tool for the spread of innovation. In *4th International Conference for Entrepreneurship, Innovation and Regional Development.* National Center for Development of Innovation and Entrepreneurial Learning.

Choi, S. Y. (2020). Industry volatility and economic uncertainty due to the COVID-19 pandemic: Evidence from wavelet coherence analysis. *Finance Research Letters*, *37*, 101783. Advance online publication. doi:10.1016/j.frl.2020.101783 PMID:33013239

Chor, D., & Manova, K. (2012). Off the cliff and back? Credit conditions and international trade during the global financial crisis. *Journal of International Economics*, *87*(1), 117–133. doi:10.1016/j.jinteco.2011.04.001

Ciglioli, S., Giovannetti, G., Marvasi, E., & Vivoli, A. (2021). (Forthcoming). The Resilience of Global Value Chains during the Covid-19 pandemic: The case of Italy. *Economia Italiana. Editrice Minerva Bancaria.*

Coldbeck, B., & Ozkan, A. (2018). Comparison of adjustment speeds in target research and development and capital investment: What did the financial crisis of 2007 change? *Journal of Business Research*, *84*, 1–10. doi:10.1016/j.jbusres.2017.10.042

Comisión Económica para América Latina y el Caribe. (2018). La convergencia entre la Alianza del Pacífico y el MERCOSUR: enfrentando juntos un escenario mundial desafiante (LC/PUB.2018/10). Author.

Comisión Económica para América Latina y el Caribe. (n.d.). *Statistical Bulletin: International trade in goods in Latin America and the Caribbean.* https://www.cepal.org/en/boletin-estadistico-de-comercio-exterior-de-bienes-en-america-latina-y-el-caribe

Concha, J., & Gómez, O. (2016). Análisis de atracción de inversión extranjera a países de la Alianza del Pacífico. *Estudios Gerenciales*, *32*(141), 369–380. doi:10.1016/j.estger.2016.11.001

Conesa, M., Lotti, G., & Powell, A. (2020). *Resilience and Fragility in Global Banking*. IDB.

Coughlin, C. C., & Well, H. J. (2011). Ethnic networks and trade: Intensive versus extensive margins. *Economics Letters*, *113*(1), 73–75. doi:10.1016/j.econlet.2011.05.023

Coulibaly, B., Sapriza, H., & Zlate, A. (2011). *Trade credit and international trade during the 2008-09 global financial crisis*. Board of Governors of the Federal Reserve System. doi:10.17016/IFDP.2011.1020

Creutzfeldt, B. (2018). *China's Engagement with Regional Actors: The Pacific Alliance*. Wilson Center, Latin *American Programmer.*

Curran, E. (2020). Urgent Demand for Medical Equipment is Making Air Cargo Fees "Absolutely Crazy". *Bloomberg*. https://www.bloomberg.com/news/articles/2020-03-30/-absolutely-crazy-air-cargo-fees-highlight-supply-chain-squeeze

D'Amato, A. (2020). Capital structure, debt maturity, and financial crisis: Empirical evidence from SMEs. *Small Business Economics*, *55*(4), 919–941. doi:10.100711187-019-00165-6

Damer, B. (2008). Meeting in the ether: A brief history of virtual worlds as a medium for user-created events. *Artifact*, *2*(2), 94–107. doi:10.1080/17493460903020877

Daskalakis, N., Balios, D., & Dalla, V. (2017). The behaviour of SMEs' capital structure determinants in different macroeconomic states. *Journal of Corporate Finance*, *46*, 248–260. doi:10.1016/j.jcorpfin.2017.07.005

Davies, E., McConn-Palfreyman, W., Williams, J., & Lovell, G. (2020). The Impact of COVID-19 on Staff Working Practices in UK Horseracing. *Animals (Basel)*, *10*(11), 1–18. doi:10.3390/ani10112003 PMID:33143200

De BackerK.YamanoN. (2011). International comparative evidence on global value chains. SSRN 2179937. doi:10.2139srn.2179937

Debaere, P., & Mostashari, S. (2010). Do tariffs matter for the extensive margin of international trade? An Empirical Analysis. *Journal of International Economics*, *81*(2), 163–169. doi:10.1016/j.jinteco.2010.03.005

Deb, R., Samalia, H. V., & Prusty, S. K. (2020). The role of informal competition in driving export propensity of emerging economy firms. *The International Journal of Sociology and Social Policy*, *40*(1/2), 184–203. doi:10.1108/IJSSP-06-2019-0131

Delisle, J. (2003). SARS, greater China, and the pathologies of globalization and transition. *Orbis*, *47*(4), 587–604. doi:10.1016/S0030-4387(03)00076-0 PMID:32287394

Demirgüç-Kunt, A., Peria, M. S. M., & Tressel, T. (2020). The global financial crisis and the capital structure of firms: Was the impact more severe among SMEs and non-listed firms? *Journal of Corporate Finance*, *60*, 101514. doi:10.1016/j.jcorpfin.2019.101514

Derudder, B., Hoyler, M., & Taylor, P. J. (2011). Goodbye Reykjavik: International banking centres and the global financial crisis. *Area*, *43*(2), 173–182. doi:10.1111/j.1475-4762.2010.00968.x

Derudder, B., Taylor, P. J., Witlox, F., & Catalano, G. (2003). Hierarchical Tendencies and Regional Patterns in the World City Network: A Global Urban Analysis of 234 Cities. *Regional Studies*, *37*(9), 875–886. doi:10.1080/0034340032000143887

DeYoung, H. (2020). Napa Green: Funding Nonprofit Social Ventures In Crisis. *Wine Business Journal*, *4*(2), 54–83.

Di Stefano, E. (2021). COVID-19 and Global Value Chains: The Ongoing Debate. *Bank of Italy Occasional Paper*, (618).

Díez, L. (2020). *Reticencias en Rioja a la vendimia en verde: «Es preferible guardar la uva».* https://nuevecuatrouno.com/2020/06/21/ayudas-vendimia-verde-rioja-insuficiente-plazos-escasos/

Dimson, E., Rousseau, P., & Spaenjers, C. (2015). The price of wine. *Journal of Financial Economics*, *118*(2), 431–449. doi:10.1016/j.jfineco.2015.08.005

Dixit, A. K., & Grossman, G. M. (1982). Trade and protection with multistage production. *The Review of Economic Studies*, *49*(4), 583–594. doi:10.2307/2297288

Dollar, D. y Kraay, A. (2001). Comercio exterior, crecimiento y pobreza, Finanzas y Desarrollo. *Revista trimestral del FMI*, *38*(3).

Dollar, D., & Kraay, A. (2001). *Growth is Good for the Poor.* Policy Research Working Paper No. 2587, World Bank.

Doraiswamy, S., Abraham, A., Mamtani, R., & Cheema, S. (2020). Use of Telehealth During the COVID-19 Pandemic: Scoping Review. *Journal of Medical Internet Research*, *22*(12), 1–15. doi:10.2196/24087 PMID:33147166

Drewes, M., Daumann, F., & Follert, F. (2021). Exploring the sports economic impact of COVID-19 on professional soccer. *Soccer and Society*, *22*(1-2), 125–137. doi:10.1080/14660970.2020.1802256

Dullien, S., Kotte, D. J., Márquez, A., & Priewe, J. (Eds.). (2010). The financial and economic crisis of 2008-2009 and developing countries. UNCTAD United Nations.

Dumitrecsu, E. I., & Hurlin, C. (2012). Testing for Granger non-causality in heterogeneous panels. *Economic Modelling*, *29*(4), 1450–1460. doi:10.1016/j.econmod.2012.02.014

Dunning, J. H. (1999). Globalization and the Theory of MNE Activity. Discussion Papers in International Investment and Multinationals, Series B, 11(264).

Durán, J. (2001). *Estrategia y Economía de la Empresa Multinacional.* Pirámide.

Dutt, P., Mihov, I., & Van Zandt, T. (2013). The effect of WTO on the extensive and intensive margins of trade. *Journal of International Economics*, *91*(2), 204–219. doi:10.1016/j.jinteco.2013.08.001

Eaton, J., & Kortum, S. (2002). Technology, geography and trade. *Econometrica*, *70*(5), 1741–1779. doi:10.1111/1468-0262.00352

Echavarría, J., González, A., López, E., & Rodríguez, N. (2012). Choques internacionales reales y financieros y su impacto sobre la economía colombiana. *Ensayos sobre Política Económica*, *30*(69), 14-66.

Edge, M., Ghosh, S., & Liang, Y. (2020). *The Evolution of Virtual Trade Shows: A Literature Review from the UK Medical Device Industry*. European Marketing Academy.

Ege İhracatçı Birlikleri. (2021). *Aegean Exporters Union*. Retrieved from https://www.eib.org.tr/en/

Eichenbaum, M. S., Rebelo, S., & Trabandt, M. (2020). *The macroeconomics of epidemics (No. w26882)*. National Bureau of Economic Research. doi:10.3386/w26882

Elliott, K. A., & Freeman, R. B. (2003). *Can labor standards improve under globalization?* Peterson Institute Press.

Engel, J., & Taglioni, D. (2017). The middle-income trap and upgrading along global value chains. *Global Value Chain Report*, 119-139.

Erkut, B. (2016a). Entrepreneurship and Economic Freedom: Do Objective and Subjective Data Reflect the Same Tendencies? *Entrepreneurial Business and Economics Review*, *4*(3), 11–26. doi:10.15678/EBER.2016.040302

Erkut, B. (2016b). Structural similarities of economies for innovation and competitiveness - a decision tree based approach. *Studia Oeconomica Posnaniensia*, *4*(5), 85–104. doi:10.18559/SOEP.2016.5.6

Ermolina, A. (2016). Business environment as the determinant of economic growth. *J. for International Business and Entrepreneurship Development*, *9*(4), 417. doi:10.1504/JIBED.2016.080020

Eurostat. (2020). *International trade data*. Retrieved May 9, 2021, from https://ec.europa.eu/eurostat/web/main/data/database

Evenett, S. J. (2020). Sicken thy neighbour: The initial trade policy response to COVID-19. *World Economy*, *43*(4), 828–839. doi:10.1111/twec.12954

Evenett, S. J., & Fritz, J. (2017). *Europe fettered: The impact of crisis-era trade distortions on exports from the European Union*. CEPR Press.

Ezcurra, R., & Rodríguez-Pose, A. (2013). Does Economic Globalization affect Regional Inequality? A Cross-country Analysis. *World Development*, *52*(December), 92–103. doi:10.1016/j.worlddev.2013.07.002

Fama, E. F., & French, K. R. (1996). Multifactor explanations of asset pricing anomalies. *The Journal of Finance*, *51*(1), 55–84. doi:10.1111/j.1540-6261.1996.tb05202.x

FAO - Food and Agriculture Organization. (2020a). *Q&A: COVID-19 pandemic - impact on food and agriculture*. Available in: http://www.fao.org/2019-ncov/q-and-a/en/

Farole, T., & Winkler, D. (2014). The Role of Mediating Factors for FDI Spillovers in Developing Countries: Evidence from a Global Dataset. *Making foreign direct investment work for Sub-Saharan Africa: Local spillovers and competitiveness in global value chains, 59*.

Federici, D., & Parisi, V. (2012). *Corporate taxation and exports*. MPRA.

Feenstra, R. C., & Hanson, G. H. (1996). Globalization, outsourcing, and wage inequality (No. w5424). National Bureau of Economic Research.

Felbermayr, G. J., & Kohler, W. (2006). Exploring the Intensive and extensive margins of world trade. *Review of World Economics, 142*(4), 642–674. doi:10.100710290-006-0087-3

Feldstein, M. (2000). *Aspects of Global Economic Integration: Outlook for the Future.* NBER, Working Paper No. 7899.

Feng, G. F., Yang, H. C., Gong, Q., & Chang, C. P. (2021). What is the exchange rate volatility response to COVID-19 and government interventions? *Economic Analysis and Policy, 69*, 705–719. doi:10.1016/j.eap.2021.01.018

Fernandes, N. (2020). *Economic effects of coronavirus outbreak (COVID-19) on the world economy.* IESE Business School Working Paper, No. WP-1240-E.

FernandesN. (2020). *Economic effects of coronavirus outbreak (COVID-19) on the world economy.* Available at SSRN 3557504. doi:10.2139srn.3557504

Fernandez-Stark, K., Bamber, P., & Gereffi, G. (2014). Global value chains in Latin America: A development perspective for upgrading. Global value chains and world trade: Prospects and challenges for Latin America, 79-106.

Fernandez-Stark, K., & Gereffi, G. (2019). Global value chain analysis: a primer. In *Handbook on Global Value Chains.* Edward Elgar Publishing. doi:10.4337/9781788113779.00008

Ffrench-Davis, R., & Heresi, R. (2014). *La economía chilena frente a la crisis financiera: respuestas contra-cíclicas y desafíos pendientes.* Universidad de Chile, Departmento de Economía.

Findlay & O'Rourke. (2007). *Power and Plenty. Trade, War and the World Economy in the second millennium.* Princeton University Press.

Findlay, R., & O'Rourke, K. (2008). *Power and Plenty: Trade, War, and the World Economy in the Second Millennium.* Princeton University Press.

Fitzgerald, E. V. K. (1978). The Fiscal Crisis of the Latin American State. In J. F. J. Toye (Ed.), *Taxation and Economic Development* (pp. 125–158). Frank Cass.

Flach, L., Irlacher, M., & Unger, F. (2019). *Corporate Taxes and Multi-Product Exporters: Theory and Evidence from Trade Dynamics.* CESifo Working Paper Series, 7809.

Flach, L., & Gräf, F. (2020). The impact of trade agreements on world export prices. *Review of International Economics, 28*(1), 168–208. doi:10.1111/roie.12446

Flam, H., & Helpman, E. (1987). Vertical product differentiation and north-south trade. *The American Economic Review, 77*(5), 810–822.

Foley, C. F., & Manova, K. (2015). *International trade, multinational activity, and corporate finance.* National Bureau of Economic Research, w20604.

Foo, L., Chin, M., Tan, K., & Phuah, K. (2020). The impact of COVID-19 on tourism industry in Malaysia. *Current Issues in Tourism*, 1–5. doi:10.1080/13683500.2020.1777951

Foster, K. (2020). The Future of the Pacific Alliance. *Harvard International Review, 24*(March). https://hir.harvard.edu/the-future-of-the-pacific-alliance/

Foster, N., Poeschl, J., & Stchrer, R. (2011). The impact of preferential trade agreements on the margins of international trade. *Economic Systems, 35*(1), 84–97. doi:10.1016/j.ecosys.2010.11.004

Fosu, A. K. (2003). Political Instability and Export Performance in Sub-Saharan Africa. *The Journal of Development Studies, 39*(4), 68–83. doi:10.1080/713869426

Frankel, J., & Romer, D. (1999, June). Does Trade Cause Growth? *The American Economic Review*, *89*(3), 379–399. doi:10.1257/aer.89.3.379

Frank, M. Z., & Goyal, V. K. (2009). Capital structure decisions: Which factors are reliably important? *Financial Management*, *38*(1), 1–37. doi:10.1111/j.1755-053X.2009.01026.x

Friedmann, J. (1986). The World City Hypothesis. *Development and Change*, *17*(1), 69–83. doi:10.1111/j.1467-7660.1986.tb00231.x

Friedman, T. (2000). *The Lexus and the Olive Tree*. Anchor Books.

Fuentes-Fernández, R. (2020). Grandes Vinos: The "Over the Rainbow" initiative & corporate philanthropy during a tragedy. *Wine Business Journal*, 82-93.

Gajjar, A., & Parmar, B. J. (2020). The Impact of COVID-19 on Event Management Industry in India. *Global Journal of Management and Business Research*, 37–43. doi:10.34257/GJMBRFVOL20IS2PG37

Gao, Y. J., Whalley, J., & Ren, Y. (2014). Decomposing China's export growth into extensive margin, export quality and quantity effects. *China Economic Review*, *29*, 19–26. doi:10.1016/j.chieco.2014.02.001

García Parra, P. (2018). La Alianza del Pacífico y Colombia ante la escalada China. *Estudios Politicos*, *52*(52), 15–35. doi:10.17533/udea.espo.n52a02

Garcia-Appendini, E., & Montoriol-Garriga, J. (2013). Firms as liquidity providers: Evidence from the 2007–2008 financial crisis. *Journal of Financial Economics*, *109*(1), 272–291. doi:10.1016/j.jfineco.2013.02.010

García-Fernández, F., & Cordero-Borjas, A. (2010). Proceso de gestión del conocimiento en Carabobo (Venezuela) y Tamaulipas (México). *Pensamiento & Gestión*, *28*, 132–154.

García, P., & Pérez, C. (2017). Desigualdad, inflación, ciclos y crisis en Chile. *Estudos Econômicos*, *44*(2), 185–221. doi:10.4067/S0718-52862017000200185

García-Pérez de Lema, D., Gálvez-Albarracín, E., & Maldonado-Guzmán, G. (2016). Efecto de la innovación en el crecimiento y el desempeño de las Mipymes de la Alianza del Pacífico. Un estudio empírico. *Estudios Gerenciales*, *32*(141), 326–335. doi:10.1016/j.estger.2016.07.003

Garzón, J. (2015). *Latin American regionalism in a multipolar world.* EUI Working Papers.

Garzón, J., & Nolte, D. (2018). The new minilateralism in regional economic governance. Cross regionalism and the Pacific Alliance. In Handbook of South American Governance. Routledge.

Gazel, S. (2016). Finansal gelişme ve ekonomik büyüme ilişkisi: 1990-2014 yılları zordaki onlu ülkeler uygulaması. *Business and Economics Research Journal*, *7*(3), 39–52. doi:10.20409/berj.2016321807

Geigenmüller, A. (2010). The role of virtual trade fairs in relationship value creation. *Journal of Business and Industrial Marketing*, *25*(4), 284–292. doi:10.1108/08858621011038243

Gereffi, G., & Fernandez-Stark, K. (2016). *Global value analysis: a primer* (2nd ed.). Center on Globalization Gobernance & Competitiveness.

Gereffi, G., & Wu, X. (2020). Global Value Chains, Industrial Hubs, and Economic Development in the Twenty-first Century. In The Oxford Handbook of Industrial Hubs and Economic Development. OUP.

Gereffi, G. (1996). Global commodity chains: New forms of coordination and control among nations and firms in international industries. *Competition & Change*, *1*(4), 427–439. doi:10.1177/102452949600100406

Gereffi, G. (1999). International trade and industrial upgrading in the apparel commodity chain. *Journal of International Economics*, *48*(1), 37–70. doi:10.1016/S0022-1996(98)00075-0

Gereffi, G. (2014). Global value chains in a post-Washington Consensus world. *Review of International Political Economy*, *21*(1), 9–37. doi:10.1080/09692290.2012.756414

Gereffi, G. (2020). What does the COVID-19 pandemic teach us about global value chains? The case of medical supplies. *Journal of International Business Policy*, *3*(3), 287–301. doi:10.105742214-020-00062-w

Gereffi, G., & Fernandez-Stark, K. (2010). *The offshore services value chain: developing countries and the crisis*. The World Bank. doi:10.1596/1813-9450-5262

Gereffi, G., Humphrey, J., & Sturgeon, T. (2005). The governance of global value chains. *Review of International Political Economy*, *12*(1), 78–104. doi:10.1080/09692290500049805

Gertler, M., & Gilchrist, S. (2018). What happened: Financial factors in the great recession. *The Journal of Economic Perspectives*, *32*(3), 3–30. doi:10.1257/jep.32.3.3

Giacalone, R. (2016). Nuevas propuestas regionales en el tablero latinoamericano. In N. Mellado (Ed.), *Latinoamérica: inserción global e integración regional* (pp. 201–224). Lerner.

Giannetti, C. (2015). Unit roots and the dynamics of market shares: An analysis using an Italian banking micro- panel. *Empirical Economics*, *48*(2), 537–555. doi:10.100700181-013-0795-1

Gil-Alana, L., & Poza, C. (2020). The impact of COVID-19 on the Spanish tourism sector. *Tourism Economics*, 1–8.

Gilpin, R. (2001). *Global Political Economy: Understanding the International Economic Order*. Princeton University Press. doi:10.1515/9781400831272

Girma, S., & Wakelin, K. (2007). Local productivity spillovers from foreign direct investment in the UK electronics industry. *Regional Science and Urban Economics*, *37*(3), 399–412. doi:10.1016/j.regsciurbeco.2006.11.006

Gnangnon, K. (2012). Does structural economic vulnerability matter for public indebtedness in developing countries. *Serie Etudes Et Documents Du Cerdi*, *36*, 1–34.

Gokcekus, O., & Sonan, S. (2017). *Corruption Perceptions in North Cyprus: 2017 Report*. Academic Press.

Gokcekus, O., Henson, J., Nottebaum, D., & John, A. W.-S. (2012). Impediments to trade across the Green Line in Cyprus. *Journal of Peace Research*, *49*(6), 863–872. doi:10.1177/0022343312452286

Goldin, I., & Reinert, K. (2007). *Globalización para el desarrollo*. Banco Mundial.

Golgeci, I., Yildiz, H. E., & Andersson, U. R. (2020). The rising tensions between efficiency and resilience in global value chains in the post-COVID-19 world. *Transnational Corporations Journal, 27*(2).

González, V. M. (2015). The financial crisis and corporate debt maturity: The role of banking structure. *Journal of Corporate Finance*, *35*, 310–328. doi:10.1016/j.jcorpfin.2015.10.002

Gopalakrishna, S., & Lilien, G. L. (2012). Trade shows in the business marketing communications mix. In *Handbook of business-to-business marketing*. Edward Elgar Publishing. doi:10.4337/9781781002445.00022

Gopinath, G. (2020). The great lockdown: Worst economic downturn since the great depression. *IMF Blog, 14*.

Gopinath, G., Boz, E., Casas, C., Díez, F. J., Gourinchas, P. O., & Plagborg-Møller, M. (2020). Dominant currency paradigm. *The American Economic Review*, *110*(3), 677–719. doi:10.1257/aer.20171201

Gössling, S. (2021). Tourism, technology and ICT: A critical review of affordances and concessions. *Journal of Sustainable Tourism*, *29*(5), 733–750. doi:10.1080/09669582.2021.1873353

Gottlieb, U., & Bianchi, C. (2017). Virtual trade shows: Exhibitors' perspectives on virtual marketing capability requirements. *Electronic Commerce Research and Applications*, *21*, 17–26. doi:10.1016/j.elerap.2016.12.004

Graham, E. (2000). *Fighting the wrong enemy antiglobal activists and multinational enterprises*. Institute for International Economics.

Gray, R. (2020). Agriculture, transportation, and the COVID-19 crisis. *Canadian Journal of Agricultural Economics*, *68*(2), 239–243. doi:10.1111/cjag.12235

Grechi, D., Ossola, P., & Tanda, A. (2017). The European tourism industry in crisis: A stock market perspective. *Tourism Analysis*, *22*(2), 139–148. doi:10.3727/108354217X14888192562203

Greene, W. H. (2012). *Econometric Analysis* (7th ed.). Pearson Education.

Greene, W. H. (2012). *Econometric analysis* (7th ed.). Prentice-Hall International.

Grossman, G. M., & Rossi-Hansberg, E. (2008). Trading tasks: A simple theory of offshoring. *The American Economic Review*, *98*(5), 1978–1997. doi:10.1257/aer.98.5.1978

Grubel, H. G., & Lloyd, P. J. (1971). The empirical measurement of intra-industry trade. *The Economic Record*, *47*(4), 494–517. doi:10.1111/j.1475-4932.1971.tb00772.x

Grunwald, J., & Flamm, K. (1985). The global factory: Foreign assembly in international trade, Brookings Institution. *Washington D., C*, 1985.

Gruszczynski, L. (2020). The COVID-19 pandemic and international trade: Temporary turbulence or paradigm shift? *European Journal of Risk Regulation*, *11*(2), 337–342. doi:10.1017/err.2020.29

Guan, W. J., Ni, Z. Y., Hu, Y., Liang, W. H., Ou, C. Q., He, J. X., Liu, L., Shan, H., Lei, C., Hui, D. S. C., Du, B., Li, L., Zeng, G., Yuen, K.-Y., Chen, R., Tang, C., Wang, T., Chen, P., Xiang, J., ... Zhong, N. S. (2020). Clinical characteristics of corona virus disease 2019 in China. *The New England Journal of Medicine*, *382*(18), 1708–1720. doi:10.1056/NEJMoa2002032 PMID:32109013

Guerrieri, P., & Pietrobelli, C. (2004). Industrial districts' evolution and technological regimes: Italy and Taiwan. *Technovation*, *24*(11), 899–914. doi:10.1016/S0166-4972(03)00048-8

Guo, P., Zhu, H., & You, W. (2018). Asymmetric dependence between economic policy uncertainty and stock market returns in G7 and BRIC: A quantile regression approach. *Finance Research Letters*, *25*, 251–258. doi:10.1016/j.frl.2017.11.001

Gurgul, H., & Lach, L. (2014). Globalization and economic growth: Evidence from two decades of transition in CEE. *Economic Modelling*, *36*(January), 99–107. doi:10.1016/j.econmod.2013.09.022

Gutiérrez-Escobar, R., Aliaño-González, M. J., & Cantos-Villar, E. (2021). Wine Polyphenol Content and Its Influence on Wine Quality and Properties: A Review. *Molecules (Basel, Switzerland)*, *26*(3), 718. doi:10.3390/molecules26030718 PMID:33573150

Ha, J., Stocker, M. M., & Yilmazkuday, H. (2019). *Inflation and exchange rate pass-through*. Policy Research Working Paper WPS 8780.

Hachette, D. (2000). *La reforma comercial. La transformación económica de Chile*. Centro de Estudios Públicos.

Hailu, G. (2020). Economic thoughts on COVID-19 for Canadian food processors. *Canadian Journal of Agricultural Economics*, *68*(2), 163–169. doi:10.1111/cjag.12241

Hakim, C. (1982). *Secondary analysis in social research: A guide to data sources and methods with examples*. Allen and Unwin/Unwin Hyman.

Hall, S. (2020). *This is How COVID-19 is Affecting the Music Industry. World Economic Forum*. Available online at: https://www.weforum.org/agenda/2020/05/this-is-how-covid-19-is-affecting-the-music-industry/

Hanna, D., & Huang, Y. (2004). The impact of SARS on Asian economies. *Asian Economic Papers*, *3*(1), 102–112. doi:10.1162/1535351041747978

Hansen, K. (2000). From selling to relationship marketing at international trade fairs. *Journal of Convention & Exhibition Management*, *2*(1), 37–53. doi:10.1300/J143v02n01_03

Hanssens, H., Derudder, B., Taylor, P. J., Hoyler, M., Ni, P., Huang, J., Yang, X., & Witlox, F. (2010). The changing geography of globalized service provision, 2000-2008. The Service Industries Journal. doi:10.1080/02642069.2010.503887

Haro, J. (2020). *Los aranceles de Trump dejan a España en desventaja ante otros socios de la UE*. https://www.eleconomista.es/economia/noticias/10720845/08/20/Los-aranceles-de-Trumpdejan-a-Espana-en-desventaja-ante-otros-socios-de-la-UE.html

Helpman, E., & Krugman, P. R. (1985). *Market structure and foreign trade: Increasing returns, imperfect competition, and the international economy*. MIT Press.

Helpman, E., Melitz, M., & Rubinstein, Y. (2008). Estimating trade flows: Trading partners and trading volumes. *The Quarterly Journal of Economics*, *123*(2), 441–487. doi:10.1162/qjec.2008.123.2.441

Hernández Bernal, J. A., & Muñoz Angulo, L. G. (2015). Comercio y evolución de la Alianza del Pacífico. *Equidad & Desarrollo*, (24), 97–118. doi:10.19052/ed.3682

Höhler, J., & Lansink, A. (2020). Measuring in the impact of COVID-19 on stock prices and profits in the food supply chain. *Agribusiness*, *37*(1), 171–186. doi:10.1002/agr.21678 PMID:33362339

Hong, Y., Cai, G., Mo, Z., Gao, W., Xu, L., Jiang, Y., & Jiang, J. (2020). The impact of COVID-19 on tourist satisfaction with B&B in Zhejiang, China: An importance–performance analysis. *International Journal of Environmental Research and Public Health*, *17*(10), 3747. doi:10.3390/ijerph17103747 PMID:32466326

Hoque, M. E., & Zaidi, M. A. S. (2020). Global and country-specific geopolitical risk uncertainty and stock return of fragile emerging economies. *Borsa Istanbul Review*, *20*(3), 197–213. doi:10.1016/j.bir.2020.05.001

Hossain, S. (2020). Impacts of COVID-19 on the agri-food sector: Food security policies of Asian productivity organization members. *Journal of Agricultural Sciences*, *15*(2), 116–132. doi:10.4038/jas.v15i2.8794

Hu, L., & Olivieri, M. (2021). How to Leverage Digital Marketing in B2B: A Study on Italian SMEs During the Covid-19 Outbreak. In *Digital Marketing & eCommerce Conference* (pp. 112–120). Springer. doi:10.1007/978-3-030-76520-0_12

Hummels, D., Ishii, J., & Yi, K. M. (2001). The nature and growth of vertical specialization in world trade. *Journal of International Economics*, *54*(1), 75–96. doi:10.1016/S0022-1996(00)00093-3

Hummels, D., & Klenow, P. J. (2005). The variety and quality of a nation's exports. *The American Economic Review*, *95*(3), 704–723. doi:10.1257/0002828054201396

Humphrey, J., & Schmitz, H. (2002). How does insertion in global value chains affect upgrading in industrial clusters? *Regional Studies*, *36*(9), 1017–1027. doi:10.1080/0034340022000022198

Hung, N. T. (2020). Directional Spillover Effects Between BRICS Stock Markets and Economic Policy Uncertainty. *Asia-Pacific Financial Markets*, 1–20. doi:10.100710690-020-09328-y

Hutchinson, A. (2020). *More nations are looking to use cell phone data to track the COVID-19 outbreak, raising privacy concerns*. Social Media Today.

Hwang, J. K., Dimkpah, Y., & Ogwu, A. I. (2014). Impacts of the 2008 financial crisis on South American equity markets. *International Business & Economics Research Journal*, *13*(3), 573–580. doi:10.19030/iber.v13i3.8594

Iamsiraroj, S., & Ulubasoglu, M. (2015). Foreign direct investment and economic growth: A real relationship or wishful thinking? *Economic Modelling*, *51*(December), 200–213. doi:10.1016/j.econmod.2015.08.009

ILO. (2020). *ILO Monitor: COVID-19 and the World of Work*. https://www.ilo.org/wcmsp5/groups/public/dgreports/dcomm/documents/briefingnote/wcms_738753.pdf

IMF. (2020). *World Economic Outlook*. Retrieved May 9, 2021, from https://www.imf.org/en/Data

Inomata, S. (2017). *Analytical frameworks for global value chains: An overview*. Global Value Chain Development Report.

Inter American Development Bank. (2017). Nuevas tendencias en los tratados comerciales en América Latina. *Módulo*, *1*, 1–57.

International Monetary Fund. (2021). *Chile: Staff Concluding Statement of the 2021 Article IV Mission*. Retrieved from: https://www.imf.org/en/News/Articles/2021/03/09/mcs030921-chile-staff-concluding-statement-of-the-2021-article-iv-mission?cid=em-COM-123-42756

International Monetary Fund. (n.d.). *Data*. https://www.imf.org/en/Data

International Trade Administration of the US. (2021). Retrieved from https://www.trade.gov/virtual-fair

IPD. (2020 November). Retrieved from Press Release, https://www.importpromotiondesk.com/fileadmin/user_upload/Publikationen/pressemitteilungen/201124_IPD_Press_Release_Virtual_Matchmaking.pdf

Itskhoki, O., & Mukhin, D. (2017). *Exchange Rate Disconnect in General Equilibrium*. NBER Working Paper 23401, National Bureau of Economic Research.

Ivanov, I., Kabaivanov, S., & Bogdanova, B. (2016). Stock market recovery from the 2008 financial crisis: The differences across Europe. *Research in International Business and Finance*, *37*, 360–374. doi:10.1016/j.ribaf.2016.01.006

Jaipuria, S., Parida, R., & Ray, P. (2020). The impact of COVID-19 on tourism sector in India. *Tourism Recreation Research*, 1–16.

James, H. (2001). *The End of Globalization: Lessons from the Great Depression*. Harvard University Press.

Javorcik, B. (2020, Apr. 3). Coronavirus will Change the Way the World Does Business for Good Businesses will be Forced to Rethink their Global Value Chains. *Valor Econômico*.

Jednak, S., & Jednak, D. (2018). Financial Integration: Crisis and Economic Development. In Regaining Global Stability After the Financial Crisis (pp. 67-87). IGI Global.

Jednak, S., Kragulj, D., & Bulajic, M. (2018). A comparative analysis of development in Southeast European countries. *Technological and Economic Development of Economy*, *24*(1), 253–270. doi:10.3846/20294913.2016.1212438

Jones, R. W., & Kierzkowski, H. (1988). *The Role of Services in Production and International Trade: A Theoretical Framework*. The Institute for Research on Public Policy.

Kalafsky, R. V., & Gress, D. R. (2013). Trade Fairs as an Export Marketing and Research Strategy: Results from a Study of K orean Advanced Machinery Firms. *Geographical Research*, *51*(3), 304–317. doi:10.1111/1745-5871.12019

Kang, K. (2018). The Effect of immigrants on the extensive and intensive margins of trade. *Applied Economics Letters*, *25*(2), 92–95. doi:10.1080/13504851.2017.1299092

Kannadhasan, M., & Das, D. (2020). Do Asian emerging stock markets react to international economic policy uncertainty and geopolitical risk alike? A quantile regression approach. *Finance Research Letters*, *34*, 101276. Advance online publication. doi:10.1016/j.frl.2019.08.024

Kanna, R., & Rajasekaran, S. (2020). The Impact of COVID-19 on Future Orthopaedic Practice. *Journal of Hand and Microsurgery*, *2*, 44–120.

Kano, L., Tsang, E. W., & Yeung, H. W. C. (2020). Global value chains: A review of the multi-disciplinary literature. *Journal of International Business Studies*, *51*(4), 1–46. doi:10.105741267-020-00304-2

Kapri, K. (2019). Impact of political instability on firm-level export decisions. *International Review of Economics & Finance*, *59*, 98–105. doi:10.1016/j.iref.2018.08.008

Karagiannis, D., & Metaxas, T. (2020). Sustainable Wine Tourism Development: Case Studies from the Greek Region of Peloponnese. *Sustainability*, *12*(12), 5223. doi:10.3390u12125223

Kaya, T., Erkut, B., & Thierbach, N. (2019). Entrepreneurial Intentions of Business and Economics Students in Germany and Cyprus: A Cross-Cultural Comparison. *Sustainability*, *11*(5), 1437. doi:10.3390u11051437

Keen, S. (1995). Finance and economic breakdown: Modeling Minsky's "financial instability hypothesis". *Journal of Post Keynesian Economics*, *17*(4), 607–635. doi:10.1080/01603477.1995.11490053

Kehoe, T. J., & Ruhl, K. J. (2013). How Important is the new goods margin in international trade? *Journal of Political Economy*, *121*(2), 358–392. doi:10.1086/670272

Keynes, J. M. (1936). *The general theory of employment, interest and money*. Macmillan Cambridge University Press.

Khan, K., Zhao, H., Zhang, H., Yang, H., Shah, M. H., & Jahanger, A. (2020). The impact of COVID-19 pandemic on stock markets: An empirical analysis of world major stock indices. *The Journal of Asian Finance, Economics, and Business*, *7*(7), 463–474. doi:10.13106/jafeb.2020.vol7.no7.463

Kimmel, A. J. (Ed.). (2005). *Marketing communication: New approaches, technologies, and styles*. Oxford University Press on Demand.

Kindleberger, Ch. (1974). *Međunarodnaekonomija*. Beograd, Srbija: VukKaradžić.

Kirchgeorg, M., Jung, K., & Klante, O. (2010). The future of trade shows: Insights from a scenario analysis. *Journal of Business and Industrial Marketing*, *25*(4), 301–312. doi:10.1108/08858621011038261

Klassen, R. D., & Whybark, D. C. (1994). Barriers to the management of international operations. *Journal of Operations Management*, *11*(4), 385–396. doi:10.1016/S0272-6963(97)90006-1

Koenig, P. (2009). Agglomeration and the export decisions of French firms. *Journal of Urban Economics*, *66*(3), 186–195. doi:10.1016/j.jue.2009.07.002

Kose, M., Sugawara, N., & Terrones, M. (2020). *Global Recessions Policy Research Working Paper 9172*. World Bank, Prospects Group. https://openknowledge.worldbank.org/handle/10986/33415

Kotler, P. (1999). *Marketing Management: The Millennium Edition*. Prentice Hall.

Kotler, P., & Armstrong, G. (2007). *Principles of Marketing* (12th ed.). Academic Press.

KPMG. (2021, April). *Incentive Snippets*. Retrieved from https://assets.kpmg/content/dam/kpmg/sg/pdf/2021/04/Incentive-Snippets-Issue-16.pdf

Kragulj, D. (2020). *Ekonomija – Osnovimikroekonomskeimakroekonomskeanalize*. Beograd, Srbija: Kragulj.

Kragulj, D., Parežanin, M., & Jednak, S. (2018). Effects of Trade Liberalisation in the SEE Countries: CEFTA 2006 Agreement. In Globalization and Trade Integration in Developing Countries (pp. 1-26). IGI Global.

Krugman, C., & Wright, R. R. (2006). *Global Meetings and Exhibitions* (Vol. 28). Wiley.

Krugman, P. (1980). Scale economies, product differentiation, and the pattern of trade. *The American Economic Review*, *70*(5), 950–959.

Krugman, P. R. (1979). Increasing returns, monopolistic competition, and international trade. *Journal of International Economics*, *9*(4), 469–479. doi:10.1016/0022-1996(79)90017-5

Krugman, P. R. (1980). Scale Economies, product differentiation, and the pattern of trade. *The American Economic Review*, *70*(5), 950–959.

Krugman, P. R. (1981). Intraindustry specialization and the gains from trade. *Journal of Political Economy*, *89*(5), 959–973. doi:10.1086/261015

Kumar, A., Luthra, S., Mangla, S. K., & Kazançoğlu, Y. (2020). COVID-19 impact on sustainable production and operations management. *Sustainable Operations and Computers*, *1*, 1–7.

Kumarasamy, D., & Singh, P. (2018). Access to Finance, Financial Development and Firm Ability to Export: Experience from Asia-Pacific Countries. *Asian Economic Journal*, *32*(1), 15–38. doi:10.1111/asej.12140

Kummritz, V., Taglioni, D., & Winkler, D. (2017). *Economic upgrading through global value chain participation: which policies increase the value added gains?* The World Bank. doi:10.1596/1813-9450-8007

Kupferschmidt, K. (2020). Preprints bring 'firehose' of outbreak data. *Science*, *367*(6481), 963–964. doi:10.1126cience.367.6481.963 PMID:32108094

Kutlay, K. (2017). Kuzey Kıbrıs'ta Banka Karlığını Etkileyen Faktörler: Ampirik bir Çalışma. *International Conference on "Scientific Cooperation for the Future in Economics and Administrative Sciences"*, 231–237.

Kuwayama, M. (2019). *Pacific Alliance: A Latin American Version of "Open Regionalism" in Practice*. Discussion Paper Series, DP2019-02, Research Institute for Economics & Business Administration, Kobe University. https://www.rieb.kobe-u.ac.jp/academic/ra/dp/English/DP2019-02.pdf

La Porta, R., Lopez-de-Silanes, F., Shleifer, A., & Vishny, R. W. (2000). Agency problems and dividend policies around the world. *The Journal of Finance*, *55*(1), 1–33. doi:10.1111/0022-1082.00199

Lai, C. C., Shih, T. P., Ko, W. C., Tang, H. J., & Hsueh, P. R. (2020). Severe acute respiratory syndrome coronavirus 2 (SARS-CoV-2) and coronavirus disease-2019 (COVID-19): The epidemic and the challenges. *International Journal of Antimicrobial Agents*, *55*(3), 105924.

Laing, J. H., & Frost, W. (2017). Journeys of well-being: Women's travel narratives of transformation and self-discovery in Italy. *Tourism Management*, *62*, 110–119. doi:10.1016/j.tourman.2017.04.004

Lámbarry Vilchis, F. (2016). Análisis estructural de la red económica de exportaciones e importaciones de la Alianza del Pacífico y el Mercado Común del Sur. *Estudios Gerenciales*, *32*(141), 319–325. doi:10.1016/j.estger.2016.10.004

Lascurain, M., & Villafuerte, L. F. (2016). Primera globalización económica y las raíces de la inequidad social en México. *Ensayos de Economía, 26*(48), 67–90.

Lawless, M. (2010). Deconstructing gravity: Trade costs and extensive and intensive margins. *The Canadian Journal of Economics. Revue Canadienne d'Economique*, *43*(4), 1149–1172. doi:10.1111/j.1540-5982.2010.01609.x

Lechtenberg, D. (2020). The impact of Covid-19 on the alternative fuels industry. *ZKG International*, *73*(7-8), 24–27.

Lee-Kelly, L., David, G., & Nada, F. A.-S. (2004). Virtual Exhibitions: An Ex-ploratory Study of Middle East Exhibitors' Dispositions. *International Marketing Review*, *21*(6), 634–643. doi:10.1108/02651330410568051

Lejárraga, I. (2019) The Pacific Alliance As an Instrument for Insertion into Global Value Chains: Lessons from a Progressive and Pragmatic Approach. In The Pacific Alliance in a World of Preferential Trade Agreements. Springer. doi:10.1007/978-3-319-78464-9_4

Lengyel, M. (2004). The Latin American Countries and the World Trading System: Addressing Institutional Barriers to Development. In M. Lengyel & V. Ventura-Dias (Eds.), *Trade Policy Reform in Latin America: Multilateral Rules and Domestic Institutions* (pp. 191–217). Palgrave/MacMillan. doi:10.1057/9780230523760_9

Leslie, D., & Reimer, S. (1999). Spatializing commodity chains. *Progress in Human Geography*, *23*(3), 401–420. doi:10.1177/030913259902300304

Levchenko, A. A., Lewis, L. T., & Tesar, L. L. (2010). The collapse of international trade during the 2008–09 crisis: In search of the smoking gun. *IMF Economic Review*, *58*(2), 214–253. doi:10.1057/imfer.2010.11

Leviastuti, A. (2020). Does the ease of starting a new business affect country's financial vulnerability? Evidence from eight European economies. *Jurnal Teknik Industri*, *22*(2), 123–132. doi:10.9744/jti.22.2.123-132

Licona Michel, A., Rangel Delgado, J., & González García, J. (2020). Article. *México y la Cuenca del Pacífico*, *9*(25), 21–49. doi:10.32870/mycp.v9i25.597

Li, L. Y. (2010). Antecedents and effect of internet implementation for trade shows. J.Bus. Indus. *Market*, *25*(4), 272–283.

Lileeva, A., & Trefler, D. (2010). Improved Access to Foreign Markets Raises Plant-Level Productivity… for Some Plants. *The Quarterly Journal of Economics*, *125*(3), 1051–1099. doi:10.1162/qjec.2010.125.3.1051

Lintner, J. (1956). Distribution of incomes of corporations among dividends, retained earnings, and taxes. *The American Economic Review*, *46*(2), 97–113.

Li, P. F. (2014). Global temporary networks of clusters: Structures and dynamics of trade fairs in Asian economies. *Journal of Economic Geography*, *14*(5), 995–1021. doi:10.1093/jeg/lbu009

Liu, H., Manzoor, A., Wang, C., Zhang, L., & Manzoor, Z. (2020). The COVID-19 outbreak and affected countries stock markets response. *International Journal of Environmental Research and Public Health*, *17*(8), 2800. Advance online publication. doi:10.3390/ijerph17082800 PMID:32325710

Liu, L., Wang, E. Z., & Lee, C. C. (2020). Impact of the COVID-19 pandemic on the crude oil and stock markets in the US: A time-varying analysis. *Energy Research Letters*, *1*(1). Advance online publication. doi:10.46557/001c.13154

Liu, L., & Zhang, T. (2015). Economic policy uncertainty and stock market volatility. *Finance Research Letters*, *15*, 99–105. doi:10.1016/j.frl.2015.08.009

Llorente & Cuenca. (2016). *La diversificación de las exportaciones en América Latina.* https://ideas.llorenteycuenca.com/wp-content/uploads/sites/5/2016/10/161006_DI_IR_divers_productiva_ESP.pdf

Loayza, N. V., & Raddatz, C. (2007). The structural determinants of external vulnerability. *The World Bank Economic Review*, *21*(3), 359–387. doi:10.1093/wber/lhm018

López, A. (2021). *Alivio en el sector vitivinícola español por el Acuerdo post-Brexit entre la UE y el Reino Unido*. http://www.sevi.net/es/3582/2000/15837/Alivio-en-el-sector-vitivin%C3%ADcola-espa%C3%B1ol-por-el-Acuerdo-post-Brexit-entre-la-UE-y-el-Reino-Unido.htm

Lu, Y. (2020, Dec.). Wine report 2020. *Statista Consumer Market Outlook*.

Luo, Y., & Zhang, C. (2020). Economic policy uncertainty and stock price crash risk. *Research in International Business and Finance*, *51*, 101112. Advance online publication. doi:10.1016/j.ribaf.2019.101112

Lüthi, S., Thierstein, A., & Goebel, D. (2010). Intra-firm and extra-firm linkages in the knowledge economy: The case of the emerging mega-city region of Munich. *Global Networks*, *10*(1), 114–137. doi:10.1111/j.1471-0374.2010.00277.x

Lu, Y., & Zheng, Q. (2020). Twitter public sentiment dynamics on cruise tourism during the COVID-19 pandemic. *Current Issues in Tourism*, *24*(7), 892–898. doi:10.1080/13683500.2020.1843607

Macciocchi, D., Lanini, S., Vairo, F., Zumla, A., Moraes Figueiredo, L. T., Lauria, F. N., ... Ippolito, G. (2016). Short-term economic impact of the Zika virus outbreak. *The New Microbiologica*, *39*(4), 287–289. PMID:28004846

Maciejewski, M., & Wach, K. (2019). What determines export structure in the EU countries? The use of gravity model in international trade based on the panel data for the years 1995-2015. *Journal of International Students*, *12*(1).

Majeed, M. (2016). Economic growth, inequality and trade in developing countries. *International Journal of Development Issues*, *15*(3), 240–253. doi:10.1108/IJDI-02-2016-0011

Maliszewska, M., Mattoo, A., & Van Der Mensbrugghe, D. (2020). The potential impact of COVID-19 on GDP and trade: A preliminary assessment. *World Bank Policy Research Working Paper*, (9211).

Maneenop, S., & Kotcharin, S. (2020). The impacts of COVID-19 on the global airline industry: An event study approach. *Journal of Air Transport Management*, *89*(101920), 1–6. PMID:32874021

Mangan, D. (2020). Covid-19 and labour law in the United Kingdom. *Eur. Lab. Law J.*, *11*, 332–346. doi:10.1177/2031952520934583

Manova, K. (2008). Credit constraints, equity market liberalization and international trade. *Journal of International Economics*, *76*(1), 33–47. doi:10.1016/j.jinteco.2008.03.008

Manova, K. (2013). Credit constraints, heterogeneous firms, and international trade. *The Review of Economic Studies*, *80*(2), 711–744. doi:10.1093/restud/rds036

Marcet, M. (2020). La economía chilena frente a la pandemia del COVID-19: fortalezas, desafíos y riesgos. *Seminario Visión Económica 2021*. https://www.bcentral.cl/contenido/-/detalle/la-economia-chilena-frente-a-la-pandemia-del-covid-19-fortalezas-desafios-y-riesgos-mario-marcel

Markusen, J. R. (2013). Expansion of trade at the extensive margin: A general gains-from-trade result and illustrative examples. *Journal of International Economics*, *89*(1), 262–270. doi:10.1016/j.jinteco.2012.04.007

Maskell, P., Bathelt, H., & Malmberg, A. (2004). *Temporary clusters and knowledge creation: the effects of international trade fairs, conventions and other professional gatherings*. Academic Press.

Maya-Muñoz, G. (2002). Colombia 1990-2000: Globalización y crisis. *Ensayos de Economía, 12*(20-21). https://revistas.unal.edu.co/index.php/ede/article/view/23930

Ma, Z., & Cheng, L. (2005). The effects of financial crises on international trade. In *International Trade in East Asia* (pp. 253–286). University of Chicago Press. doi:10.7208/chicago/9780226379005.003.0009

McDermaid, M., & Newton, S. (2020). Paradise Ridge Winery: Can a tragedy strengthen a brand? *Wine Business Journal, 4*(2), 5–28.

McEwan, K., Marchand, L., Shang, M., & Bucknell, D. (2020). Potential implications of COVID-19 on the Canadian pork industry. *Canadian Journal of Agricultural Economics, 68*(2), 201–206. doi:10.1111/cjag.12236

McGrew, A. (1990). A Global Society. In *Modernity and Its Futures*. Polity Press.

McKibbin, W., & Fernando, R. (2020). The economic impact of COVID-19. *Economics in the Time of, COVID-19*, 45.

McLuhan, H. M. (1962). *La Glaxia Gutemberg*. Available on the web: http://www.ub.edu/procol/sites/default/files/La-Galaxia-Gutenberg-Marshall-Mcluhan-.pdf

Melitz, M. J. (2003). The Impact of Trade on Intra-Industry Reallocations and Aggregate Industry Productivity. *Econometrica, 71*(6), 1695–1725. doi:10.1111/1468-0262.00467

Mellizo, A. (2019). *Pacific Alliance: Five Challenges in the medium and long term.* EFE/EPA. https://www.efe.com/efe/english/world/50000262

Mensi, W., Hammoudeh, S., Reboredo, J. C., & Nguyen, D. K. (2014). Do global factors impact BRICS stock markets? A quantile regression approach. *Emerging Markets Review, 19*, 1–17. doi:10.1016/j.ememar.2014.04.002

Mesa, R., González, J., & Aguirre, Y. (2009). Se "esfumó" el crecimiento económico colombiano en 2009: Análisis de la coyuntura y perspectivas 2010. *Perfil de Coyuntura Económica, 14*, 69–111.

Mete, M., Pekmez, G., & Kıyançiçek, C. (2016). Effect of 2008 financial crisis on fragile eight: Theoretical review. *Electronic Journal of Social Sciences, 15*(57), 689–709.

Mian, A., & Sufi, A. (2015). *House of debt: How they (and you) caused the Great Recession, and how we can prevent it from happening again*. University of Chicago Press.

Michaely, M. (1996). *Trade Preferential Agreements in Latin America: An Ex-Ante Assessment.* Policy Research Working Paper 1583. The World Bank. https://core.ac.uk/download/pdf/6645169.pdf

Milberg, W., & Winkler, D. (2010). Trade, crisis, and recovery: restructuring global value chains. *Global value chains in a postcrisis world: A development perspective*, 23-72.

Milberg, W., & Winkler, D. (2013). *Outsourcing Economics: Global Value Chains in Capitalist Development.* Cambridge University Press. doi:10.1017/CBO9781139208772

Mimouni, K., Temimi, A., Goaied, M., & Zeitun, R. (2019). The impact of liquidity on debt maturity after a financial crisis: Evidence from the Gulf Cooperation Council region. *Emerging Markets Finance & Trade, 55*(1), 181–200. doi:10.1080/1540496X.2018.1425835

Minsky, H. P. (1977). The financial instability hypothesis: An interpretation of Keynes and an alternative to "standard" theory. *The Challenge (Karachi), 20*(1), 20–27. doi:10.1080/05775132.1977.11470296

Miroudot, S. (2020). Resilience versus robustness in global value chains: Some policy implications. *COVID-19 and trade policy: Why turning inward won't work*, 117-130.

Mishra, P. K., & Mishra, S. K. (2020). Corona Pandemic and Stock Market Behaviour: Empirical Insights from Selected Asian Countries. Millennial Asia. 10.1177%2F0976399620952354.

Mitchell, J., Keane, J., & Coles, C. (2009). *Trading up: How a value chain approach can benefit the rural poor. COPLA Global.* Overseas Development Institute.

Mohanty, P., Dhoundiyal, H., & Choudhury, R. (2020). *Events Tourism in the Eye of the COVID-19 Storm: Impacts and Implications* (1st ed.). Apple Academic Press.

Mohapatra, S., Priyanka, V., Mohapatra, S., Kohli, I., & Mishra, R. K. (2020). Impact Of Corona Virus Covid-19 On the Global Economy. *International Journal of Agricultural and Statistics Sciences*, *16*(2), 771–778.

Molano, G. (2007, September-December). El interregionalismo y sus límites. *Estudios Internacionales. Revista del Instituto de Estudios Internacionales de la Universidad de Chile*, (158), 12.

Molle, W. (2006). *The Economics of European Integration: theory, practice, policy* (5th ed.). Routledge.

Monreal-Pérez, J., & Geldres-Weiss, V. V. (2019). *A configurational approach to the impact of trade fairs and trade missions on firm export activity.* BRQ Business Research Quarterly. doi:10.1016/j.brq.2018.11.001

Montoya-Uribe, D. A., Gonzalez-Parias, C. H., & Duarte-Herrera, L. K. (2016). Situación y retos de Colombia en materia de comercio exterior, en el marco de la Alianza del Pacífico. *Revista Entramado*, *12*(1), 50–65. doi:10.18041/entramado.2016v12n1.23128

Morady, F., & Kapucu, H. (Eds.). (2017). *Development & Growth: Economic Impacts of Globalization. Global Studies, No. 3.* IJOPEC Publication. doi:10.5281/zenodo.1291756

Mora, J. U. (2016). La Alianza del Pacífico y Mercosur: Evidencias de convergencia económica. *Estudios Gerenciales*, *32*(141), 309–318. doi:10.1016/j.estger.2016.10.005

Morton, J. (2020). On the susceptibility and vulnerability of agricultural value chains to COVID-19. *World Development*, *136*(105132), 1–4. PMID:32836692

Movahedi, M., & Shahbazi, K. (2020). *Firms' export decisions: self-selection versus trial-and-error. Economics: The Open-Access, Open-Assessment E-Journal.* doi:10.5018/economics-ejournal.ja.2020-22

Mukerji, P. (2009). Trade liberalization and the extensive margin. *Scottish Journal of Political Economy*, *56*(2), 141–166. doi:10.1111/j.1467-9485.2009.00478.x

Munich Security Report. (2020). *Westlessness.* Disponible en: https://securityconference.org/en/publications/munich-security-report-2020/

Muûls, M. (2015). Exporters and credit constraints. *Journal of International Economics*, *95*(2), 333–343. doi:10.1016/j.jinteco.2014.12.003

Naim, M. (1999). *Fads and Fashion in Economic Reforms: Washington Consensus or Washington Confusion.* Working Draft of a Paper Prepared for the IMF Conference on Second Generation Reforms, Washington, DC. https://www.imf.org/external/pubs/ft/seminar/1999/reforms/naim.htm

Naude, M., Santos-Paulino, W., & Mcgillivary, A. (2009). *Vulnerability in developing countries.* United Nations University Press.

Neaime, S. (2016). Financial crises and contagion vulnerability of MENA stock markets. *Emerging Markets Review*, *27*, 14–35. doi:10.1016/j.ememar.2016.03.002

Neilsno, J., & Pritchard, B. (2010). Fairness and ethicality in their place: The regional dynamics of fair trade and ethical sourcing agendas in the plantation districts of South India. *Environment & Planning A*, *42*(8), 1833–1851. doi:10.1068/a4260

Nikitina, O. (2021). Convention and Exhibition Industry: Digitalization and Strategic Leadership During the COVID-19 Crisis and After the Pandemic. In *1st International Scientific Conference "Legal Regulation of the Digital Economy and Digital Relations: Problems and Prospects of Development" (LARDER 2020)* (pp. 215-220). Atlantis Press.

Nippani, S., & Washer, K. M. (2004). SARS: A non-event for affected countries' stock markets? *Applied Financial Economics*, *14*(15), 1105–1110. doi:10.1080/0960310042000310579

Nitsch, V. (2009). Die another day: Duration in German import trade. *Review of World Economics*, *145*(1), 133–154. doi:10.100710290-009-0008-3

Notteboom, T., Pallis, T., & Rodrigue, J. (2021). Disruptions and resilience in global container shipping and ports: The COVID-19 pandemic versus the 2008–2009 financial crisis. *Maritime Economics & Logistics*, 1–32.

Nwachukwu, T. (2019). A global financial crises and international trade – the impact on Nigerian exports. *International Journal of Economics and Financial Management*, *4*(4), 1–19.

Observatory of Economic Complexity. (n.d.). *Country's profiles.* https://oec.world/en/profile/country

Ocampo, J. (2005). ¿Por qué fue tan severa la crisis económica de fines de los años noventa? *Coyuntura Económica: Investigación Económica y Social,* (1093). https://www.repository.fedesarrollo.org.co/handle/11445/916

Ocampo, J. (2011). ¿Cómo fue el desempeño de América Latina durante la crisis financiera global? *Revista de Ensayos Económicos. Banco Central de la República de Argentina*, *61*(62), 1–28.

OECD. (2013). *Multidimensional Review of Myanmar* (Vol. 1). Initial Assesment.

OECD. (2013). *OECD Economic Outlook, Volume 2013 Issue 1.* OECD Publishing. . doi:10.1787/eco_outlook-v2013-1-en

OIV. (2020). *Estadísticas.* https://www.oiv.int/es/statistiques/recherche

Okore, O. A., & Onoh, J. O. (2013). The impact of capital account liberalization on economic growth in Nigeria. *European Journal of Business and Management*, *5*(2), 34–40.

Olingo Allan. (2020). *Economy hit hard as services slow down; Daily Nation.* Nation Media Group.

Olney, W. W. (2016). Impact of corruption on firm-level export decisions. *Economic Inquiry*, *54*(2), 1105–1127. doi:10.1111/ecin.12257

Opler, T., Pinkowitz, L., Stulz, R., & Williamson, R. (1999). The determinants and implications of corporate cash holdings. *Journal of Financial Economics*, *52*(1), 3–46. doi:10.1016/S0304-405X(99)00003-3

Organization for Economic Co-operation and Development. (2018). *OECD Economic Surveys: Chile 2018.* OECD Publishing.

Organization for Economic Co-operation and Development. (2021). *OECD Economic Surveys: Chile 2021.* OECD Publishing.

Ortiz, C. (2017). La Alianza del Pacífico como actor regional: factores de éxito para la cohesión regional hacia la proyección internacional. *Desafíos*, *29*(1), 49-77. http:// doi:10.12804/revistas.urosario.edu.co/desafios/a.4885

Palomares, G. (2006). *Relaciones internacionales en el siglo XXI.* Tecnos.

Palumbo, F., & Herbig, P. A. (2002). Trade shows and fairs: An important part of the international promotion mix. *Journal of Promotion Management*, *8*(1), 93–108. doi:10.1300/J057v08n01_09

Parežanin, M., Jednak, S., & Kragulj, D. (2016). The Impact of FDI on the Economic Growth of Serbia. *Management: Journal of Sustainable Business and Management Solutions in Emerging Economies*, *21*(78), 25–32.

Parisi, M. L. (2017). Labor market rigidity, social policies and the labor share: Empirical evidence before and after the big crisis. *Economic Systems*, *41*(4), 492–512. doi:10.1016/j.ecosys.2017.08.003

Parra, C., & Salazar, N. (2000). La crisis financiera y la experiencia internacional. *Boletines de Divulgación Económica*, 1. https://colaboracion.dnp.gov.co/CDT/Estudios%20Econmicos/La%20crisis%20financiera%20y%20la%20experiencia%20internacional.pdf

Pastrana, E. (2016). *La Alianza del Pacífico: de cara a los proyectos regionales y las transformaciones globales*. Barcelona/Ciudad de México, Editorial Gedisa.

Patel, N. (2020). Impact on dental economics and dental healthcare utilization in COVID-19: An exploratory study. *Journal of Advanced Oral Research*, *11*(2), 128–136. doi:10.1177/2320206820941365

Pecherskaya, M. D., Mamatkulov, S. I., & Butanov, H. T. (2019). Virtual Fairs as A Modern Tool of Marketing. *Acta of Turin Polytechnic University in Tashkent*, *9*(3), 25–27.

Peck Isobel. (2021). *The Fix, A Monthly Vei Digital Digest*. Retrieved from https://cd100848-2bdf-4893-9b66-4304140e139e.filesusr.com/ugd/538ca9_e5bd224c59df40848c60f6bed902c3b5.pdf

Pegler, L., & Knorringa, P. (2007). *Integrating labour issues in global value chain analysis: Exploring implications for labour research and unions. In Trade union responses to globalisation: A review by the Global Unions Research Network*. ILO.

Peña-Vinces, J. C., Casanova, L., Guillen, J., & Urbano, D. (2016). International competitiveness of small and medium-sized enterprises: Peru, a Latin-American emerging market. *Emerging Markets Finance & Trade*, *53*(1), 150–169. doi:10.1080/1540496X.2016.1156525

Perez-Reyna, D. (2017). Crisis de 1999. In J. D. Uribe (Ed.), Historia del Banco de la República 1923-2015 (pp. 437–463). Academic Press.

Pesaran, M. H. (2004). *General diagnostic tests for cross section dependence in panels*. IZA Discussion Paper No. 1240.

Pesaran, M. H. (2007). A simple panel unit root test in the presence of cross section dependence. *Journal of Applied Econometrics*, *22*(2), 265–312. doi:10.1002/jae.951

Pesaran, M. H., Ullah, A., & Yamagata, T. (2008). A bias-adjusted LM test of error cross-section independence. *The Econometrics Journal*, *11*(1), 105–127. doi:10.1111/j.1368-423X.2007.00227.x

Piketty, T. (2014). *El capital en el siglo XXI*. Fondo de Cultura Económica.

Pinkowitz, L., Stulz, R. M., & Williamson, R. (2016). Do US firms hold more cash than foreign firms do? *Review of Financial Studies*, *29*(2), 309–348. doi:10.1093/rfs/hhv064

Pitterle, I., Haufler, F., & Hong, P. (2015). Assessing emerging markets' vulnerability to financial crisis. *Journal of Policy Modeling*, *37*(3), 484–500. doi:10.1016/j.jpolmod.2015.03.010

Polanco, R. (2015). *Chilean Trade and Investment Agreements with Southern Countries: From Bilateral Treaties to the Pacific Alliance*. SECO/WTI Academic Cooperation Project Working Paper Series, 1.

Polat, A. Y. (2020). Borç vadesi ve finansal kriz: Türkiye örneği. *Erciyes Üniversitesi İktisadi ve İdari Bilimler Fakültesi Dergisi*, (1), 118–130. doi:10.18070/erciyesiibd.846318

Pöllmann, M. P. (2013). *Process definition for innovation in trade fairs* (Doctoral dissertation). Edinburgh Napier University.

Ponte, S. (2008). Developing a vertical dimension to chronic poverty research: Some lessons from global value chain analysis. *Chronic Poverty Research Centre Working paper*, (111).

Power, D., & Jansson, J. (2008). Cyclical clusters in global circuits: Overlapping spaces in furniture trade fairs. *Economic Geography*, *84*(4), 423–448. doi:10.1111/j.1944-8287.2008.00003.x

Pradhan, S., Ghose, D., & Shabbiruddin. (2020). Present and future impact of COVID-19 in the renewable energy sector: A case study on India. *Energy Sources. Part A, Recovery, Utilization, and Environmental Effects*, 1–11. doi:10.1080/15567036.2020.1801902

Pramiyanti, A., Mayangsari, I. D., Nuraeni, R., & Firdaus, Y. D. (2020). Public perception on transparency and trust in government information released during the COVID-19 pandemic. *Asian Journal for Public Opinion Research*, *8*(3), 351–376.

Prasad, E. S., Rogoff, K., Wei, S-J., & Ayan Kose, M. (2003). Effects of Financial Globalization on Developing Countries: Some Empirical Evidence. Washington, DC: IMF.

Price, G. N., & Adu, D. P. (2021). Was trade openness with China an initial driver of cross-country human coronavirus infections? *Journal of Economic Studies (Glasgow, Scotland)*, *ahead-of-print*(ahead-of-print). Advance online publication. doi:10.1108/JES-10-2020-0497

Prochile. (2019). *Liderazgo de Chile en las exportaciones mundiales*. Departamento de Estudios. https://www.prochile.gob.cl/documento-biblioteca/liderazgo-de-chile-en-las-exportaciones-mundiales-2018/#:~:text=Sin%20ir%20m%C3%A1s%20lejos%2C%20Chile,y%20algas%20de%20uso%20industrial

Prokopijević, M. (2005). *Evropskaunija: Uvod*. Službeniglasnik.

PWC. (2020). *Perspectives from the Global Entertainment & Media Outlook 2020–2024*. Retrieved from https://www.pwc.com/gx/en/entertainment-media/outlook-2020/perspectives.pdf

Radelet, S., & Sachs, J. (2000). The onset of the East Asian financial crisis. In P. Krugman (Ed.), *Currency crises* (pp. 105–162). University of Chicago Press.

Rafael, D. (2021). *Más impuestos al vino y pérdida de competitividad, riesgos de la era post Brexit para el sector agroalimentario*. https://www.eleconomista.es/empresas-finanzas/agro/noticias/10997429/01/21/Mas-impuestos-al-vino-y-perdida-de-competitividad-riesgos-de-la-era-post-Brexit-para-el-sector-agroalimentario.html

Rahmanov, F., Aliyeva, R., Rosokhata, A., & Letunovska, N. (2020). Tourism management in Azerbaijan under sustainable development: Impact of COVID-19. *Marketing and Management of Innovations*, *3*(3), 195–207. doi:10.21272/mmi.2020.3-14

Rajan, R. G., & Zingales, L. (1995). What do we know about capital structure? Some evidence from international data. *The Journal of Finance*, *50*(5), 1421–1460. doi:10.1111/j.1540-6261.1995.tb05184.x

Ramírez-Pasillas, M. (2010). International trade fairs as amplifiers of permanent and temporary proximities in clusters. *Entrepreneurship and Regional Development*, *22*(2), 155–187. doi:10.1080/08985620902815106

Ramos, J. (2008). El desarrollo exportador chileno: evolución y perspectivas. *Documento de Trabajo de Economía de la Universidad de Chile*, 289. http://repositorio.uchile.cl/handle/2250/144171

Rawat, A. S., & Arif, I. (2018). Does geopolitical risk drive equity price returns of BRIC economies? Evidence from quantile on quantile estimations. *Journal of Finance and Economics Research*, *3*(2), 24–36. doi:10.20547/jfer1803202

Řehák, A. (2008). *Analysis of perspective trends in trade fairs.* Univerzita Tomáše Bati ve Zlíně.

Reid, M. (2020, July). Peru is heading towards a dangerous new populism. *The Economist.* https://www.economist.com/the-americas/2020/07/23/peru-is-heading-towards-a-dangerous-new-populism

Reid, M. (2021, April). Two extremists vie in a run-off for Peru's presidency. *The Economist.* https://www.economist.com/the-americas/2021/04/15/two-extremists-vie-in-a-run-off-for-perus-presidency

Reinhart, C. M., & Rogoff, K. S. (2008). This time is different: A panoramic view of eight centuries of financial crises (No. w13882). National Bureau of Economic Research.

Reinhart, C., & Rogoff, K. (2009). *The aftermath of financial crises.* NBER Working Paper Series, 14656. https://www.nber.org/papers/w14656

Reinhart, C. M., & Rogoff, K. S. (2013). Banking Crises: An Equal Opportunity Menace. *Journal of Banking & Finance, 37*(November), 4557–4573. doi:10.1016/j.jbankfin.2013.03.005

Reinhart, C. M., & Savastano, M. A. (2003). The realities of modern hyperinflation. *Finance & Development, 40*(2), 20–23. https://www.elibrary.imf.org/view/journals/022/0040/002/article-A007-en.xml

Remolar, I., Garcés, A., Rebollo, C., Chover, M., Quirós, R., & Gumbau, J. (2015). Developing a virtual trade fair using an agent-oriented approach. *Multimedia Tools and Applications, 74*(13), 4561–4582. doi:10.100711042-013-1822-0

Republic of Turkey Ministry of Trade. (2021). Retrieved from https://ticaret.gov.tr/destekler/ihracat-destekleri/pazara-giriste-dijital-faaliyetlerin-desteklenmesi

Rinallo, D., Borghini, S., & Golfetto, F. (2010). Exploring visitor experiences at trade shows. *Journal of Business and Industrial Marketing, 25*(4), 249–258. doi:10.1108/08858621011038207

Ritzer, G. (2011). *Globalization: The Essentials.* Wiley-Blackwell.

Robinson, J. (2005). Urban geography: World cities, or a world of cities. *Progress in Human Geography, 29*(6), 757–765. doi:10.1191/0309132505ph582pr

Rodriguez, F., & Rodrik, D. (2000). *Trade Policy and Economic Growth: A Skeptics Guide to the Cross-National Evidence.* NBER Working Paper N° 7081.

Rodríguez, J. A. (2021). Situación económica, política fiscal y pandemia en Colombia. *Revista de Economia Institucional, 23*(44), 249–263.

Rodríguez, M. P., Cortez, K., & Méndez, A. B. (2019). Financial and Economic Convergence in Pacific Alliance Countries. In M. Blanco-Jimenez & J. C. Álvarez (Eds.), *Regional Integration in Latin America* (pp. 45–60). Emerald Publishing Limited. doi:10.1108/978-1-78973-159-020191004

Rodrik, D. (2000). How far will international economic integration go? *Journal of Economic Perspective, 14*(1), 177-186.

Rodrik, D. (2007). *One Economics Many Recipes, Globalization, Institutions and Economic Growth.* Princeton University Press. doi:10.1515/9781400829354

Rosales, O., & Kuwayama, O. (2012). *China y América Latina y el Caribe. Hacia una relación económica y comercial estratégica.* Comisión Económica para América Latina y el Caribe (CEPAL). https://www.redalc-china.org/monitor/images/pdfs/Investigacion/15_Rosales_2012.pdf

Rosson, P. J., & Seringhaus, F. R. (1995). Visitor and exhibitor interaction at industrial trade fairs. *Journal of Business Research, 32*(1), 81–90. doi:10.1016/0148-2963(94)00012-4

Rotunno, L., & Vézina, P. L. (2012). Chinese networks and tariff evasion. *World Economy*, *35*(12), 1772–1794. doi:10.1111/j.1467-9701.2012.01452.x

Roy, H., Gupta, V., Faroque, A., & Patel, A. (2020). The impact of COVID-19 on the foodservice industry in Vancouver, British Columbia, Canada. *Anatolia*, *32*(1), 157–160. doi:10.1080/13032917.2020.1857803

Rozmainsky, I., & Rodionova, T. (2021). The financial fragility hypothesis and the debt crisis in Italy in the 2010s. *Terra Economicus*, *19*(1), 6–16. doi:10.18522/2073-6606-2021-19-1-6-16

Sachs, J., Tornell, A., & Velasco, A. (1996). Financial crises in emerging markets: The lessons from 1995. Paper no. w5576, National Bureau of Economic Research. doi:10.3386/w5576

Şafaklı, O. V. (2002). KKTC'de Banka Krizleri açısından Kamu Finansmanının Etkinliği. *Uludağ Üniversitesi İktisadi ve İdari Bilimler Fakültesi Dergisi*, *21*(2), 65–84.

Şafaklı, O. V. (2006). KKTC'nin olası AB üyeliği karşısında Kamu Bankalarının Stratejik Analizi. *Ç.Ü. Sosyal Bilimler Enstitüsü Dergisi*, *15*(1), 313–332.

Şafaklı, O. V., & Özdeşer, H. (2002). An Analysis of the Cooperatives in the Turkish Republic Of Northern Cyprus in the Process of EU. *XVII. International Turkish Cooperative Congress on Globalization and Cooperatives*.

Saini, S., Bansal, A., & Sadhana, R. K. (2020). A study on the impact of corona virus (Covid-19) on the global food industry. *International Journal in Management and Social Science*, *8*(6).

Sala-i-Martin, X. (2002). *The Distributing rise of global income inequality*. NBER Working Paper No. 8904.

Sala-i-Martin, X. (2006). *Globalización y reducción de la pobreza*. FAES.

SalesRoads. (2021). *White Paper, The State Of Trade Show Lead Generation*. Retrieved from https://salesroads.com/resource/trade-show-lead-gen/

Salisu, A. A., & Vo, X. V. (2020). Predicting stock returns in the presence of COVID-19 pandemic: The role of health news. *International Review of Financial Analysis*, *71*, 101546. Advance online publication. doi:10.1016/j.irfa.2020.101546

Salvatore, D. (2020). Growth and trade in the United States and the world economy: Overview. *Journal of Policy Modeling*, *42*(4), 750–759. doi:10.1016/j.jpolmod.2020.03.001 PMID:32362694

Sama, S., Quinn, M., Galligan, C., Karlsson, N., Gore, R., Kriebel, D., & Lindberg, J. (2020). Impacts of the COVID-19 Pandemic on Home Health and Home Care Agency Managers, Clients, and Aides: A Cross-Sectional Survey, March to June, 2020. *Home Health Care Management & Practice*, *33*(2), 125–129. doi:10.1177/1084822320980415

Sandretto, R. (2002) Globalization and National Sovereignty Defense of an iconoclastic view. In *Seventh International Scientific Conference. The problems of Economic Integration of Ukraine into the European Union.* Globalization and New Economy.

Sanna-Randaccio y Veurgeles, R. (2003). Global Innovation strategies of MNE's: implications for host economies. In J. Cantwell & J. Molero (Eds.), *Multinational Enterprises*. Innovative Strategies and Systems of Innovation, New Horizons in International Business.

Sapir, J. (2011). *La Démondialisation*. Éditions du Seuil.

Sapir, J. (2016). Jacques Sapir: Donald Trump, président de la démondialisation? *Le Figaro*. Available on web: https://www.lefigaro.fr/vox/monde/2016/11/10/31002-20161110ARTFIG00233-jacques-sapir-donald-trump-president-de-la-demondialisation.php

Sapir, J. (2016). Jacques Sapir: Donald Trump, President of the Demondialisation? *Le Figaro*. http://www.lefigaro.fr/vox/monde/2016/11/10/31002-20161110ARTFIG00233-jacques-sapir-donald-trump-president-de-la-demondialisation.php

Sapir, J. (2011). *La demondialisation*. Seuil.

Sarmento, M., Farhangmehr, M., & Simões, C. (2015). A relationship marketing perspective to trade fairs: Insights from participants. *Journal of Business and Industrial Marketing*, *30*(5), 584–593. doi:10.1108/JBIM-01-2013-0024

Sarmento, M., & Simões, C. (2019). Trade fairs as engagement platforms: The interplay between physical and virtual touch points. *European Journal of Marketing*, *53*(9), 1782–1807. doi:10.1108/EJM-10-2017-0791

Sar, T. T., Aernan, P. T., & Houmsou, R. S. (2010). H1N1 Influenza Epidemic: Public Health Implications for Nigeria. *International Journal of Virology*, *6*, 1–6.

Sassen, S. (1991). The global city: New York, London, Tokyo. Princeton.

Sedky Herve. (2021). *The Fix, A Monthly Vei Digital Digest*. Retrieved from https://cd100848-2bdf-4893-9b66-4304140e139e.filesusr.com/ugd/538ca9_e5bd224c59df40848c60f6bed902c3b5.pdf

Seifert, B., & Gonenc, H. (2016). Creditor rights, country governance, and corporate cash holdings. *Journal of International Financial Management & Accounting*, *27*(1), 65–90. doi:10.1111/jifm.12033

Seifert, B., & Gonenc, H. (2018). The effects of country and firm-level governance on cash management. *Journal of International Financial Markets, Institutions and Money*, *52*, 1–16. doi:10.1016/j.intfin.2017.12.001

Şeker, A. (2020). The impacts of liner shipping connectivity and economic growth on international trade case of European countries and Turkey. In G. Ç. Ceyhun (Ed.), *Handbook of research on the applications of international transportation and logistics for world trade* (pp. 139–150). IGI Global. doi:10.4018/978-1-7998-1397-2.ch008

Seraphin, H., & Dosquet, F. (2020). Mountain tourism and second home tourism as post COVID-19 lockdown placebo? *Worldwide Hospitality and Tourism Themes*, *12*(4), 485–500. doi:10.1108/WHATT-05-2020-0027

Seringhaus, F. H., & Rosson, P. J. (2000, Apr.). Exhibitors at international trade fairs: The influence of export support. *LTA*.

Sharda, R., Sikolia, D., Thomas, J., & Sambasivan, R. (2012). A Design Science Approach to Virtual World Implementation of Trade Fairs. Pacific Asia. *Journal of the Association for Information Systems*, *4*(2), 4.

Sharif, A., Aloui, C., & Yarovaya, L. (2020). COVID-19 pandemic, oil prices, stock market, geopolitical risk and policy uncertainty nexus in the US economy: Fresh evidence from the wavelet-based approach. *International Review of Financial Analysis*, *70*, 101496. Advance online publication. doi:10.1016/j.irfa.2020.101496

Sharma, A., & Nicolau, J. (2020). An open market valuation of the effects of COVID-19 on the travel and tourism industry. *Annals of Tourism Research*, *83*(102990), 1–4. PMID:32834220

Sharpe, W. F. (1964). Capital asset prices: A theory of market equilibrium under conditions of risk. *The Journal of Finance*, *19*(3), 425–442.

Shelburne, R. C. (2010). The global financial crisis and its impact on trade: the world and the european emerging economies. *United Nations Economic Commission for Europe-Discussion Papers Series, 2*.

Shepherd, B. (2016). Infrastructure, trade facilitation, and network connectivity in Sub-Saharan Africa. *Journal of African Trade*, *3*(1-2), 1–22. doi:10.1016/j.joat.2017.05.001

Shereni, N. C., Ncube, F. N., & Mazhande, P. (2021). Exhibitors' preference at trade fairs: The case of Zimbabwe International Trade Fair (ZITF). *Journal of Convention & Event Tourism*, 1–21. doi:10.1080/15470148.2021.1893241

Shi, X., & Xu, Z. (2020). *Export Tax Refund and the Misreporting of Chinese Exporters*. Academic Press.

Shiau, H. L., Chang, Y. H., & Yang, Y. J. (2018). The cash holdings and corporate investment surrounding financial crisis: The cases of China and Taiwan. *Chinese Economy*, *51*(2), 175–207. doi:10.1080/10971475.2018.1447833

Shih, S. (1996). *Me-Too is Not My Style: Challenge Difficulties, Break through Bottlenecks, Create Values*. The Acer Foundation.

Shikimi, M., & Yamada, K. (2019). Trade and financial channels as the transmission mechanism of the financial crisis. *International Review of Economics & Finance*, *63*, 364–381. doi:10.1016/j.iref.2019.04.008

Shousha, S. (2019). *The dollar and emerging market economies: Financial vulnerabilities meet the international trade system.* International Finance Discussion Papers 1258.

Siba, E., & Gebreeyesus, M. (2017). Learning to export and learning from exporting: The case of Ethiopian manufacturing. *Journal of African Economies*, *26*(1), 1–23. doi:10.1093/jae/ejw022

SICE. (2020). *Foreign Trade Information System.* Organization of American States (OAS). sice.oas.org

Siche, R. (2020). What is the impact of COVID-19 disease on agriculture? *Scientia Agropecuaria*, *11*, 3–6.

Siemieniako, D., & Gębarowski, M. (2017). B2B trade fairs and promise management as a relationship marketing concept. *Journal of Customer Behaviour*, *16*(3), 237–261. doi:10.1362/147539217X15071081721116

Silva, J. M. C. S., Tenreyno, S., & Wei, K. (2014). Estimating the extensive margin of trade. *Journal of International Economics*, *93*(1), 67–75. doi:10.1016/j.jinteco.2013.12.001

Silva, T. C., Muniz, F. J., & Tabak, B. M. (2021). Indirect and direct effects of the subprime crisis on the real sector: Labor market migration. *Empirical Economics*, 1–32. PMID:33897095

Sinani, E., & Meyer, K. E. (2004). Spillovers of technology transfer from FDI: The case of Estonia. *Journal of Comparative Economics*, *32*(3), 445–466. doi:10.1016/j.jce.2004.03.002

Singh, P., & Maiti, D. (2019). ICT, Access to Finance and Firm Exports: A Cross-Country Study. In D. Maiti, F. Castellacci, & A. Melchior (Eds.), *Digitalisation and Development: Issues for India and Beyond* (pp. 161–181). Springer.

Situma, S. P. (2012). The effectiveness of trade shows and exhibitions as organizational marketing tool (analysis of selected companies in Mombasa). *International Journal of Business and Social Science*, *3*(22), 219–230.

Siu, A., & Wong, Y. R. (2004). Economic impact of SARS: The case of Hong Kong. *Asian Economic Papers*, *3*(1), 62–83.

Smith, T. M., Gopalakrishna, S., & Smith, P. M. (2004). The complementary effect of trade shows on personal selling. *International Journal of Research in Marketing*, *21*(1), 61–76. doi:10.1016/j.ijresmar.2003.04.003

Sohrabi, C., Alsafi, Z., O'neill, N., Khan, M., Kerwan, A., Al-Jabir, A., ... Agha, R. (2020). World Health Organization declares global emergency: A review of the 2019 novel coronavirus (COVID-19). *International Journal of Surgery, 76*, 71-76.

Solberg, C. A. (1991). Export promotion and trade fairs in Norway: are there better ways? *International Perspectives on Trade Promotion and Assistance*, 119-125.

Solomon, S., Rao, G. P., & Swapna, M. (2020). Impact of COVID-19 on Indian sugar industry. *Sugar Tech*, *22*(4), 547–551. doi:10.100712355-020-00846-7 PMID:32837056

Song, K., & Lee, Y. (2012). Long-term effects of a financial crisis: Evidence from cash holdings of East Asian firms. *Journal of Financial and Quantitative Analysis*, *47*(3), 617–641. doi:10.1017/S0022109012000142

Song, Y., Liu, T., Li, Y., & Ye, B. (2020). The influence of COVID-19 on grid parity of China's photovoltaic industry. *Environmental Geochemistry and Health*, 1–16. doi:10.100710653-020-00701-4 PMID:32857234

Spillan, J. E., & Virzi, N. (2017). Business Opportunities in the Pacific Alliance: The Economic Rise of Chile, Peru, Colombia, and Mexico. Springer. doi:10.1007/978-3-319-54768-8

Stallings, B., & Studart, R. (2006), *Financiamiento para el desarrollo: América Latina desde una perspectiva comparada.* Libros de la CEPAL No. 90.

Statistics, A. B. O. (2020). *Jobs by Industry Sub-division.* Available online at: https://www.abs.gov.au/statistics/labour/employment-and-unemployment/labour-force-australia-detailed-quarterly/latest-release

Steinberg, F. (2005). *Cooperación y Conflicto en el Sistema Comercial Multilateral: La Organización Mundial de Comercio como Institución de Gobernanza Económica Global* (Tesis Doctoral). Presentada en el Departamento de Análisis Económico: Teoría Económica e Historia Económica de la Facultada de Ciencias Económicas y Empresariales de la Universidad Autónoma de Madrid, España.

Steinberg, F. (2007). *Cooperación y Conflicto Cooperación Internacional en la era de la Globalización.* Ediciones Akal.

Stellian, R., & Danna-Buitrago, J. (2019). Revealed comparative advantages and regional specialization: Evidence from Colombia in the Pacific Alliance. *Journal of Applied Econometrics*, *22*(1), 349–379. doi:10.1080/15140326.2019.1627722

Stiglitz, J. (2003). *Globalization and its Discontents.* W.W. Norton Company.

Stockhammer, E. (2012). Financialization, income distribution and the crisis. Investigación Económica, 71(279).

Stone, R. J. (1993). Virtual reality: toys or tools of the trade? In *Aslib Proceedings.* MCB UP Ltd. doi:10.1108/eb051321

Straw, W., & Glennie, A. (2012). The Third Wave of Globalization. In *IPPR Review on the Future of Globalization.* Institute for Public Policy Research.

Subsecretaría de Relaciones Económicas Internacionales - SUBREI. (2020). *Informe Anual de Comercio exterior de Chile, 2019.* Dirección de Estudios. https://www.subrei.gob.cl/docs/default-source/estudios-y-documentos/reporte-trimestral/comercio-exterior-de-chile-anual-2019.pdf?sfvrsn=1eb0bb58_0

Subsecretaría de Relaciones Económicas Internacionales - SUBREI. (2021a). *Informe anual de Comercio exterior de Chile, 2020.* Dirección de Estudios.

Subsecretaría de Relaciones Económicas Internacionales - SUBREI. (2021b). *Ficha país.* https://www.subrei.gob.cl/estudios-y-documentos/ficha-pais

Süreç, Y., & Eminer, F. (2019). *Rekabet Edebilirlik Raporu.* Academic Press.

Surendranath, R. (2010). The Role of Sovereign Wealth Funds in Global Financial Intermediation. *Thunderbird International Business Review*, *52*(6), 589–604. doi:10.1002/tie.20381

Süygün, S. (2019). Promotion Of International Trade. In Dynamics of Globalization at the Crossroads of Economics (pp. 35-43). Peter Lang GmbH, Internationaler Verlag der Wissenschaften.

Svirydzenka, K. (2016). Introducing a new broad-based index of financial development. *IMF Working Papers, 16*, 1.

Swiss Economic Institute. (2013). *Press Release, KOF Index of Globalization 2013.* Author.

Tamarauntari, M. K., & Diseye, B. T. (2013). Macroeconomic Uncertainty and Foreign Portfolio Investment: Evidence from Nigeria. *IISTE*, *3*(12), 229–236.

Tamrat, W. (2021). Enduring the impacts of COVID-19: Experiences of the private higher education sector in Ethiopia. *Studies in Higher Education*, *46*(1), 59–74. doi:10.1080/03075079.2020.1859690

Tatoğlu, F. Y. (2013). *İleri Panel Veri Analizi*. Beta Yayıncılık.

Taylor, P. (2004). *World City Network: A global urban analysis*. doi:10.4324/9780203634059

TC Ticaret Bakanlığı. (2020). *Pazar Bilgileri*. Academic Press.

Tekin, H. (2020a). Firm size and dividend policy of European firms: Evidence from financial crises. *Marmara Journal of European Studies*, *28*(1), 109–121.

Tekin, H. (2020b). How optimal cash changed by the global financial crisis? A multi-country analysis. *Economics and Business Letters*, *9*(2), 114–123. doi:10.17811/ebl.9.2.2020.114-123

Tekin, H. (2020c). Market differences and adjustment speed of debt, equity, and debt maturity. *Australian Journal of Management*. Advance online publication. doi:10.1177/0312896220968266

Tekin, H., & Polat, A. Y. (2020a). Agency theory: A review in finance. *Anemon: Journal of Social Sciences of Mus Alparslan University*, *8*(4), 1323–1329.

Tekin, H., & Polat, A. Y. (2020b). *Do market differences matter on dividend policy?* Borsa Istanbul Review. doi:10.1016/j.bir.2020.10.009

Tekin, H., & Polat, A. Y. (2020c). Is saving vital? Evidence from the financial crisis. *Economics and Business Letters*, *9*(2), 124–134. doi:10.17811/ebl.9.2.2020.124-134

Tekin, H., & Polat, A. Y. (2020d). The global financial crisis and capital structure decisions of Turkish SMEs: A review. *International Journal of Management Economics and Business*, *16*(3), 513–535. doi:10.17130/ijmeb.798509

Tekin, H., & Polat, A. Y. (2021a). Adjustment speed of debt maturity: Evidence from financial crises in East Asia. *Bulletin of Monetary Economics and Banking*, *24*(1), 71–92.

Tekin, H., & Polat, A. Y. (2021b). *Is leverage a substitute or outcome for governance? Evidence from financial crises*. International Journal of Emerging Markets. doi:10.1108/10.1108/IJOEM-03-2020-0297

Tello, M. D. (2012). Peru: Integration, sectoral specialization and synchronization with international gross domestic product cycles. *CEPAL Review*, *106*(106), 89–106. doi:10.18356/84420f4d-en

Telukdarie, A., Munsamy, M., & Mohlala, P. (2020). Analysis of the Impact of COVID-19 on the Food and Beverages Manufacturing Sector. *Sustainability*, *12*(22), 9331. doi:10.3390u12229331

Thatcher, A., Zhang, M., Todoroski, H., Chau, A., Wang, J., & Liang, G. (2020). Predicting the Impact of COVID-19 on Australian Universities. *Journal of Risk and Financial Management*, *13*(9), 1–20. doi:10.3390/jrfm13090188

The World Bank. (2016). *Turkish Cypriot Community: Workforce Development*. Author.

The World Bank. (2019). *World Bank Enterprise Survey for Turkish Cypriot Community*. enterprisesurveys.org.

Thoumi, F. E. (2002). Illegal Drugs in Colombia: From Illegal Economic Boom to Social Crisis. *The Annals of the American Academy of Political and Social Science*, *582*(1), 102–116. doi:10.1177/000271620258200108

Ticaret Dairesi. (2019). *İhracat İstatistik Raporu*. Academic Press.

Tiwari, A. K., Jana, R. K., & Roubaud, D. (2019). The policy uncertainty and market volatility puzzle: Evidence from wavelet analysis. *Finance Research Letters*, *31*. doi:10.1016/j.frl.2018.11.016

Tiwari, P., Séraphin, H., & Chowdhary, N. (2020). Impacts of COVID-19 on tourism education: Analysis and perspectives. *Journal of Teaching in Travel & Tourism*, 1–26. doi:10.1080/15313220.2020.1850392

Tobin, J. (1978). A Proposal for International Monetary Reform. *Eastern Economic Journal*, *4*(3-4), 153–159.

Topcu, M., & Gulal, O. S. (2020). The impact of COVID-19 on emerging stock markets. *Finance Research Letters*, *36*, 101691. Advance online publication. doi:10.1016/j.frl.2020.101691 PMID:32837378

Torres, G. A. (2011). La crisis colombiana de finales del siglo XX: ¿Un choque real o financiero? *Perfil de Coyuntura Económica*, *18*, 79–96.

Tramontana, A. R., George, B., Hurt, A. C., Doyle, J. S., Langan, K., Reid, A. B., ... Slavin, M. (2010). Oseltamivir resistance in adult oncology and hematology patients infected with pandemic (H1N1) 2009 virus, Australia. *Emerging Infectious Diseases*, *16*(7), 1068.

Tugores, J. (2002). *Economía internacional, globalización e integración regional*. McGraw-Hill.

Turan Katircioglu, S. (2006). Causality between agriculture and economic growth in a small nation under political isolation. *International Journal of Social Economics*, *33*(4), 331–343. doi:10.1108/03068290610651643

UFI. (2019). *Global Economic Impact of Exhibitions, 2019 Edition*. Retrieved from https://www.ufi.org/wp-content/uploads/2019/04/Global-Economic-Impact-of-Exhibitions_b.pdf

UFI. (2021). *Global Exhibition Barometer, 26th edition*. Retrieved from https://www.ufi.org/wp-content/uploads/2021/01/26th_UFI_Global_Barometer_january_2021.pdf

UFI. (2021). *Media Release*. Retrieved from https://www.ufi.org/wp-content/uploads/2021/02/MR_UFI-releases-figures-stating-the-impact-of-COVID-19_4february2021.pdf

Urrutia, M., & Llano, J. (2011). La crisis internacional y cambiaria de fin de siglo en Colombia. *Revista Desarrollo y Sociedad*, (67), 11–48. doi:10.13043/dys.67.1

Valéri, P. (1945). Política del espíritu. Losada.

Van Bergeijk, P. A. G., & Brakman, S. (2010). *The gravity model in international trade: advances and applications*. Cambridge Univ Pr. doi:10.1017/CBO9780511762109

Van Hoang, T. H., Gurău, C., Lahiani, A., & Seran, T. L. (2018). Do crises impact capital structure? A study of French micro-enterprises. *Small Business Economics*, *50*(1), 181–199. doi:10.100711187-017-9899-x

Van Senten, J., Engle, C., & Smith, M. (2021). Effects of COVID-19 on US aquaculture farms. *Applied Economic Perspectives and Policy*, 1–13.

Varón, O., Ríos, H. F. & Chávez, N. M. (2017). Budgetary deficit and inflation: case the Pacific Alliance. *Dimensión empresarial*, *16*(1), 135-146. doi:10.15665/dem.v16i1.1899

Vasiljeva, M., Neskorodieva, I., Ponkratov, V., Kuznetsov, N., Ivlev, V., Ivleva, M., Maramygin, M., & Zekiy, A. A. (2020). Predictive Model for Assessing the Impact of the COVID-19 Pandemic on the Economies of Some Eastern European Countries. *J. Open Innov. Technol. Mark. Complex*, *6*, 92.

Verick, S., & Islam, I. (2010). *The Great Recession of 2008-2009: Causes, Consequences and Policy Responses*. Discussion Paper No. 4934. IZA Forschungsinstitut zur Zukunft der ArbeitInstitute for the Study of Labor.

Vial, J. (2020). *Situación actual y perspectivas de la economía chilena.* Seminario Banco de España, 17 de febrero 2020, Madrid, España. https://www.bcentral.cl/es/web/banco-central/contenido/-/details/situacion-actual-y-perspectivas-de-la-economia-chilena-joaquin-vial-vicepresidente-madrid

Vieyra Medrano, J. A. (2000). Reconversión industrial, gran empresa y efectos territoriales: El caso del sector automotriz en México. *EURE. Revista Latinoamericana de Estudios Urbano Regionales, 26*(77), 25–47. doi:10.4067/S0250-71612000007700002

Vik, Å. S., Nørbech, B. C., & Jeske, D. (2018). Virtual career fairs: Perspectives from Norwegian recruiters and exhibitors. *Future Internet, 10*(2), 19. doi:10.3390/fi10020019

Villaécija, R. (2019). *Los aranceles de Trump amenazan a España: 400 millones en aceite y 300 en vino.* https://www.elmundo.es/economia/macroeconomia/2019/10/03/5d95bf0621efa04e508b457f.html

Villar, L., & Rincón, H. (2000). *The Colombian Economy in the Nineties: Capital Flows and Foreign Exchange Regimes.* Paper presented at the Conference on "Critical Issues in Financial Reform: Latin American- Caribbean and Canadian Perspectives", University of Toronto. https://www.banrep.gov.co/sites/default/files/publicaciones/archivos/borra149.pdf

Vogel, J., & Ajoudani, A. (2020). Virtual Conferences in Times of COVID-19: Embracing the Potential. *IEEE Robotics & Automation Magazine, 27*(3), 19–19. doi:10.1109/MRA.2020.3008838

Vysin, M. (2017). *The role of development cooperation for upgrading in Uganda's organic fruit value chain* (Doctoral dissertation). Uniwien.

Wagner, A. F. (2020). What the stock market tells us about the post-COVID-19 world. *Nature Human Behaviour, 4*(5), 440–440. doi:10.103841562-020-0869-y PMID:32242087

Wagner, J. (2019). Access to Finance and Exports – Comparable Evidence for Small and Medium Enterprises from Industry and Services in 25 European Countries. *Open Economies Review, 30*(4), 739–757. doi:10.100711079-019-09534-w

Waiho, K., Fazhan, H., Ishak, S., Kasan, N., Liew, H., Norainy, M., & Ikhwanuddin, M. (2020). Potential impacts of COVID-19 on the aquaculture sector of Malaysia and its coping strategies. *Aquaculture Reports, 18*(100450), 1–6. doi:10.1016/j.aqrep.2020.100450

Wang, Q., Chen, D., & Chang, C. (2021). The impact of COVID-19 on stock prices of solar enterprises: A comprehensive evidence based on the government response and confirmed cases. *International Journal of Green Energy, 18*(5), 443–456. doi:10.1080/15435075.2020.1865367

WEF. (2019). *The travel & tourism competitiveness report 2019-travel and tourism at a tipping point.* http://www3.weforum.org/docs/WEF_TTCR_2019.pdf

Westerlund, J. (2007). Testing for error correction in panel data. *Oxford Bulletin of Economics and Statistics, 69*(6), 709–748. doi:10.1111/j.1468-0084.2007.00477.x

WHO. (2020). *Coronavirus disease (COVID-19) Pandemic.* World health Organization. https://www.who.int/emergencies/diseases/novel-coronavirus-2019

Wignaraja, G. (2013). Can SMEs participate in global production networks? In D. K. Elms & P. Low (Eds.), *Global value chains in a changing world* (pp. 279–312). World Trade Organization.

Williamson, J. G. (2013). *Trade and Poverty: When the Third World Fell Behind.* MIT Press Books.

Williamson, J. (2003). The Washington Consensus and Beyond. *Economic and Political Weekly, 38*(15), 1475–1481.

Wittwer, G., & Anderson, K. (2020). COVID-19 and global beverage markets: Impacts on Australian wine industry. *Wine & Viticulture Journal*, *35*(3), 61–66.

Wolf, M. (2005). *Why Globalization Works*. Yale Nota Bene.

World Bank Group. (2020). *World Bank Open Data*. Retrieved May 10, 2021, from https://data.worldbank.org/

World Bank. (2016). *World Bank Data*. http://data.worldbank.org/?display=default

World Bank. (2019). *World development report 2020: Trading for development in the age of global value chains*. The World Bank.

World Bank. (2020). *COVID-19 Outbreak: Capital Markets Implications and Response. Equitable Growth, Finance and Institutions: COVID-19 Notes, Finance Series*. https://pubdocs.worldbank.org/en/776691586478873523/COVID-19-Outbreak-Capital-Markets.pdf

World Bank. (2020a). *Latin America and Caribbean results*. Retrieved from https://www.worldbank.org/

World Bank. (2020b). *Mexico's international trade*. Retrieved from https://wits.worldbank.org/

World Bank. (n.d.). *World Development Indicators* [Data set]. https://databank.worldbank.org/

World Health Organization. (2020a). *Corona virus disease (COVID-19): situation report, 165*. WHO.

World Health Organization. (2020b). *Corona virus disease (COVID-19): situation report, 114*. WHO.

World Health Organization. (2020c). *Corona virus disease (COVID-19): situation report, 198*. WHO.

World Trade Organization. (n.d.). *Aid for Trade*. https://www.wto.org/english/tratop_e/devel_e/a4t_e/aid4trade_e.htm

WTO. (2020). *Covid-19 and Agriculture: A Story of Resilience, Information Note*. https://www.wto.org/english/news_e/news20_e/agri_27aug20_e.htm

WTO. (2020). *Trade shows signs of rebound from COVID-19, recovery still uncertain*. Press release. https://www.wto.org/english/ news_e/pres20_e/pr862_e.htm

WTO. (2021a). *World Trade Primed for Strong but Uneven Recovery after COVID-19 pandemic shock*. https://www.wto.org/english/news_e/pres21_e/pr876_e.htm

WTO. (2021b). https://www.wto.org/english/tratop_e/covid19_e/agric_report_e.pdf

WTO. (2021c). https://www.wto.org/english/tratop_e/covid19_e/covid19_e.htm

WTO. (2021d). https://www.wto.org/english/tratop_e/covid19_e/trade_related_goods_measure_e.htm

Wu, A., Peng, Y., Huang, B., Ding, X., Wang, X., Niu, P., & Jiang, T. (2020). Genome composition and divergence of the novel coronavirus (2019-nCoV) originating in China. *Cell Host & Microbe*, *27*(3), 325–328.

Wu, Y., Xu, X., Chen, Z., Duan, J., Hashimoto, K., Yang, L., & Yang, C. (2020). Nervous system involvement after infection with COVID-19 and other coronaviruses. *Brain, Behavior, and Immunity*, *87*, 18–22.

Wynne, M., & Kersting, E. (2009). Trade, globalisation and the financial crisis. *Economics Letters*, *4*(nov).

Yahya, W. (2015). Macroeconomic factors and foreign portfolio investment volatility: A case of South Asian countries. *Future Business Journal*, *1*(1-2), 65–74. doi:10.1016/j.fbj.2015.11.002

Yang, C.-H. (2018). Exports and innovation: The role of heterogeneity in exports. *Empirical Economics*, *55*(3), 1065–1087. doi:10.100700181-017-1312-8

Yang, Y., Liu, H., & Chen, X. (2020). COVID-19 and restaurant demand: Early effects of the pandemic and stay-at- home orders. *International Journal of Contemporary Hospitality Management*, *13*(12), 3809–3834. doi:10.1108/IJCHM-06-2020-0504

Yang, Y., Peng, F., Wang, R., Guan, K., Jiang, T., Xu, G., Sun, J., & Chang, C. (2020). The deadly coronaviruses: The 2003 SARS pandemic and the 2020 novel coronavirus epidemic in China. *Journal of Autoimmunity*, *109*, 102434. Advance online publication. doi:10.1016/j.jaut.2020.102434 PMID:32143990

Yazir, D., Şahin, B., Yip, T., & Tseng, P. (2020). Effects of COVID-19 on maritime industry: A review. *International Maritime Health*, *71*(4), 253–264. doi:10.5603/IMH.2020.0044 PMID:33394490

Ye, M., Meng, B., & Wei, S. J. (2015). Measuring smile curves in global value chains (No. 530). Institute of Developing Economies, Japan External Trade Organization (JETRO).

Yeats, A. J. (1998). *What can be expected from African regional trade arrangements? Some empirical evidence.* Some Empirical Evidence (November 1998). World Bank Policy Research Working Paper, (2004).

Yi, K. M. (2003). Can vertical specialization explain the growth of world trade? *Journal of Political Economy*, *111*(1), 52–102. doi:10.1086/344805

Yin, L., Yang, Q., & Su, Z. (2017). Predictability of structural co-movement in commodity prices: The role of technical indicators. *Quantitative Finance*, *17*(5), 795–812. doi:10.1080/14697688.2016.1225977

Yoo, J. (2019). Better legal institutions: An intertemporal effect on export composition. *Economic Bulletin*, *39*(4), 1–8.

Youssef, M., Mokni, K., & Ajmi, A. N. (2021). Dynamic connectedness between stock markets in the presence of the COVID-19 pandemic: Does economic policy uncertainty matter? *Financial Innovation*, *7*(1), 1–27. doi:10.118640854-021-00227-3

Yüksel, E., & Saridoğan, E. (2011). Uluslararası Ticaret Teorileri ve Paul R. Krugman'ın Katkıları. *Öneri Dergisi*, *9*(35), 199-206.

Zaremba, A., Aharon, D. Y., Demir, E., Kizys, R., & Zawadka, D. (2021). COVID-19, government policy responses, and stock market liquidity around the world: A note. *Research in International Business and Finance*, *56*, 101359. Advance online publication. doi:10.1016/j.ribaf.2020.101359 PMID:33343055

Zeitun, R., Temimi, A., & Mimouni, K. (2017). Do financial crises alter the dynamics of corporate capital structure? Evidence from GCC countries. *The Quarterly Review of Economics and Finance*, *63*, 21–33. doi:10.1016/j.qref.2016.05.004

Zhang, D., Hu, M., & Ji, Q. (2020). Financial markets under the global pandemic of COVID-19. *Finance Research Letters*, *36*, 101528. Advance online publication. doi:10.1016/j.frl.2020.101528 PMID:32837360

Zhang, D., Lei, L., Ji, Q., & Kutan, A. M. (2019). Economic policy uncertainty in the US and China and their impact on the global markets. *Economic Modelling*, *79*, 47–56. doi:10.1016/j.econmod.2018.09.028

Zhu, Y. W., Bathelt, H., & Zeng, G. (2020). Are trade fairs relevant for local innovation knowledge networks? Evidence from Shanghai equipment manufacturing. *Regional Studies*, *54*(9), 1250–1261. doi:10.1080/00343404.2019.1695046

About the Contributors

Ahu Coşkun Özer was born in Istanbul in 1981, graduated from Marmara University with a bachelor's degree in 2004, graduated from Marmara University with a master's degree in theory of economics in 2007. In 2012, Dr. Özer graduated from Ph.D. in Istanbul University, started to work as a research assistant in 2011, has been working as an assistant professor for 7 years at the Marmara University Vocational School of Social Sciences in Foreign Trade Program. Her research areas are international economics, foreign trade, economics, business, and entrepreneurship.

* * *

Burcu Berke is associate professor at department of economics in Nigde Omer Halisdemir University, Niğde, Turkey. Dr. Berke teaches International Economics and Development economics courses. She received the B.S. degree in Public Finance, Uludag University, Turkey in 2002; Master degree in Economics from Akdeniz University, Turkey, in 2004; and finally, she obtained PhD. Degree in Economics from Akdeniz University, Turkey, in 2011. Her main areas of research interest are Open Macroeconomics, International Economics and Applied Econometrics.

Adriana Cabello Cerna is Lecturer Instructor at Department of Management Control and Information System, University of Chile. She is a Ph.D. (c) in Business Administration at Universidad de Chile and she holds her Master in International Management from University of Zaragoza, España. She is a researcher and instructor in accounting and corporate governance.

Burak Erkut is an assistant professor at the Faculty of Economics, Administrative and Social Sciences of Bahçeşehir Cyprus University. He is a fellow of the Institute for Research in Economic and Fiscal Issues.

Sudeshna Ghosh has a Ph.D. in Economics and works as an Associate Professor at the Scottish Church College Kolkata, India, in the Department of Economics. She teaches data analysis, development studies and interdisciplinary studies. Her research interests include trade and tourism development, development economics, and time series econometrics. She published over 35 research papers in various national and international journals related to the above fields including in Quality & Quantity; Arthaniti: Journal of Economic Theory and Practice; International Journal of Tourism Research; Asia Pacific Journal of Tourism Research & Tourism Management.

Sandra Jednak is employed at the Faculty of Organizational Sciences, University of Belgrade as a Full Professor. She has published scientific research papers in international and national monographs, journals and conferences proceedings. Her teaching areas are an introduction to economics, macroeconomics, microeconomics, economic development and EU. Her research focus is on economic development, energy economics, knowledge economy, international economics and higher education.

Dragana Kragulj is a Full Professor of Economics at Faculty of Organizational Sciences at University of Belgrade. She graduated from the Faculty of Economics, University of Belgrade, where she also got her MSc degree and PhD degree. She was a Head of Department of Economics, Business Planning and International Management. Also, she was a Head of Centre for Economic and Business Research. She has published two monographs, several editions of different textbooks of Economics and over 100 peer-reviewed papers. The areas of her research interest include macroeconomic problems, prices, market, inflation, economic development, investment, agriculture, energy economics, process of transition, international economic integrations, the European Union.

Reenu Kumari is an Assistant Professor in the Department of Business and Management Studies, Meerut Institute of Engineering and Technology, Meerut, India. She has received Ph.D. from the Indian Institute of Technology, Roorkee. She has qualified for UGC NET (JRF) in 2011. She has thirteen-year experience in teaching as well as research also. Her area of specialization is Finance & Accounting. Her interest is FDI, Education, Economic Growth, Digitalization, and Trade Openness. She has written and published many research papers in national & international journals and Conferences. She has an editor in "International Journal of Applied Marketing and Management (IJAMM)". She has reviewed in various journals including Sage, Emerald, Inderscience, Elsevier. International Journal of Emerging Markets (IJoEM), Management Research Review (MRR), International Journal of Comparative Management (IJoCM), the Third PAN-IIM World Management Conference, Human Development and Capabilities (JoHDC), The social science Journal (SSJ), Transnational Corporations Review (TCR), South Asian Journal of business studies.

Jahir Lombana is Associate Professor and Senior Researcher at the Universidad del Norte (Barranquilla-Colombia). Ph.D. in Economics at the University of Goettingen (Germany), Master in International Studies at the University of Chile. Specialist in International Relations at the University of Chile with an undergraduate degree in Economics at the Universidad del Rosario in Bogotá (Colombia). He was specialized professional at the Ministry of Foreign Trade in Colombia, Director / Editor of the Internet portal specialized in foreign trade of fresh fruits and vegetables: www.freshplaza.es and www.freshplaza.com; project consultant in Europe and Latin America in organizations such as the Friedrich Ebert Foundation (Germany), Food and Agriculture Organization of the United Nations for (FAO), the Institute of Agricultural Studies INRA (France), the Colombian Banana Association AUGURA (Colombia), the Northern Cattlemen's Association ASOGANORTE (Colombia). In research and teaching his areas of interest are: competitiveness, international trade, management skills and agribusiness. Where he has several writings and is an active topic in the courses he teaches. In addition, he has supported regional agroindustry projects by the execution of recent research financed by the National Planning Department in Colombia.

Bartolomé Marco-Lajara (PhD) is Professor at the University of Alicante. His research interests are strategic management and tourism management. He is the author of several books, book chapters and international articles related to the areas above mentioned. He is a member of the Tourism Research Institute at the University of Alicante since its foundation and the main researcher of the European project 'Next Tourism Generation Alliance' at his University, as well as of the public competitive project for the creation of the Tourist Observatory of the Valencian Community (Spain). He has taken part in others public and private projects, such as the development of the strategic plan of the Alicante province for the period 2010-2020. He is the Head of the Department of Management at the University of Alicante, and previously was the Assistant Dean of the Economics Faculty for the Business Degree.

Javier Martínez-Falcó is a Teaching Assistant of Management at University of Alicante. In the research field, he focuses his interest on topics related to Regional Science and Strategic Management, particularly in the area of knowledge management, on which he has written numerous publications. He is currently a member of the research group Strategic Management, Knowledge, and Innovation in a Global Economy (DECI-GLOBAL).

Lorena Palacios-Chacón is Full Time Assistant Professor of International Business at Instituto Tecnológico y de Estudios Superiores de Monterrey (ITESM). Dr. Palacios-Chacon earned her Ph.D. in management from the University of Puerto Rico, and her two bachelors in economics and finance and international trade from the Sergio Arboleda University. One of her main interest is the writing of teaching cases, she has participated in a number of conferences, having won multiple best case awards. She is member of the Board of Directors of the Latin American Case Association (ALAC). Dr. Palacios-Chacon has written books and articles in the areas of internationalization of the firm, financial deepening in Colombia, the processes of offshore and outsourcing of companies and international economic integration between countries. She is initiating a line of research in multinationals from emerging markets, specially Multilatinas.

Miloš Parežanin is employed at the Faculty of Organizational Sciences, University of Belgrade. He graduated from the Faculty of Economics, University of Belgrade in 2009. Currently he is a Ph.D. candidate at the same faculty. He has participated in several scientific national and international conferences. His research interests include foreign direct investment, energy economics, competitiveness of the economy, European integration, economic development.

Lorena Ruiz-Fernández is a Postgraduate Teaching Assistant (TA) of Management at University of Alicante (Spain). Her research interests are on strategic management and more specific on dynamic capabilities view, innovation and intellectual capital. Moreover, she is the author of different papers related to these topics and she has participated in several international conferences.

Nestor Salcedo is a Ph.D. fellow in Business Economics at Universitat Autònoma de Barcelona. He holds his MRes and MBA degrees from ESAN Graduate School of Business and a BSc in Architecture from the National University of Engineering (Peru). He is a researcher and instructor in corporate governance and information technology (IT). His research focuses on Iberoamerican corporate governance, board leadership structures, IT investments, using new institutional theories.

Ayberk Şeker is an Assistant Professor in the field of the International Trade. Skilled in Import-Export Management, Economic Integration, International Trade Organizations, High-Technology Export. He is graduated from Yıldız Technical University, Bachelors Degree in Political Science and International Relations, Istanbul, Turkey; Yalova University, M.A. and Ph.D. in International Trade and Finance, Yalova, Turkey. Also, he had worked as a custom inspector for two years before the academic profession.

Osman Seraceddin Sesliokuyucu is an Assistant Professor in the department of Aviation Management at Suleyman Demirel University, Turkey. He received his BSc. in Economics at Marmara University, his MSc. in International Trade and Logistics, and Ph.D. in Economics at Gaziantep University, Turkey. His Ph.D. thesis focused on the Upgrading in Global Value Chain and its relationship with Countries Infrastructures. He published papers about air transport, global value chains, value co-creation, and the adoption of new processes. He pursues his research in air transport, air passenger behavior, information technology, international trade, and value co-creation and co-destruction.

Pedro Seva-Larrosa (PhD) is an assistant professor of Management at the University of Alicante (Spain). His research interests are focused on the fields of Strategic Management, Business Location and Regional Science. As a researcher he is very interested in the agglomeration of companies, especially in the food and beverage industry, although his research also addresses other economic activities. He is co-author of some book chapters and has published several papers in leading journals as Business Ethics, Papers in Regional Science, International Journal of Emerging Markets, Journal of Regional Research, Competitiveness Review, among other. Currently, he is part of the DECI-GLOBAL research group and participates in the European Project THE NEXT TOURISM GENERATION ALLIANCE.

Ashwani Sharma is an Assistant Professor in the Department of Business & Management Studies at Meerut Institute of Engineering & Technology, Meerut, India. He has eleven years of Experience in the field of teaching and research and also expertise in marketing and Digital Marketing. He received his Ph.D from CCS University, Meerut, and MBA from Dr. A.P.J. Abdul Kalam Technical University, Lucknow and Post Graduate Diploma in Educational Administration (PGDEA) from UPRTOU Allahabad. His research interests include cashless Commerce, E-Commerce ,Digital economy , International trade. He has published a number of research papers in national and international journals. He has Received a Copyright of Design Thinking Model for Startups.

Hasan Tekin is a lecturer at Karabuk University, Turkey. He received his Ph.D. in Finance from University of Bradford, UK. His research topics include capital structure, corporate governance, cash holdings, dividend payouts and financial crises. His research has appeared in journals such as Australian Journal of Management, Borsa Istanbul Review, Bulletin of Monetary Economics and Banking, Economics Business Letters, International Journal of Emerging Markets.

José G. Vargas-Hernández, M.B.A., Ph.D., Member of the National System of Researchers of Mexico and a research professor at University Center for Economic and Managerial Sciences, University of Guadalajara. Professor Vargas-Hernández has a Ph. D. in Public Administration and a Ph.D. in Organizational Economics. He has undertaken studies in Organisational Behaviour and has a Master of Business Administration, published four books and more than 200 papers in international journals and reviews (some translated to English, French, German, Portuguese, Farsi, Chinese, etc.) and more than 300 essays in national journals and reviews. He has obtained several international Awards and recognition.

Index

www.ingramcontent.com/pod-product-compliance
Lightning Source LLC
LaVergne TN
LVHW062152300926
849161LV00010B/2650